MW01001366

The Politics of Hope

and

The Bitter Heritage

James Madison [signature]

THE JAMES MADISON LIBRARY IN AMERICAN POLITICS
Sean Wilentz, General Editor

The James Madison Library in American Politics of the Princeton University Press is devoted to reviving important American political writings of the recent and distant past. American politics has produced an abundance of important works—proclaiming ideas, describing candidates, explaining the inner workings of government, and analyzing political campaigns. This literature includes partisan and philosophical manifestos, pamphlets of practical political theory, muckraking exposés, autobiographies, on-the-scene reportage, and more. The James Madison Library issues fresh editions of both classic and now-neglected titles that helped shape the American political landscape. Up-to-date commentaries in each volume by leading scholars, journalists, and political figures make the books accessible to modern readers.

The Conscience of a Conservative by Barry M. Goldwater

The New Industrial State by John Kenneth Galbraith

Liberty and the News by Walter Lippmann

The Politics of Hope and The Bitter Heritage: American Liberalism in the 1960s by Arthur M. Schlesinger, Jr.

The Politics of Hope

and

The Bitter Heritage

American Liberalism in the 1960s

Arthur M. Schlesinger, Jr.

With a new foreword by **Sean Wilentz**

PRINCETON UNIVERSITY PRESS
PRINCETON AND OXFORD

Copyright © 2008 by Princeton University Press
Foreword Copyright © 2008 by Sean Wilentz

The Politics of Hope Copyright © 1949, 1953, 1955, 1957, 1958,
1959, 1960, 1962 by Arthur M. Schlesinger, Jr.
The Bitter Heritage Copyright © 1966 by Houghton Mifflin
Company and © 1967, 1968 by Arthur M. Schlesinger, Jr.

Requests for permission to reproduce material from this work
should be sent to Permissions, Princeton University Press

Published by Princeton University Press,
41 William Street, Princeton, New Jersey 08540
In the United Kingdom: Princeton University Press,
3 Market Place, Woodstock, Oxfordshire OX20 1SY
All Rights Reserved

Permissions for previously published material can be found at the
end of this book

The Politics of Hope first published 1963
The Bitter Heritage first published 1967; Revised Edition, with new
final chapter, published 1968
The Politics of Hope and The Bitter Heritage, for The James
Madison Library in American Politics, published 2008

Library of Congress Control Number 2007933225
ISBN 978-0-691-13475-8

British Library Cataloging-in-Publication Data is available

This book has been composed in Sabon with Didot and Helvetica
Neue display

Printed on acid-free paper. ∞

press.princeton.edu

Printed in the United States of America

10 9 8 7 6 5 4 3 2 1

Contents

Foreword
Sean Wilentz

Arthur M. Schlesinger, Jr.'s *The Politics of Hope* and *The Bitter Heritage* mark, in retrospect, the triumph and the downfall of 1960s liberalism. *The Politics of Hope* was published in 1963, when Schlesinger, having left Harvard, was working in the White House as special assistant to President John F. Kennedy.[1] It is filled with excitement and wonder. "We have awakened as from a trance," he wrote, "and we have awakened so quickly and sharply that we can hardly remember what it was like when we slumbered. Our complaints now are that we have not made more progress, not that our capacity for progress is extinct." The book did not once mention Vietnam, a place about which most Americans then knew little or nothing.

Four years later, when the first edition of *The Bitter Heritage* appeared, Kennedy was dead, Schlesinger had returned to the academy, and everybody had heard of Vietnam. Schlesinger perceived what he called an honorable, negotiated "middle course" out of the war, but he knew that by 1967 President Lyndon B. Johnson's heedless military escalation had dashed many liberal dreams, including Johnson's own envisaged Great Society. "The fight for equal opportunity for the Negro, the war against poverty, the struggle to save the cities, the improvement of our schools—all must be starved for the sake of Vietnam," Schlesinger glumly observed. *The Bitter Heritage* is not exactly a cry of de-

---

[1] Schlesinger had obtained an official leave of absence from Harvard when he began serving in the White House in February 1961. He resigned his professorship when the leave expired in 1962.

feat, but its prevailing tone is tragic, and it says precious little about hope.

It is remarkable how quickly history shifted in the 1960s. The sheer pace of momentous events, most of them unanticipated, now seems crushing. This new combined edition of Schlesinger's books brings the ideas and debates of those bewildering times vividly back to life. It also prompts fresh reflection about the nature of 1960s American liberalism, why it flourished, and why it collapsed.

●●●

By the time he started work at the White House in February 1961, Schlesinger, still in his early forties, was an influential political writer as well as a Pulitzer Prize–winning historian and professor. His father, the esteemed Harvard historian Arthur Schlesinger, Sr., and his remarkable mother, Elizabeth Bancroft Schlesinger, had given him a childhood filled with books, ideas, and political argument. Young Arthur's Harvard undergraduate senior thesis on the Jacksonian-era political agitator Orestes Brownson was so strong that it soon appeared as a book.

The historical work that first earned Schlesinger major distinction and recognition, *The Age of Jackson*, developed a bold reinterpretation of Jacksonian liberalism, placing Andrew Jackson's presidency on a line of development with F.D.R. and the New Deal, which Schlesinger passionately supported. *The Age of Jackson* reached the best-seller lists and made Schlesinger an instant celebrity upon its publication in 1945. No one could fault the author's impressive scholarship or his brilliant literary style; more than sixty years later, the book remains essential reading for students as well as professional scholars. Still, a few writers complained that Schlesinger's historical judgments too often reflected his own present-day political beliefs. One critic observed that, much as the great nineteenth-century historian George Bancroft, a Democratic partisan, had voted for Andrew Jackson on every page of his monumental history of the United States, every page of *The Age of Jackson* was a vote for Franklin D. Roosevelt.

The charge, Schlesinger later conceded, had some merit, as did the link between Schlesinger and Bancroft. Schlesinger always suspected he had some kin connection to Bancroft through his mother's family. Indeed, he began what became *The Age of Jackson* intending to write Bancroft's biography. But the connection was in fact deeper. Bancroft had balanced his prodigious scholarly endeavors with a full-fledged political career inside the Democratic Party. In 1838, President Van Buren appointed him the collector of the Port of Boston, which made him the boss of the Massachusetts Democratic organization. Bancroft went on to run (unsuccessfully) for governor of Massachusetts, then served President James K. Polk, first as secretary of the navy and later as minister to Great Britain. Although Schlesinger had no ambitions for elective public office, he was drawn to Bancroft's example of helping to make history as well as to write about it.

Good fortune, and Schlesinger's amazing reserves of energy, took him far as a political adviser and insider. After serving in the Office of War Information and the Office of Strategic Services during the Second World War, he threw himself, during the late 1940s, into efforts to sustain the New Deal legacy against what he and others saw as the threat posed by left-wing, pro-Soviet elements inside the liberal camp. In 1948, he worked hard for President Harry S. Truman and against the splinter Progressive Party candidate, Roosevelt's former vice president Henry Wallace, whose campaign converged with the political line of the Communist Party. A year earlier, Schlesinger had joined with several prominent Democratic leaders, including Eleanor Roosevelt and Hubert Humphrey, to found Americans for Democratic Action (A.D.A.), a national organization devoted to promoting liberal ideas and fending off American Communist influence. And in 1949, Schlesinger published his liberal anticommunist manifesto, *The Vital Center*, which quickly became the political bible of American Cold War liberals.[2]

The Vital Center is more concerned with the mind and soul of politics than it is with specific positions or policies. Arguing on behalf of what he called the "free [L]eft" (sometimes called the "Non-Communist Left," or NCL for short), Schlesinger contended that American liberals and conservatives, despite their sharp differences, had an overriding common interest in fighting the major forms of modern tyranny—communism and fascism. After the defeat of the Axis powers, Schlesinger was naturally most concerned with the Soviet Union, and with warning his fellow liberals to resist communism's deceptions about liberating the downtrodden.

Schlesinger brought to bear the insights of religious as well as political thinkers, notably the theologian (and fellow A.D.A. founder) Reinhold Niebuhr. Niebuhr's conception of original sin and universal human frailty appealed deeply to Schlesinger, who turned it, in *The Vital Center*, into a secular argument

[2] The book's central thesis had its origins in the politics of 1948. See Schlesinger, "Not Left, Not Right, But a Vital Center," *New York Times Magazine*, April 4, 1948.

against historical determinism and political messianism of every variety. To succeed, Schlesinger insisted, American liberals would have to appreciate better the ironies and paradoxes of history, fight for their causes with a humbling sense of all humanity's limitations (especially their own), and vaunt pragmatism over dogma, flexibility over certitude.

In 1952, Schlesinger thought he had found a Democratic candidate, Governor Adlai Stevenson of Illinois, who could become an excellent liberal president in this realistic mold. Although Schlesinger had serious qualms about certain of Stevenson's stances (above all, his coolness on civil rights), overall he thought Stevenson well-equipped to carry on the New Deal legacy and the politics of reform without succumbing to dogmatic illusions. Twice matched against the intensely popular Dwight D. Eisenhower, Stevenson's aspirations proved hopeless. Still, Schlesinger gained enormous political experience and expertise in Stevenson's 1952 and 1956 campaigns, serving as head of research and speechwriter as well as publicist and *kibitzer*. All the while, and throughout the rest of the 1950s, Schlesinger also taught his history courses at Harvard, wrote a torrent of articles and reviews (including film reviews), and completed three thick and highly praised volumes in a projected multivolume history of the New Deal, entitled *The Age of Roosevelt*.

The essays in *The Politics of Hope* date from the dozen years after *The Vital Center*, although nearly one-third of them first appeared between 1957 and 1960, when Schlesinger was beginning to focus on yet another presidential campaign. The topics covered range widely, from the historiography of the American Civil War and the writings of the historian of the American West Bernard DeVoto, to the torments and joys of an American middle-class family vacationing in postwar Europe. The essays likewise vary greatly in style: some are polemical, others reflective and philosophical, still others wry and humorous. Schlesinger, a man of abundant curiosity as well as superhuman vitality, could write expertly on numerous subjects and in different tones of voice. But *The Politics of Hope* coheres around a few basic themes, each connected to American liberalism's evolution into the 1960s.

First, the book is concerned with political leadership and its place in liberal and democratic politics. In 1945, the sudden death of F.D.R.—the embodiment of liberal and even national hopes through the Great Depression and the Second World War—caused liberal Democrats an enormous problem. As long as F.D.R. was in the White House, they had few questions about the necessity for great leaders. But now, in what Schlesinger called "an age without heroes"—lacking leaders on the order of Churchill and Gandhi as well as Roosevelt—Schlesinger puzzled over the problematic properties of heroic greatness. Detecting a basic bafflement in democratic theory with regard to leadership, Schlesinger considered the dangers heroic figures posed to freedom, before concluding that a tempered belief in individual greatness was a necessary antidote to fatalism and lethargy. "An age without great men," he said (twenty years later, he would have written "great men and women"), "is one which acquiesces in the drift of history."

Next, Schlesinger explored the relation of ideas and intellectuals to political democracy. Abjuring the self-important, supposedly objective, and then-voguish academic social sciences (notably in his witty evisceration of one premier example, a team-produced study of *The American Soldier*), he assessed how individual thinkers—from Niebuhr to the ex-Communist-turned-informer Whittaker Chambers—had either engaged with or evaded politics. With subtlety and modulation, Schlesinger evaluated the kind of detachment commended by the eminent political commentator Walter Lippmann. Schlesinger found much to admire in Lippmann's ideal of "men who have stood apart, who refused to be anxious or too much concerned, who were cool and inquiring and had their eyes on a longer past and a longer future."[3] Yet Schlesinger also insisted that political parties and movements that disparaged or ignored ideas and intellectuals would ruin democracy. And he was concerned that intellectuals seeking tranquil contemplation might end up choosing abject and self-destructive political withdrawal. "Much as the highbrow . . . may dislike politics," he wrote, "he cannot escape or reject it."

A third theme in the book was the changing political mood at the end of the 1950s, abroad and at home. The Sino-Soviet rift, as well as independent stirrings within the Soviet European bloc, showed Schlesinger that the monolithic Communist world of the 1930s and 1940s had broken down, replaced by a new polycentrism that opened genuine opportunities for Western diplomats sagacious enough to discern them. Inside the United States, he sensed that the political exhaustion produced by the Great Depression and the Second World War was giving way to a new idealism which would address persisting inequalities and injustices. Schlesinger contended that the empty materialism and consumerism of the Eisenhower years—chronicled in such widely read books as *The Affluent*

---

[3] Lippmann, "The Scholar in a Troubled World" (1932), quoted in Schlesinger, *The Politics of Hope* (1963), present edition p. 194.

Society, by his close friend and political collaborator John Kenneth Galbraith—had run out of steam. Americans, he thought, were searching for a larger sense of purpose and meaning in their lives. Insofar as Schlesinger viewed the much-discussed "New Conservatism" of Russell Kirk and other writers (reviewed in another essay) as a derivative, incoherent exercise in nostalgia, he had great hopes that the changing political climate would lead to a full-blown liberal revival.

Schlesinger was a broad thinker about politics and history and not a technical policy expert, and in *The Politics of Hope* he provided no blueprint for rebuilding liberal American government. He did, though, offer some basic philosophical guidelines. Any new liberalism, Schlesinger said, would necessarily build upon the revolution in American national government completed by the New Deal, with its provisions for the public good like Social Security. But New Deal liberalism, Schlesinger noted, had arisen at a time very different from the 1960s, and in response to economic collapse. Any revived liberalism would have to gear itself to the problems of an economy of abundance. It would have to advance the Cold War policy of containment of Communism hammered out in the late 1940s, but also understand and exploit the continuing changes within the Communist world. It would have to pursue its goals in a spirit of pragmatism, humility, and skepticism—always remembering, Schlesinger wrote, that "history is not a redeemer, promising to solve all human problems in time." But it would also have to honor the obligation to face up to social conflicts produced by great moral issues. Finally, Schlesinger suggested, the new liberalism needed a leader who could articulate and act on these precepts.

The Politics of Hope discusses miscellaneous other

topics, including contemporary British drama, the middle-brow affirmations of *Time* magazine, and the so-called crisis of American masculinity, a much fretted-over matter at the time. (Schlesinger ascribed whatever "crisis" existed not to the emancipation of American women, the common antifeminist bugaboo, but to the rise of cultural conformity and homogenization.) The entire book, though, is suffused with the hope to which its title (borrowed from Emerson) refers—and with Schlesinger's mounting confidence that the kind of humane but disillusioned liberalism he had championed for so long was about to have its chance. By the time the collection appeared, Schlesinger's confidence seemed vindicated, at least in his own mind. He had found his indispensable leader in John F. Kennedy. As an active member of President Kennedy's administration, he was getting his greatest opportunity to help make history as well as to write about it.

In one of the essays included in *The Politics of Hope*, "The New Mood in Politics," Schlesinger predicted cheerily that "the '60s will probably be spirited, articulate, inventive, incoherent, turbulent, with energy shooting off in all directions." By the beginning of 1963, events were already proving him correct—more so than he could have expected. But the final outcomes would break liberals' hearts.

•••

There is a famous story about how Schlesinger, newly arrived at the White House in February 1961, asked the president what exactly his duties were. Kennedy replied that he wasn't sure himself. But Schlesinger's connections to Kennedy, and his ambition for public service, were stronger than the anecdote might suggest. Schlesinger had known Kennedy for years before the

1960 campaign, from the Washington and Cambridge soirée circuit, and he had found the senator attractive and not unintelligent, if a little on the conservative side. In the spring of 1959, though, Kennedy, gearing up for a presidential run, invited Schlesinger down from Cambridge to talk politics at the Kennedy family's summer compound in Hyannis Port, and the two began getting to know each other in earnest. By the start of the 1960 presidential election season, Schlesinger later remarked, he nostalgically favored Adlai Stevenson, ideologically favored the liberal senator from Minnesota (and A.D.A stalwart) Hubert Humphrey, for whom he was still writing occasional speeches—but realistically he favored Kennedy.

As part of the general election effort, Schlesinger wrote a quickie book, really an extended pamphlet, entitled *Kennedy or Nixon: Does It Make Any Difference?*, aimed at educated liberals and independents who were wary of Kennedy's youth and wealth, as well as past positions they disliked. (These included Kennedy's failure to confront vigorously his demagogic Senate colleague from Wisconsin, Joseph R. McCarthy.) After Kennedy's narrow victory, Schlesinger's correspondence and private journal show that he fervently hoped to receive an appointment in the new White House. A few possibilities fell by the wayside (including appointment as national security adviser, a post that went to his Harvard colleague McGeorge Bundy) before Schlesinger took up general duties as special assistant to the president.

Schlesinger had much to offer Kennedy as an adviser. He was the administration's in-house historian, who kept a running account of an insider's view of events, preserved in his copious journals. He was available to provide his scholarly expertise to a singular historically minded president, with contributions that ranged from historical insight on major problems to quickly retrieved quotations to insert into speeches. Because he had particular knowledge of Latin America, Schlesinger was consulted (and given special assignments) concerning Latin American affairs. (He was privy to the top-secret meetings in early 1961 that led to the disastrous invasion at Cuba's Bay of Pigs, an operation Schlesinger opposed. He would forever regret that he did not voice his opposition more forcefully.) Schlesinger's activities in A.D.A. and elsewhere had made him an acute observer of the complexities and nuances of leftist and liberal political movements at home and abroad. Schlesinger also served as a liaison between the White House and American intellectuals—a duty he fulfilled in part as the organizer of the so-called Hickory Hill seminars, which invited prominent thinkers to talk with members of the administration at the Virginia home of the president's brother, Attorney General Robert F. Kennedy.

One role Schlesinger might not have anticipated was as a contact man inside the White House for dissidents abroad, especially those who might be broadly construed as part of the "free [L]eft," or NCL, that he had written about in *The Vital Center*. It was only natural that these rebels would see in Schlesinger an influential friend. But the contacts often led to disappointment for all concerned.

In 1963, a new crisis began to intrude on the administration—the smoldering conflict in Vietnam—but Schlesinger had already been in contact for years with exiled nationalist opponents of the Ngo Dinh Diem regime in South Vietnam. These dissidents, chiefly leaders of the Democratic Party of Vietnam (or *Viet-Nam Dan-Chu Dan*), now relocated to Paris, were implacably pro-American, anticommunist foes of the insurgent Viet Cong and Ho Chi Minh's government in North Vietnam, yet were also revolted by Diem. In July 1961, one of the party's founders and its current president, Nguyen Thai Binh, wrote to Schlesinger from Paris on behalf of those he called the Free Nationalist Vietnamese to express disappointment with continued U.S. support for Diem's "tyrannical, incapable, and corrupt" government. (Binh also wrote, on the same date, to the leading official on Vietnam at the National Security Council [N.S.C.], Bundy's assistant Walter W. Rostow, but the correspondence petered out in October.) Binh wrote more letters to Schlesinger over the coming months to press his case for a change in American policy "before Communism is looked upon as a welcome relief" in Vietnam. "We stand resolutely anti-Communist," Binh said, "and we are disheartened to see continuing evidence of the Communist position in South Vietnam strengthened, ironically, through the well meaning financial aid from the United States."[4]

---

[4] Binh to Schlesinger, July 18 and September 17, 1961. This correspondence and all of the archival material cited below (unless otherwise indicated) come from White House Files, Boxes WH-19, WH-44, Arthur M. Schlesinger, Jr. Papers, John F. Kennedy Presidential Library and Museum, Boston, MA. Binh's correspondence with Rostow consists of Binh to Rostow, July 18, August 28, October 10, 23, 1961, and Rostow to Binh, August 17, 1961, White House Central Files, Box 75, Vietnam, CO312, 1/20/61–11/30/61, Kennedy Library. The small Democratic Party of Vietnam was founded in 1955, shortly after Diem's rise to power, but was banned in 1957. Binh also sent copies of a book he wrote on behalf of the party, *Vietnam: The Problem and a Solution*, to Special Assistant to the President Kenneth O'Donnell and to Pierre Salinger. Binh to O'Donnell, December 1961, Binh to Salinger, December 1961, O'Donnell to Binh, February 3, 1962, White House Central Files, Box 75, Vietnam, CO312, 12/1/61–4/15/62, Kennedy Library.

Also from Paris, the exiled essayist, poet, and historian Tran Van Tung—once a close friend and supporter of Diem's but now the Democratic Party of Vietnam's leading light and, officially, its executive secretary—wrote Schlesinger on several occasions. In a final pair of letters, composed in mid-October 1963, Tung noted Schlesinger's "continuing interest in the Viet-Nam dilemma" and forwarded two documents— a speech Tung had delivered to American reporters and a copy of a letter he had just sent President Kennedy, pleading with Kennedy to withdraw U.S. support for Diem and his corrupt cronies and relatives. Tung called for the Americans to back instead the formation of a new government of "competent" nationalist leaders, beginning with a roundtable conference of civilians and key army officers aimed at working out an anticommunist program for reform. "History rules against the opinion of those militarists who claim that force is all that is necessary to defeat guerrilla insurgencies," Tung warned.[5]

Schlesinger initially knew nothing of either Binh or Tung, and little enough about administration policy on Vietnam, and so he replied to Binh's early letters in a noncommittal way and to Tung's not at all.[6] But he

[5] Tung to Schlesinger, October 15 and 18, 1963; Tung to Kennedy, October 16, 1963. Two years earlier, Tung also wrote to Rostow and directly to Kennedy, and received a friendly but bland and evasive official reply from Rostow in response to both letters. Tung to Rostow, October 30, 1961; Tung to Kennedy, November 5, 1961; Rostow to Tung, November 25, 1961, White House Central Files, Box 75, Vietnam, CO312, 1/20/61–11/30/61, Kennedy Library.

[6] Schlesinger to Binh, August 29, September 27, October 30, and November 15, 1961. Obviously nonplussed by the first letter he received from Tung, Schlesinger forwarded it to Bundy, with a handwritten note: "Some one who understands our policy should answer this!" Route Slip, Office of the Special Assistant to the President,

also made sure that the letters came to the attention of other top administration officials. He forwarded two of Binh's to Robert Johnson of the N.S.C. staff at the end of October 1961, noting that although he could not identify the author, "his letters make a good deal of sense." He also forwarded one of Binh's letters from mid-September 1961 to Rostow, with an attached memorandum inquiring into the whereabouts of the foremost anti-Diem dissident and head of the semi-clandestine Free Democratic Party (or *Dang Dan-Chu Tu-Do*), the Harvard-trained physician Dr. Phan Quang Dan. (Binh's letter had mentioned, ominously, that Dan seemed to have disappeared completely.)[7] Soon after, Schlesinger forwarded additional letters to

---

November 9, 1961, White House Central Files, Box 75, Vietnam, CO312, 1/20/61–11/30/61, Kennedy Library.

[7] Schlesinger to Johnson (memorandum), October 30, 1961; Schlesinger to Rostow (memorandum), September 23, 1961. Dan had been elected to the national legislature in 1959, but Diem had him arrested soon after. Dan's disappearance, following a failed anti-Diem coup on November 11, 1960, led to protests from, among others, the International Commission of Jurists. After Diem's fall, Dan emerged as one of South Vietnam's most popular politicians, an elected member of the country's Constituent Assembly, and a thorn in the side of the country's succession of military rulers. In December 1966, he nearly died when an explosion wrecked his car in Saigon in an assassination attempt, probably executed by the Viet Cong. An intellectual as well as a politician (in the mid-1970s, he completed a lengthy monograph on the environment and people of Vietnam), Dan went on to serve briefly as minister of state for external affairs and then as deputy minister of health, social welfare, and relief; minister of social welfare; and deputy prime minister, chiefly responsible for the relocation of Vietnamese peasant refugees left homeless by the fighting. Dan departed Vietnam in the evacuation scramble that preceded the fall of Saigon in April 1975. On Dan's activities under Diem's regime, see Robert G. Seigliano, "Political Parties in South Vietnam Under the Republic," *Pacific Affairs*, 33 (1960): 339–40.

Bundy, observing (perhaps in keeping with the then-prevalent White House tone) that he had "no doubt that Tran-Van-Tung and Nguyen-Thai-Binh are disaffected intellectuals, etc.," but adding that "they make a literate and not altogether unimpressive case."[8]

Relations between Schlesinger and his correspondents, and Schlesinger's sympathy for their position, seem to have warmed as the Diem regime's repression intensified. In March 1962, Tung arrived in Washington to commence what he described as a national goodwill tour, and he visited with Schlesinger and his wife. A year later, Schlesinger, now alerted by many sources as well as his correspondents, was so put off by Ambassador Frederick E. "Fritz" Nolting, Jr.'s upbeat reports from Saigon that, in a memorandum to N.S.C. staff member and fellow skeptic Michael V. Forrestal, he described one Nolting letter as among "the most dismal documents I have ever encountered."[9]

Letters and documents sent by the Vietnamese dissidents to Schlesinger continued to circulate sporadically inside the White House until the final week of October 1963, when Forrestal abruptly told Schlesinger that "[a]t this stage, I think we want to keep our traffic bland."[10] A few days later, on November 1, a coup organized by South Vietnamese generals, with U.S. approval, overthrew the Diem government. Diem and his younger brother, Ngo Dinh Nhu, were apprehended and, though promised safe passage, summarily exe-

[8] Schlesinger to Bundy (memorandum), November 15, 1961.

[9] Tung to Schlesinger, October 18, 1963; Schlesinger to Forrestal (memorandum), March 9, 1963. Tung's tour in 1962 gained some notice in the national press. See, for example, Carroll Kilpatrick, "Ngo's Foe Cites Need of Reform," *Washington Post*, March 25, 1962.

[10] Forrestal to Schlesinger, October 24, 1963.

cuted, their mutilated bodies dumped in an unmarked grave next to the home of Nolting's recent replacement as U.S. ambassador, Henry Cabot Lodge. A military junta immediately took over. The coup was expected, but Diem and Nhu's brutal deaths shocked President Kennedy—and he began considering American withdrawal from the conflict, although only in the vaguest, most wistful of terms.[11]

Although their paramount hopes for Diem's ouster came to pass—to their relief and elation—the Vietnamese dissidents' approaches to Schlesinger for political support never lost a pervasive pathos.[12] Schlesinger, although inside the consultation loop, was not a major figure in making U.S. policy in Southeast Asia. Even if he had been, there is no reason to think that the administration would have paid much heed to some obscure political exiles, no matter how courageous, who lacked any clear and substantive influence inside South Vietnam. Additionally, many of those who did make U.S. policy, including Ambassador Nolting, were perfectly content to stick by Diem, at least through 1961 and 1962. Only in 1963, when Diem's brutal crackdown on Buddhist protests provoked an enormous social and political crisis, was a change of American policy at hand. Even then, with the exception of

[11] Some of Kennedy's advisers found his reaction surprising. "What did he expect?" former general Maxwell Taylor reportedly whispered after seeing the president blanch upon hearing the news of the assassinations. On these events and, more generally, on Schlesinger, the Kennedys, and Vietnam, see Jeff Shesol, *Mutual Contempt: Lyndon Johnson, Robert Kennedy, and the Feud That Defined a Decade* (New York: W. W. Norton & Co., 1997), esp. pp. 252–58, 266–67.

[12] For joyous reaction to the coup, see Tung to Bundy, November 4, 1963; Tung to Kennedy, November 8, 1963, White House Central Files, Box 75, Vietnam, CO312, 7/1/63– , Kennedy Library.

some long-skeptical officials (especially Forrestal, Undersecretary of State W. Averell Harriman, and Assistant Secretary of State for Far Eastern Affairs Roger Hilsman), most responsible Washington officials held out hope until the bitter end that Diem could be persuaded to reform his government and back off from repressive policies.[13] And despite the shocking circumstances of Diem's overthrow, it was almost certain that, barring an unlikely total withdrawal, the United States would stand by South Vietnam's new military rulers as long as they showed no signs of embracing a softer, noncommunist "neutralist" position. Civilian nationalist reformers and democrats inside South Vietnam—preeminently Dr. Phan Quang Dan—soon enough found themselves back in opposition, now criticizing a string of unsteady but strong-arming military governments.[14]

[13] There was, to be sure, some disquiet within the administration before the situation completely fell apart. In February 1963, for example, Forrestal and Hilsman recommended cautiously "expanding the contacts between U.S. personnel in Saigon and non-communist elements of the Vietnamese opposition"—in part to increase American alternatives "in the event of an accident which results in a shift in the government." See Forrestal to Harriman (memorandum), February 8, 1963.

[14] In an assessment of the situation in Saigon in mid-August 1963, Richard Helms of the CIA recommended to Hilsman that, in the event of a coup and the installation of a military junta, the United States should urge the generals to utilize Diem's sitting vice president, Nguyen Ngoc Tho, "even if only as a front man"—but, failing in that, "the best, if not the only U.S. Government course, would be to recognize the status quo and take all possible steps to influence the junta to install a broadly based government which would also utilize competent civilians." Helms went on to list eight prominent civilians who might play a role in a new government, all but one of them officials or former officials in the Diem government. The exception, the oppositionist Pham Khac Suu, was a former member of

Schlesinger's fleeting Vietnam involvements did have some minor significance—and they contained a bitter irony. There turned out to be, as Schlesinger might have hoped, men such as Binh and Tung in and around the Vietnam situation who at least looked like representatives of Schlesinger's "free [L]eft." Their politics seemed aligned with Schlesinger's own—those of a third force, standing between Communism and anti-Communist authoritarianism, that Schlesinger and others in the Kennedy White House sought to promote around the world as best they could. But in many places, as in Vietnam, those elements remained—or at least appeared to remain—politically marginal. And despite the qualms of many officials, the main thrust of Kennedy's Cold War realism in foreign policy was officially to back the most stable and viable regimes possible, even if they were unsavory, in order to beat back threats of Communist subversion.[15] Only when those

---

the cabinet of the French-backed emperor Bao Dai who had been imprisoned following an abortive coup against Diem in 1960 and who would go on to serve briefly as president of South Vietnam in 1964–65. Memorandum From the Deputy Director for Plans, Central Intelligence Agency, to the Assistant Secretary of State for Far Eastern Affairs, August 16, 1963, Department of State, Vietnam Working Group Files: Lot 67 D 54, POL 26, Coup Rumors. Secret. Also posted online at http://www.presidency.ucsb.edu/vietnam/showdoc.php?docid=2.

[15] In May 1961, Vice President Johnson returned from Saigon with an uneven report for the president—yet publicly, he had toasted Diem as "the Winston Churchill of Asia." The following year, Attorney General Robert Kennedy, holding stronger hopes for the possibilities of counterinsurgency and reform in Vietnam, read an official statement at the Saigon airport praising the premier as "brave and patriotic" and expressing the U.S. government's "full confidence" in him. A year later, Kennedy was more skeptical about counterinsurgency in general and about Diem in particular.

regimes were no longer viable, such as Diem's in 1963, would the United States back the strongest anticommunist alternative.

The irony fully surfaced only in later years. Early in his presidency, Kennedy said he thought the Vietnam crisis was essentially a political and not a military matter—yet he allowed the major influence pertaining to the American involvement to shift from the State Department to the Pentagon. Falling into what had already become a familiar syndrome, he believed his advisers' best-case scenarios and enlarged the American military commitment, persuaded that one last push would crush the Viet Cong once and for all. At the end of 1961, there were fewer than fifteen hundred U.S. military advisers in Vietnam; by the time Kennedy was murdered less than two years later, there were more than fifteen thousand. Although the president steadfastly refused to send American troops to Vietnam, debates within the administration, until the eve of Diem's ouster, had become dominated by military and not political concerns.

President Kennedy's assassination in Dallas only three weeks after the Saigon coup would forever leave open to speculation and debate what his future Vietnam policies might have been. In any event, Schlesinger, distraught at Kennedy's death, would no longer have a hand in shaping policy on any issue. After staying on to serve President Johnson during the immediate period of transition, Schlesinger quit the White House in February 1964. He set to work in his Georgetown home on the mixture of history, reportage, and memoir that became *A Thousand Days: John F. Kennedy in the White House.*

After Johnson won the 1964 election, his administration, led by many of Kennedy's top foreign policy appointees, drastically escalated U.S. military involvement in Vietnam. The administration might have acted differently had it known about and heeded (or been willing to heed) Tung's warning to Schlesinger in 1963, about how history disproved "that force is all that is necessary to defeat guerrilla insurgencies." As it happened, Schlesinger would have to issue that warning himself, years later, in *The Bitter Heritage*.

•••

After completing *A Thousand Days* (for which he would receive a second Pulitzer Prize), Schlesinger moved from Washington, briefly to the Institute for Advanced Study in Princeton, and then to Manhattan, to take up a distinguished teaching position at the Graduate Center of the City University of New York in 1966. There, in the coming years, he would become part of a glamorous set of New York–based writers, artists, and critics that *Time* labeled (in the style Schlesinger had pilloried in *The Politics of Hope*) the "swinging soothsayers." Yet by the time Schlesinger got his feet back on the ground, the Vietnam War had escalated into a major American military commitment and become the all-consuming issue in American politics. The liberals' heady days celebrating the Civil Rights Act of 1964 and the Voting Rights Act of 1965, and embarking on Johnson's Great Society programs (sketched out for L.B.J. in part by Schlesinger's friend Galbraith) gave way to bitter contention. The numbers of American combat troops in Vietnam had risen from zero in 1963 to 400,000 at the end of 1966 (and would reach more than half a million six months later). The aerial bombardment of North Vietnam begun in March 1965, under the name "Operation Rolling Thunder," continued to rain tons of explosives on

North Vietnam, despite brief pauses. Restiveness at home was generating a growing antiwar movement, most conspicuously on the nation's campuses, but also spreading outward. Revulsion over the war badly divided the Democratic Party and revived the so-called anti-anticommunist American Left.

For Schlesinger, the war raised conflicting thoughts and emotions. On the one hand, he believed it would be worse than dishonorable for the Americans to renege on their commitments, delivered repeatedly, to the anticommunist South Vietnamese—men and women who would almost certainly be either killed or imprisoned if the Viet Cong won an outright military victory. Demands from some quarters that the United States withdraw immediately from Vietnam—or, as Schlesinger later put it, "scuttle and run"—were unthinkable. Many of the policies that led to the new mess had taken shape early on during the Kennedy administration. Those policies, albeit greatly enlarged, were now being prosecuted and passionately defended by many Kennedy men whom Johnson had held over, including Secretary of State Dean Rusk and Secretary of Defense Robert McNamara. And though Schlesinger came to detest Rusk (whom he had never held in high regard), he was sensitive about publicly criticizing the White House, and President Johnson in particular, too harshly.

On the other hand, Schlesinger believed that the increased emphasis on military outcomes had obscured what Johnson himself said was the desired goal of the United States—not an outright military victory for American and South Vietnamese forces, but a negotiated settlement. As long as the political and diplomatic dimensions of the Vietnam situation receded before the military dimension, the war would drag on endlessly, killing untold numbers of Americans and Vietnamese (North and South) to no discernible good purpose. At home, furthermore, the war had already drained away the federal monies and the will necessary to sustain, let alone enlarge upon, the social programs planned under Kennedy's New Frontier and Johnson's Great Society.

Schlesinger also worried that the war would cause a domestic political backlash from hard-line right-wingers. Having militarized America's involvement within certain limits—ruling out, above all, the use of nuclear weapons—the Johnson White House ran the risk of provoking ultraconservative attacks on Democrats and liberals as half-hearted in the defense of freedom. President Johnson may have thought that, by escalating American military involvement in Vietnam, he was staving off the Right, insuring that no one would ever accuse his administration of ceding Vietnam to the Communists as Truman's administration had been faulted for "losing" China. In reality, Schlesinger thought, Johnson, by fighting the war the way he was, actually heightened the possibilities of a right-wing crusade against "backstabbing" liberals, like the one Joseph McCarthy had pursued amid the Korean War at the start of the 1950s.

With the Johnson White House showing no signs of changing its policies, and with the antiwar movement growing, Schlesinger ceased trying to defend the war, broke with the Johnson administration, and published *The Bitter Heritage*. Not unlike his instant production on Kennedy and Nixon during the 1960 campaign, it was more of a pamphlet than a treatise. But despite its brevity, Schlesinger's book managed to fill in a great deal about the political background to the Vietnam conflict, and offered a forceful case for changing policies without abandoning the basic terms of Cold War liberalism.

Schlesinger showed, first, that America's involvement with Vietnam dated back twenty-five years, to the Second World War, when President Roosevelt offered proposals, ultimately fruitless, for forming a protectorate in Southeast Asia to replace French colonial rule. Schlesinger then sketched how the elements that led to the current impasse had gradually fallen into place. In 1954, President Eisenhower announced his support for the so-called domino theory in order to justify Western military intervention in Southeast Asia. That same year, the United States sponsored the creation of the Southeast Asia Treaty Organization, later cited (falsely) as an American commitment that bound the Johnson administration to escalate the war.

Schlesinger's loyalties to the Kennedy administration did not stop him from discussing how it had contributed to letting the situation get out of hand, and how J.F.K. himself had aggravated matters by declaring, rashly, in his State of the Union message of 1963 that "[t]he spearpoint of aggression has been blunted in South Vietnam." Yet Schlesinger was inclined to place most of the blame on the inaccurate and wishful reports Kennedy received from his top advisers, especially Secretary of State Rusk, Ambassador Nolting, and the military. (He did note the contrary reports by newspapermen such as David Halberstam of the *New York Times*, who abhorred what they witnessed of the Diem regime, although Schlesinger left it unclear what Kennedy may or may not have made of those reports.) Although he endeavored to be judicious, Schlesinger also occasionally slipped into berating President Johnson—a man, he wrote, "who can hardly understand the eastern seaboard of his own country," yet who presumed to think he could understand the eastern seaboard of Asia.

For the most part, though, Schlesinger stuck by his conviction, announced early in the book, that there was no one great villain to blame over Vietnam. Instead, policymakers had fallen prey to rigid thinking, poor intelligence, false historical analogizing, and reckless pride. Updating a theme he had introduced in *The Politics of Hope*, Schlesinger knocked aside the still-ubiquitous domino theory by showing how the divisions within the Communist world had rendered such thinking obsolete. He also refuted another common claim—that failing to stop Ho Chi Minh and the Viet Cong cold would be an act of appeasement on the order of the appeasement of Hitler at Munich in 1938. Above all, he argued that the Johnson administration had lost touch with the necessary humility and caution required of any liberal democratic nation, lest it conflate its honorable goals with the conceits of omnipotence and omniscience. On this, Schlesinger turned for wisdom to some remarks of President Kennedy's, "that we cannot right every wrong or reverse every adversary—and that therefore there cannot be an American solution to every world problem."

This was not to say, Schlesinger insisted, that America should scuttle and run. "[H]olding the line in South Vietnam is essential," Schlesinger wrote, out of moral obligations to our allies in South Vietnam. But there was little sense in continuing to pursue the current policy of escalation. Schlesinger's proposed "middle course" included halting the bombing campaign, entering into serious negotiations over South Vietnam's political future (with the Viet Cong a party to the talks), and ending the barbaric policy of handing captured prisoners over to South Vietnamese officials, who would subject them to torture. More generally, he advised ceasing to allow the existing military junta, headed by the swaggering air force marshal Nguyen Cao Ky, to determine so much of American policy. Perhaps, if he recalled his own White House correspondence, Schlesinger had it in mind for the Americans to ally more closely with dissident leaders like Dr. Phan Quang Dan.

• • •

Schlesinger's proposals, not surprisingly, got nowhere with the Johnson White House. A year after *The Bitter Heritage* appeared, Schlesinger was deeply involved in another presidential campaign for a new liberal hero, President Kennedy's brother Robert, who won election to the Senate from New York in 1964. Tortured by his own conflicting thoughts and feelings, R.F.K. had been turning against Johnson's escalation policies since 1965, and at the end of 1967, he called, not for the first time, for a cessation of American bombing. After his colleague from Minnesota Eugene McCarthy ran strong as an antiwar candidate in the New Hampshire Democratic primary, Kennedy decided in mid-March 1968 to make his own run at the nomination.

Two weeks after Kennedy's announcement, President Johnson suddenly withdrew his name from contention and announced a bombing halt. Schlesinger went to work on a revised edition of *The Bitter Heritage*, adding a new chapter on the lessons of Vietnam. The new chapter avoided any mention of Kennedy's candidacy but instead focused on Johnson's March 31 speech renouncing renomination and on the president's professed intention to intensify the search for a peaceful settlement. For Schlesinger, it seemed that

Johnson truly had recognized the war's failure—and the possibility loomed that American foreign policy had reached a major turning point, rejecting the excessive universalism and "obsessive anti-communism" that had overtaken it. Superficially, Schlesinger appeared to have retreated from the tough-minded Cold War liberalism he had done so much to articulate since the late 1940s. In fact, he was taking his tough-mindedness and his sense of irony a step further, acknowledging once again that dogmatism and pride can disfigure all ideals—including his own.

"Nothing," he wrote, "has exalted America more than [its] sense of world mission—this decent and admirable feeling of responsibility for the welfare of others. It had led to acts of national generosity unparalleled in the history of man. Yet little is more dangerous than a sense of world mission pushed too far or perceived too absolutely." The liberalism of the 1960s had become prey to the very vices it had warned against— retrospectively, a fine Schlesingerian irony. Yet Schlesinger remained optimistic in the spring of 1968 that American liberalism could learn from and remedy its mistakes. His political champion for redirecting the liberal cause was the chastened but still-growing Robert F. Kennedy.

When Kennedy won the California primary in early June, it was plausible to think he might actually become the Democratic candidate—and the next president. But on the night of Kennedy's California victory, a youthful, embittered Palestinian gunman, enraged at his support for Israel, cut him down. Another of Schlesinger's lessons in *The Bitter Heritage*, about the tragic, excruciating inscrutability of history, had once more crushed, with a merciless impassivity, his politics of hope. And in November, with antiwar and proadministration Democrats deeply divided, Republican candidate Richard M. Nixon barely defeated Johnson's loyal vice president, Hubert Humphrey, ushering in a long era of conservative politics.

Six years later, in another of history's enigmatic twists, Nixon was undone by Watergate. But the liberalism of the 1960s had reached a political and intellectual crisis in 1968 from which it never recovered. The Democratic Party had already given up much of its southern political base earlier in the decade, when Kennedy and Johnson endorsed the civil rights movement. The Vietnam War further split the Democrats, creating fundamental differences over America's role as a world power that have not healed forty years later. And when American liberalism did seem to be making a political comeback in the 1990s, it had to be reinvented yet again—not only to adjust to the changes wrought during the administrations of Ronald Reagan and George H. W. Bush, but also to address the problems of a world even more different from that of the 1960s than the 1960s had been from the 1930s.

Through it all, Arthur M. Schlesinger, Jr., remained an engaged, passionate voice for the liberal values by which he stood, always bringing history to bear on the present, until his death at age 89 in 2007. Some critics accused him of not adapting his own politics of hope sufficiently to changing times; others accused him of changing his politics, especially over foreign policy, too much. Later historians and biographers will debate these matters. Without question, though, Schlesinger approached public affairs, of the past and the present, with a remarkably consistent liberalism, tempered by an abiding sense of tragedy and irony—a way of thinking that he had worked out in the 1940s and 1950s, and that became one of the spiritual as well as intellectual pillars of 1960s liberalism.

Long after the New Frontier and the Great Society have passed into history, long after the basic facts of political life of the 1960s have changed utterly, Schlesinger's complicated, clarifying idealism retains compelling wisdom. Writing in *The Bitter Heritage* of history's opaqueness, Schlesinger sounded a note that might just as easily have appeared in *The Politics of Hope*:

> [W]e can agree that history should lead statesmen to a profound and humbling sense of human frailty— to a recognition of the fact, so insistently demonstrated by experience and so tragically destructive of our most cherished certitudes, that the possibilities of history are far richer and more various than the human intellect is likely to conceive. This, and the final perception that while the tragedy of history implicates us all in the common plight of humanity, we are never released, despite the limits of our knowledge and the darkness of our understanding, from the necessity of meeting our obligations.

In the middle of a cruel century, Schlesinger fashioned a humane, confident American liberalism that understood the moral blindness and arrogance of supposing that the future will yield easily to its acumen. That it finally fell victim to these human frailties makes that liberalism more pertinent, not less—as a paradoxical caution as well as an inspiration. It is one of Schlesinger's many intellectual achievements that deserve to endure.

• • •

The combined James Madison Library edition contains *The Politics of Hope* as it was originally published in 1963. There have been two previous editions of *The Bitter Heritage*—one published in 1967, the other published the following year, with a new final chapter. I have included here the second edition. Typographical and obvious wording errors found in the older editions of both books have been silently amended.

I am grateful to several friends and colleagues for their advice and assistance in writing this foreword. Above all, Diana Kimball provided some indispensable and timely research assistance. I also wish to thank Sven Beckert, David Elliott, John Lewis Gaddis, Hue-Tam Ho Tai, Ben Kiernan, and Stephen Schlesinger, as well as the archivists and staff at the John F. Kennedy Presidential Library and Museum. I was fortunate to be able to complete the work during a stint as the Mrs. Giles Whiting Foundation Fellow at the extraordinary Dorothy and Lewis B. Cullman Center for Writers and Scholars at the New York Public Library. To the center's director, Jean Strouse, her entire staff, the librarians of the NYPL, and all of the center's fellows, a big tip of the cap.

S. W.

THE
POLITICS
OF HOPE

For Katharine, Stephen, Christina, and Andrew

Contents

Introduction

Mankind, Emerson once said, is divided between the party of Conservatism and the party of Innovation, between the Past and the Future, between Memory and Hope. Neither Memory nor Hope provides by itself an entirely persuasive basis for political action. But the distinction expresses a deep contrast in human temperament and purpose. Some people resent change and others welcome it. Some are satisfied with what we have; others think we can do better. "It is," wrote Emerson, "the counteraction of the centripetal and centrifugal forces. Innovation is the salient energy; Conservatism the pause on the last movement." Some believe that life's the fool of time and time must have a stop. Others believe that time will forever outstrip our pretenses and outwit our platitudes—that, as Bacon put it, "He that will not apply new remedies must expect new evils; for time is the greatest innovator."

A good many of the pieces that follow were written by an American liberal in the United States in the 1950's—written, that is, from the viewpoint of Hope in an age of Memory. They were written in the belief that, contrary to the view then held by many Americans and (apparently) by most people outside America, the America of the '50's did not necessarily represent the triumphant culmination of the American experiment; that America, as a nation, had not necessarily solved all its problems or achieved all its objectives; that the promise of American life had not found perfect fulfillment in a consensus of togetherness and a rhetoric of moralism and self-congratulation; that the American people would not be satisfied forever with a diet of clichés and pieties; that they could not, from now on, be counted as permanently hostile to style, wit, intellect, innovation, and idealism; that the impulses of Hope, gathering beneath the surface, would soon break out and launch the United States into a new and more entertaining epoch.

I could not believe that my country had ground to a halt because, as an historian, and especially as the son of my father, I was well aware of the existence of a cyclical rhythm in our national affairs. The basic fallacy has always been to suppose that the current state of things represents the essence of the American reality. But our reality has always been dialectic. A generation ago my father traced back the historic alternation between Innovation and Conservatism to the start of the American republic.[1] By this analysis, the '50's, far from expressing a final capitulation of America to the *status quo*, were rather an entirely predictable decade of Memory after two decades of active and exhausting Hope. So far as the historian was concerned, there was no reason to suppose, because we acquiesced for a season, that acquiescence would ever after be the American way.

The correctness of this cyclical view has been shown, I think, by the long way we have already come in the '60's. We are beginning to recover the qualities which the rest of the world—and many Americans too, some with relief, others with foreboding—imagined that we had forsworn forever. We no longer seem an old nation, tired, complacent and self-righteous. We no longer suppose that our national salvation depends on stopping history in its tracks and freezing the world in

[1] The essay, originally published in the *Yale Review* in 1939, is reprinted as "The Tides of National Politics" in *Paths to the Present* (New York, 1949).

its present mold. Our national leadership is young, vigorous, intelligent, civilized, and experimental—and rare in this world in being any of these things. Our mistakes these days tend to be the mistakes of rationality, not the mistakes of complacency.

Self-righteousness has ceased to be the main instrument of our diplomacy. Instead, idealism sends thousands of young Americans to the ends of the world as farmers or teachers or engineers for the Peace Corps. The life of the mind enjoys a new freedom and a new status. There has never been such official interest in and support of the arts. Wit has become respectable; it is even presidential now. Satire has burst out of the basements of San Francisco and Greenwich Village. People feel free to make jokes about anybody or anything. The word "togetherness" has passed from the language. Few would describe American society any longer in last decade's condescending vocabulary of conformism and homogenization.

In short, the older American faith in leadership and diversity and contention and individualism and experiment and irreverence is beginning to reassert itself. We are Sons of Liberty once again; or, at least, we admit this as a legitimate ambition. We have awakened as from a trance; and we have awakened so quickly and sharply that we can hardly remember what it was like when we slumbered. Our complaints now are that we have not made more progress, not that our capability for progress is extinct. The peculiarities of the '50's, some of which are recounted in the pages to follow, have almost the air of a forgotten nightmare.

It is important not to overdo this. Self-congratulation is as dangerous for the party of Hope as for the party of Memory. It would be premature to suppose that we are approaching the millennium—that the day is imminent when all turmoil will be over, when Satan will be cast into the life of fire and brimstone, and mankind will behold a new heaven and a new earth. It would not only be premature; it would be wrong. By American tradition, the party of Hope is humane, skeptical, and pragmatic. It has no dogma, no sense of messianic mission, no belief that mortal man can attain Utopia, no faith that fundamental problems have final solutions. The empiricism of the American party of Hope stands in sharp contrast to the millennialism which still inflames the ideologists, whether of the American right or of the European and Asian left—the notion that a golden age existed in the past, or will exist in the future, which mankind can achieve through the proper combination of incantations and exorcisms.

José Figueres, the Latin American patriot, calls his *finca* in the Costa Rican uplands "La Lucha Sin Fin"— the struggle without end. Freedom is inseparable from struggle; it is a process, not a conclusion. And freedom, as Brandeis said, is the great developer; it is both the means employed and the end attained. This, I believe, states the essence of the Politics of Hope—this and the understanding that the struggle itself offers not only a better life for others but a measure of fulfillment, even of pleasure, for oneself.

I am indebted to Paul Brooks of Houghton Mifflin for suggesting this book and to Anne Barrett and Helen Phillips for seeing the volume through the press. I am also indebted to my father for continuing counsel and tolerance; and my father and I are both indebted to John F. Kennedy for vindicating the cyclical theory of American politics.

Arthur M. Schlesinger, Jr.

Part I

Leadership and History

1.

On Heroic Leadership and the Dilemma of Strong Men and Weak Peoples
(1960)

Political life in the 20th century has been marked by a certain tendency toward one-man rule. This tendency has experienced setbacks and even reverses, and one is by no means justified in concluding an irresistible drive toward Caesarism. Nonetheless, the resort to the semi-heroic leader has become a sufficiently common phenomenon to deserve consideration. Such resort has taken place in the new nations, where the thrust toward modernization has often seemed to require national discipline of a sort best stimulated and enforced by a powerful personality: one need only mention Egypt, Thailand, Pakistan, Burma, Iraq, the Sudan, Tunisia, Lebanon, Indonesia, Cuba, Ghana, Guinea. Such resort has also taken place in older nations where strong personal leadership has seemed the only way to suspend divisive conflicts and avert social disintegration: for example, France.

The question inevitably arises of the implications for democracy of this reliance on the heroic (or pseudo-heroic) individual. How far is heroic leadership necessary and under what conditions? How far legitimate? Is it compatible with democracy? At what stage does it become a menace? How can one distinguish heroic leadership which supports democracy from that which threatens democracy? In what circumstances, in short, if any, can believers in democracy accept the heroic leader?

I should like to examine these questions by discussing (1) the place of the heroic leader in classical democratic theory, (2) the problem of heroic leadership in the 20th century, and (3) the criteria for reconciling heroic leadership and democracy.

I

The heroic leader has always constituted an anomaly in democratic theory. Since democratic theory arose historically as a protest against theses of the "divine right" of particular personalities, its early proponents naturally put their major emphasis on the sufficiency of the people (or a majority thereof) as against the need for heroic leadership. Most democratic theory derives from Locke; and, in Locke's account, the people assert their rightful control over the state through a process essentially of spontaneous combustion. "The people," he wrote, "generally ill-treated and contrary to right, will be ready upon any occasion to ease themselves of a burden that sits heavy upon them. They will wish and seek for the opportunity, which in the change, weakness, and accidents of humane affairs, seldom delays long to offer itself."[1] This analysis of the requirements of a revolutionary situation proposed no special role for leadership; it stands in marked contrast to, for example, the writings of Blanqui or to Lenin in *What Is to Be Done?* The Lockian assumption was that the people were endowed with sufficient purpose and intelligence to produce out of themselves, so to speak, the initiatives necessary both for successful revolution and for effective government thereafter.

Conventional democratic theory has accepted the

[1] Locke, *Second Treatise of Civil Government.*

Lockian bias on this matter ever since. If one defines democracy as a system in which the majority under constitutional procedures freely chooses among competing persons for limited-term control of the state, then the inescapable drift of democratic theory is against investing too much significance in any particular competitor.

Other inherent factors have reinforced this tendency to minimize the problem of leadership. Thus democratic theory has resisted emphasis on leadership on ideological grounds—because this emphasis has seemed to imply that some men should lead and others should follow, a proposition which clashes with the traditional democratic commitment to equality and to majoritarianism. It has resisted this emphasis on moral grounds—because it has seemed to overlook the democratic conviction that power corrupts. It has resisted this emphasis on emotional grounds—because it irritates that populist strain in democracy which often includes an envy of superior persons.

Most important of all, it has resisted this emphasis on compelling practical grounds—because it has seemed to encourage the erosion of democracy. Since Lockian theory assumed the omni-competence of majorities, most post-Lockian attempts to rehabilitate the idea of leadership have begun precisely by asserting the incompetence of majorities. Rousseau, it is true, argued the case for heroic pro-democratic leadership in the instances of the Legislator, who was to constitute the state, and the Dictator, who might be called upon to save it; but these were both emergency functions, and his theory made no provision for leadership as a continuing feature of democratic society.[2] In any event,

[2] Cf. *The Social Contract*, Book II (chap. 7) and Book IV (chap. 6).

his limited vindication of leadership seemed only further evidence of the perils of leadership theory since his whole system led so easily toward totalitarian democracy. And most ideologists of leadership have been, like Carlyle and Lenin, polemicists against democracy: they have invoked the supposed ignorance, fecklessness, and instability of the crowd as a chief reason for according special respect to leaders. Historically, the idea of leadership has thus become associated with elitist philosophies; leadership theory has seemed a weapon to be employed by reactionaries or revolutionaries against Lockian democracy. And history seems fully to have corroborated this supposed association. The *Führerprinzip*, the cult of personality, the rituals of hero worship, have too often led to the suppression of freedom, the establishment of authoritarianism, and the destruction of democracy.

All these considerations, both inherent and historical, have thus produced the implicit assumption in classical democratic theory that numerical majorities provide a substitute for heroic leadership, and that too much speculation about the need for leadership may be subversive of democracy.

II

It is evident that one confronts here a curious discrepancy between democratic theory and democratic practice, because in practice democracy as a form of government has accepted—indeed, has regularly required and demanded and produced—heroic leaders. There are several reasons why democracy has employed in practice what it has rejected in principle.

For one thing, democracy involves a *functional* need for strong leadership. When one gives political power to the masses, one risks the hopeless diffusion of decision and purpose—unless leadership arises to offset the centrifugal effects of the dispersion of political power. From the start, democracies have been able to concert their energies and focus their aspirations only as strong individuals embodied and clarified the tendencies of their people. This functional need for strong leadership is distinct from the technical need for expertise produced by the growing complexities of industrial society. Thus Andrew Jackson was a strong President of the United States at a time when the administrative problems of government were sufficiently easy that he could plausibly describe official duties as "so plain and simple that men of intelligence may readily qualify themselves for their performance." When times moved beyond that state of beatitude imagined by William Jennings Bryan where any man of good heart could write a currency law, the problem of democratic leadership became more specialized and more urgent; but it did not essentially change.

Democracy's functional need for leadership was recognized at an early point in the United States. In the 70th *Federalist* paper, Alexander Hamilton addressed himself to this issue with characteristic cogency, setting forth an argument which was not inconsistent with Locke—with which, indeed, Locke might have agreed—but which Locke never made. Hamilton began by citing, as "not without its advocates," the idea that "a vigorous Executive is inconsistent with the genius of Republican government." This seemed to him wrong; more than that, he continued, believers in republican government (by which Hamilton meant representative government controlled by the majority) could not admit the truth of this idea "without at the same time admitting the condemnation of their own principles."

After all, Hamilton said, "a feeble Executive implies a feeble execution of the government. A feeble execution is but another phrase for a bad execution; and a government ill executed, whatever it may be in theory, must be, in practice, a bad government." If people really believed in republican government, they must surely wish that government to be efficiently executed. Therefore, "energy in the Executive is a leading character in the definition of good government. It is essential to the protection of the community against foreign attacks; it is not less essential to the steady administration of the laws; to the protection of property against those irregular and high-handed combinations which sometimes interrupt the ordinary course of justice; to the security of liberty against the enterprises and assaults of ambition, of faction, and of anarchy." The way to preserve freedom, Hamilton wrote, was not to enfeeble the Executive but to strengthen the residual power of the people against the Executive.

If any are disposed to reject the testimony of Hamilton because of incipient traces of elitism in his thought, it should be noted that on this point he and Thomas Jefferson were in substantial agreement. As Jefferson wrote to John Adams in 1813, "There is a natural aristocracy among men. The grounds for this are *virtue and talents*. The natural aristocracy I consider to be the most precious gift of nature, *for the instruction, the trusts, and the government of society.*" Jefferson added: "May we not even say, that form of government is best, which provides the most effectually for a pure selection of the natural *'aristoi'* into the offices of government?"[3] Lincoln, too, faced the question when

[3] Hamilton, *Federalist* No. 70; Jefferson to Adams, October 28, 1813.

he asked whether all republics must necessarily have "this inherent and fatal weakness." "Must a government," he asked, "of necessity be too strong for the liberties of its people, or too weak to maintain its own existence?"[4] His own administration gave that question an effective answer.

It can be further contended that democracy involves not only a functional but a *moral* need for strong leadership. The Lockian bias in favor of the people as against the leaders implied a certain denigration of the role of the individual in history; and subsequent defenders of democracy rashly reduced the role to the point where the individual no longer mattered and where impersonal forces, working through the masses, took control of human events.

Yet this line of argument ends up in an historical determinism which deprives history of its moral dimension by depriving the individual of accountability for his acts. Such an historical philosophy, in its ultimate implications, profoundly contradicts the democratic faith in the freedom, dignity, and responsibility of man. A convinced democrat must therefore make the case against fatalism; but to do so, to restore the moral dimension to history, one must contend for the potency of human choice: individual decisions have to make a difference to history after all. This does not mean the decisions of *all* individuals; but it does mean those of *some;* and those individuals who do make a difference become the emblems and proof of man's freedom. As Emerson said in *Representative Men,* his astute Yankee response to the romantic braggadocio of *Heroes and Hero-Worship,* "Great men exist that there may be greater men." The heroic leader has the

[4] Lincoln, Message to Congress, July 4, 1861.

Promethean responsibility to affirm human freedom against the supposed inevitabilities of history. As he does this, he combats the infection of fatalism which might otherwise paralyze mass democracy. Without heroic leaders, a society would tend to acquiesce in the drift of history. Such acquiescence is easy enough; the great appeal of fatalism, indeed, is as a refuge from the terrors of responsibility. A purposeful and vital democracy must rest on a belief in the potency of choice—on the conviction that individual decisions do affect the course of events.

Hamilton and Emerson thus modified classical democratic theory by assigning a positive role to leadership. In so doing, they interpreted the experience of democracy in the United States. The American political system, though misconceived by some as made up of three coordinate branches of equal powers, has worked best as a presidential system. Only strong Presidents have been able to overcome the tendencies toward inertia inherent in a structure so cunningly composed of checks and balances. Great Britain, too, has tempered pure Lockianism by an implicit recognition of the role of positive leadership, though in the main the presidential system seems better designed than the parliamentary system to give force to the Hamilton conception of "executive energy."

III

The United States and Britain, being empirical nations, were thus prepared to grant some recognition to the role of leadership. On the other hand, being empirical nations, they were not concerned with incorporating their deviations into a basic reconstruction of democratic theory. And on the continent of Europe, where people cared about ideology and the conventional democratic view lingered in its purity, democrats continued to cling to multi-party parliamentarianism, to mistrust leadership and to feel that dominant personalities imperiled free institutions.

For a long time, the relationship between democracy and leadership was a question of political philosophy. But toward the end of the 19th century the sociology of politics began to displace political theory as the means of getting at political truth; and the discussion of leadership entered a new phase. Pareto and Mosca contended for the pivotal role of elites in history; Michels set forth the iron law of oligarchy in the belief that he was demonstrating scientifically that "every system of leadership is incompatible with the most essential postulates of democracy";[5] and, in particular, Max Weber proposed a theory of authority which has had a hypnotic effect on subsequent analysis.

Weber's contention, of course, was that there were three pure types of legitimate authority: *traditional,* as in a tribe; *rational,* as in a bureaucracy; and *charismatic,* as under a spell. As a student of history, I must confess to a certain uneasiness at this attempt to conduct historical inquiries in terms of "ideal types"; and, as an observer of politics, I am bound to protest against the extent to which Weber's types seem to have pre-empted the discussion of leadership. For Weber's typology neither derives from nor applies to a study of democratic society. Most authority in a democracy rests neither on traditional nor on rational nor on charismatic bases. No doubt the exercise of authority in a democracy often contains traces of all elements in Weber's triad; but, in essence, the political leader in a

[5] Robert Michels, *Political Parties*, p. 400.

democracy behaves neither like the tribal chieftain, who confines himself to a repetition of practices sanctioned by immemorial custom; nor like the bureaucrat, who dwells in a world of strict and rational routines and rules; nor like the charismatic leader, who demands and receives unconditional assent and obedience. The grounds of the democratic leader's authority rest characteristically on his capacity to gain *conditional* support from enough interests and people to put together a *temporary* majority; his method is characteristically a pragmatic balancing of forces, appeals, and policies: none of this finds room in Weber's system. For this reason the Weberian categories have reinforced the European inability to cope intellectually with the problems of democratic leadership.

The concept of charisma is perhaps the most mischievous of Weber's contributions to the study of authority. For Weber charisma, in its purity, is clearly a pre-industrial concept: "the further back we look in history, the more we find this [charismatic basis for authority] to be the case." On one occasion, he referred to Robespierre's glorification of reason as "the *last* form" which charisma has assumed in its long road of varied and rich destinies; and, in the main, charisma is for him a specific feature of the world of myth and sorcery. Weber writes: "The legitimacy of charismatic rule thus rests upon the belief in magical powers, revelations, and hero worship. The source of these beliefs is the 'proving' of the charismatic quality through miracles, through victories, and other successes. . . . Such beliefs and the claimed authority resting on them therefore disappear . . . as soon as the charismatically qualified person appears to be devoid of his magical power or forsaken by his god."

The particular characteristics of charismatic authority, as defined by Weber, further emphasize its irrelevance to the modern technical world. Thus charismatic authority has nothing to do with day-to-day administration. It is "specifically outside the realm of everyday routine and the profane sphere. . . . Both rational and traditional authority are specifically forms of everyday routine control of action, while the charismatic type is the *direct antithesis* of this. Bureaucratic authority is specifically rational, in the sense of being bound to intellectually analysable rules; while charismatic authority is specifically irrational in the sense of being foreign to all rules." Charisma is equally "foreign to economic considerations." The staff of a charismatic leader has no structure or allocation of responsibility. "There is no such thing as 'appointment' or 'dismissal,' no career, no promotion. . . . There is no hierarchy. . . . There is no such thing as a definite sphere of authority and of competence." Charisma, in short, is prophetic, mystical, unstable, irrational, and, by Weber's definition, incapable of dealing with the realities of modern industrial society.[6]

Weber does make a vague effort to rescue the concept of charisma for modern purposes by describing a process which he calls the "routinisation of charisma"—i.e., the acceptance by charismatic leaders of everyday administrative necessities. But the effect of the routinization process is evidently to transform charisma into traditionalism or into bureaucratic rationalism—into the forms of authority, in short, which Weber had previously defined as the "specific" antithesis of charisma. As soon as charisma becomes organ-

[6] Gerth and Mills, *From Max Weber*, pp. 267, 272, 296; and Weber, *The Theory of Social and Economic Organisation*, pp. 360–62.

ized and rationalized, it ceases—by Weber's admission—to be charismatic and becomes its opposite. If this is so, it only demonstrates the more conclusively the uselessness of charisma as a concept with which to analyze leadership in more complicated cases than those of medicine men, warrior chieftains, and religious prophets.

It is worthwhile to argue this point at length because of the role the concept of charisma continues to play in discussions of leadership. Surely the only western leader since Robespierre who qualifies as charismatic in Weber's full sense is Hitler. Perhaps cases could be made out for Napoleon, Mussolini, Lenin, or Stalin—though, even if these men had charisma for certain associates or followers, their essential success was not due to divine afflatus of a charismatic—i.e., compulsive, thaumaturgic, unorganized, irrational—sort but precisely to highly conscious and rational organization. And to apply the adjective to leaders in a democracy—to Gladstone or Lloyd George or Churchill or Wilson or Roosevelt or even to Bismarck or De Gaulle—is to drain the concept of all meaning.

Most contemporary usage of the word charismatic (outside parts of Africa and Asia, where Weber's strict definition still applies) is metaphorical; the word has become a chic synonym for "heroic" or for "demagogic" or even just for "popular." Indeed, so far as Weber was concerned, individual leadership itself was a vanishing factor in a world increasingly dominated by the remorseless "march of bureaucracy." Charisma, which stood for individual spontaneity in his system, was losing out inexorably in the contest with bureaucratization; in Weber's vision of the future, the methodical rationalization of life decreed that heroic leaders be replaced by anonymous administrators. This thesis of bureaucratic determinism has great value in directing our attention to certain features common to all industrial societies, whatever their ideological disagreements; but it obviously greatly underrates the persistence of politics, even in the most advanced bureaucratic states; and it has little relevance at all to the question of leadership in a democracy.

To sum up: the original political theory of democracy minimized the role of heroic leadership. In the United States and Great Britain, empirical considerations modified classical democratic ideology in the direction of an acceptance of leadership as an organic part of the democratic process; but no new grand synthesis appeared to supersede the earlier, anti-leadership formulations of the democratic position. On the continent of Europe, the conventional ideology, crystallized in the parliamentary system and unmodified by experience, continued to inculcate a distrust of heroic leadership. In the meantime, leadership theory had become, in Europe at least, identified with anti-democratic social philosophies.

As a consequence, the conventional political theory of democracy remained unprepared to deal with the problems of leadership. And the intellectual position of defenders of democracy was further demoralized by the Weberian analysis of authority in terms which excluded democratic leadership and by the Weberian vision of a future in which individual leadership wouldn't matter much anyway.

IV

Today, therefore, in spite of the insights of Hamilton and Emerson and of the examples of a score of statesmen from Washington to Churchill, democratic theory still stands baffled and irresolute before the phenomenon of leadership. It remains unprepared to explain the necessities of heroic leadership; and it can thus provide little guidance to countries which see no alternative but resort to such leadership.

The problem of heroic leadership appears most urgent in the so-called underdeveloped countries seeking to compress centuries of social experience into a single generation and to advance from the ox cart to the steel mill in a single leap. The passion for forced-draft modernization imposes on these nations an exceedingly difficult and tangible economic problem: that is, to produce as much as possible and consume as little as possible so there will be savings enough to maintain a high rate of capital investment. It imposes on them also a less tangible but equally difficult social problem: that is, to revolutionize ways of work and life hardened in centuries of custom without at the same time inciting anxieties or releasing ambitions which will destroy national cohesion. The need in these new nations, in short, is for social discipline which will see traditional societies through the ordeal and tumult of transition into relatively modern industrial states.

What political system is best adapted to bring about the necessary combination of discipline and progress? In countries like Britain and the United States, with plenty of time and resources, with traditions of education and self-government, without major population problems, and with a belief in strong leadership, multiparty democracy was able to do the job—though even in these countries the suffrage, for example, was extended slowly (if far more slowly than necessary) and did not become universal for adults until after the First World War. But few of the new nations of the mid-20th century are comparably blessed: they are desperately in a hurry, their resources are inadequate compared to their populations, their level of education is low, their civic traditions are feeble, and modernization threatens nearly all the traditional institutions which hold society together. In such conditions, it is hardly surprising that heroic leadership should seem the most effective means of charging semiliterate people with a sense of national and social purpose.

The real division in these countries is not between left and right; it is between hard and soft—between leadership which has the will to do what must be done to lay the foundations for economic growth and leadership which falters before the vested interests of traditional society or the peremptory challenges of rising social groups. This desire for *effectiveness* accounts, of course, for the vast appeal of Communism to the peoples of underdeveloped countries. (Ironically Communism's historic destiny, despite the expectations of Marx, appears to be as a technique for rapid modernization in the agrarian world, not as a guarantee of Utopia in the industrial world.) For similar reasons, non-Communist countries seeking modernization have recourse to dominating personalities—Kemal, Diem, Sukarno, Ayub, Bourguiba, Nkrumah, Magsaysay, Muñoz, Nyerere, Mboya, and Nasser, Castro, Mao. Even in a nation like India, which has made an extraordinary effort to establish and use representative institutions, one feels that democracy would not have had its relative success if it had not been for the personal authority of Nehru. The use of the heroic leader as a focus for purpose in the epoch of transition is an obvious convenience for a new nation. The question is whether it can be reconciled to the theory and practice of democracy.

And, as I have already noted at the start, the resort to heroic leadership is not just a phenomenon of the new nations. European nations, struggling with problems beyond their control, watching national energies dissipate in the merry-go-round of multi-party democracy, have sought discipline and purpose in the strong leader. De Gaulle's return to power in France is only the most spectacular example of a mood which has found milder expression in Adenauer of Germany, in the confusion which has overtaken Italy since the death of De Gasperi, and even—it has been solemnly argued—in the benign "father image" of Eisenhower in the United States.

This rush to heroic leadership does obvious damage to the classical theory of democracy. Some writers have concluded from it that democracy as a system of government is moribund. Amaury de Riencourt has thus contended in *The Coming Caesars* that expanding democracy leads to imperialism and that imperialism inevitably ends in the destruction of democracy; further, that, as society grows more equalitarian, it tends increasingly to vest absolute power in the hands of a leader. "Caesarism is therefore the logical outcome of a double current . . . the growth of a world empire that cannot be ruled by republican institutions, and the gradual extension of mass democracy, which ends in the destruction of freedom and in the concentration of supreme power in the hands of one man." And even those who see no massive historic inevitabilities in these tendencies can legitimately wonder whether powerful leaders or elites are ever likely to relinquish their power peaceably; and how people are supposed to qualify themselves for self-government in any other way than through undergoing the experience of governing themselves.

"The attempt to make dictatorship serve the ends of democracy," wrote Michels, "is tantamount to the endeavour to utilise war as the most efficient means for the defence of peace, or to employ alcohol in the struggle against alcoholism."

V

Yet is the situation so truly hopeless? Does the contemporary resort to heroic leadership signify the existence of irresistible social tendencies with which democracy cannot cope and which will surely destroy it? Or is it possible to reconcile the existing situation to some degree at least with democratic theory and propose criteria by which heroic leadership which helps democracy can be distinguished from that which hurts it?

Let me return for a moment to Rousseau; for his discussions of the Legislator and the Dictator cover precisely the two cases of one-man rule described in the previous section. The founding of a state, Rousseau wrote in his *Contrat social,* required a Lawgiver, "an extraordinary figure in the State," a person of superior intelligence and character who could, if necessary, claim divine sanction for his recommendations. His mission was to constitute the state and was complete as soon as the state became a going concern; but for that period he was indispensable, and his personal role was thus legitimate. This was Rousseau's first defense of dramatic individual intervention into the democratic process; the second came about because the Legislator, however wise, could not provide for everything in advance; "the ability to foresee that some things cannot be foreseen is a very necessary quality." While only the gravest danger could justify any fundamental change in public order, Rousseau wrote, still it would be an error to make laws and institutions so rigid that they could never be suspended. Every society may confront the need for a Dictator. "Where the peril is of such proportions that the machinery of law is an actual obstacle in dealing with it, then a single ruler must be appointed who can reduce all law to silence and temporarily suspend the sovereign authority. . . . It is obvious that the People's first concern must be to see that the State shall not perish. Thus, the suspension of legal authority does not imply its abolition." So too Jefferson: "To lose our country by a scrupulous adherence to written law, would be to lose the law itself, with life, liberty, property and all those who are enjoying them with us; thus absurdly sacrificing the end to the means. . . . The line of discrimination between cases may be difficult; but the good officer is bound to draw it at his own peril, and throw himself on the justice of his country and the rectitude of his motives."[7]

Yet, even within these limits, how can one know? How can one be sure whether a heroic constitutional leader might not use his exceptional authority to abolish the constitution? How can one be sure that the Legislator will content himself with the giving of the laws and will not seize power to serve his own interests? that the Dictator will turn back the authority confided him? that the suspension of legal authority does not imply its abolition?

There is no guaranteed answer to any of these questions. But one can perhaps suggest certain things to watch which might enable a society to judge whether strong leadership is being employed to establish democracy or to establish itself.

[7] Letter to J. B. Colvin, September 20, 1810.

Here the situation differs as between old and new nations. In a country with functioning representative institutions, the contraction of individual rights and freedoms is justified only under the direst necessity. While the Executive should wield all his powers under the constitution with energy, he should not be able to abrogate the constitution except in face of war, revolution, or economic chaos. If crisis can be met no other way, it must be met that way; but his extraordinary authority must be confined to what is necessary to meet the crisis, and, once the crisis is met, then that extraordinary authority must disappear. Above all, the assumption of exceptional powers must not be made too easy: provisions like Article 48 in the Weimar constitution can become an invitation to dictatorship (which is not to suggest, of course, that the absence of Article 48 would have prevented Hitler from coming to power). Even if the power of the national parliament is diminished for the duration of the crisis, parliament should continue to sit, to watch, and to register its views. Great Britain or the United States in wartime suggest that this temporary devolution of power can take place without permanent harm to democratic institutions.[8]

VI

The problem of the new countries is more complex. For what makes short-run authoritarianism possible in Britain and the United States is precisely the strength of the antecedent tradition of liberty. Such nations can risk an interlude of crisis because the great preponderance of national values and institutions can be relied

[8] For a thoughtful discussion see Clinton Rossiter, *Constitutional Dictatorship*.

on to require reversion once the crisis is over. A nation without an antecedent tradition of liberty is obviously far more vulnerable to the encroachments of tyranny. In such countries, therefore, one must examine rigorously and vigilantly both the *ideology* and the *acts* of the leadership.

Ideology includes both the explicit commitments of the regime and the values implied by its performance. If the avowed philosophy of the regime, for example, is purposefully authoritarian, if the regime takes every opportunity to decry democracy, individual freedom, and free institutions, then there seems little hope that its ultimate impact may be democratic. Of course, prodemocratic slogans are no guarantee of pro-democratic actions; yet an ideology which explicitly identifies itself, however nominally, with values of law and of individual freedom and dignity may plant seeds which could ultimately ripen among the people into demands that the regime honor its public professions.

The question of implicit ideology revolves around the relationship between the leader and his people. A leader can embody democratic or totalitarian values in his personal style. The essence of the totalitarian leader is the demand for absolute obedience. He regards the members of his society as means to an end, and the end his own aggrandizement and glorification. The democratic leader, on the other hand, must strive to regard the members of his society as ends in themselves. Their compliance with his proposals should come not through fear or through faith but through free and rational choice. "The instructed few may not be safe leaders," said Woodrow Wilson, "except in so far as they have communicated their instruction to the many, except in so far as they have transmuted their thought into a common, a popular thought. . . . The dynamics of [democratic] leadership lie in persuasion." Persuasion—not manipulation; or, as Maritain puts it, "The question is: are the people to be *awakened* or to be *used*?"[9] The emergence of a cult of personality, for example, is an obvious danger sign. The first rule of democracy is to distrust all leaders who begin to believe their own publicity.

One way in certain instances to reduce the chances of personal tyranny is to vest power not in an individual but in a party. This may seem a frail hope in a century when parties have shown themselves as cruel and implacable—and far longer-lived—than individuals. Yet the broadly-based party or coalition of parties may become a means by which a wide variety of people find opportunity for and access to power within an ostensibly authoritarian society. The example of the Partido Revolucionario Institucional in Mexico is instructive. The PRI was the party of the Mexican Revolution; for all practical purposes, it remains today the only political party in Mexico. Yet Mexico as a nation has gradually acquired free institutions and individual liberties. These include the liberties of political opposition. But the opposition parties never get anywhere; somehow the major interests in society have found satisfactory representation within the PRI itself. The Congress Party in India seems to be playing a comparable role. For nations which need stability as well as freedom, the solution of a loose and capacious "central" party may offer the best hope. To those, like myself, who believe a two-party system offers far better guarantees of freedom, this solution will not be adequate. Yet we would all be more than happy if the new nations all enjoyed the

[9] Woodrow Wilson, *Leaders of Men*, pp. 41–42, 59; Maritain, *Man and the State*, p. 142.

measure of freedom which exists under this system in Mexico or India. Every nation has to work out forms of freedom consistent with its own culture and traditions.

The ideology of the regime, both explicit and implicit, is thus of first importance. The acts of the regime, of course, are almost as important. "When societies first come to birth," said Montesquieu, "it is the leaders who produce the institutions of the republic. Later, it is the institutions which produce the leaders." A regime genuinely desirous of moving in a democratic direction will concentrate on developing appropriate institutions. It will increase both the quantity and the quality of education. It will work for an equitable distribution of income and rising mass living standards. It will demand the emancipation of women and children. It will encourage a free and honest press. It will train public administrators. It will eliminate graft and corruption. It will pull men of talent and vigor from every class of the population into the governing process. It will begin to offset the executive power by building responsible and representative governmental institutions, starting with a national legislature. It will work to establish the supremacy of law and to strengthen the mechanisms of political opposition.

Many of these things, of course, are required by a policy of modernization, whether the leadership is trying to build a democratic or an authoritarian regime. That is why, in the end, the question of ideology has its special significance. For in spite of the determinists, whether Weberians or Marxists, the modern high-technology society will not necessarily generate a determinate and uniform political structure. It will probably assume a variety of political forms and support a variety of political institutions. Because this is so, it means that a nation will retain a certain freedom of choice.

That freedom is, of course, severely limited by the traditions of the nation, by its economic and strategic situation, and by manifold other circumstances. Yet a precious margin remains for human decision.

VII

The future remains indeterminate. Heroic leadership can lead toward democracy or away from it—depending on what the leader does with his power, and what his people permit or encourage him to do. What is plainly required is a reconstruction of democratic theory to enable us to come to terms with the problem of leadership—to enable us to decide which styles of leadership democrats can use and which they must fight. The classical democratic ideology nourishes us all; but, maintained in rigid purity, it has been an abundant source of trouble. By denying positive leadership a role within the democratic frame, it has tied the hands of democratic societies; by discouraging leadership, it has encourged crisis. As Raymond Aron has said of France, "The Republic was so afraid of great men that it was forced, from time to time, to have recourse to saviours." And the classical ideology has misled people not only about their leaders but about themselves. The citizen in a democracy simply cannot play the role in which the classical philosophy has cast him. In particular, it has assigned him a power and initiative in theory which he cannot achieve in practice; and the consequent gap between expectations and actualities unquestionably contributes to the political frustration and estrangement pervading modern democracies.[10]

[10] See M. B. Levin, *The Alienated Voter*, a most illuminating study of political alienation in Boston, Massachusetts.

Political alienation becomes another emotion driving the masses to saviors.

Thus the classical ideology generates frustrations which threaten democracy itself. To escape this, democratic theory must be revised to accept the theoretical insights of Hamilton and Emerson, which means to incorporate the practical experience of all working democracies. An adequate democratic theory will recognize that democracy is not self-executing; that leadership is not the enemy of self-government but the means by which it can be made to work; and that Caesarism has been more often produced by the failure of weak government than by the success of strong ones. Thurman Arnold once spoke of "the absurd idea that dictatorships are the result of a long series of small seizures of power on the part of a central government." The exact opposite was true: "every dictatorship which we know flowed into power like air into a vacuum because the central government, in the face of a real difficulty, declined to exercise authority." So, too, Plato saw tyranny as the consequence not of responsible authority but of anarchy. As democracy itself develops a realistic conception of the indispensable place of leadership in the democratic process—the indispensable role of leadership as witness to man's freedom—it will be in a better position to judge the pretensions of heroic leaders, and it will probably experience far less need for them.

2.

The Decline of Greatness
(1958)

Ours is an age without heroes—and, when we say this, we suddenly realize how spectacularly the world has changed in a generation. Most of us grew up in a time of towering personalities. For better or for worse, great men seemed to dominate our lives and shape our destiny. In the United States we had Theodore Roosevelt, Woodrow Wilson, Franklin Roosevelt. In Great Britain, there were Lloyd George and Winston Churchill. In other lands, there were Lenin, Stalin, Hitler, Mussolini, Clemenceau, Gandhi, Kemal, Sun Yat-sen. Outside of politics there were Einstein, Freud, Keynes. Some of these great men influenced the world for good, others for evil; but, whether for good or for evil, the fact that each had not died at birth made a difference, one believed, to everyone who lived after them.

Today no one bestrides our narrow world like a colossus; we have no giants who play roles which one can imagine no one else playing in their stead. There are a few figures on the margin of uniqueness, perhaps: Adenauer, Nehru, Tito, De Gaulle, Chiang Kai-shek, Mao Tse-tung. But there seem to be none in the epic style of those mighty figures of our recent past who

The previous piece discussed the need for strong leadership in developing countries and suggested that such leadership was not necessarily incompatible with the democratic process. This piece, written two years earlier, discusses the decline of strong leadership in the developed countries and suggests that a revival of such leadership is essential to save freedom.

seized history with both hands and gave it an imprint, even a direction, which it otherwise might not have had. As De Gaulle himself remarked on hearing of Stalin's death, "The age of giants is over." Whatever one thought, whether one admired or detested Roosevelt or Churchill, Stalin or Hitler, one nevertheless felt the sheer weight of such personalities on one's own existence. We feel no comparable pressures today. President Eisenhower, with all his pleasant qualities, has more or less explicitly renounced any desire to impress his own views on history. The Macmillans, Khrushchevs, and Gronchis have measurably less specific gravity than their predecessors. Other men could be in their places as leaders of America or Britain or Russia or Italy without any change in the course of history. Why ours should thus be an age without heroes, and whether this condition is good or bad for us and for civilization are topics worthy of investigation.

Why have giants vanished from our midst? One must never neglect the role of accident in history; and accident no doubt plays a part here. But too many accidents of the same sort cease to be wholly accidental. One must inquire further. Why should our age not only be without great men but even seem actively hostile to them? Surely one reason we have so few heroes now is precisely that we had so many a generation ago. Greatness is hard for common humanity to bear. As Emerson said, "Heroism means difficulty, postponement of praise, postponement of ease, introduction of the world into the private apartment, introduction of eternity into the hours measured by the sitting-room clock." A world of heroes keeps people from living their own private lives.

Moreover, great men live dangerously. They introduce extremes into existence—extremes of good, extremes of evil—and ordinary men after a time flinch from the ultimates and yearn for undemanding security. The Second World War was the climax of an epoch of living dangerously. It is no surprise that it precipitated a universal revulsion against greatness. The war itself destroyed Hitler and Mussolini. And the architects of victory were hardly longer-lived. After the war, the British repudiated Churchill, and the Americans (with the adoption of the 22nd Amendment), Roosevelt. In due course, the French repudiated De Gaulle (they later repented, but it took the threat of civil war to bring him back); the Chinese, Chiang Kai-shek; and the Russians, Stalin. Khrushchev, in toppling Stalin from his pedestal, pronounced the general verdict against the uncommon man: the modern world, he said, had no use for the "cult of the individual." And, indeed, carried to the excesses to which the worshipers of Hitler and Stalin carried it, even to the much milder degree to which admirers of Roosevelt and Churchill sometimes carried it, the cult of the individual was dangerous. No man is infallible, and every man needs to be reminded of this on occasion. Still, our age has gone further than this—it objects not just to hero worship but to heroes. The century of the common man has come into its own.

This term, "common man," suggests the deeper problem. There is more involved than simply a dismissal of those colossi whom the world identified with a season of blood and agony. The common man has always regarded the great man with mixed feelings—resentment as well as admiration, hatred as well as love. The Athenian who refused to vote for Aristides because he was so tired of hearing him called "the Just" expressed a natural reaction. Great men make small men aware of their smallness. Rancor is one of the unavowed but potent emotions of politics; and one must never forget that the envy of the have-nots can be quite as consuming when the haves have character or intelligence as it is when they have merely material possessions.

Modern democracy inadvertently gave envy new scope. While the purpose of democracy was to give everyone a fair chance to rise, its method enabled rancorous men to invoke "equality" as an excuse for cutting all down to their own level. "I attribute the small number of distinguished men in political life," wrote Alexis de Tocqueville after visiting the United States in the 1830's, "to the ever-increasing despotism of the majority. . . . The power of the majority is so absolute and irresistible that one must give up one's rights as a citizen and almost abjure one's qualities as a human being, if one intends to stray from the track which it prescribes." James Bryce even titled a chapter in his *American Commonwealth,* "Why Great Men Are Not Chosen President."

History has shown these prophets unduly pessimistic. Distinguished men do enter American politics; great men have been chosen President. Democracy demonstrates a capability for heroic leadership quite as much as it does a tendency toward mediocrity. Yet Tocqueville and the others were correct enough in detecting the dislike of great men as a permanent potentiality in a democracy. And the evolution of industrial society appears to have given this sentiment new force. More and more of us live and work within great organizations; an influential book has already singled out the organization man as the American of the future. The bureaucratization of American life, the decline of the working class, the growth of the white-collar class, the rise of suburbia—all this has meant the increasing homogeneity of American society. Though we continue to speak of ourselves as rugged individualists, our actual life has grown more and more collective and anonymous. As a Monsanto Chemical film put it, showing a group of technicians at work in a laboratory: "No geniuses here; just a bunch of average Americans working together." Our ideal is increasingly smooth absorption into the group rather than self-realization in the old-fashioned, strong-minded, don't-give-a-damn sense. Where does the great man fit into our homogenized society?

"The greatness of England is now all collective," John Stuart Mill wrote a century ago: "individually small, we only appear capable of anything great by our habit of combining." He might have been writing about contemporary America; but where we Americans are inclined to rejoice over the superiority of the "team," Mill added somberly, "It was men of another stamp than this that made England what it has been; and men of another stamp will be needed to prevent its decline."

But was Mill right? Do individuals really have impact on history? A powerful school of philosophers has denied any importance at all to great men. Such thinkers reject heroes as a childish hangover from the days when men ascribed everything to the action of gods. History, they assert, is not made by men, but by inexorable forces or irrevocable laws: if these forces or laws do not manifest themselves through one individual, they will do so through another. What has happened already has comprehensively and absolutely decided what will happen in the future. "If there is a single human action due to free will," wrote Tolstoi, "no historical law exists, and no conception of historical events can be formed." If all this is so, obviously the presence or absence of any particular "hero" at any particular time cannot make the slightest difference.

This view of history is a form of fatalistic determinism; and Tolstoi's *War and Peace* offers one of its most eloquent statements. Why, Tolstoi asked, did millions of men in the time of Napoleon, repudiating their common sense and their human feelings, move from west to east, slaughtering their fellows? The answers provided by historians seemed to him hopelessly superficial. His own answer was: "The war was bound to happen simply because it was bound to happen"; all previous history predetermined it. Where did this leave the great men? In Tolstoi's view, they were the most deluded figures of all. Great men, he said, "are but the labels that serve to give a name to an event and, like labels, they have the least possible connection with the event itself." The greater the man, "the more conspicuous is the inevitability and predestination of every act he commits." The hero, said Tolstoi, "is the slave of history."

There are many forms of historical fatalism. Toynbee and Spengler, with their theory of the inexorable growth and decay of civilizations, represent one form. The Marxists, with their theory that changes in the modes of production control the course of history, represent another. When Khrushchev denounced the practice of making "a hero" out of "a particular leader" and condemned the cult of the individual as "alien to the spirit of Marxism-Leninism," he was speaking the true spirit of his faith. And Marxism is not the only form of economic determinism; there are also, for example, economic determinists of the laissez-faire school who believe that all civilization is dependent on rigid adherence to a certain theory of the sacredness of private property.

Fatalists differ greatly among themselves. But, however much they differ, they unite in the conclusion that the individual plays no role of his own in history. If they are right, then nothing could matter less whether or not this is an age without heroes.

But they are not right. The philosophy of historical fatalism rests on serious fallacies. For one thing, it supposes that because a thing happens it had to happen. But causation is one matter; predestination another. The construction of a causal explanation after an event merely renders that event in some sense intelligible. It does not in the least show that this particular event, and no other, had to take place; that nothing else could possibly have occurred in its stead. The serious test of the fatalist case must be applied before the event. The only conclusive proof of fatalism would lie in the accurate prediction of events that have not yet happened. And to say, with Tolstoi, that all prior history predetermines everything that follows is to say nothing at all. It is to produce an explanation which applies equally to everything—and thus becomes so vague and limitless as to explain nothing.

Fatalism raises other difficulties. Thus it imputes reality to mystical historical "forces"—class, race, nation, the will of the people, the spirit of the times, history itself. But there are no such forces. They are merely abstractions or metaphors with no existence except in the mind of the beholder. The only evidence for them is deduction from the behavior of individuals. It is therefore the individual who constitutes the basic unit of history. And, while no individual can be wholly free—and, indeed, recent discoveries of the manifold ways in which we are unconsciously conditioned should constitute a salutary check on human vanity—one must assume the reality of an area of free choice until that assumption is challenged not by metaphysical affirmation but by verifiable proof—that is, consistently accurate prediction of the future.

Fatalism, moreover, is incompatible with human psychology and human morality. Anyone who rigorously accepted a deterministic view of life, for example, would have to abandon all notions of human responsibility, since it is manifestly unfair to praise or punish people for acts which are by definition beyond their control. But such fatalism is belied by the assumption of free choice which underlies every move we make, every word we utter, every thought we think. As Sir Isaiah Berlin observes of determinism, "If we begin to take it seriously, then, indeed, the changes in our language, our moral notions, our attitudes toward one another, our views of history, of society and of everything else will be too profound to be even adumbrated." We can no more imagine what the universe of the consistent determinist would be like than we can imagine what it would be like to live in a world without time or one with seventeen-dimensional space.

The historian concerned with concrete interpretation of actual events can easily demonstrate the futility of fatalism by trying to apply it to specific historical episodes. According to the extreme determinist view, no particular individual can make the slightest difference. As slaves of history, all individuals are, so to speak, interchangeable parts. If Napoleon had not led his armies across Europe, Tolstoi implies, someone else would have. William James, combating this philosophic fatalism, once asked the determinists whether they really believed "the convergence of sociological pressures to have so impinged on Stratford-on-Avon about April 23, 1564, that a W. Shakespeare, with all his mental peculiarities, had to be born there." And did they further believe, James continued, that "if the aforesaid W. Shakespeare had died of cholera infantum, another mother at Stratford-on-Avon would needs have engendered a duplicate copy of him to restore the sociologic equilibrium?" Who could believe such stuff? Yet, if the determinists do not mean exactly this, how can they read the individual out of history?

In December 1931 a British politician, crossing Fifth Avenue in New York between 76th and 77th streets around ten-thirty at night, was knocked down and gravely injured by an automobile. Fourteen months later an American politician, sitting in an open car in Miami, Florida, was fired on by an assassin; a man standing beside him was killed. Would the next two decades of history have been the same had Contasini's car killed Winston Churchill in 1931 and Zangara's bullets killed Franklin Roosevelt in 1933? Suppose, in addition, that Adolf Hitler had been killed in the street fighting during the Munich *Putsch* of 1923, and that Lenin and Mussolini had died at birth. Where would our century be now?

Individuals, of course, must operate within limits. They cannot do everything. They cannot, for example, propel history into directions for which the environment and the human material are not prepared: no genius, however heroic, could have brought television to ancient Troy. Yet, as Sidney Hook has convincingly argued in his thoughtful book *The Hero in History,* great men can count decisively "where the historical situation permits of major alternative paths of development."

This argument between fatalism and heroism is not one on which there is a lot to be said on both sides. The issue is far too sharp to be straddled. Either history is rigidly determined and foreordained, in which case individual striving does not matter; or it is not, in which case there is an essential role for the hero. Analysis of concrete episodes suggests that history is, within limits, open and unfinished; that men have lived who did what no substitute could ever have done; that their intervention set history on one path rather than another. If this is so, the old maxim "There are no indispensable men" would seem another amiable fallacy. There is, then, a case for heroes.

To say that there is a case for heroes is not to say that there is a case for hero worship. The surrender of decision, the unquestioning submission to leadership, the prostration of the average man before the Great Man—these are the diseases of heroism, and they are fatal to human dignity. But, if carried too far, hero worship generates its own antidote. "Every hero," said Emerson, "becomes a bore at last." And we need not go too far. History amply shows that it is possible to have heroes without turning them into gods.

And history shows, too, that when a society, in flight from hero worship, decides to do without great men at all, it gets into troubles of its own. Our contemporary American society, for example, has little use for the individualist. Individualism implies dissent from the group; dissent implies conflict; and conflict suddenly seems divisive, un-American, and generally unbearable. Our greatest new industry is evidently the production of techniques to eliminate conflict, from positive thoughts through public relations to psychoanalysis, applied everywhere from the couch to the pulpit. Our national aspiration has become peace of mind, peace of soul. The symptomatic drug of our age is the tranquilizer. "Togetherness" is the banner under which we march into the brave new world.

Obviously society has had to evolve collective institutions to cope with problems that have grown increasingly complex and concentrated. But the collective approach can be overdone. If Khrushchev worried because his collectivist society developed a cult of the individual, maybe Americans should start worrying as our so-called individualist society develops a cult of the group. We instinctively suppose that the tough questions will be solved by an interfaith conference or an interdisciplinary research team or an interdepartmental committee or an assembly of wise men meeting at Arden House. But are not these group tactics essentially means by which individuals hedge their bets and distribute the irresponsibilities? And do they not nearly always result in the dilution of insight and the triumph of mishmash? If we are to survive, we must have ideas, vision, courage. These things are rarely produced by committees. Everything that matters in our intellectual and moral life begins with an individual confronting his own mind and conscience in a room by himself.

A bland society will never be creative. "The amount of eccentricity in a society," said John Stuart Mill, "has generally been proportional to the amount of genius, mental vigor and moral courage it contained. That so few now dare to be eccentric marks the chief danger of the time." If this condition frightened Mill in Victorian England, it should frighten us much more. For our national apotheosis of the group means that we systematically lop off the eccentrics, the originals, the proud, imaginative, lonely people from whom new ideas come. What began as a recoil from hero worship ends as a conspiracy against creativity. If worship of great men brings us to perdition by one path, flight from great men brings us there just as surely by another. When we do not admire great men, then our instinct for admiration is likely to end by settling on ourselves. The one thing worse for democracy than hero worship is self-worship.

A free society cannot get along without heroes, because they are the most vivid means of exhibiting the power of free men. The hero exposes to all mankind unsuspected possibilities of conception, unimagined resources of strength. "The appearance of a great man," wrote Emerson, "draws a new circle outside of our largest orbit and surprises and commands us." Carlyle likened ordinary, lethargic times, with their unbelief and perplexity, to dry, dead fuel, waiting for the lightning out of heaven to kindle it. "The great man, with his free force direct out of God's own hand, is the lightning. . . . The rest of men waited for him like fuel, and then they too would flame."

Great men enable us to rise to our own highest potentialities. They nerve lesser men to disregard the world and trust to their own deepest instinct. "In picking out from history our heroes," said William James, "each one of us may best fortify and inspire what creative energy may lie in his own soul. This is the last justification of hero worship." Which one of us has not gained fortitude and faith from the incarnation of ideals in men, from the wisdom of Socrates, from the wondrous creativity of Shakespeare, from the strength of Washington, from the compassion of Lincoln, and above all, perhaps, from the life and the death of Jesus? "We feed on genius," said Emerson. "Great men exist that there may be greater men."

Yet this may be only the smaller part of their service. Great men have another and larger role—to affirm human freedom against the supposed inevitabilities of history. The first hero was Prometheus, who defied the gods and thus asserted the independence and autonomy of man against all determinism. Zeus punished Prometheus, chaining him to a rock and encouraging a vulture to pluck at his vitals.

Ever since, man, like Prometheus, has warred against history. It has always been a bitter and remorseless fight; for the heavy weight of human inertia lies with fatalism. It takes a man of exceptional vision and strength and will—it takes, in short, a hero—to try to wrench history from what lesser men consider its preconceived path. And often history tortures the hero in the process, chains him to a rock and exposes him to the vulture. Yet, in the model of Prometheus, man can still hold his own against the gods. Brave men earn the right to shape their own destiny.

An age without great men is one which acquiesces in the drift of history. Such acquiescence is easy and seductive; the great appeal of fatalism, indeed, is as a refuge from the terror of responsibility. Where a belief in great men insistently reminds us that individuals can make a difference, fatalism reassures us that they can't. It thereby blesses our weakness and extenuates our failure. Fatalism, in Berlin's phrase, is "one of the great alibis" of history.

Let us not be complacent about our supposed capacity to get along without great men. If our society has lost its wish for heroes and its ability to produce them, it may well turn out to have lost everything else as well.

3.

The Causes of the Civil War
A Note on Historical Sentimentalism
(1949)

The Civil War was our great national trauma. A savage fraternal conflict, it released deep sentiments of guilt and remorse—sentiments which have reverberated through our history and our literature ever since. Literature in the end came to terms with these sentiments by yielding to the South in fantasy the victory it had been denied in fact; this tendency culminated on the popular level in *Gone with the Wind* and on the highbrow level in the Nashville cult of agrarianism. But history, a less malleable medium, was constricted by the intractable fact that the war had taken place, and by the related assumption that it was, in William H. Seward's phrase, an "irrepressible conflict," and hence a justified one.

As short a time ago as 1937, for example, even Professor James G. Randall could describe himself as "unprepared to go to the point of denying that the great American tragedy could have been avoided." Yet in a few years the writing of history would succumb to the psychological imperatives which had produced *I'll Take My Stand* and *Gone with the Wind;* and Professor Randall would emerge as the leader of a triumphant new school of self-styled "revisionists." The publication of two vigorous books by Professor Avery Craven—*The Repressible Conflict* (1939) and *The Coming of the Civil War* (1942)—and the appearance of Professor Randall's own notable volumes on Lincoln—*Lincoln the President: Springfield to Gettysburg* (1945), *Lincoln and the South* (1946), and *Lincoln the Liberal Statesman* (1947)—brought about a profound reversal of the professional historian's attitude toward the Civil War. Scholars now denied the traditional assumption of the inevitability of the war and boldly advanced the thesis that a "blundering generation" had transformed a "repressible conflict" into a "needless war."

The swift triumph of revisionism came about with very little resistance or even expressed reservations on the part of the profession. Indeed, the only adequate evaluation of the revisionist thesis that I know was made, not by an academic historian at all, but by that illustrious semi-pro, Mr. Bernard DeVoto; and Mr. De-Voto's two brilliant articles in *Harper's* in 1945 unfortunately had little influence within the guild. By 1947 Professor Allan Nevins, summing up the most recent scholarship in *Ordeal of the Union,* his able general history of the 1850's, could define the basic problem of the period in terms which indicated a measured but entire acceptance of revisionism. "The primary task of statesmanship in this era," Nevins wrote, "was to furnish a workable adjustment between the two sections, while offering strong inducements to the southern people to regard their labor system not as static but evolutionary, and equal persuasions to the northern people to assume a helpful rather than scolding attitude."

This new interpretation surely deserves at least as meticulous an examination as Professor Randall is prepared to give, for example, to such a question as whether or not Lincoln was playing fives when he received the news of his nomination in 1860. The following notes are presented in the interests of stimulating such an examination.

The revisionist case, as expounded by Professors Randall and Craven, has three main premises.

First: that the Civil War was caused by the irresponsible emotionalization of politics far out of proportion to the real problems involved. The war, as Randall put it, was certainly not caused by cultural variations nor by economic rivalries nor by sectional differences; these all existed, but it was "stupid," as he declared, to think that they required war as a solution. "One of the most colossal of misconceptions" was the "theory" that "fundamental motives produce war. The glaring and obvious fact is the artificiality of war-making agitation." After all, Randall pointed out, agrarian and industrial interests had been in conflict under Coolidge and Hoover; yet no war resulted. "In Illinois," he added, "major controversies (not mere transient differences) between downstate and metropolis have stopped short of war."

Nor was slavery the cause. The issues arising over slavery were in Randall's judgment "highly artificial, almost fabricated. . . . They produced quarrels out of things that would have settled themselves were it not for political agitation." Slavery, Craven observed, was in any case a much overrated problem. It is "perfectly clear," he wrote, "that slavery played a rather minor part in the life of the South and of the Negro."

What then was the cause of war? "If one word or phrase were selected to account for the war," wrote Randall, ". . . it would have to be such a word as fanaticism (on both sides), misunderstanding, misrepresentation, or perhaps politics." Phrases like "whipped-up crisis" and "psychopathic case" adorned Randall's explanation. Craven similarly described the growing sense of sectional differences as "an artificial creation of inflamed minds." The "molders of public opinion steadily created the fiction of two distinct peoples." As a result, "distortion led a people into bloody war."

If uncontrolled emotionalism and fanaticism caused the war, how did they get out of hand? Who whipped up the "whipped-up crisis"?

Thus the second revisionist thesis: that sectional friction was permitted to develop into needless war by the inexcusable failure of political leadership in the '50's. "It is difficult to achieve a full realization of how Lincoln's generation stumbled into a ghastly war," wrote Randall. ". . . If one questions the term 'blundering generation,' let him inquire how many measures of the time he would wish copied or repeated if the period were to be approached with a clean slate and to be lived again."

It was the politicians, charged Craven, who systematically sacrificed peace to their pursuit of power. Calhoun and Adams, "seeking political advantage," mixed up slavery and expansion; Wilmot introduced his "trouble-making Proviso as part of the political game"; the repeal clause in the Kansas-Nebraska Act was "the afterthought of a mere handful of politicians"; Chase's "Appeal to the Independent Democrats" was "false in its assertions and unfair in its purposes, but it was politically effective"; the "damaging" section in the Dred Scott decision was forced "by the political ambitions of dissenting judges." "These uncalled-for moves and this irresponsible leadership," concluded Craven, blew up a "crack-pot" crusade into a national conflict.

It is hard to tell which was under attack here—the performance of a particular generation or democratic politics in general. But, if the indictment "blundering generation" meant no more than a general complaint that democratic politics placed a premium on emotionalism, then the Civil War would have been no more nor less "needless" than any event in our blundering history. The phrase "blundering generation" must consequently imply that the generation in power in the '50's was *below* the human or historical or democratic average in its blundering.

Hence the third revisionist thesis: that the slavery problem could have been solved without war. For, even if slavery were as unimportant as the revisionists have insisted, they would presumably admit that it constituted the real sticking-point in the relation between the sections. They must show therefore that there were policies with which a nonblundering generation could have resolved the slavery crisis and averted war; and that these policies were so obvious that the failure to adopt them indicated blundering and stupidity of a peculiarly irresponsible nature. If no such policies could be produced even by hindsight, then it would seem excessive to condemn the politicians of the '50's for failing to discover them at the time.

The revisionists have shown only a most vague and sporadic awareness of this problem. "Any kind of sane policy in Washington in 1860 might have saved the day for nationalism," remarked Craven; but he did not vouchsafe the details of these sane policies; we would be satisfied to know about one.[1] Similarly Randall declared that there were few policies of the '50's he would wish repeated if the period were to be lived over again; but he was not communicative about the policies he would wish pursued. Nevins likewise blamed

[1] It is fair to say that Professor Craven seems in recent years to have modified his earlier extreme position; see his article "The Civil War and the Democratic Process," *Abraham Lincoln Quarterly*, June 1947.

the war on the "collapse of American statesmanship," but restrained himself from suggesting how a non-collapsible statesmanship would have solved the hard problems of the '50's.

In view of this reticence on a point so crucial to the revisionist argument, it is necessary to reconstruct the possibilities that might lie in the back of revisionism. Clearly there could be only two "solutions" to the slavery problem: the preservation of slavery or its abolition.

Presumably the revisionists would not regard the preservation of slavery as a possible solution. Craven, it is true, has argued that "most of the incentives to honest and sustained effort, to a contented, well-rounded life, might be found under slavery. . . . What owning and being owned added to the normal relationship of employer and employee is very hard to say." In describing incidents in which slaves beat up masters, he has even noted that "happenings and reactions like these were the rule [sic], not the exception." But Craven would doubtless admit that, however jolly this system might have been, its perpetuation would have been, to say the least, impracticable.

If, then, revisionism has rested on the assumption that the nonviolent abolition of slavery was possible, such abolition could conceivably have come about through internal reform in the South; through economic exhaustion of the slavery system in the South; or through some government project for gradual and compensated emancipation. Let us examine these possibilities.

1. *The internal reform argument.* The South, the revisionists have suggested, might have ended the slavery system if left to its own devices; only the abolitionists spoiled everything by letting loose a hysteria which caused the southern ranks to close in self-defense.

This revisionist argument would have been more convincing if the decades of alleged antislavery feeling in the South had produced any concrete results. As one judicious southern historian, Professor Charles S. Sydnor, recently put it, "Although the abolition movement was followed by a decline of antislavery sentiment in the South, it must be remembered that in all the long years before that movement began no part of the South had made substantial progress toward ending slavery. . . . Southern liberalism had not ended slavery in any state."

In any case, it is difficult for historians seriously to suppose that northerners could have denied themselves feelings of disapproval over slavery. To say that there "should" have been no abolitionists in America before the Civil War is about as sensible as to say that there "should" have been no anti-Nazis in the 1930's or that there "should" be no anti-Communists today. People who indulge in criticism of remote evils may not be so pure of heart as they imagine; but that fact does not affect their inevitability as part of the historic situation.

Any theory, in short, which expects people to repress such spontaneous aversions is profoundly unhistorical. If revisionism has based itself on the conviction that things would have been different if only there had been no abolitionists, it has forgotten that abolitionism was as definite and irrevocable a factor in the historic situation as was slavery itself. And, just as abolitionism was inevitable, so too was the southern reaction against it—a reaction which, as Professor Clement Eaton has ably shown, steadily drove the free discussion of slavery out of the South. The extinction of free discussion meant, of course, the absolute extinction of any hope of abolition through internal reform.

2. *The economic exhaustion argument.* Slavery, it

has been pointed out, was on the skids economically. It was overcapitalized and inefficient; it immobilized both capital and labor; its one-crop system was draining the soil of fertility; it stood in the way of industrialization. As the South came to realize these facts, a revisionist might argue, it would have moved to abolish slavery for its own economic good. As Craven put it, slavery "may have been almost ready to break down of its own weight."[2]

This argument assumed, of course, that southerners would have recognized the causes of their economic predicament and taken the appropriate measures. Yet such an assumption would be plainly contrary to history and to experience. From the beginning the South has always blamed its economic shortcomings, not on its own economic ruling class and its own inefficient use of resources, but on northern exploitation. Hard times in the 1850's produced in the South, not a reconsideration of the slavery system, but blasts against the North for the high prices of manufactured goods. The overcapitalization of slavery led not to criticisms of the system but to increasingly insistent demands for the reopening of the slave trade. Advanced southern writers like George Fitzhugh and James D. B. DeBow were even arguing that slavery was adapted to industrialism. When Hinton R. Helper did advance before the Civil War an early version of Craven's argument, asserting that emancipation was necessary to save the southern economy, the South burned his book. Nothing in the historical record suggests that the southern ruling class was preparing to deviate from its traditional pattern of

[2] This, at least, was the belief in 1949. Subsequent investigations by Alfred Conrad and John Meyer challenge the assumption that slavery was becoming uneconomic.

self-exculpation long enough to take such a drastic step as the abolition of slavery.

3. *Compensated emancipation.* Abraham Lincoln made repeated proposals of compensated emancipation. In his annual message to Congress of December 1, 1862, he set forth a detailed plan by which states, on an agreement to abolish slavery by 1900, would receive government bonds in proportion to the number of slaves emancipated. Yet, even though Lincoln's proposals represented a solution of the problem conceivably gratifying to the slave-holder's purse as well as to his pride, they got nowhere. Two-thirds of the border representatives rejected the scheme, even when personally presented to them by Lincoln himself. And, of course, only the pressure of war brought compensated emancipation its limited hearing of 1862.

Still, granted these difficulties, does it not remain true that other countries abolished slavery without internal convulsion? If emotionalism had not aggravated the situation beyond hope, Craven has written, then slavery "might have been faced as a national question and dealt with as successfully as the South American countries dealt with the same problem." If Brazil could free its slaves and Russia its serfs in the middle of the 19th century without civil war, why could not the United States have done as well?

The analogies are appealing but not, I think, really persuasive. There are essential differences between the slavery question in the United States and the problems in Brazil or in Russia. In the first place, Brazil and Russia were able to face servitude "as a national question" because it was, in fact, a national question. Neither country had the American problem of the identification of compact sectional interests with the survival of the slavery system. In the second place, there was no race problem at all in Russia, and, though there was a race problem in Brazil, the more civilized folkways of that country relieved racial differences of the extreme tension which they breed in the South of the United States. In the third place, neither in Russia nor in Brazil did the abolition of servitude involve constitutional issues; and the existence of these issues played a great part in determining the form of the American struggle.

It is hard to draw much comfort, therefore, from the fact that other nations abolished servitude peaceably. The problem in America was peculiarly recalcitrant. The schemes for gradual emancipation got nowhere. Neither internal reform nor economic exhaustion contained much promise for a peaceful solution. The hard fact, indeed, is that the revisionists have not tried seriously to describe the policies by which the slavery problem could have been peacefully resolved. They have resorted instead to broad affirmations of faith: if only the conflict could have been staved off long enough, then somehow, somewhere, we could have worked something out. It is legitimate, I think, to ask how? where? what?—at least, if these affirmations of faith are to be used as the premise for castigating the unhappy men who had the practical responsibility for finding solutions and failed.

Where have the revisionists gone astray? In part, the popularity of revisionism obviously parallels that of *Gone with the Wind*—the victors paying for victory by pretending literary defeat. But the essential problem is why history should be so vunerable to this literary fashion; and this problem, I believe, raises basic questions about the whole modern view of history. It is perhaps stating the issue in too portentous terms. Yet I cannot escape the feeling that the vogue of revisionism is connected with the modern tendency to seek in optimistic sentimentalism an escape from the severe demands of moral decision; that it is the offspring of our modern sentimentality which at once evades the essential moral problems in the name of a superficial objectivity and asserts their unimportance in the name of an invincible progress.

The revisionists first glided over the implications of the fact that the slavery system was producing a closed society in the South. Yet that society increasingly had justified itself by a political and philosophical repudiation of free society; southern thinkers swiftly developed the anti-libertarian potentialities in a social system whose cornerstone, in Alexander H. Stephens' proud phrase, was human bondage. In theory and in practice, the South organized itself with mounting rigor against ideas of human dignity and freedom, because such ideas inevitably threatened the basis of their own system. Professor Frank L. Owsley, the southern agrarian, has described inadvertently but accurately the direction in which the slave South was moving. "The abolitionists and their political allies were threatening the existence of the South as seriously as the Nazis threaten the existence of England," wrote Owsley in 1940; ". . . Under such circumstances the surprising thing is that so little was done by the South to defend its existence."

There can be no question that many southerners in the '50's had similar sentiments; that they regarded their system of control as ridiculously inadequate; and that, with the book-burning, the censorship of the mails, the gradual illegalization of dissent, the South was in process of creating a real machinery of repression in order more effectively "to defend its existence." No society, I suppose, encourages criticism of its basic institutions. Yet, when a democratic society acts in self-defense, it does so at least in the name of human dignity and freedom. When a society based on bond slavery acts to eliminate criticism of its peculiar institution, it outlaws what a believer in democracy can only regard as the abiding values of man. When the basic institutions are evil, in other words, the effect of attempts to defend their existence can only be the moral and intellectual stultification of the society.

A society closed in the defense of evil institutions thus creates moral differences far too profound to be solved by compromise. Such a society forces upon everyone, both those living at the time and those writing about it later, the necessity for a moral judgment; and the moral judgment in such cases becomes an indispensable factor in the historical understanding.

The revisionists were commendably anxious to avoid the vulgar errors of the post-Civil War historians who pronounced smug individual judgments on the persons involuntarily involved in the tragedy of the slave system. Consequently they tried hard to pronounce no moral judgments at all on slavery. Slavery became important, in Craven's phrase, "only as a very ancient labor system, probably at this time rather near the end of its existence"; the attempt to charge this labor system with moral meanings was "a creation of inflamed imaginations." Randall, talking of the Kansas-Nebraska Act, could describe it as "a law intended to subordinate the slavery question and hold it in *proper* proportion" (my italics). I have quoted Randall's even more astonishing argument that, because major controversies between downstate and metropolis in Illinois stopped short of war, there was reason to believe that the Civil War could have been avoided. Are we to take it that the revisionists seriously believe that the downstate-metropolis fight in Illinois—or the agrarian-industrial fight in the Coolidge and Hoover administrations—were in any useful sense comparable to the difference between the North and South in 1861?

Because the revisionists felt no moral urgency themselves, they deplored as fanatics those who did feel it, or brushed aside their feelings as the artificial product of emotion and propaganda. The revisionist hero was Stephen A. Douglas, who always thought that the great moral problems could be solved by sleight-of-hand. The phrase "northern man of southern sentiments," Randall remarked, was "said opprobriously . . . as if it were a base thing for a northern man to work with his southern fellows."

By denying themselves insight into the moral dimension of the slavery crisis, in other words, the revisionists denied themselves a historical understanding of the intensities that caused the crisis. It was the moral issue of slavery, for example, that gave the struggles over slavery in the territories or over the enforcement of the fugitive slave laws their significance. These issues, as the revisionists have shown with cogency, were not in themselves basic. But they were the available issues; they were almost the only points within the existing constitutional framework where the moral conflict could be faced; as a consequence, they became charged with the moral and political dynamism of the central issue. To say that the Civil War was fought over the "unreal" issue of slavery in the territories is like saying that the Second World War was fought over the "unreal" issue of the invasion of Poland. The democracies could not challenge fascism inside Germany any more than opponents of slavery could challenge slavery inside the South; but the extension of slavery, like the extension of fascism, was an act of aggression which made a moral choice inescapable.

Let us be clear what the relationship of moral judgment to history is. Every historian, as we all know in an argument that surely does not have to be repeated in 1949, imports his own set of moral judgments into the writing of history by the very process of interpretation; and the phrase "every historian" includes the category "revisionist." Mr. DeVoto in his paraphrases of the revisionist position has put admirably the contradictions on this point: as for "moral questions, God forbid. History will not put itself in the position of saying that any thesis may have been wrong, any cause evil. . . . History will not deal with moral values, though of course the Republican radicals were, well, culpable." The whole revisionist attitude toward abolitionists and radicals, repeatedly characterized by Randall as "unctuous" and "intolerant," overflows with the moral feeling which is so virtuously excluded from discussions of slavery.

An acceptance of the fact of moral responsibility does not license the historian to roam through the past ladling out individual praise and blame: such an attitude would ignore the fact that all individuals, including historians, are trapped in a web of circumstance which curtails their moral possibilities. But it does mean that there are certain essential issues on which it is necessary for the historian to have a position if he is to understand the great conflicts of history. These great conflicts are relatively few because there are few enough historical phenomena which we can confidently identify as evil. The essential issues appear, moreover, not in pure and absolute form, but incomplete and imperfect, compromised by the deep complexity of history. Their proponents may often be neurotics and fanatics, like the abolitionists. They may attain a social importance only when a configuration of nonmoral factors—economic, political, social, military—permit them to do so.

Yet neither the nature of the context nor the pretensions of the proponents alter the character of the issue. And human slavery is certainly one of the few issues of whose evil we can be sure. It is not just "a very ancient labor system"; it is also a betrayal of the basic values of our Christian and democratic tradition. No historian can understand the circumstances which led to its abolition until he writes about it in its fundamental moral context. "History is supposed to understand the difference between a decaying economy and an expanding one," as Mr. DeVoto well said, "between solvency and bankruptcy, between a dying social idea and one coming to world acceptance. . . . It is even supposed to understand implications of the difference between a man who is legally a slave and one who is legally free."

"Revisionism in general has no position," DeVoto continues, "but only a vague sentiment." Professor Randall well suggested the uncritical optimism of that sentiment when he remarked, "To suppose that the Union could not have been continued or slavery outmoded without the war and without the corrupt concomitants of war is hardly an enlightened assumption." We have here a touching afterglow of the admirable 19th-century faith in the full rationality and perfectibility of man; the faith that the errors of the world would all in time be "outmoded" (Professor Randall's use of this word is suggestive) by progress. Yet the experience of the 20th century has made it clear that we gravely overrated man's capacity to solve the problems of existence within the terms of history.

This conclusion about man may disturb our complacencies about human nature. Yet it is certainly more in accord with history than Professor Randall's "enlightened" assumption that man can solve peaceably all the problems which overwhelm him. The unhappy fact is that man occasionally works himself into a log-jam; and that the log-jam must be burst by violence. We know that well enough from the experience of the last decade. Are we to suppose that some future historian will echo Professor Nevins' version of the "failure" of the 1850's and write: "The primary task of statesmanship in the 1930's was to furnish a workable adjustment between the United States and Germany, while offering strong inducements to the German people to abandon the police state and equal persuasions to the Americans to help the Nazis rather than scold them"? Will some future historian adapt Professor Randall's formula and write that the word "appeaser" was used "opprobriously" as if it were a "base" thing for an American to work with his Nazi fellow? Obviously this revisionism of the future (already foreshadowed in the work of Charles A. Beard) would represent, as we now see it, a fantastic evasion of the hard and unpleasant problems of the '30's. I doubt whether our present revisionism would make much more sense to the men of the 1850's.

The problem of the inevitability of the Civil War, of course, is in its essence a problem devoid of meaning. The revisionist attempt to argue that the war could have been avoided by "any kind of sane policy" is of interest less in its own right than as an expression of a characteristically sentimental conception of man and of history. And the great vogue of revisionism in the historical profession suggests, in my judgment, ominous weaknesses in the contemporary attitude toward history.

We delude ourselves when we think that history teaches us that evil will be "outmoded" by progress and that politics consequently does not impose on us the necessity for decision and for struggle. If historians are to understand the fullness of the social dilemma they seek to reconstruct, they must understand that sometimes there is no escape from the implacabilities of moral decision. When social conflicts embody great moral issues, these conflicts cannot be assigned for solution to the invincible march of progress; nor can they be by-passed with "objective" neutrality. Not many problems perhaps force this decision upon the historian. But, if any problem does in our history, it is the Civil War.

To reject the moral actuality of the Civil War is to foreclose the possibility of an adequate account of its causes. More than that, it is to misconceive and grotesquely to sentimentalize the nature of history. For history is not a redeemer, promising to solve all human problems in time; nor is man capable of transcending the limitations of his being. Man generally is entangled in insoluble problems; history is consequently a tragedy in which we are all involved, whose keynote is anxiety and frustration, not progress and fulfillment. Nothing exists in history to assure us that the great moral dilemmas can be resolved without pain; we cannot therefore be relieved from the duty of moral judgment on issues so appalling and inescapable as those involved in human slavery; nor can we be consoled by sentimental theories about the needlessness of the Civil War into regarding our own struggles against evil as equally needless.

One must emphasize, however, that this duty of judgment applies to issues. Because we are all implicated in the same tragedy, we must judge the men of the past with the same forbearance and charity which we hope the future will apply toward us.

4.

Probing the American Experience
(1958)

It has become a commonplace in the United States to talk about the "boom" in history. There are indeed abundant evidences of a revival of interest in the past and especially in the American past. Historical novels, of course, have always been popular in America. But now there are book clubs dedicated exclusively to the distribution of nonfictional historical writing. A new magazine, *American Heritage,* with amiable historical essays surrounded by expensive illustrations, has a circulation as large as the *Atlantic Monthly* and several times that of the *New Republic.* Thousands of American families make pilgrimages to the colonial restoration at Williamsburg every year. Children's books go in more than ever for historical heroes and episodes: one series—Random House's Landmark Books—has sold nearly five million copies in less than a decade. A third of American colleges now require American history for a degree; and most large universities offer graduate degrees in a new area called (optimistically perhaps) American Civilization. With the centennial of the American Civil War impending in 1961, one must dig in against a landslide of books of the battles, generals, and politicians—not to speak of the symbols, myths, social structure, interpersonal relationships, and sex habits—of the Union and the Confederacy.

But there is something lacking. Just as the current American religious revival has everything except religion, so the historical revival seems to have nearly everything except history. It mostly deals not in the critical reconstruction of the past, which is the historian's business, but in pseudo-history—in antiquarianism, monuments, shrines, American primitives, patriotic self-approbation, and nostalgia. So, just as serious neo-orthodox theologians regard the Billy Grahams and Norman Vincent Peales with revulsion, serious technical historians tend to recoil from the historical boom, reject the popular audience, and retire to their own specializations with redoubled zeal.

There is nothing new about this separation between the technical historian and the cultivated public. In spite of a splendid early tradition—from George Bancroft to Henry Adams—of brilliant nonprofessionals addressing wide audiences on historical topics, the onward march of German professionalism proved irresistible in the United States in the last years of the 19th century. The result was the triumph of the Ph.D. system, the beginning of commitment to narrow specialization, the establishment of the monograph as the ordained medium of historical publication, and the steady withdrawal of the technical historian from general intellectual discourse. These are still dominating characteristics of the historical profession in America. Professional historians who write for audiences larger than their graduate students risk the disdain, if not the active hostility, of many of their colleagues.

Nevertheless, there is some indication that the authority of the monograph is declining. One notes a new readiness on the part of some of our best professionals to undertake comprehensive, multi-volume works— Dumas Malone's biography of Thomas Jefferson, for example, Arthur Link's of Woodrow Wilson, Frank Freidel's of Franklin Roosevelt; or, even more to the point, Allan Nevins' volumes (*Ordeal of the Union* and *The Emergence of Lincoln*) superseding James Ford Rhodes on the 1850's, the distinguished climax of the career of an excellent historian whose reputation within the profession would doubtless be twice as great if he had written half as much.

As the focus widens, as the historian moves beyond the minute factual problem, he can no longer keep larger questions of historical interpretation out of his consideration. The lively minds in the profession are already displaying a marked readiness to experiment in historical method. At the moment, the kinetic field in American historiography is certainly intellectual history; and intellectual history is providing the means not just of pursuing its own purposes—the origin and impact of ideas—but of restoring fertility to apparently exhausted tracts of conventional history. Seen through the perspective of ideas, political history, constitutional history, and institutional history acquire a new force and vitality. Richard Hofstadter, for example, has shown brilliantly in *The Age of Reform* how intellectual history can rejuvenate political history. Some historians are even approaching such jaded subjects as the frontier and Jacksonian democracy through the analysis of myth and metaphor, writing history as if it were a branch of the New Criticism; Henry Nash Smith's imaginative *Virgin Land* was the first significant work of this sort, and Marvin Meyers' *The Jacksonian Persuasion* a recent example.

The rise of intellectual history has been accompanied by a growing interest on the part of younger historians in the ideas and techniques (sometimes, alas, in the vocabulary) of the so-called "behavioral sciences." These sciences—sociology, social psychology, social anthropology—have been much pushed by the foundations; the Ford Foundation has even set up a center at

Stanford University where historians and behavioral scientists are encouraged to engage in intellectual cohabitation. For some historians, the behavioral sciences have proved a rather heady potion. For example, that influential work *The Authoritarian Personality* of T. W. Adorno and associates beguiled one or two into attributing racial intolerance primarily to rigid parental authority, as if parents south of the Mason-Dixon line were notably more authoritarian than parents in Massachusetts or Minnesota. Similarly the phenomenon of McCarthyism is traced to "status anxiety" in that stimulating book *The New American Right*; yet this ascription seems both unhistorical and naïve in view of the fact that McCarthyism perished with the Korean War while status anxiety remains as acute as ever.

The ultimate intellectual implication of the behavioral sciences is rather ominous for history. The deeper thrust of the "behavioralist" approach seems to be to expel ideas and free choice from history and reduce everything to a set of reflexes conditioned, according to the school, by class or status or ethnic group or the traumas of infancy. This is often accompanied by a passion for quantification carrying with it the unspoken assumption that problems not susceptible to quantitative resolution are not worth consideration. (The behavioral scientists thus play rather the role in the United States that Professor Butterfield attributes to Sir Lewis Namier and his followers in England.) Nonetheless, the practical effect of the exposure of historians to the behavioral sciences should be for the good. Already the experience has opened up a new range of issues to history—questions of social mobility, acculturation, status tension, and social myth. Anything which makes American historians *think* cannot help benefiting the profession.

Still, if intellectual history and the behavioral sciences are causing a valuable ferment, the dismal fact remains that at present the professional historian does not matter much in the general intellectual life of the United States, in the sense that men like Berlin, Taylor, Namier, Brogan, Butterfield, Toynbee, Trevor-Roper count for something outside the profession in England (or, indeed, in the sense that Beard, Becker, and Turner counted for something a generation ago in America). The American historian seems too often unreflective, pedantic, and sterile. He does not ask himself the questions likely to produce answers that would make a difference to society. The editor of the *American Historical Review* recently wrote a little sadly about the essays submitted to his journal last year, "But a handful attempted to formulate, and test with evidence, new and fertile hypotheses which might enrich our understanding of the past." "Bold new views," he added, were especially lacking among those writing in the field of American history. Last December Professor William L. Langer startled the American Historical Association by appealing in his presidential address to his colleagues to read Freud.

Part of the reason for the aridity of technical history is the suffocating effect of false conceptions of professional decorum—the fear that the historian corrupts himself when he writes for a non-professional audience. The aridity is also the consequence of an educational system geared to the production each year of enough teachers to meet the needs of American mass education. As Oscar Handlin has put it, "The profession does not aim to produce more than a few score original creative scholars. Rather its objective is to supply the thousands of teachers with the cachet of the Ph.D. that the hundreds of collegiate institutions and advanced secondary schools demand of it." Doubtless another reason is the fact that historians, too, have succumbed to the homogenizing atmosphere of the age of Eisenhower. I don't mean that they have been enlisted, like physicists, in the cold war; there has been neither the effort to do this on the part of government nor the desire on the part of the profession. But, for one reason or another, historians have relaxed from their skepticism of the '20's and '30's and flinch from the searching question and the iconoclastic conclusion.

If historians are doing little to illuminate the deeper issues of the American experience, neither, it must be said, are contemporary American political writers. Political journalism, in particular, has gone into a melancholy decay. A comparison of Robert Donovan's uncritical "inside" book about the Eisenhower administration with the similar and far more critical "inside" works of Ernest Lindley about the first Roosevelt term, and of Joseph Alsop about the second, illustrates the decline. Under the influence of *Time*, the relentless notation of external detail (the color of a man's suit, the condition of his hair, and what he had for dinner) has created a spurious conception of journalistic "truth" which has driven out analysis and ideas. Some of the columnists still do well—Walter Lippmann has never in a long and uncommonly articulate life been more wise and trenchant than in the last two years; Mr. Alsop continues lively and apocalyptic; Doris Fleeson writes an astute daily commentary; James Wechsler, James Reston, Marquis Childs, William V. Shannon, and the *New Republic*'s T.R.B. (Richard Strout) are generally worth reading. Murray Kempton contributes an intermittently brilliant column to the New York *Post,* and Richard Rovere writes penetratingly of politics for the *New Yorker.* One political journalist—

Samuel Lubell—has had far more impact than any political scientist in making people reconsider the electoral processes of American politics. But these are exceptions in a generally boring flow of articles and books on the political situation. As for more pretentious political writing, the hothouse attempt to breed a New Conservatism in the United States has produced stillborn results, and liberalism has not yet emancipated itself from the doctrines of the 1930's.

Where the historian and the political writer have abdicated, other voices are making themselves heard on the central problems of American society. Economists like J. K. Galbraith and Adolf Berle, theologians like Reinhold Niebuhr, sociologists like David Riesman, social critics like William H. Whyte, Jr., literary critics like Edmund Wilson and Lionel Trilling—such men are doing much more than historians or political writers to explore the deeper preoccupations of American culture and attempt a fresh assessment of the meaning of the American experience. Out of their work there is already emerging a new portrait of America. As this begins to take shape, one may legitimately hope that it will stimulate historians and political writers to a more thoughtful, imaginative, and astringent conception of their purposes.

5.
The Statistical Soldier
(1949)

Too many obvious frauds were at last committed in the name of sociology. At the same time, the allied breeds of social psychology and social anthropology began to promise new and exciting forms of cross-fertilization. So the old and toothless beast was put out to pasture. In its place has come its more carnivorous son, known in his more modest mood under some such name as "social relations," or, more often, in a tone of majestic simplicity, as "social science."

The historical eye perhaps finds little new in this transformation. Sociology has whored after the natural sciences from the start; certain persons have always been able to convince themselves that these passions were requited; and the result has been to beguile the sociologists into egotistic and self-evidently absurd theorizations. Such efforts bring the whole study into mild disrepute and lead the younger practitioners to try to flee the family disgrace by hanging out some new and deceptive shingle. The champions of "social science" today have hardly advanced beyond Lester Ward or Comte in the grandiosity of their promises.

But they have far surpassed such a lonely and self-respecting figure as Ward in the persistence and success of their showmanship. Bursting onto university campuses after the war, overflowing with portentous if vague hints of mighty wartime achievements (not, alas, to be disclosed because of security), fanatical in their zeal and shameless in their claims, they persuaded or panicked many university administrations into giving their studies top priorities. Needless to say, they scored an even more brilliant success with the foundations. Certain foundation directors even decided that virtually all their funds for research in the social sciences should be expended on projects of the "social science" variety; the individual scholar, so far as they were concerned, was through.

The mark of the beast is today eloquent through our academic life: the remorseless jargon (certain social scientists in one great university recently produced a solemn memorandum entitled "Toward a Common Language in the Social Sciences" — English not apparently being adequate); the notion that a knowledge of the Trobriand Islander or the Sioux is the first requisite for the study of modern America or Russia; the idea of research by committee, six men always being accounted better than one and the responsibility being distributed like the credit lists in a Hollywood film; the fetish of "interdisciplinary" projects; the proliferation of apparatus, each new gadget more elaborate and expensive than the rest: the whole happily subsidized by the foundations, carrying to triumphant completion their ancient hope of achieving the bureaucratization of American intellectual life.

Well, the "social science" machinery has been grinding away for some years now. Occasionally skeptics approach the devout and say with proper humility: You have basked in the smile of deans and in the favor of foundations. You are discovering the secrets of the ages. We wish to share in the new enlightenment you are bringing us. But what, oh wise one, should we read? Can you name a single book that would give some idea of the great revelations which lie in wait? The oracle at that point used to become muffled. Then one began to hear of *The American Soldier.* This work, one was told, was the real stuff; this would settle the doubts.

The American Soldier is now 50 per cent with us, the first two of four large volumes having been published by the Princeton University Press. These volumes represent the analysis by what the jacket describes as "a brilliant group of sociologists and social psychologists" of materials collected by the Research Branch, Information and Education Division, United States Army. These materials, primarily surveys of attitude and opinion, were gathered to assist the Army in the best utilization of its manpower during the war. The first volume deals with problems of adjustment during army life; the second with the problems of combat and its aftermath. Volumes three and four will deal primarily with technical and methodological questions.

It should be said, first of all, that these volumes give an entirely convincing picture of the great usefulness to the Army of the Research Branch. One can only admire the resourcefulness with which the tests were devised and the courage with which the heads of the Branch opposed Army policies they considered unwise. Nor can one do anything but praise the prevailing modesty and clarity with which the results of the research are written up. There can be no question either that the problems and methods embraced under the "social science" rubric include much of very great importance to the study of human behavior, and that these studies should be prosecuted.

But to say this is not to satisfy the social relations hucksters. Indeed, the more basic questions are raised, not by the relatively innocuous practice of "social science," but by its mystique — its pretensions to new knowledge and to new certitude, its pretensions ultimately to a body of knowledge with the same properties of verifiability and predictability as modern physical theory. Turning to *The American Soldier*, one can legitimately ask: (1) Does this kind of research yield anything new? and (2) Does what it does yield constitute a higher and more certain form of knowledge?

The answer to the first question is easy. Most of *The American Soldier* is a ponderous demonstration in Newspeak of such facts as these: new recruits do not like noncoms; front-line troops resent rear-echelon troops; combat men manifest a high level of anxiety as compared to other soldiers; married privates are more likely than single privates to worry about their families back home. Indeed, one can find little in the 1200 pages of text and the innumerable surveys which is not described more vividly and compactly, and with far greater psychological insight, in a small book entitled *Up Front* by Bill Mauldin. What Mauldin may have missed will turn up in the pages of Ernie Pyle.

The authors of *The American Soldier* show a sporadic and apprehensive recognition of their lack of originality. One contributor writes defensively that perhaps Conrad could communicate the "feel" of a hurricane better, but that meteorology has its uses too. A more aggressive contributor, describing writers in his barbarous patois as "insightful observers," comments that their "recorded observations and insights are, however, fragmentary, relatively unsystematic, and nonquantitative. What can therefore be added is further systematization, based upon a quantitative treatment of many soldiers' responses."

"Social science," thus, does not discover; it systematizes through quantification and thereby places knowledge on a truly "scientific" basis. Such an undertaking involves a technique; and the technique you must believe in to accept *The American Soldier* is polling. Recent criticism by such persons as Lindsay Rogers and Harry S. Truman has shaken our faith in the infallibility of the pollsters. Indeed, given a conflict between a poll and an "insightful observer," even the authors of *The American Soldier* generally (see, e.g., Volume II, page 29) reinterpret the poll in order to bring it into line with common sense. The individual human experience is supposed to vanish away in the whirl of punch cards and IBM machines. Yet an indissoluble residue of subjectivity remains. "There is no escape," even *The American Soldier* concedes, "from the need for using 'good judgment' in interpretations." So, beneath the disguise of Superman, we gradually discern the "insightful observer" whom we had previously consigned to an unimportant place on the library shelf.

What does "good judgment" (or even "'good judgment'") mean to the social psychologist? One cannot escape the impression that their whole system of interpretation is inherently deficient in two crucial aspects: in a sense of individual psychology and in a sense of history. A comparison of the chapter in *The American Soldier* on "Morale Attitudes of Combat Flying Personnel in the Air Corps" with the studies of such Air Force psychiatrists as Grinker, Hastings, and Bond shows how incomparably richer and more illuminating the depth method of the psychiatrist is than the polls of the social psychologist. As for history, the authors of *The American Soldier* have almost achieved the tour de force of writing about the American in the Second World War with practically no reference to the historical context from which he came. Nor do the few random sallies in this direction inspire confidence. When someone writes that "the intellectual history of the period between the two world wars was one of a developing climate of opinion distrustful of committing oneself to causes," it can only be concluded that he has never heard of communism, fascism or the New Deal. One comes to feel, indeed, that the American soldier existed, neither in life nor in history, but in some dreary statistical vacuum. One ends by wondering whether the whole theory of social quantification does not involve so systematic an abstraction from the total experience of man as to squeeze out the more meaningful factors in individual behavior in the sleight-of-hand which pretends to eliminate — but cannot — the insight of the observer.

The American Soldier is an entirely harmless book. The Army certainly wasted no money in maintaining the Research Branch, even if the Social Science Research Council might have done better to subsidize the same number of individual scholars. "Social science" as a whole is perhaps doing no present harm, except as it engrosses money and energy which might be put more wisely to other uses. But it might eventually do great harm in obscuring from ourselves the ancient truths concerning the vanity of human wishes, and the distortions worked by that vanity upon the human performance.

If *The American Soldier* represents the highest achievement of the new "science" of human behavior, then we have a considerable distance to go before resigning ourselves to a regime of total manipulation. Its practitioners are in the stage of alchemy, not of chemistry. Probably that is why they proclaim so loudly that they are on the verge of discovering the philosopher's stone.

Part II
Liberalism and Policy

6.
Liberalism in America
A Note for Europeans
(1956)

In a sense all of America is liberalism. "The great advantage of the American," Tocqueville wrote over a century ago, "is that he has arrived at a state of democracy without having to endure a democratic revolution and that he is born free without having to become so." With freedom thus a matter of birthright and not of conquest, the American assumes liberalism as one of the presuppositions of life. With no social revolution in his past, the American has no sense of the role of catastrophe in social change. Consequently, he is, by nature, a gradualist; he sees few problems which cannot be solved by reason and debate; and he is confident that nearly all problems can be solved. It is characteristically American that every war in American history has been followed by an outburst of historical "revisionism" seeking to prove that the war was unnecessary.

It is this birthright liberalism of American society which justified the European political thinkers two centuries ago who saw in America the archetype of primal political innocence. Here, at last, men were free to inscribe their own aspirations in society without the clog or corruption of the accumulated evils of history. "In the beginning," as Locke put it, "all the world was America." This was, of course, an overstatement, since no American could escape the history he brought with him from Europe, any more than he could escape the peculiar stamp of the American experience, especially the ever-receding frontier. But, though extreme, the view was not entirely misleading. The American *tabula rasa* may not have been totally blank; but it lacked one determining phenomenon in particular of the European scene—that is, feudalism. As a young American political scientist, Professor Louis Hartz of Harvard, has brilliantly argued in his recent book *The Liberal Tradition in America,* the absence of feudalism is a basic factor in accounting for the pervasive liberalism of the American political climate.

The absence of feudalism meant the absence of a static and confining social order, and it meant equally the absence of a profound social passion to uproot and destroy that order. It deprived America simultaneously of traditions of reaction and of revolution. The American Revolution was thus a revolution of limited liability, aiming at national independence more than at social change. And since independence, American political conflict has taken place in an atmosphere—sometimes felt rather than understood—of consensus. The tensions of the French Revolution still vibrate in the Fourth Republic; but Thomas Jefferson could dispel most of the apprehensions of "the Glorious Revolution of 1800" by proclaiming in his inaugural, "We are all Republicans, all Federalists." There have been few periods of more embittered political feeling in America than the age of Andrew Jackson; but Tocqueville, seeing America in the perspective of France, could not but feel the differences between the Jacksonians and the Whigs to be superficial and trivial.

American historians have not always drawn so mellow a picture of American political history; but these historians, Mr. Hartz argues with some justice, have too often ignored the framework of consensus in their zest for conflict. American campaign oratory, Hartz warns, should never be taken for a sober description of issues; American partisan enthusiasm gives an air of violence to sham battles which the observer would nonetheless be sadly mistaken if he takes for war *à l'outrance*. And this combination of verbal violence and underlying accord further helps explain the semantic obscurity of American politics. Every one, in one mood or another, has claimed to be a liberal or a conservative—even Franklin D. Roosevelt to be a conservative, even Herbert Hoover to be a liberal. Such words in the American consensus tend to be counters in a game rather than symbols of impassable divisions of principle.

Up to this point, Mr. Hartz is surely right. The American political tradition is essentially based on a liberal consensus. Even those Americans who privately reject the liberal tradition—like the Communists of the '30's and '40's or the McCarthyites of the '50's—can succeed only as they profess a relationship to liberalism. They wither and die in a liberal society when their antiliberal purposes are fully exposed and understood.

But this invocation of consensus does not perhaps tell the whole story. As historians of the '30's saw the American past too much in terms of conflict, so there is a danger that historians and political scientists today may see the past too much in terms of agreement.

For, however much Americans have united on fundamentals, there still remain sharp and significant differences—the differences which divided a Jefferson from a Hamilton, a Jackson from a Daniel Webster, a William Jennings Bryan from a McKinley, a Franklin Roosevelt from a Hoover. Nor have those been local and fleeting differences. Rather they have been differences to which time has given a sense of continuity, so that two identifiable traditions have emerged in American politics, and the liberal tradition, at least, has been animated by a vigorous sense in each period that it is the bearer of a cause which stretches back to Jefferson and the beginning of the Republic. The conflict within the liberal consensus between "liberalism" and "conservatism" has been one of the sources of creativity and advance in American history. Any account of American politics which leaves it out impoverishes and distorts the American past.

The use of words like "liberalism" and "conservatism" immediately raises questions of definition. The absence of a feudal tradition, of course, has gravely affected the character of American "conservatism." It has deprived American conservatism of the instinct to be responsible as well as the instinct to kill, of both decorum and of terror, reducing it, on the whole, to expressions—or, rather, ejaculations—of individual or class self-interest. In recent years a school of New Conservatives has sought to rehabilitate the tradition of American conservatism. But, since many of the New Conservatives take positions on immediate issues which are closer to the views of American liberals than of American conservatives, the semantic confusion has only been compounded.

Accepting the theory of America as essentially a liberal society, how can one distinguish the liberal and conservative tendencies within that society? Some of the New Conservatives tell us that the liberal believes in the perfectibility of men, while the conservative has a conviction of human fallibility and of original sin. Yet no one has preached more effectively to this generation of the reality of human imperfection than the liberal (in politics, at least) Reinhold Niebuhr, while it was Andrew Carnegie, a conservative, who used to say of man that there was no "conceivable end to his march to perfection." And it would be hard to argue, for example, that the words of Dwight D. Eisenhower, the conservative, show a greater sense of the frailty of human striving or the tragedy of the human condition than those of the liberal Adlai Stevenson.

Similarly, it is difficult to believe that the crucial distinction lies in the attitude toward the role of the state. Thus the conservatives Alexander Hamilton and John Quincy Adams and the liberal Franklin D. Roosevelt agreed in advocating government direction of the economy, while the liberal Thomas Jefferson and the conservative Herbert Hoover agreed in wishing to limit the power of the state.

Nor does the distinction lie in the question of civil freedom. Some liberals have been majoritarians with a limited concern for the rights of minorities; some conservatives have been valiant defenders of the liberties of conscience and expression. Nor does it even really lie in the question of private property. While conservatives have been the more vigilant champions of private property, liberals have perhaps stood more consistently for the rights of property in Locke's original sense of a product of nature with which man mixes his labor.

All this ambiguity and even interchangeability of position testify once again to the absence of deep differences of principle in American society. "Each is a great half," wrote Emerson of the liberal and the conservative, "but an impossible whole. Each exposes the abuses of the other but in a true society, in a true man, both must combine." In elaborating on the character of each "great half," Emerson went on to define the diverging tendencies which liberalism and conservatism have embodied within the American consensus. His distinction, I think, is still useful today.

For Emerson the basic difference was between the party of the past and the party of the future, between the party of memory and the party of hope. It is still true that the American liberal believes that society can and should be improved, and that the way to improve it is to apply human intelligence to social and economic problems. The conservative, on the other hand, opposes efforts at purposeful change—especially when they threaten the existing distribution of power and wealth—because he believes that things are about as good as they can be reasonably expected to be, and that any change is more likely than not to be for the worse.

The liberal belief in working for change does not mean that he regards human reason as an infallible or incorruptible instrument, or that he thinks Utopia is just around the corner. But it does mean that he feels that history never stands still, that social change can better the quality of people's lives and happiness, and that the margin of human gain, however limited, is worth the effort.

Nor will the conservative in all cases and occasions resist change. But he inclines to accept it only when the intellectual case for it is overwhelming and the political pressure for it irresistible. Up to that point, he clings stubbornly to that which he knows and to which he is habituated. "The castle which conservatism is set to defend," said Emerson, "is the actual state of things, good and bad."

Enough should have been said by now to indicate that liberalism in the American usage has little in common with the word as used in the politics of any European country, save possibly Britain. Liberalism in America has been a party of social progress rather than of intellectual doctrine, committed to ends rather than to methods. When a laissez-faire policy seemed best calculated to achieve the liberal objective of equality of opportunity for all—as it did in the time of Jefferson—liberals believed, in the Jeffersonian phrase, that that government is best which governs least. But, when the growing complexity of industrial conditions required increasing government intervention in order to assure more equal opportunities, the liberal tradition, faithful to the goal rather than to the dogma, altered its view of the state.

The process of redefining liberalism in terms of the social needs of the 20th century was conducted by Theodore Roosevelt and his New Nationalism, Woodrow Wilson and his New Freedom, and Franklin D. Roosevelt and his New Deal. Out of these three great reform periods there emerged the conception of a social welfare state, in which the national government had the express obligation to maintain high levels of employment in the economy, to supervise standards of life and labor, to regulate the methods of business competition, and to establish comprehensive patterns of social security. This liberal conception won, in a sense, its greatest triumph in the election of 1952 when the Republican party, as the party of conservatism, accepted as permanent the changes wrought in the American scene by a generation of liberal reform.

The ideological content of modern American liberalism has been less coherent than its political and administrative evolution. The two Roosevelts and Wilson were ideologists only in the broadest and loosest sense. Their oratory dealt in mood and in program rather than in philosophy; and, with inspired eclecticism, they drew on all types and sources for their ideas and policies. In the 1920's, however, a liberal ideology did begin to crystallize, deriving its main tenets from the philosophy of John Dewey and from the economics of Thorstein Veblen. Dewey, with his faith in human rationality and in the power of the creative intelligence, gave this ideological liberalism a strong belief in the efficacy of overhead social planning; and this bent was reinforced by Veblen, who detested the price system and the free market and thought that the economy could be far more efficiently and sensibly operated by a junta or soviet of engineers.

This liberal ideology, with its commitment to central governmental planning, was shattered, however, by the experience of the New Deal. Men in the Dewey-Veblen tradition tended to regard the New Dealers as hopeless improvisers and opportunists, engaged in the futile patching of an old system when they should have been consecrated to the triumphant creation of a new one. But in time it began to appear that the somewhat helter-skelter, catch-as-catch-can improvisations of the New Deal were more true to the helter-skelter, catch-as-catch-can conditions of American society than any rational central *Gosplan* could have been. What at first seemed the vices of pragmatism and expediency in the New Deal came later to be regarded as among its greatest virtues.

In this process, Dewey and Veblen lost their hold on American liberalism. They have been more or less replaced in recent years as guiding influences by Reinhold Niebuhr and John Maynard Keynes. Niebuhr, the neo-orthodox theologian, has provided a more realistic and searching picture of man than Dewey's image of a rational and cooperative planner. The Niebuhr restatement of the Christian conception of human nature has made it easier for the present generation to understand the suprarational extremities of cruelty and of sacrifice in this tragic century. And Keynes has made available a far more useful, flexible, and intelligent set of economic ideas than those of Veblen. The Keynesian emphasis on indirect controls—on fiscal and monetary policy—rather than on direct, physical, quantitative controls of the Veblen type has persuaded American liberalism that central economic management may be reconciled with the decentralization of decision and the technical advantages of a price system and a free market.

The broad liberal objective is a balanced and flexible "mixed economy," thus seeking to occupy that middle ground between capitalism and socialism whose viability has so long been denied by both capitalists and socialists. American liberalism, it should be emphasized, is antisocialist, where socialism retains its classical connotation of state ownership of the basic means of production and distribution. This is partly because American liberals doubt whether bases for political opposition and freedom can survive when all power is vested in the state; liberty, if it is to be guaranteed by anything but the self-restraint of the rulers, must have resources of its own inaccessible to the state. And the antisocialism of American liberals derives also from an estimate of the administrative difficulties of a socialist system. If substantial abundance and equality of opportunity can be achieved through a system of mixed enterprise, why throw up a rigid and oppressive structure of state bureaucracy? The humane, as distinct from the institutional, goals of socialism can be better achieved, American liberals feel, through diversifying ownership rather than concentrating it.

American liberalism believes that in this respect it has made a major contribution to the grand strategy of freedom. Where both capitalists and socialists in the 1930's were trying to narrow the choice to either/or—

either laissez-faire capitalism or bureaucratic social-ism—the New Deal persisted in its vigorous faith that human intelligence and social experiment could work out a stable foundation for freedom in a context of se-curity and for security in a context of freedom. That faith remains the best hope of free society today.

Contemporary American liberalism thus has no overpowering *mystique*. It lacks a rhapsodic sense. It has jettisoned many illusions. Its temper is realistic, even skeptical. Its objectives are limited. It is mistrust-ful of utopianism, perfectionism, and maximalism. It abhors the maudlin sloganism of the popular front of the '30's. It refuses to believe that lofty aspiration ex-cuses cruel oppression. In particular, it lacks patience for those who can pronounce societies "progressive" which develop huge and terrible systems of forced labor and deny freedom of expression and movement to the bulk of their populations.

Some Europeans feel that this realistic mood is an expression of weariness and defeat, if not a confession of cowardice. Yet American liberalism feels that real-ism is the source of strength, and that illusion, while productive of momentary enthusiasm, will be in the end a source of catastrophe. And American liberalism can point to concrete national gains even in the period of the cold war—to the great strides toward achieving better opportunities for Negroes, to the maintenance of high levels of employment, to the extension of the system of social security, to the eventual defeat of Sen-ator McCarthy; not to speak of such extraordinary world initiatives as the Marshall Plan and Point Four.

Even under a conservative administration, these lib-eral impulses will continue to have effect. Even the Re-publican party, on the whole, is "conservative" only in the special American sense. For all its tendencies toward ignorance and self-righteousness, that party is far from blind reactions and will, in the end, accept the arbitrament of reason and debate.

One can understand how the excesses of certain American politicians in recent years may have shaken world faith in the essential liberality of the American political tradition. Yet that tradition and its liberality rest on something deeper and solider than official rhetoric or pious hope. American liberalism, in the broad sense, is an expression of the total national experience—a fact which will doubtless become evident to the world again when American liberalism, in the more restricted sense, returns to political power.

7.
The Politics of Nostalgia
(1955)

No intellectual phenomenon has been more surprising in recent years than the revival in the United States of conservatism as a respectable social philosophy. For decades liberalism seemed to have everything its way. The bright young men were always liberals; the thoughtful professors were generally liberals; even conservatives, like the late Senator Taft, began in despair to avow themselves liberals.

But in the last year or two, it has all seemed to change. Fashionable intellectual circles now dismiss liberalism as naïve, ritualistic, sentimental, shallow. With a whoop and a roar, a number of conservative prophets have materialized out of the wilderness, exhuming conservatism, revisiting it, revitalizing it, preaching it—Russell Kirk, saber in hand, a cavalier on a black horse; Peter Viereck, rearing high on a charger while he fires his six-shooter vigorously in all directions; Clinton Rossiter, cool and businesslike, driving an unassuming Ford: all with dozens of disciples deploying behind them, and many more well-wishers cheering them on from the sidelines. Today, we are told, the bright young men are conservatives; the thoughtful professors are conservatives; even a few liberals, in their own cycle of despair, are beginning to avow themselves conservatives.

Since we seem to be in the midst of a counter-revolution in political philosophy, it would be well to examine the new gospel. For even if the prophets of the New Conservatism speak by no means with a single voice, yet they have been articulate and reasonably coherent in sketching a common outline of faith.

To begin with, they feel that liberalism had its chance and failed. Much of the mess and wreckage of the contemporary world have resulted, in their belief, from illusions inculcated by liberalism. They condemn liberalism for its optimism, its emotional thinness, its disdain for the past, its faith in the application of intelligence to social problems. In its place they propose a return to the time-hallowed principles of conservatism. They feel that continuity, tradition, prescription, order, inequality, a prejudice against change, and reverence for authority are the hallmarks of the good society. They contend that the only hope for America lies in the speedy elevation of these conservative principles to the highest place in our national life.

Their favorite sage is the great British conservative Edmund Burke. They could not, of course, go to a better master; for no Anglo-Saxon political philosopher has written more penetratingly or profoundly about the nature of civil society and the processes of social change. And they rightly see that there flows from Burke the grand tradition of British conservatism, adorned by such names as Coleridge, Shaftesbury, Disraeli, and Winston Churchill—a tradition inspired by a belief in the organic character of society, where power implies responsibility and where all classes should be united in harmonious union by a sense of common trust and mutual obligation.

This tradition, it can be easily seen, represents the ethical afterglow of feudalism. In medieval days, inequality of rank and condition was tempered (in theory, at least) by a sense of the reciprocal duties of status. Society was a living moral unity, not just a bundle of cold commercial relationships.

The conservative prophets fully acknowledged their feudal antecedents. Burke, lamenting the passing of the age of chivalry, cried that the age of sophisters, economists, and calculators had succeeded, and the glory of Europe was therefore extinguished forever. Disraeli regarded the principle of feudalism as "the ablest, the grandest, the most magnificent and benevolent that was ever conceived by sage or practiced by patriot." The essence of British conservatism has been, in short, to try to apply the social values of feudalism to the emerging problems of modern business society.

In making this effort, the humanitarian aristocrats inevitably collided with the laissez-faire liberalism of the rising business community. To their natural disdain for these parvenu merchants and manufacturers, the socially minded aristocrats began to add a disposition to call in the state to redress the balance of society on behalf of the poor. Thus Shaftesbury demanded legislative intervention to protect factory workers from the greed of their employers. Thus Disraeli expounded what Karl Marx scornfully described as "feudal socialism," seeking to rally the oppressed behind the leadership of a benevolent government and a socially responsible aristocracy. Thus Lord Randolph Churchill developed the doctrines of Tory democracy under the slogan "Trust the people." And thus his son Winston became a leading figure in the great Liberal reforms before the First World War.

It is essentially a romantic nostalgia for this great tradition which animates the New Conservatives of contemporary America. Some of them, it must be admitted, have tried to give their conservatism a native line of descent, but the search for philosophic roots in a business society only results in stringing together a collection of incompatible names—the Adamses, Alexander Hamilton, John C. Calhoun, Theodore Roosevelt, Irving Babbitt, most of whom cordially detested the others—in an unconvincing and thoroughly artificial genealogy. The deeper passion of the New Conservatives, one feels, is for the rich, humane, and somber sentiments of European conservatism, based on culture, morality, and tradition, not on the accumulation of money. They want a ruling class, but one composed of responsible patricians, not of successful shopkeepers.

Yet obvious difficulties arise when the attempt is made to transplant the philosophy of aristocratic British conservatism to the United States. The faith of Burke and Disraeli emerged from a concrete social situation in a specific country. It represented the distillation and the legacy of centuries of British experience, including particularly the centuries of feudalism. And in the British ruling class it has had a continuing instrument to execute its purposes. Aristocratic leadership requires, in the first instance, the existence of an aristocracy.

The American experience has been quite another story. We had no feudal system; how can we expect to have feudal traditions? We have no aristocracy in the British sense; how can we expect to enjoy aristocratic leadership? For better or worse, our upper classes base their position not on land or tradition or a sense of social responsibility but on the folding stuff. They constitute not an aristocracy but a plutocracy.

This has been by no means a disadvantage for our country. Because our business class has suffered few social impediments in the way of its scramble for wealth, we have built here a dynamic and expanding economy which has done far more for the masses of the people than the protective and restrictionist economic life fostered by the feudal conservatism of Europe. But the very qualities of unbridled and creative acquisitiveness that account for the economic contributions of American business seem to disqualify it as a governing class. Very little that has happened since January 20, 1953, would render obsolete Henry Cabot Lodge's observation of half a century ago: "The businessman dealing with a large political question is really a painful sight. It does seem to me that businessmen, with a few exceptions, are worse when they come to deal with politics than men of any other class."

Conservatism founded on land is committed to permanence in a community and responds to social motives. Conservatism founded on money is fickle, selfish, and irresponsible; its chief object is to protect what it has and, if possible, to make more. The aristocrat, ideally at least, wants to protect the poor because in the end he regards the nation, rich and poor alike, as a single family. The plutocrat generally regards the poor as legitimate objects of exploitation, like any other commodity; as for the nation, its welfare, he believes, is assured so long as nobody interferes with the unlimited pursuit of his own self-interest. "A merchant's desire," that sturdy Tory Dr. Johnson once remarked, "is not of glory, but of gain; not of public wealth, but of private emolument; he is, therefore, rarely to be consulted on questions of war or peace, or any designs of wide extent and distant consequence." His characteristic faith is that what is good for General Motors is good for the country.

On May 28, 1903, a young British aristocrat, son of the most passionate of Tory democrats, left the British

Conservative party because he feared that the business community was taking it over. Under this commercial influence, he told the House of Commons, the Tory party was becoming a new party, "like perhaps the Republican Party of the United States . . . rigid, materialist, and secular." Thus Winston Churchill expressed his sense of the difference between government by aristocrats and government by businessmen.

A favorite object of New Conservative derision is the liberal reformer who wishes to remake society by imposing on it abstract ideological schemes that bear no relation to concrete social circumstances. Yet what else are the New Conservatives themselves doing when they propose to apply the tradition of British conservatism, that worthy child of feudalism and aristocracy, to the nonfeudal, nonaristocratic, dynamic, progressive business society of the United States? Liberals, heaven knows, have been foolishly romantic, but few have recently been so romantic as to suppose that American businessmen, after reading a few edifying tracts, are going to start behaving like the British landed gentry.

Involuntarily the New Conservatives acknowledge this, even if they do not let the acknowledgment disturb their argument. When they leave the stately field of rhetoric and get down to actual issues of social policy, they tend quietly to forget about Burke and Disraeli and to adopt the views of the American business community. The pull of the American situation, in other words, forces them into a leap from Tory fantasy into Republican reality.

No one illustrates this more compactly than Russell Kirk, author of *The Conservative Mind* and *A Program for Conservatives*. Of all the New Conservatives, he seems the most devoted to Burke. Yet when he is not chastising liberal professors in the style of Burkean conservatism for the sins of rationalism and optimism, he is engaged in vehement warfare in the style of laissez-faire liberalism against the whole idea of humanitarian reform. The Federal school-lunch program, he suggests, is a "vehicle for totalitarianism." The Social Security system "bears nearly all the marks of a remorseless collectivism." The United Auto Workers "has scarcely any more element of volition in it than the most arbitrary totalitarian state." We have injured our political order, he tells us, by adopting universal suffrage, direct primaries, and the popular election of Senators. On the subject of Senator McCarthy, he endorses the statement of the Messrs. Buckley and Bozell that McCarthyism is "a movement around which men of good will and stern morality can close ranks."

As for the idea of disposing of our public-power projects to the utilities, first proposed by Charles E. Wilson of General Electric and recently adopted with respect to TVA by the task force of the Hoover Commission, Professor Kirk describes this admiringly as "conservatism intelligently applied to our present discontents." If carried out, he suggests, it would be "the most important reversal of the drift toward a repressive collectivism which any nation has experienced in many years."

How far all this is from Disraeli with his legislation on behalf of trade unions, his demand for government intervention to improve working conditions, his belief in due process and civil freedom, his support for the extension of the suffrage, his insistence on the principle of compulsory education! If there is anything in contemporary America that might win the instant sympathy of men like Shaftesbury and Disraeli, it could well be the school-lunch program. But for all his talk about mutual responsibility and the organic character of society, Professor Kirk, when he gets down to cases, tends to become a roaring Manchester liberal of the Herbert Hoover school.

Coningsby, the aristocratic champion of the poor and oppressed in Disraeli's famous novel of the same name, cries, "I would make these slum-landlords skip." The people the New Conservatives seem interested in making skip are New Dealers, trade-union leaders, reformers, and, evidently, all those who can read without moving their lips. ("When a man is both a professor and an intellectual," says Professor Kirk, "he is loathsome; when he is professor and intellectual and ideologist rolled into one, he is unbearable.") One can find very little in any of the New Conservatives' writings—Professor Viereck's aside—calculated to upset a slum landlord.

So the New Conservatism has strong interior tendencies toward schizophrenia. It attempts to unite the feudal traditions of British conservatism with the laissez-faire policies of American business. The offspring is a hybrid that retains little contact with the realities of either nation. The schizophrenia, it should be said, is by no means so noticeable in all the New Conservatives as it is in Professor Kirk. Professor Rossiter, for example, abjures a good deal of both the Burkean mystique and the laissez-faire dogmatism; indeed, he occupies such moderate positions on social issues that it is hard to tell why he styles himself a conservative rather than a liberal.[1] But the inner contradictions so visible in Professor Kirk would seem inherent in the whole enterprise of rehabilitating philosophical conservatism—or, at least, in the whole attempt to transplant aristo-

[1] Professor Rossiter has subsequently ceased doing so.

cratic British conservatism to the business society of the United States.

The New Conservatism is thus severed from the American reality. The inevitable result is to condemn it to irrelevance in American life. If it has any significance today, it should be as a means of assisting the new conservative Administration in Washington to interpret its mandate and to devise genuinely conservative policies. But while liberal leaders always have their entourages of brain trusters and eggheads, nothing would be more incongruous than a New Conservative at a White House stag dinner, seated perhaps between a utilities executive and a football coach. Indeed, most New Conservatives are more at ease with their liberal colleagues and critics than they would be in an atmosphere where Locke is the name of a South African golf player and Burke the winner of the United States Open in 1931.

The further paradox is that the aristocratic champion of the oppressed, in the Coningsby manner, is not an unfamiliar figure in the United States. But he is rarely to be found in the conservative party. From Jefferson and Jackson to the Roosevelts, Stevensons, and Harrimans of the 20th century, the country squire has played an important role in American politics, summoning the commoners to battle against the forces of entrenched greed. Some day an enterprising graduate student will write a Ph.D. thesis on "The Contributions of Groton School to the American Left." This strain of aristocratic radicalism is, I suppose, our nearest counterpart to the tradition of Disraeli. But while the patrician Jeffersons and Roosevelts seek to restrain business rule as members of the liberal party, the conservative party in our country is essentially the party of business, dominated by what Theodore Roosevelt (who knew them well) once described as "men very powerful in certain lines and gifted with the 'money touch,' but with ideals which in their essence are merely those of so many glorified pawnbrokers."

The relationship with the business community must be the acid test of the New Conservatism. The New Conservatives can combat the business community, or they can seek to convert it, or they can base themselves squarely on it. (Or they can, like Peter Viereck, forsake politics and conceive the New Conservatism as essentially a moral and cultural movement: "In America," Professor Viereck wisely writes, "the conservative today can best start by being unpolitical.") Still, if they feel they have political contributions to make, the one thing they cannot do is to ignore the business community—and that, unfortunately is what most of them do.

In Britain, of course, "feudal socialism" has so successfully infiltrated the Conservative party under the Churchill-Eden-Butler leadership that Tory orators helped win the recent election with the claim that they had built more houses, planned more hospitals, and generated more social welfare than the Socialists. But it seems unlikely that the New Conservatives, even if they wanted to do so, are going to persuade the Republicans to out–New Deal the New Dealers. And there seems little disposition on the part of the New Conservatives to follow the Jefferson-Roosevelt country squire tradition of making the merchants and bankers skip.

If conversion and opposition are thus ruled out, the New Conservatism, if it wishes to seek political reality, must accept the brutal fact that the only possible executor of a conservative tradition in American political life is the American business community. There could be a real intellectual challenge here in working out a social philosophy that would explain the purposes and the achievements of American capitalism. But it is not a social philosophy to be worked out in terms of Burke and Disraeli, or of Adams and Calhoun.

One somehow doubts the challenge will be taken up. For the New Conservatism is essentially the politics of nostalgia. Its emotions are honorable, generous—and irrelevant. It is a hothouse growth, carefully cultivated in the academies by men who dream they dwelt in marble halls. What matters in America is not the conservatism of the professors but the conservatism of the industrialists, bankers, and politicians—and in this case, the practical conservatives do not even maintain diplomatic relations with their own eggheads.

So long as the New Conservatism remains in its present elegiac mood, one can only feel that it is the wrong doctrine in the wrong country in the wrong century directed against the wrong enemies.

8.
The New Mood in Politics
(1960)

At periodic moments in our history, our country has paused on the threshold of a new epoch in our national life, unable for a moment to open the door, but aware that it must advance if it is to preserve its national vitality and identity. One feels that we are approaching such a moment now—that the mood which has dominated the nation for a decade is beginning to seem thin and irrelevant; that it no longer interprets our desires and needs as a people; that new forces, new energies, new values are straining for expression and for release. The Eisenhower epoch—the present period of passivity and acquiescence in our national life—is drawing to a natural end.

As yet, the feeling is inchoate and elusive. But it is beginning to manifest itself in a multitude of ways: in freshening attitudes in politics; in a new acerbity in criticism; in stirrings, often tinged with desperation, among the youth; in a spreading contempt everywhere for reigning clichés. There is evident a widening restlessness, dangerous tendencies toward satire and idealism, a mounting dissatisfaction with the official priorities, a deepening concern with our character and objectives as a nation.

Let me list some expressions of the discontent, the desire for reappraisal, the groping for something better:

The rise of the Beat Generation is plainly in part the result of the failure of our present society to provide ideals capable of inspiring the youth of the nation.

The revival in the last two or three years of satire (not altogether to be dismissed by the appellation "sick humor") is another expression, as in the '20's, of contempt for the way things currently are going.

The religious boom (Billy Graham, etc.) suggests the widespread yearning for spiritual purpose of some sort in life.

The top book on the fiction best-seller list for many months was Pasternak's *Doctor Zhivago*—again a symptom of the felt need for some kind of spiritual affirmation.

A book like J. K. Galbraith's *The Affluent Society* sells fifty thousand copies in hard cover; David Riesman's *The Lonely Crowd* and W. H. Whyte's *The Organization Man* sell hundreds of thousands in paper-back—all this means that our intellectuals are beginning to draw the new portrait of America out of which new political initiatives will in due course come, and that people are responding to their portrayal.

Somehow the wind is beginning to change. People—not everyone by a long way, but enough to disturb the prevailing mood—seem to seek a renewal of conviction, a new sense of national purpose. More and more of us, I think, are looking for a feeling of dedication, for a faith that what we are doing is deeply worth-while—the kind of inspiration and lift we had for a while in the '30's and again during the Second World War.

The threats of communism and nuclear catastrophe ought perhaps to be enough to give us this sense of purpose, but they don't seem to. Certainly the goal of adding to our material comforts and our leisure time has not filled our lives. Are we not beginning to yearn for something beyond ourselves? We are uncertain but expectant, dismayed but hopeful, troubled but sanguine. It is an odd and baffled moment in our history—a moment of doubt and suspense and anticipation. It is as if increasing numbers of Americans were waiting for a trumpet to sound.

At bottom, perhaps, we are seeking a new articulation of our national values in the belief that this will bring about a new effectiveness in our national action. For national purpose is not something that is enshrined in monuments or preserved in historic documents. It acquires meaning as part of an ongoing process; its certification lies not in rhetoric but in performance. The values of the '50's have been, to a great degree, self-indulgent values. People have been largely absorbed in themselves—in their own careers, their own lives, their own interests. We tend to cover up our self-absorption by saying that what is good for our own interests is good for the country; but this is a gesture of piety. In fact, we start from our own concerns and work outward, rather than start from the national needs and work inward.

The badge of our self-indulgence has been the contemporary orgy of consumer goods. The chairman of the President's Council of Economic Advisers, Dr. Raymond J. Saulnier, recently stated his concept of the role of the American economy: "Its ultimate purpose is to produce more consumer goods. This is the goal. This is the object of everything that we are working at; to produce things for consumers." Not to produce better people or better schools or better health or better national defense or better opportunities for cultural and spiritual fulfillment—but to produce more gadgets and gimmicks to overwhelm our bodies and distract our minds. As against what we self-righteously condemn as the godless materialism of the Communists we seem to have dedicated ourselves to a godly materialism of our own.

But materialism—the belief that the needs of life can be fulfilled by material opulence—is not enough. It will not truly achieve for our own citizens what Herbert Croly used to call the promise of American life, for that is a moral and spiritual promise. And it will not offer an effective counterfaith—or even an effective counterbalance—against communism. Under the spell of materialism, our nation has allocated its abundance to private satisfaction rather than to public need, with the result that the wealthiest nation in the world suddenly seems to be falling behind in education, falling behind in science, falling behind in technology, falling behind in weapons, falling behind in our capacity to stir the minds and hearts of men. Russia, a much poorer nation, more than makes up for its smaller annual output by its harder sense of national purpose.

Our situation would be troubling enough if there were no world civil war. But the existence of the world civil war trebles every bet. We are coming to realize that we need a new conviction of national purpose not only as a matter of taste but as a matter of desperate necessity. And so the time is drawing near for a revision of our national priorities, a revaluation of our national values, a renewal of our national purpose. This process of reorientation will be the mainspring of the politics of the '60's. As we commit ourselves to this vast challenge, we will cross the threshold into what promises to be one of the exciting and creative epochs in our history.

Now there is little to be gained in denouncing the values of the '50's as meager and mean. It is important rather to understand why we have dallied with such values—why our nation, in a time of danger, should have lowered its sights, renounced older concepts of high national purpose, and elevated private consumer satisfaction into a controlling national ethic. There is, I believe, no insoluble mystery here. Nor can we properly shift the blame for our condition from ourselves to our leaders. Certainly our leadership has failed in this decade to develop our potentialities of national power and to meet the onward rush of national needs. But it has just as certainly succeeded in expressing the moods and wishes of the electorate.

What accounted for the torpor of the '50's? The answer, I think, is plain enough. The basic cause was the state of national exhaustion produced by the two preceding decades of continuous crisis. During the '30's, '40's and into the '50's the American people went through the worst depression of their history, the worst hot war of their history, the worst cold war of their history, the most frustrating limited war of their history. During these decades, two aggressive Presidents kept demanding from us a lively interest in public policy and kept confronting us with tough problems of national decision. But no nation can live in tension indefinitely. By the early '50's, the American people had had it. We were weary and drained. We were tired of subordinating the reality of our daily lives to remote and abstract national objectives. We wanted a vacation from public responsibilities. We wanted to take up the private strands of existence, to bury ourselves in family, home, career.

The politics of the '50's were, in consequence, the politics of fatigue. Twenty years of intense public activity, first at home, then abroad, had left the nation in a state of moral and emotional exhaustion. Lull was the natural and predictable result. President Eisenhower was the perfect man for the new mood. Where his predecessors had roused the people, he soothed them; where they had defined issues sharply, he blurred them over; where they had called for effort and action, he counseled patience and hoped things would work themselves out. Perhaps his particular contribution to the art of politics was to make politics boring at a time when the people wanted any excuse to forget public affairs. The nation needed an interval of repose in order to restore its physiological balance, and repose was what President Eisenhower gave them.

In so doing, he was playing his part in the larger rhythm of our politics. For the national life has always alternated between epochs of advance and epochs of consolidation, between times of action and times of passivity. We began the 20th century with two decades of active and insistent leadership under the dominating Presidents—Theodore Roosevelt and Woodrow Wilson. These Presidents raised the national sights. They stood for a crusading fervor in politics, directed first to reform at home and then to carrying the gospel of democracy to the world. After two decades of this, the people could stand it no longer: 1920 was like 1952. They wanted "normalcy," and that is what they got from Warren G. Harding and his successors.

And so the '20's were the decade of "normalcy." The politics of purpose gave way to the politics of lassitude. The nation swung from affirmative government to negative government. But, after a time, negative government began to seem insufficient. As the national energies began to be replenished, people started to tire of the official mood of aimlessness and complacency. Moreover, new problems, nurtured by the years of indifference, began to emerge—problems which required direction and vigor in their solution. The Wall Street crash and its aftermath provided dramatic evidence that drift was not enough as a national policy. The time had come for the reconquest of purpose.

And so the cyclical rhythm has continued. In the '30's and '40's we had decades of purpose until we were tired again; in the '50's quiescence and respite until problems heaped up and batteries began to be recharged. If this rhythm continues according to schedule, the '60's and '70's should be decades of affirmation until we fall back into drift in the '80's. The pattern of American politics has been an alternation between periods of furious performance which accomplish a lot of things but finally wear the people out to periods of stagnation which go on until new issues accumulate, flagging national energies revive, and forward motion can be resumed. There is no reason to suppose now that this pendular motion has suddenly come to a full stop.

The question remains whether the nation could afford that holiday from responsibility in the '50's which its every nerve demanded—whether it was wise to choose this point to rest on its oars. No doubt the condition of national weariness made it hard to exercise vigorous leadership in any case; but this scarcely excuses our leaders from not having tried harder. When America "took five," so to speak, in the 1880's or the 1920's, it didn't much matter. But the 1950's were fatal years for us to relax on the sidelines. The grim and unending contest with communism was the central international fact of the decade, and the Communists took no time out to flop in the hammock. We did, and we have paid a cruel price for it.

In our decade of inertia, we squandered, for example, a commanding weapons lead until our own officials now frankly concede that by the early '60's the Soviet Union, a nation supposedly far behind our own in economic and technological sophistication, will have a superiority in the thrust of its missiles and in the penetration of outer space. In this same decade, we came up with no new ideas in foreign policy (or, rather, with no new *good* ideas—our new ideas have either been busts, like the Baghdad Pact and the Eisenhower Doctrine, or else were, fortunately, never carried out, like unleashing Chiang Kai-shek and massive retaliation). This period of sterility in our conduct of foreign affairs stands in particular contrast to the astonishing decade of creativity which preceded it, from the Atlantic Charter to NATO and from Lend-Lease to Point Four.

The policy of drift not only lost us essential margins of power in the competition of coexistence. It also got us into trouble at home—and in so doing further damaged our power position relative to the Communist world. For most of this decade, for example, our national economic growth slowed down dangerously. Between 1947 and 1953 our gross national product increased at an average annual rate of 4.6 per cent; between 1953 and 1958 the average annual rate of increase was only about 1.6 per cent. (We are doing much better, of course, in 1959, but, even adding this in, the average annual rate of increase recently has been only about 2.5 per cent.) The Soviet economy, according to the Central Intelligence Agency, continues to roar along at an average annual rate of 9.5 per cent.

These have been years of enormous population growth in the United States. By 1960 we will have nearly 30,000,000 more people than in 1950—an increase of almost 3,000,000 a year. The annual appearance of millions of new boys and girls automatically creates needs for new hospitals, new houses, new schools, new communities; the relentless expansion is straining our facilities to the utmost. And these new

boys and girls constitute our most valuable natural re-
source. Our future will depend on their knowledge,
their education, their health, their strength, on the opportunities open to them to develop their abilities.
From the viewpoint not only of humanity and equity
but of national power, these people should be a major
object of national investment.

And it is precisely these new boys and girls who
have been most forgotten during the consumer goods
infatuation. We have chosen in this decade to invest
not in people but in things. We have chosen to allocate
our resources to undertakings which bring short-run
profits to individuals rather than to those which bring
long-run profits to the nation. "A nation that spends
more per capita upon advertising than upon education," Barbara Ward has written, "has somewhere lost
the path to the future." While our population billows,
our national leadership has made only the most feeble
efforts to enlarge our community services and facilities—schools, medical care, housing, urban and suburban planning, social security, roads, recreation, water
resources, and energy development—to assure decent
opportunities for these new children.

The result is the weird and intolerable suggestion
that the United States, the richest country in the history
of the world, can't "afford" an educational system
worthy of its children, can't "afford" as many ICBM's
as the less affluent Soviet Union, can't "afford" a
proper resources policy, can't even, heaven help us,
"afford" a decent postal system. Does anyone really
suppose that we don't have the money to do these
things? Of course we have. It isn't that we can't afford
it; it is that we choose to expend our resources elsewhere. Under a system where the production and con-
sumption of consumer goods is regarded as the be-all

and end-all of existence, where everyone's making a fast buck is supposed to insure the common good, where private interests take priority over the public interests, the public sector—everything from schools to missiles—is systematically starved. If something does not pay its way in the market place, it is felt to be hardly worth doing at all. Is our land really dedicated to the notion that only things which pay their way deserve to survive? If so, we are doomed, because very little of genuine importance—from education to defense—pays its own way in the market.

Our trouble is not that our capabilities are inadequate. It is that our priorities—which means our *values*—are wrong. While consumer goods heap up in our attics and basements, while our advertising system knocks itself out trying to create new wants which will require the manufacture of new consumer goods, while more and more of our resources are absorbed in this mad business of chasing our own tail, the public framework of society, on which everything else rests, is overstrained by population growth and undercut by neglect. Our communities grow more chaotic, our schools more crowded, our teachers more overworked and underpaid, our roads more dangerous, our national parks more unkempt, our weapons development and foreign aid more catastrophically inadequate. While we overstuff ourselves as individuals, we let the national plant run down. And it is the national plant—above all, it is our national investment in people (education, health, welfare, equal opportunity)—on which our future depends. We are heading for the classical condition of private opulence and public squalor. Let no one forget that through history this condition has led to the fall of empires.

I suppose there might be an argument for the consumer-goods ethos if it produced a happy society. Certainly the consumer-goods age has made possible for the first time the democratization of human comfort. No one in his senses would wish to abolish the benefits of mass production and mass distribution. But consumer goods as the underpinning of life are one thing; as the main object of life, another. When the production of consumer goods occupies the top priority in society, it sets in motion a process which can only be described as the institutionalization of the situation described in *Macbeth*: "Nought's had, all's spent, / Where our desire is got without content." The consumer-goods economy depends on a system of calculated and organized obsolescence.

In the '20's, another consumer-goods era, people became progressively disturbed by the official notion that material abundance was the answer to everything. As the decade wore on, dissatisfaction mounted. Then with the depression the rejection of drift and the reinstatement of national purpose became not only a preference but a necessity. Similarly today we are entering the phase of psychological restlessness and spiritual discontent.

Concrete issues already exist around us in abundance. What is needed is vision to unite these issues and to endow them with a broader meaning. These include such questions as:

The revitalization of our community life (better planning of cities and suburbs, slum clearance, decent housing, urban renewal, area development).

The reconstruction of our educational system.

The improvement of medical care and of care for the aged.

The assurance of equal rights for minorities.

The freedoms of speech, expression, and conscience.

The development of our natural resources.

The control of inflation.

The improvement of social security.

The refinement of our mass media and the elevation of our popular culture.

The provision of adequate foreign aid.

The prosecution of our weapons effort.

And, though we do not confront a depression, the competition of the Communist world serves the same purpose of converting a preference into an imperative.

This is the challenge of the '60's: the reorganization of American values. If we are going to hold our own against communism in the world, if we are going to build a satisfying life at home for ourselves and our children, the production of consumer goods will have to be made subordinate to some larger national purpose. As more and more people perceive the nature of our dilemma, they will demand the revival of public leadership, until in time the gathering discontent will find a national voice, like Theodore Roosevelt in 1901 and Franklin Roosevelt in 1933, and there will be a breakthrough into a new political epoch.

The hallmark of the '50's has been the belief that what is good for one's own private interest is good for all. Charles E. Wilson gave this idea its classic formulation when he suggested that what was good for General Motors was good for the country. And many critics of Wilson have seemed to object less to the principle of Wilson's law than to his choice of beneficiary. Too many tend to assume that what is good for what we care about is good for the country; if we don't like business, then we suppose, if government would only cater to labor or to the farmers, everything would be all right.

But people can't fool themselves indefinitely into supposing that the national interest is only the extension of whatever serves their own power and pocketbook. I believe that millions already feel that the road to national salvation no longer lies in pushing their own claims to the uttermost. Farmers dislike the excesses of the farm program. Workers begin to wonder whether higher wages are the answer to everything. Businessmen know that everything else in society cannot be sacrificed to their own profits.

If the hallmark of the '50's has been the belief in the sanctity of private interests, the hallmark of the '60's, I suggest, may well be the revival of a sense of the supremacy of the public interest—along with the realization that private interests and the public interest often come into harsh conflict. Theodore Roosevelt once said, "Every man holds his property subject to the general right of the community to regulate its use to whatever degree the public welfare may require." If unlimited private indulgence means that there are not enough resources left for national defense or for education or medical care or decent housing or intelligent community planning, then in a sane society private indulgence can no longer be unlimited.

The new attitude toward the public interest will bring in its wake a host of changes. There will be a change, for example, in the attitude toward government. One of the singular developments of the last decade was the rise of the notion that government was somehow the enemy. This was not George Washington's attitude toward government, nor Alexander Hamilton's, nor Andrew Jackson's, nor Abraham Lincoln's. The great American statesmen have all seen government as one means by which a free people achieves its purposes. But in the '50's we tended to suppose that a man engaged in making money for himself was in nobler work than a man serving the community (and that the more money he made, the greater his wisdom and virtue). That attitude will diminish in the '60's. Young men will go into public service with devotion and hope as they did in the days of T.R., Wilson and F.D.R. Government will gain strength and vitality from these fresh people and new ideas.

Of course, affirmative government *per se* can no more be a sufficient end for a good society than consumer goods *per se*. The object of strengthening government is to give force to the idea of public interest and to make possible the allocation of resources to necessary public purposes. There is no other way to meet the competition of communism. There is no other way to bring about a higher quality of life and opportunity for ordinary men and women.

This point—the quality of life—suggests the great difference between the politics of the '60's and the politics of the '30's. The New Deal arose in response to economic breakdown. It had to meet immediate problems of subsistence and survival. Its emphasis was essentially quantitative—an emphasis inevitable in an age of scarcity. But the '60's will confront an economy of abundance. There still are pools of poverty which have to be mopped up; but the central problem will be increasingly that of fighting for individual dignity, identity, and fulfillment in an affluent mass society. The issues of the new period will not be those involved with refueling the economic machine, putting floors under wages, and farm prices, establishing systems of social security. The new issues will be rather those of education, health, equal opportunity, community planning—the issues which make the difference between defeat and opportunity, between frustration and fulfillment, in the everyday lives of average persons. These issues will determine the quality of civilization to which our nation aspires in an age of ever-increasing wealth and leisure. A guiding aim, I believe, will be the insistence that every American boy and girl have access to the career proportionate to his or her talents and characters, regardless of birth, fortune, creed, or color.

The beginning of a new political epoch is like the breaking of a dam. Problems which have collected in the years of indifference, values which have suffered neglect, energies which have been denied full employment—all suddenly tumble as in a hopeless, swirling flood onto an arid plain. The chaos of the breakthrough offends those who like everything neatly ordered and controlled; but it is likely to be a creative confusion, bringing a ferment of ideas and innovations into the national life. Thus the '60's will probably be spirited, articulate, inventive, incoherent, turbulent, with energy shooting off wildly in all directions. Above all, there will be a sense of motion, of leadership, and of hope.

When this happens, America will be herself again. She will deal affirmatively and imaginatively with her problems at home. More than that, she will justify once again her claim to leadership of free peoples—a claim which cannot be founded on wealth and power alone, but only on wealth and power held within a framework of purpose and ideals.

Very little in history is inevitable. The cyclical rhythm we have identified in our national affairs offers no guarantee of national salvation. It will work only as men and women rise to a towering challenge. But nothing is stronger than the aspiration of a free people. If the energy now bottled up in American society can win its release in the decade ahead, we will reverse the downward curve of American power and charge the promise of American life with new meaning. From the vantage point of the '60's, the '50's, instead of marking a stage in the decline and fall of the American republic, will seem simply a listless interlude, quickly forgotten, in which the American people collected itself for greater exertions and higher splendors in the future.

Part III

Men and Ideas

9.
Reinhold Niebuhr's Role in American Political Thought and Life
(1956)

American liberalism—if by liberalism we assume the tradition of Jefferson and Jackson—has retained through American life a constancy of political purpose while undergoing a succession of changes in philosophical presuppositions. The generation which fought the American Revolution had, on the whole, a realistic image of human limitation. "Every man by Nature," said a petition from Pittsfield, Massachusetts, in 1776, "has the seeds of Tyranny deeply implanted within."[1] This realism pervaded the sessions of the Constitutional Convention in 1787, dominated the *Federalist* papers, ruled the thought of such Jeffersonians as James Madison, and was still to be found in such Jacksonians as Nathaniel Hawthorne.

But early in the 19th century a new and more cheerful estimate of human potentiality began to suffuse liberal thought. The rising optimism about man derived from many sources: from the new mystique of democracy and the common man, welling up from the American and French Revolutions; from the beneficent and harmonizing role newly assigned to individual self-interest by the laissez-faire economics of Adam Smith; from the passionate new romantic faith in human innocency, in self-reliance, and in the perfectibility of

[1] Oscar and Mary F. Handlin, *Commonwealth, a Study of the Role of Government in the American Economy: Massachusetts, 1774–1861* (New York: New York University Press, 1947), p. 5.

man, a faith stimulated by English poetry, French political thought, and German philosophy; and above all from the new circumstances of life and opportunity in 19th-century America. It has become fashionable in a more somber age to patronize or ridicule the optimism. But it is hard to deny that it was more true to the needs of the American life than the mechanical and exaggerated pessimism of the increasingly sterile Calvinism it displaced, and harder to deny that it released the energy of the nation to serve invaluable political and social ends.

If the tragedy of the Civil War momentarily disturbed this optimism, the extraordinary economic expansion of the years after the war quickly quenched any nascent doubt or disillusion. Andrew Carnegie's interpretation of human evolution would have served for liberals and conservatives alike. "Man was not created with an instinct for his own degradation," Carnegie wrote, "but from the lower he had risen to the higher forms. Nor is there any conceivable end to his march to perfection. His face is turned to the light; he stands in the sun and looks upward."[2] In much this mood, American liberalism marched through its Populist and Progressive phases. The faith even survived, in important aspects, at least, the agony and slaughter of the First World War.

For an important segment of the liberal community, optimism after the First World War found its warrant in two converging streams of thought. One was the Social Gospel. The other was the social application of the instrumentalist version of American pragmatism, associated with John Dewey. While differing in their ori-

[2] Andrew Carnegie, *Autobiography*, John C. Van Dyke, ed. (Boston; Houghton Mifflin, 1920), p. 339.

gins, both currents of thought combined to vindicate a common attitude toward man and society—a radiant sense of optimism and of hope, a conviction of the manageability of human tensions and the plasticity of human nature. In this sanguine climate, the old liberal optimism acquired new religious and scientific guarantees.

By 1920 the Social Gospel had, of course, a long history. Beginning in the '80's as the beleaguered conviction of a disreputable minority, it had sought to rescue 19th-century Protestantism from its individualistic and reactionary interpretation of Christianity and to restore contact with the working classes. By the first decade of the 20th century, it had won its way to respectability within the Protestant churches. And by this time Walter Rauschenbusch, its most penetrating theologian, had begun his work of systematizing its implications for traditional Christian thought. For Rauschenbusch the conception of the Kingdom of God was central in an approach both to religion and to society; the Kingdom represented not just the final end of man but man's historical hope. "Does not the Kingdom of God consist of this," Rauschenbusch asked, "that God's will shall be done on earth, even as it is now in heaven?" The Kingdom meant, he said, "a growing perfection in the collective life of humanity, in our laws, in the customs of society, in the institutions of education, and for the administration of mercy." The Kingdom was "humanity organized according to the will of God"; it would be "brought to its fulfillment by the power of God in his own time." This would require first, faith; then knowledge, "a scientific comprehension of social life"; then, as Rauschenbusch, a convinced socialist, concluded, a revolutionary mission and a dedicated class: "If the banner of the Kingdom of God is to enter through the gates of the future, it will have to be carried by the tramping hosts of labor."[3]

Rauschenbusch had no naïve expectations that social change would abolish the sinfulness of man; he never wholly lost his tragic sense. But many followers of the Social Gospel read his affirmations more enthusiastically than they did his reservations. After the First World War, it was widely believed in Social Gospel circles that the Kingdom of God could be realized on earth, within history; that its laws were identical with the laws of human nature and society; that the Christian ethic and the commandment of love were directly applicable to social and political questions; and that Christian policies offered practical alternatives to secular policies in specific situations. Charles M. Sheldon's question—"What would Jesus do?"—was considered the key which would unlock social and political perplexity. Such a document as the report of the Federal Council's Committee on the War and the Religious Outlook, *The Church and Industrial Reconstruction* (1920), provided a measured but unambiguous summation of the Social Gospel premises:

> Mankind in all its relations . . . must be organized according to the will of God, as revealed in Christ. The entire social order must be Christianized. The world as a whole is the subject of redemption . . . By the Kingdom Jesus means a social order which is

[3] D. R. Sharpe, *Walter Rauschenbusch* (New York: Macmillan, 1942), p. 62; V. P. Bodein, *The Social Gospel of Walter Rauschenbusch* (New Haven: Yale University Press, 1944), p. 2; Rauschenbusch, *A Theology for the Social Gospel* (New York: Macmillan, 1917), p. 142; Rauschenbusch, *Christianity and the Social Crises* (New York: Book Stall, 1907), p. 194; Rauschenbusch, *Christianizing the Social Order* (New York: Macmillan, 1912), p. 449.

not merely of man's devising, but which it is God's purpose to establish in the world . . . Is such an ideal practicable? Beautiful though it may be, can it ever be anything more than another Utopia? To this question the Christian answer is definite and unmistakable. This ideal can, indeed, be realized.[4]

Politics, in short, could incarnate the absolute.

Nor was the task of applying Christian law to immediate problems deemed overly difficult. Christianity seemed not only transcendent; it was utilitarian. It was not only the religion of ultimate judgment and repentance; it also, properly interpreted, had the immediate answers on prohibition, foreign policy, wages-and-hours legislation and universal military training. And, as Rauschenbusch had suggested, sociology might further mitigate the conflicts of social policy. Scientific studies of social issues, undertaken in the light of the Christian ethic, would show how the simple moralism of the Gospels would resolve the complex issues of industrial society. "There is every reason to believe," observed officials of the Federal Council in 1928, "that science can now adopt social ideals as specifications of a great task to be accomplished for humanity and proceed by the scientific method to assist in evolving a new industrial order which shall be increasingly characterized by righteousness and peace."[5]

As for individual human beings, they were essentially mild, good, and reasonable, and would in time

[4] Pp. 6, 9, 32.

[5] Labor Sunday Message, *Federal Council Bulletin*, September 1928; see the discussion in D. B. Meyer, "The Protestant Social Liberals in America, 1919–1941," Ph.D. thesis, Harvard University, pp. 247–49. I am indebted to Mr. Meyer's brilliant thesis both for information and for insight concerning Reinhold Niebuhr and his place in the development of Protestant social thought.

respond to the sociological argument, especially when fortified by the Christian appeal. The parable of the leaven explained how the principle of love would gradually conquer an evil world. The Kingdom of God was thus identical with historical progress. Neither egoism in man nor power in society need be serious obstacles; they could be bypassed by following the paths of love in human relations, of nonviolence in political relations, and of pacifism in international relations. For most of the Social Gospel, the onward march of democratic idealism would assure the Kingdom. For the radical minority, the Kingdom was the classless society of Marxist anticipation, to be won by the tramping hosts of labor.

The Social Gospel thus supplied democratic idealism with a religious sanction. At the same time, John Dewey was providing it with a humanistic and secular rationale. In a series of influential books in the '20's Dewey affirmed in naturalistic terms the capacity of man to achieve beneficent social change through education and experiment. Social progress could be reliably attained, Dewey emphasized, by the planned and experimental techniques which had won such brilliant success in the natural sciences. In fine, the organized social intelligence could be counted on to work out definite solutions to the great political and economic issues.

If all this were so, why was society still so far from man's ideal? The answer, Dewey suggested, was primarily ignorance, which made man unaware of his potentialities, and prejudice, which prevented him from acting scientifically to realize them; the answer, in short, was the cultural lag. And as the remedy for ignorance was education, so the remedy for prejudice was science.

These views, it is obvious, ran closely parallel to the Social Gospel. Indeed, Robert E. Fitch has recently argued that Dewey should be considered "the Last Protestant."[6] Dewey's individualism, his rationalism, his belief in the primacy of experience, his faith in education and in tolerance, his utopianism—all these, in a sense, might be taken as Protestantism at the end of its journey. Certainly the social philosophy of Dewey and the commandments of the Social Gospel fused happily in a common conviction that human and political tensions, however widespread or exasperating, could be dissolved in the end by reason or by love. The result was a prevailing liberal climate which Reinhold Niebuhr impatiently sought in 1936 to reduce to a set of propositions:

a. That injustice is caused by ignorance and will yield to education and greater intelligence.

b. That civilization is becoming gradually more moral and that it is a sin to challenge either the inevitability or the efficacy of gradualness.

c. That the character of individuals rather than social systems and arrangements is the guarantee of justice in society.

d. That appeals to love, justice, good-will and brotherhood are bound to be efficacious in the end. If they have not been so to date we must have more appeals to love, justice, good-will and brotherhood.

[6] R. E. Fitch, "John Dewey—The Last Protestant," *Pacific Spectator,* Spring 1953. Reinhold Niebuhr, in reviewing Dewey's *A Common Faith*, suggested that Dewey's credo came "closer than Dr. Dewey is willing to admit to the primary tenets of prophetic religion" (*Nation*, September 26, 1934).

e. That goodness makes for happiness and that the increasing knowledge of this fact will overcome human selfishness and greed.

f. That wars are stupid and can therefore only be caused by people who are more stupid than those who recognize the stupidity of war.[7]

This was the developing atmosphere of American liberalism when in 1915, at the age of twenty-three, Niebuhr, fresh from the Yale Divinity School, came to a small church in industrial Detroit. Spurred by vigorous and incisive intelligence, he combined his pastoral duties with eager attention to the intellectual challenges and controversies of the day. The wretchedness of life on the industrial frontier quickened an already live interest in social problems. Niebuhr was, in a real sense, a child of the Social Gospel. He was soon serving on the Mayor's Commission on Interracial Relations and on the Detroit Council of Churches' Industrial Relations Commission. He became a member of the Fellowship for a Christian Social Order and of the Fellowship of Reconciliation. He was active in the Federal Council; he was a circuit rider to the colleges and universities; and he was a prolific contributor to the *World Tomorrow* and the *Christian Century*. He responded deeply to the social passion; and his first book, published in 1927—*Does Civilization Need Religion?*—while critical of easy assumptions concerning the capacity of people or of institutions to transcend self-interest, was still safely within the Social Gospel presuppositions.

In a similar—if less demonstrable—sense, Niebuhr

[7] Niebuhr, "The Blindness of Liberalism," *Radical Religion*, Autumn 1936. Hereafter all citations will be to writings of Niebuhr unless otherwise attributed.

was a child of the pragmatic revolt. Nature had made him an instinctive empiricist; he had sharp political intuitions, an astute tactical sense, and an instinct for realism; and his first response to situations requiring decisions was typically as a pragmatist, not as a moralist or a perfectionist. He shared with William James a vivid sense of the universe as open and unfinished, always incomplete, always fertile, always effervescent with novelty. Where James called it a "pluralist universe," Niebuhr would call it a "dynamic universe"; but the sense of reality as untamed, streaming, provisional was vital to both. Similarly both revolted against the notion that this unpredictable universe could be caught and contained in any closed philosophical system. The burden of James's polemic was against the notion that there was any human viewpoint from which the world could appear as an absolute single fact; the crudity of experience, said James, remained an eternal element of experience. Similarly Niebuhr: "A perfectly consistent world view is bound to outrage some actual facts in the life of nature and the history of man." For James monism and absolutism were the end, the miserable culmination of what he dismissed as "tendermindedness"; and for Niebuhr: "The universe is simply not the beautiful Greek temple pictured in the philosophy of the absolutists and the monists."[8] Where James would accept the intractability of experience and the incompleteness of perception as the essence of reality, Niebuhr, committed to ultimate explanation, developed the category of "paradox" to deal with the antinomies which had formed the substance of James's "radical empiricism." The de-

[8] "A Religion Worth Fighting For," *Survey Graphic*, August 1927.

vice of paradox would become a central tactic of Niebuhr's Christian pragmatism.

Thus Niebuhr came to intellectual maturity under the influence both of the Social Gospel and of pragmatism. But, where Dewey and the social passion had agreed on the fundamentals of social strategy, Niebuhr, in the course of the '20's, began to detect a difference between what he called the "prophet" and the "statesman"—the one committed to God, the other to the sinful world. The ethic of Jesus and the dictates of pragmatic wisdom, instead of coinciding, seemed almost at times—and necessarily so—to point in opposite directions:

> It may be well for the statesman to know that statesmanship easily degenerates into opportunism and that opportunism cannot be sharply distinguished from dishonesty. But the prophet ought to realize that his higher perspective and the uncompromising nature of his judgements always has [sic] a note of irresponsibility in it. Francis of Assisi may have been a better Christian than Pope Innocent III. But it may be questioned whether his moral superiority over the latter was as absolute as it seemed. Nor is there any reason to believe that Abraham Lincoln, the statesman and opportunist, was morally inferior to William Lloyd Garrison, the prophet. The moral achievement of statesmen must be judged in terms which take account of the limitations of human society which the statesman must, and the prophet need not, consider.[9]

This insight foreshadowed a fundamental criticism of the prevailing liberal ideology. Without escaping the

[9] *Leaves from the Notebook of a Tamed Cynic*, pp. xii–xiv.

influence either of the Social Gospel or of pragmatism, Niebuhr was beginning to lose his loyalty to the current formulations of both. The Social Gospel lacked for him a sense of the relative; pragmatism lacked a sense of the absolute; their value came not in their agreement, as in the prevalent ideology, but rather in their discord; they seemed fruitful, not as a harmony but as a paradox.

Niebuhr's philosophy always bore to a degree the imprint of events; this was to be an essential source of his strength and its relevance; and his development in the '20's was visibly spurred by the crises of his experience. The aftermath of the First World War was one experience driving him to re-examine the bases of his conviction. He had supported the war, honestly if without great enthusiasm ("I think that if Wilson's aims are realized the war will serve a good purpose . . . If we must have a war I'll certainly feel better on the side of Wilson than on the side of the Kaiser"). But by 1923 he was prepared for the "whole horrible truth about the war"; "every new book," he said, "destroys some further illusion." The war, as he later wrote, "made me a child of the age of disillusionment." It convinced him that religion could be effective only if it resisted the embraces of civilization.[10]

Detroit left its mark too. More and more the "simple little moral homilies" he preached in accordance with the social passion seemed irrelevant to the brutal facts of life on the industrial frontier. Such sermons assuaged individual frustrations perhaps, but they did not change human actions or attitudes in any problem of collective behavior "by a hair's breadth." By 1927

[10] *Leaves*, pp. 14, 42; "What the War Did to My Mind," *Christian Century*, September 27, 1928.

Niebuhr was criticizing "modern religious liberalism" for its "sentimental optimism" which still spoke of "the essential goodness of men without realizing how evil good men can be." For all its partial acceptance of the thesis of the cultural lag and its tendency still to conceive religion as morality, *Does Civilization Need Religion?* sought nonetheless to re-establish transcendent religious perspectives. The Christian absolutes, far from fitting smoothly into everyday life, were "always a little absurd"; the relationship between the ultimate and the historical was one of tension rather than harmony; still, Niebuhr felt bound to assert "reality slowly approaches the ideals which are implicit in it." Yet, for all these gestures to moralism, *Does Civilization Need Religion?* was a book shot through with premonitions and misgivings over the prevalent liberal creed.[11]

The depression accelerated the process of change. Rauschenbusch had written that he could hear human virtue cracking and crumbling all around in the panic of 1893. For Niebuhr, now translated from the Detroit parish to the Union Theological Seminary in New York City, the economic collapse came as a conclusive refutation of liberal hopes. His book of 1932—*Moral Man and Immoral Society*—was a somber and powerful rejection of the Social Gospel–Dewey amalgam, with its faith in the politics of love and reason. To the champions of the Social Gospel he denied that the law of love could ever achieve social perfection; to the followers of Dewey he denied that expert knowledge could ever achieve impartial wisdom. Individual ego-

[11] "Ten Years That Shook My World," *Christian Century*, April 26, 1939; "A Religion Worth Fighting For"; *Does Civilization Need Religion?*, pp. 44–45.

ism, he asserted, was not being progressively checked by either "the development of rationality or the growth of a religiously inspired goodwill."

Scientific intelligence and moral piety, said Niebuhr, could not abolish social conflict; and those who would stake all on rational and moralistic methods ignored the limitations in human nature which must finally frustrate their efforts. An effective theory of politics must take account not only of the possibilities but of the weaknesses of man, especially the weaknesses of men in their collective behavior. The Kingdom of God would "never be fully realized" on earth; coercion was the necessary instrument of social cohesion; the realm of love was one thing and the realm of power another. Each, Niebuhr emphasized, must be approached in its own terms: "Better to accept a frank dualism in morals than to attempt a harmony between the two methods which threatens the effectiveness of both."[12]

What the Social Gospel and Dewey had joined together Niebuhr now sought to thrust asunder: love was the strategy of religion, pragmatism the strategy of society. In place of the older social passion he now affirmed what he called "Christian radicalism." His new formulations emerged in part from the discussion in the Fellowship of Socialist Christians, founded in 1930; in 1935 the Fellowship acquired its organ in *Radical Religion* (later *Christianity and Society*). For the Christian radicals the Kingdom of God was "final and absolute"; it was in some respects "equally distant from all political programs." The Kingdom offered no alternatives but perspectives; it would be a check not on policies but on pride; a source not of directives but of humility and contrition. The law of love, Niebuhr

[12] *Moral Man and Immoral Society*, pp. xi–xii, 21, 271.

contended in *An Interpretation of Christian Ethics* (1935), was relevant not as a possibility but precisely as an impossibility: the tension between the unconditional and the relative created the need and the opportunity for the grace of God. Yet the remoteness of the Kingdom of God by no means relieved Christians of the responsibilities of acting in history and in terms of the relativities of society. And political action, if perseveringly directed toward justice, could be a form of service to God. "The Kingdom of God is not of this world; yet its light illuminates our tasks in this world and its hope saves us from despair."[13]

Thus proximate political action was a Christian duty. Niebuhr vigorously attacked interpretations of the Christian religion which denied "the meaningfulness and importance of man's temporal existence, of his life in this body, of the vicissitudes of his social history, of the victories of good and evil in the rise and fall of empires and civilizations." Man remained the child of God, and no evil in human nature could completely destroy the image of God in him. Yet, "we are men and not God and we have to act even though we know that we are and will be proved by subsequent history to be sinful men in action." So no acts could escape the stain of self-interest and sin. Politics thus must always involve a choice between evils. "We use evil in every moment of our existence to hold evil in check." And political achievement must in consequence always be limited, fragmentary and incomplete. "Historic reality is never self-explanatory or self-sufficient. Both the ground and the goal of historic existence lie beyond itself . . . What is in history is always partial to specific

[13] "Socialist Decision and Christian Conscience," *Radical Religion*, Spring 1938; "The Hitler-Stalin Pact," *Radical Religion*, Fall 1939.

interests and tainted by sin." Next to rejecting the human condition in favor of the absolute, there can be no worse error than in identifying the absolute with contingent philosophies or programs. The role of the prophetic religion was to guide men in a mood of dialectical humility between the twin disasters of utopianism and defeatism, trusting in the end to the judgment and mercy and grace of God.[14]

Niebuhr's Christian radicalism thus constituted a fundamental critique of the liberalism created by the fusion of the Social Gospel and Dewey. In the political field Niebuhr rejected the Sermon on the Mount for pragmatism; even the choice between violence and nonviolence in social change, he asserted, was purely an expedient choice. But pragmatism had its limits: social redemption was impossible within history; the realm of power and sin was eternally under the judgment of the absolute; ultimately he rejected pragmatism for the Gospel. Thus he retained both the divine purpose and the pragmatic method which had characterized the liberal amalgam. But he sought to save each from the other by affirming the separateness of both.

If the politics of love was now rejected as confusing and irrelevant, how would the politics of power equip moral man to approach the problems of immoral society? Here Niebuhr's thought suffered a profound split of its own. He rendered two answers to this question— one on the level of strategy, the other on the level of tactics—and assumed that the two answers were identical. It would take him more than a decade before he fully perceived that they were different.

[14] "Christian Radicalism," *Radical Religion*, Winter 1936; "Socialist Decision and Christian Conscience"; "Pacifism and Sanctions," *Radical Religion*, Spring 1938; "Marx, Barth and Israel's Prophets," *Christian Century*, January 30, 1935.

His first answer derived from his conviction that power conflicts were the basic elements of history. Both the Social Gospel and Dewey had minimized the significance of power.[15] But for Niebuhr, power was the characteristic object of that imperialistic egoism which was man's ineradicable failing. "All life is an expression of power"; therefore all political calculations had to begin and end with power. So long as power remained in society, mankind could obviously never escape the necessity of endowing those who possess it with the largest measure of ethical self-control. But that would not, said Niebuhr in *Moral Man,* "obviate the necessity of reducing power to a minimum, of bringing the remainder under the strongest measure of social control; and of destroying such types of it as are least amenable to social control. For there is no ethical force strong enough to place inner check upon the use of power if its quantity is inordinate." He quoted Madison with approval: "The truth is that all men having power ought to be distrusted." But where did this analysis lead? If social cohesion were impossible without coercion, and coercion impossible without injustice, if self-interest could not be checked without the assertion of conflicting self-interest, what were the prospects for social harmony? If this analysis were right, Niebuhr concluded, "an uneasy balance of power would seem to become the highest goal to which society could aspire."[16]

[15] In the case of Dewey exceptions should be made for his wartime essays "Force, Violence, and Law," *New Republic,* January 22, 1916, and "Force and Coercion," *International Journal of Ethics,* April 1916. Both are reprinted in *Characters and Events* (New York: Holt, 1939). But the essence of the argument—"squeamishness about force is the mark not of idealistic but of moonstruck morals"—was ignored in his writings of the '20's.

[16] "Politics and the Christian Ethic," *Christianity and Society,* Spring 1940; *Moral Man,* pp. 164, 232.

On the level of strategy the balance of power in one form or another remained—and remains still—Niebuhr's answer to the problem of achieving a tolerable society. "The force of human egoism and the limits of the human imagination will make the struggle against the abuse of power a perpetual one," he wrote in 1933, "and will confront every society with the treble problem of decentralizing power as much as possible, of bringing power under social control and of establishing inner moral checks upon it." The urgent need, he repeated in 1934 in *Reflections on the End of an Era,* was for a political theory which would be radical "not only in the realistic nature of its analysis but in its willingness to challenge the injustices of a given social system by setting power against power until a more balanced equilibrium of power is achieved."[17]

But the statement of the end could not, for a Christian realist, solve the problem of means. The next question was what to do in America of the 1930's to attain the "more balanced equilibrium of power." And in the area of immediate action Niebuhr, under the pressure of the depression, found himself deeply attracted both to the diagnosis and to the prescriptions of Marxism. Liberalism, he crisply declared a few days before the inauguration of Franklin D. Roosevelt, was a "spent force." If anything was clear in March of 1933, it was "that capitalism is dying and . . . that it ought to die." Capitalist society could not reform itself from within; "there is nothing in history to support the thesis that a dominant class ever yields its position or privileges in society because its rule has been convicted of ineptness or injustices . . . Next to the futility of liberalism we

[17] "Optimism and Utopianism," *World Tomorrow*, February 22, 1933; *Reflections on the End of an Era*, p. 230.

may set down the inevitability of fascism as a practical certainty in every Western nation."[18]

The apocalyptic mood was dominant in *Reflections on the End of an Era*. The book throbbed with urgency and foreboding. The sickness of capitalism, Niebuhr said, was "organic and constitutional"; it was rooted in "the very nature of capitalism," in "the private ownership of the productive processes." There was no middle way; economists like Keynes might offer their advice, but they could not hope to arrest the drift toward fascism; "the drift is inevitable." The only hope was the socialization of the economy; but the rise of fascism seemed to guarantee that "the end of capitalism will be bloody rather than peaceful." Marxism thus came to seem to Niebuhr "an essentially correct theory and analysis of the economic realities of modern society, correct in its theory of class conflict, correct in regarding private ownership of the means of production as the basic causes of economic crisis and international war, correct in insisting that "communal ownership of the productive process is a basic condition of social health in a technical age."[19]

The appeal of Marxism to Niebuhr was a measure of his recoil from the optimism and moralism of Christian liberalism. One great attraction of the Marxist analysis was evidently its catastrophism. Rebounding from the liberal belief in the inevitability of progress, Niebuhr was all too susceptible to an equally extreme belief in the inevitability of catastrophe. The recurrence of the "end of an era" formula in his writings of

[18] "After Capitalism—What?" *World Tomorrow*, March 1, 1933.

[19] *Reflections*, pp. 24, 30, 53, 59; "Russia and Karl Marx," *Nation*, May 7, 1938; "Socialist Decision and Christian Conscience" (see footnotes 13 and 14).

the '30's suggests his shocked fascination with the possibility of some basic turn, some drastic judgment in history. He found the Marxist appreciation of the "fact of judgment and catastrophe in history . . . closer to the genius of Hebrew prophecy than liberalism, either secular or religious"; the notion that unjust civilizations would destroy themselves seemed only a secularized version of the prophecies of doom in which the Old Testament abounded.[20]

Thus, as Marxist catastrophism countered liberal optimism, so Marxist cynicism about the power of self-interest countered liberal sentimentalism and idealism; so Marxist collectivism, with its understanding of the need for community, countered liberal individualism; so Marxist determinism, with its sense of the implacability of history, countered the naïve liberal faith in the perfect plasticity of man and society; so the Marxist commitment to the working class countered the self-righteous complacency of the middle class. Above all, the historical and economic analysis of Marxism seemed to make increasing sense in what appeared to be an era of disintegrating capitalism.[21]

Yet Niebuhr's allegiance to Marxism was always strictly limited; and, though he was willing at various periods to consider tactical collaboration with the Communists, he never had illusions concerning the perils in their version of the Marxist faith. The fundamental Communist error, in his view, was a new form

[20] "Marx, Barth and Israel's Prophets"; see also "Christian Politics and Communist Religion" in John Lewis *et al.*, eds., *Christianity and the Social Revolution* (New York: Scribner's, 1936), especially pp. 461–63.

[21] For Niebuhr's retrospective accounts see "Communism and the Clergy," *Christian Century*, August 19, 1953; "Liberals and the Marxist Heresy," *New Republic*, October 12, 1953.

of liberal heresy: that is, the Communists found the Kingdom of God *in* history; they perceived in the Soviet Union the incarnation of the absolute. If the liberals were soft Utopians, the Communists were hard Utopians. For a season, while writing *Moral Man and Immoral Society,* Niebuhr regarded this Communist error as an indispensable myth, "a very valuable illusion for the moment; for justice cannot be approximated if the hope of its perfect realization does not generate a sublime madness in the soul." But on the reflection the madness generated by communism seemed to him less sublime than sinister. Indeed, he had already (in 1931) written about "the Religion of Communism," suggesting that "only a sentimentalist could be oblivious of the possibilities of Napoleonic ventures in the forces which are seething in Russia." By 1933 he explicitly repudiated the note of tolerance for myth on which *Moral Man* ended. By 1935 he could write ruefully: "I once thought such a faith to be a harmless illusion. But now I see that its net result is to endow a group of oligarchs with the religious sanctity which primitive priest-kings once held."[22]

His other basic objection to communism arose from his theory of power. Not only did Communist utopianism breed fanaticism and tyranny, but Communist economic reorganization gravely jeopardized the conditions of freedom. If power remained the central fact of society, and the desire for power man's ineradicable failing, then the destruction of economic privilege could hardly be expected to alter human nature to the degree that no one thereafter would desire to make selfish use of power. "The abuse of power by commu-

[22] *Moral Man*, pp. 276–77; "The Religion of Communism," *Atlantic Monthly*, April 1931; "Optimism and Utopianism"; "Religion and Marxism," *Modern Monthly*, February 1935.

nistic bureaucrats is very considerable," he wrote in *Moral Man,* "and is bound to grow as the purer revolutionary idealists are supplanted by men who have consciously sought for the possession of power . . . If the Russian oligarchy strips itself of its own power, it will be the first oligarchy of history to do so." In *Reflections* he made the indictment even more specific. The attempt to establish "an economic equilibrium through social ownership," he warned, might well create "a new disproportion of power . . . The new and stronger centres of political power will be new occasions for and temptations to injustice." By 1938, after the Moscow trials, he would state the viewpoint of "modern Christian Socialists" in blunt terms: "They want to equalize economic power but not at the price of creating political tyranny in a socialist society. They do not trust any irresponsible power in the long run, whether it is wielded by priests, monks, capitalists or commissars."[23]

He thus saw a profound contradiction between the Communist reality and his basic conviction that "all justice in human society rests upon some kind of balance of power." But, while excluding communism, he apparently saw no contradiction between his demand for a social balance of power and democratic socialism. Throughout the decade of the '30's, the socialization of property seemed to him not, of course (as it did to some of his Social Gospel friends), the means of ushering in Utopia or of establishing the Kingdom, but still the top pragmatic priority in order to achieve "a tolerable equilibrium of economic power." "We need more Christians," he cried in 1937, "who see how ab-

[23] *Moral Man,* pp. 164, 193; *Reflections,* pp. 243–44; "The Creed of Modern Christian Socialists," *Radical Religion,* Spring 1938.

solutely basic a revolution in the property system is for the sake of justice." Socializing the means of production remained for him, in a favorite phrase, "a primary requisite of social health in a technical age."[24]

In this respect Niebuhr and Dewey, despite their differences in presupposition, had no difference in program. For all their professed dislike of doctrine, they were both in this period staunch economic doctrinaires. For all their rejection of closed abstract systems, each saw the contemporary American problem in closed and abstract terms. The passionate champions of experiment, both flatly condemned the most massive and brilliant period of political and economic experimentation in American history. With a supreme political pragmatist as President, and with the most resourceful and creative economic and legal pragmatists of the time seeking patiently and tirelessly to work out a middle way between laissez faire and collectivism neither the secular pragmatist nor the Christian pragmatist managed to work up much interest. The pragmatic philosophers, abandoning pragmatism to Franklin D. Roosevelt, retreated precipitately to their own cryptoutopias. In the case of Dewey, it should be said that his disdain for the New Deal and his commitment to socialization proceeded naturally enough from his disregard for power in society and from his faith in human rationality and scientific planning; but for Niebuhr, who was realistic about man and who wanted to equilibrate power in society, the commitment to socialization was both the price of indifference

[24] Editorial comment on Dwight J. Bradley, "Radicalism and Religions of Redemption," *Radical Religion*, Spring 1938; "Ten Years That Shook My World"; review of *Toward a Christian Revolution* in *Radical Religion*, Spring 1937; "Socialist Decision and Christian Conscience."

to the achievements of piecemeal reform and a symptom of despair. Where Dewey spurned the New Deal because of his optimism about man and his belief in science, Niebuhr seems to spurn it because of his pessimism about man and his belief in catastrophe.

Early in 1935 Niebuhr took an inventory of the resources of the American democratic tradition. Middle-class politics—by which he evidently meant party politics—seemed to him hopeless, "rushing us at incredible speed from the futilities of Rooseveltian 'liberalism' to the worse confusion of a political program concocted by a radio priest and a Louisiana 'kingfish.'" The New Deal continued to figure in his writings of the period as an image of incoherent and aimless triviality; and his attitude toward what was going on in Washington in these days remained singularly lacking in concreteness and even in curiosity. This was, no doubt, because he had excluded the middle way, so to speak, by definition. Liberalism, after all, was "spent," and there was evidently no point in wasting time examining its works. Keynes, Stuart Chase, Sir Arthur Salter might insist on the necessity for democratic planning; but "the imperiled oligarchy of our day, though it may pay lip service to the sweet reasonableness of their counsels, drifts nevertheless toward fascism"; and the drift was inevitable.[25]

The "paradox" was, of course, that at these moments the imperiled oligarchy was being forced by effective democratic government to accept measures of regulation and reform which would avert fascism and lead to recovery. But Niebuhr, blinkered by doctrine, scornfully rejected the very pragmatism he called for in

[25] "Our Romantic Radicals," *Christian Century*, April 10, 1935; *Reflections*, pp. 45–46, 53.

theory. The nation, he said after the 1936 election, when he supported Norman Thomas, "has chosen a messiah rather than a political leader committed to a specific political program; and unfortunately the messiah is more renowned for his artistic juggling than for robust resolution."[26] The possibility that "artistic juggling" might be the strategy by which social power could best be distributed and balanced was not then to be considered.

Niebuhr's attitude toward the New Deal seems to have been further influenced by his indifference to New Deal economics. Like Dewey he wrote with earnest conviction on economic questions without adequately informing himself on the issues of economic policy. Indeed, like the British Socialists of 1930, he seemed almost to feel that, if socialism was excluded, one had to play the capitalist game according to strict capitalist rules; the choice was between nationalizing everything and balancing the budget; the power and resources of fiscal policy in a capitalist economy did not figure in his calculations. Thus his writings of the middle '30's showed a curious but persistent concern with the unbalanced budget and the terrifying size of the annual deficits (which actually only once—1936— exceeded $4 billion in Roosevelt's first two terms). During the recession of 1937–38, caused in great part by the reduction of government spending, Niebuhr actually urged an *increase* in taxes, which would, of course, have only reduced further the government's contribution to the economy. In 1939 he denounced deficits as a form of insulin, a medicine "which wards off dissolution without giving the patient health." And the incurable experimentalism of the New Deal clearly

[26] "The National Election," *Radical Religion*, Winter 1936.

seemed to him to stand in sorry contrast to the clear-cut logic of socialism. Roosevelt was concededly "better than most of his reactionary critics," said Niebuhr in 1938. "But no final good can come of this kind of whirligig reform." "If that man could only make up his mind to cross the Rubicon!" Niebuhr added. "A better metaphor is that he is like Lot's wife. Let him beware lest he turn into a pillar of salt."[27]

The Rubicon metaphor suggested the either/or approach which Niebuhr still maintained in face of the New Deal assumption that the mixed economy was a better means of equilibrating power than was socialism. For Roosevelt, of course, the problem was not to cross the Rubicon but to navigate down it. And in time the relative success of New Deal improvisation, especially in contrast with the melancholy results of Communist logic, began to force Niebuhr to re-examine his political presuppositions; perhaps the reflections on the end of an era had been premature. The attack on socialism in Bertrand Russell's *Power* in 1938 plainly touched an exposed nerve. In 1939, considering the question whether the capitalist system could not be made to work, Niebuhr surprisingly confessed, "It would be rather rash to give an unequivocal answer," even adding that socialists should prefer a solution of the New Deal type to a general breakdown. A year later he frankly said that "if socialization of economic power is purchased at the price of creating irresponsible and tyrannical political power, our last estate may be worse than the first." Social justice, he

[27] "The Political Campaign," *Radical Religion*, Autumn 1936; "The Administration and the Depression," Winter 1937; "Roosevelt's Merry-Go-Round," Spring 1938; "The Domestic Situation," Summer 1938; "Nicholas Murray Butler," Fall 1938; "New Deal Medicine," Spring 1939.

declared, could be achieved only if social forces were allowed considerable freedom of challenge and maneuver through an unremitting process of "political pressure and counterpressure."[28] When in June 1940 Niebuhr resigned, after a dozen years, from the Socialist party, it was the ratification of inner reservations which had made him a keen critic of the party's policies and leadership for the three years preceding. In November, while still viewing himself, in some sense, as a socialist and still insisting on "a genuine farmer-labor party" as one of "the inevitabilities of American politics," to be anticipated in 1944 or 1948, he nevertheless cast his first vote for Franklin D. Roosevelt and the Democrats.[29] After the election he joined with a group of ex-Socialists and New Dealers in founding the pragmatically oriented Union for Democratic Action.

It cannot be said, however, that domestic economic policy was the decisive reason for Niebuhr's rejection of the Socialist party and his new approval of Roosevelt. What was decisive was the issue of foreign policy, growing in size and urgency as Nazi aggression began to remake the map of Europe. Here the Socialists, committed largely to isolationism, and the Protestant ministry, committed to some degree to pacifism, seemed to show in a dismal and devastating way the consequences of moralized politics. In contrast, the canny and opportunistic political realism of Roosevelt gained new stature in his eyes; rather than merely an

[28] "Anatomy of Power," *Nation*, October 1, 1938; review of Ezekiel's *Jobs for All* in *Radical Religion*, Spring 1939; "A New Name," *Radical Religion*, Winter 1940; review of Eliot's *The Idea of Christian Society* in *Radical Religion*, Winter 1940.

[29] "An End to Illusions," *Nation*, June 29, 1940; "The Socialist Campaign," *Christianity and Society*, Summer 1940.

artistic juggler, Roosevelt seemed almost to have the dimensions of a great democratic leader.

Niebuhr had not always approved Roosevelt's attempts to build up American armed strength against fascism. In 1937 he assailed Roosevelt's naval program as "sinister"; "this Roosevelt navalism," he said, "must be resisted at all cost." The next year he called the naval program "the most unjustified piece of military expansion in a world full of such madness"—in short, evidently worse than Nazi rearmament. But after Munich it seemed to him that even world war might be better than the extension of Nazi tyranny. By 1940 Niebuhr was prepared to make magnanimous reparation. Roosevelt "anticipated the perils in which we now stand more clearly than anyone else," he wrote. "In fact there are few among us who did not make unjustified criticisms of his preparedness program, which subsequent events have proved to be conservative rather than hysterical."[30]

The pacifist program, on the other hand, now seemed to concentrate in itself all the errors of liberalism which Niebuhr had castigated for so long. It refused to accept the existence of power; by refusing to use power, it bowed out of the field of political responsibility; by retreating from responsibility, it dodged its Christian duty; and it did all this under the cover of an intolerable self-righteousness. Pacifism might be necessary as a witness and a remainder of absolute perspectives; but it could well be disastrous if it sought to intervene in pragmatic politics and to demand "all kinds of fatuous political alternatives." In *Christianity and Power Politics* (1940) he attacked the

[30] "Brief Comments," *Radical Religion*, Winter 1937; "Brief Comments," Spring 1938; "Willkie and Roosevelt," *Christianity and Society*, Fall 1940.

versions of Christian and secular perfectionism which placed a premium upon nonparticipation in conflicts; this was a "very sentimentalized" form of the Christian faith, and at variance with the profoundest insights of the Christian religion. The effort to reduce the peace of the Kingdom of God into simple historical possibility, he added, inevitably invited surrender to evil as the price of avoidance of conflict. "In waging the war and in building the peace," he said in 1942, "we need the idealism of the Christian gospel to save us from cynicism and complacency. But we also need the realism of the Christian faith to save us from sentimentality. In America at least the dangers of a perverse sentimentality have been greater than the perils of cynicism."[31]

In 1939 Niebuhr had delivered the Gifford Lectures at Edinburgh. Suitably revised and expanded, they appeared in the two great volumes of 1941 and 1943 which made up *The Nature and Destiny of Man*. Here his politics, as they had emerged from his experience of the 1930's, took their place in the full setting of his religious conviction. "We know," he wrote, "that we cannot purge ourselves of the sin and guilt in which we are involved by the moral ambiguities of politics without disavowing responsibility for the creative possibilities of justice."[32] As for democratic politics, he now found their essence in the "pressures and counter pressures, the tensions, the overt and covert conflicts by which justice is achieved and maintained." This acceptance of conflict as the consequence of power and antidote to it would stand in sharp contrast to some of

[31] "Christianity and the World Crises," *Christianity and Society*, Fall 1940; *Christianity and Power Politics*, ix–x; "The Churches and the War," *Town Meeting of the Air*, August 27, 1942.
[32] *The Nature and Destiny of Man*, II, 284.

his fellow Socialist Christians, such as Paul Tillich, who as late as 1953 would regard the "competitive society" as a basic threat to personality and community and call for "social transformation."[33]

What Niebuhr meant was spelled out in more detail in the West Foundation lectures at Stanford in 1944, published the next year under the title of *The Children of Light and the Children of Darkness*. Here he wrestled once again with his old commitment to the socialization of property. The Marxist theory was correct, he still felt, in emphasizing the "social character of industrial property"; but perhaps socialization was "too simple a solution"; and he now questioned the Marxist assumption that it would "destroy all disproportions of economic power in the community." How, indeed, could one socialize property "without creating pools of excessive social power in the hands of those who manage both its economic and political processes"? Even if social ownership were more efficient, it might be wise to sacrifice efficiency "for the sake of preserving a greater balance of forces and avoiding undue centralization of power." He was still not sure; the "logic of history" still seemed to him behind proposals for socialization, but "the logic is not unambiguous." And he later underscored the ambiguities of this historical logic by arguing that the two prerequisites for a free society were that there should be an equilibrium among class forces, and that the equilibrium should be dynamic, gradually shifting "the political institutions of the community to conform to changing economic needs and unchanging demands

[33] Paul Tillich, "The Person in a Technical Society" in J. A. Hutchison, ed., *Christian Faith and Social Action* (New York: Scribner's, 1953), pp. 144, 152.

for a higher justice."[34] This sounded a good deal more like the mixed economy and open society of the New Deal than like socialism.

The retreat from socialization was visibly reducing the gap between the ends and the means of his social thought in the '30's. Yet he was still reluctant to identify the more appropriate means in concrete economic and political terms. In 1944 he voted for Roosevelt, but again foreign rather than domestic policy was dominant. In 1947 the Fellowship of Socialist Christians changed its name to Frontier Fellowship. "We continue to be socialists," Niebuhr explained, "in the sense that we believe that the capitalist order of society stands under divine judgment and that there is no justice in modern technical society without a completely pragmatic attitude toward the institution of property. It must be socialized wherever it is of such character that it makes for injustice through inordinate centralization. . . . But the most dangerous error is the centralization of both economic and political power in the hands of a communist oligarchy."[35]

In the '30's the Socialist party had been Niebuhr's political outlet, but during the war he had worked through UDA, and after 1947 he became a leading figure in Americans for Democratic Action, a group of pragmatic liberals opposed to all dogmatisms, conservative, socialist, or communist, and dedicated to piecemeal and gradual reform. In 1948 he voted for Truman. And by 1949 he was prepared to accept the logic of his "completely pragmatic attitude." There was, he said, "a bare possibility that the kind of pragmatic po-

[34] *The Children of Light and the Children of Darkness*, pp. 74, 76, 78, 80, 82, 102.
[35] "Frontier Fellowship," *Christianity and Society*, Autumn 1948.

litical program which has been elaborated under the 'New Deal' and the 'Fair Deal' may prove to be a better answer to the problems of justice in a technical age than its critics of either right or left had assumed." Democratic socialism, even in its British version, seemed to him encumbered with dogmas almost as confusing as the dogmas of the plutocracy. The "unplanned improvisations of our early New Deal" now seemed more likely than conservatism or socialism to "grow into a purposeful pragmatism," which would make "a significant contribution to the cause of democracy."[36] It turned out not to have been necessary to cross the Rubicon after all; "whirligig reform" now seemed a viable middle way.

Niebuhr's subsequent writings elaborated this general position. When Frontier Fellowship dissolved into Christian Action in 1951, the single economic plank in the new statement of purpose only pledged government action "to maintain a high and stable level of economic activity"[37]—a position so vague that a conservative Republican would have little difficulty in accepting it. A crucial chapter of *The Irony of American History* (1952) was entitled "The Triumph of Experience over Dogma." He could now speak of "our success in establishing justice and insuring domestic tranquillity." We have, he wrote, achieved such social justice as we possess in the only way justice could be achieved in a technical society: "we have equilibrated power. We have attained a certain equilibrium in economic society itself by setting organized power against organized power. When that did not suffice we used

[36] "Plutocracy and World Responsibilities," *Christianity and Society*, Autumn 1949.

[37] "Christian Action Statement of Purpose," *Christianity and Crisis*, October 1, 1951.

the more broadly based political power to redress disproportions and disbalances in economic society." It had been, he concluded, "a pragmatic approach to political and economic questions" which would have done credit to Edmund Burke.[38] At long last the two halves of Niebuhr's social thought were together; Christian radicalism had given way, so to speak, to Christian realism; his old demand for a social balance of power had fully found its objective correlative in public policy.

Having resolved the inner contradiction in his social thought, Niebuhr was now able the better to resolve his ambivalent relations to the two creeds from which he had drawn so much strength and which he had subjected to such devastating criticism. I suggested earlier that he was, in a sense, the child both of the Social Gospel and of pragmatism, but that he had profoundly resisted the attempts of the Social Gospel to annihilate the relative, as he had profoundly resisted the attempts of pragmatism to annihilate the absolute. By 1952 the old battle with the moralistic simplicities of the Social Gospel seemed to come to an end. Reviewing the familiar defects of the Gospel, Niebuhr now dismissed them as "minor when its achievement is recognized: it delivered American Protestantism from meeting complex ethical problems of a technical civilization with an

[38] *The Irony of American History*, pp. 89, 101; see also Niebuhr's most recent and critical reconsideration of Marxism and democratic socialism, "The Anomaly of European Socialism," *Christian Realism and Political Problems*, pp. 43–51; and his vigorous affirmation of the necessity for limited government intervention in economic life along mixed-economy lines, "Coercion, Self-Interest and Love," in K. E. Boulding, *The Organizational Revolution* (New York: Harper, 1953), pp. 228–44; also his "Christian Faith and Social Action," pp. 225–42 (see note 33).

almost completely irrelevant individualistic pietism and moralism."[39]

The issues with pragmatism remained more tense and complex. Niebuhr had never ceased his polemic against Dewey—against the illusions of "social science" and the supposition that "scientific" analysis of society could produce impartial and uncontaminated results.[40] When empiricism mistook a finite for an absolute perspective, it sinned; and its sin, in Niebuhr's view, could be fraught with perilous consequence. Yet Niebuhr continued to maintain just as resolutely the supremacy of the pragmatic method in the world of contingent decision and action. Relativism was, of course, the inevitable result of his belief that original sin tainted all human perception and knowledge. The absolute was thus, by definition, unattainable; so mortal man's apprehension of truth had to be fitful, shadowy, and imperfect; he saw through the glass darkly, nor could there be a worse expression of human self-righteousness and self-deception than the attempt to endow fragmentary and corrupt perceptions with objectivity and certitude.

The great lesson of prophetic religion, he often remarked, was to show "how relative all human ideals are." Against absolutism he insisted both on the "relativity of all human perspectives" and on the sinfulness of those who claimed absolute validity and divine sanction for their opinions. He declared himself "in broad agreement with the relativist position in the matter of freedom, as upon every other social and po-

[39] "The Protestant Clergy and U.S. Politics," *Reporter*, February 19, 1952.

[40] Cf., e.g., "Faith and the Empirical Method in Modern Realism," and "Ideology and the Scientific Method," *Christian Realism*, pp. 1–14, 75–94.

litical right or principle."[41] In the '30's it had been the gospel-minded of the left who contended most aggressively that the Kingdom of God existed on earth and who sought to hypostatize the finite into the absolute. When, in the late '40's and early '50's, the main religious pressure came from the right, Niebuhr valiantly turned to oppose the attempts to identify capitalism with Christian truth or to transform necessary pragmatic resistance against Communist aggression into a "holy war" against communism.

In pointing to the dangers of what Mr. Justice Jackson has called "compulsory godliness,"[42] Niebuhr once again argued that "religion is so frequently a source of confusion in political life, and so frequently dangerous to democracy, precisely because it introduces absolutes into the realm of relative values." Religion, he warned, could be a source of error as well as wisdom and light; its proper role should be not to endorse but to question; to inculcate, not a sense of infallibility, but a sense of humility. Indeed, "the worst corruption is a corrupt religion."[43]

He still defended the line between pragmatism and faith—the lines designed to keep the absolute out of the relative but at the same time to prevent the relative from mistaking itself for the absolute. In the immediate past it had seemed most important to hold this line

[41] "Marx, Barth and Israel's Prophets"; "Moral Rearmament," *Radical Religion*, Fall 1939; "The Limits of Liberty," *Nation*, January 24, 1942.

[42] In his dissenting opinion in *Zorach* v. *Clauson*, 343 U.S. at 325.

[43] Letter to the Editor, *Reporter*, May 27, 1952; "Prayers and Politics," *Christianity and Crisis*, October 27, 1952; comment on book jacket of R. L. Roy's *Apostles of Discord* (Boston: Beacon Press, 1953).

against the simplistic followers of Dewey who wanted to sacrifice the absolute to the relative. But in the early '50's Niebuhr found himself equally involved in holding the line against the simplistic believers in religion who wanted to sacrifice the relative to the absolute.

The penetrating critic of the Social Gospel and of pragmatism, he ended up, in a sense, the powerful reinterpreter and champion of both. It was the triumph of his own remarkable analysis that it took what was valuable in each, rescued each by defining for each the limits of validity, and, in the end, gave the essential purposes of both new power and new validity. And he did this not alone in his books and articles, but in his life. No man has had as much influence as a preacher in this generation; no preacher has had as much influence in the secular world. His own authentic humility, his deep awareness of the moral precariousness of historical striving combined with his moral resoluteness about the immediate issues, the range of his compassion, the honesty of his wrath, the spontaneity of his unselfishness, and the sweetness and grandeur of his character—all these qualities succeeded in making manifest and vivid, as no more sermons or essays could, the image of Christian man.

It was almost as much his personality as his writings which thus helped accomplish in a single generation a revolution in the bases of American liberal political thought. A culture which had staked too much on illusions of optimism found itself baffled and stricken in an age dominated by total government and total war; history had betrayed its votaries. Defeatism and despair might have been a natural reaction to so devastating a disillusion—a natural reaction in the world of philosophy, at least, even if reflexes of survival have guaranteed resistance in the world of politics.

But if history refuted democratic absolutism, the resources of democratic pragmatism turned out to be greater than many people—including Niebuhr himself in certain moods—had imagined. And his "vindication of democracy and a critique of its traditional defenders" turned out—in another "paradox"—to be the supreme interpretation of the pragmatic economics and politics of the '30's for which, at the time, he had so little use. Thus Niebuhr showed that the refutation by history of democratic illusions need not turn into a refutation of democracy; that the appalled realization that man was not wholly good and reasonable need not turn into a repudiation of man as wholly evil and impotent; that men and women could act more effectively for decency and justice under the banner of a genuine humility than they had under the banner of an illusory perfectibility. His penetrating reconstruction of the democratic faith—in the context of Roosevelt's brilliant invocation of democratic resources against the perils of depression and war—absorbed and mastered the forces of disillusion and preserved the nerve of action. With his aid, that faith emerged from two anguished decades far better than before against future ordeal and challenge.

It was, I have said, the achievement both of Niebuhr the moral and political philosopher and of Niebuhr the man. If his searching realism gave new strength to American liberal democracy, or, rather, renewed sources of strength which had been too often neglected in the generations since the American Revolution, his own life and example have shown in compelling terms the possibilities of human contrition and human creativity within the tragedy of history.

10.
Walter Lippmann
The Intellectual *vs*. Politics
(1959)

At the depths of the depression (if my memory is correct), the *New Yorker's* "Talk of the Town," commenting on the reported formation of a Monarchist party in the United States, said that many Americans would be glad to settle for Walter Lippmann as king. Nor was this notion of the pundit as leader a novel one. At Harvard College nearly a quarter of a century before, Lippmann's classmate John Reed used to introduce him, not wholly satirically, as "Gentlemen, the future President of the United States!"[1] James Truslow Adams could recall discussing Lippmann in 1918 "with a distinguished American far from visionary in his judgments"; the forecast then was that Lippmann by forty might easily be governor of New York or Secretary of State.[2] Yet, for all such predictions, Lippmann throughout his life has resolutely declined entangling political commitment; and his few brushes with operating responsibility seem only to have fortified this resolution. His career, in a sense, has been a long and troubled search to define the role of the intellectual in the polity of a free society.

His broad answer to this quest has been plain enough. The office of the intellectual, Lippmann has generally

[1] Granville Hicks, *John Reed* (New York: Macmillan, 1936), p. 34.

[2] J. T. Adams, "Walter Lippmann," *Saturday Review of Literature*, January 7, 1933.

proposed, is to articulate the guiding faith which will enable society so to discipline itself and focus its purposes that its members can live effective, coherent, and fulfilled lives. To give the intellectual this function is to imply, of course, that such a central faith exists—that there is some ultimate perspective in terms of which everything else will fall into its proper place. Lippmann has believed this during most, though not all, of his life; and, in affirming the possibility of some sort of basic order and rationality in the universe, he has perhaps betrayed the fact that, of the two Harvard philosophers who influenced him most, one influenced him more profoundly than the other. Both George Santayana and William James greatly excited young Lippmann; but in the end, Santayana's realm of essences evidently struck deeper chords than James's radical empiricism. Lippmann used to say in later years that it was Santayana who saved him from becoming a pragmatist.[3]

Assuming, then, that there was a central something to articulate, that the apparent contrarieties of existence were somehow corrected and harmonized in a higher realm of essences, how would the intellectual best go about persuading the world to recognize its own rationality? The next question was the old and vexatious one of detachment *vs.* commitment. Would the intellectual help most as a free individual or as a part of a cause? by insisting on rigorous independence of mind or by entering and helping control the great practical movements of history? At Harvard, Santayana and James, wherever else they might disagree, agreed in viewing the world at a philosophic distance. Both were men informed by a critical and ironic toler-

[3] John Mason Brown, *Through These Men* (New York: Harper, 1956), p. 211.

ance of human diversity. Lippmann certainly shared this instinct for disengagement. Yet other forces of the day tugged at him. These were years of urgent social and intellectual ferment. The Progressive era was at high noon; and for a mind both sensitive and logical, the rampant humanitarianism and rationalism of the day argued against a course of total withdrawal.

It seems at first odd that a man of Lippmann's evident brilliance and promise appeared not to consider seriously the prospects of an academic career. He did stay on at Harvard for a year to serve as Santayana's assistant in a philosophy course; but from the start he seems to have accepted a destiny as a commentator rather than as a professional philosopher. As a thinker deeply responsive to the complex equilibrium of intellectual forces around him, he chose the role of helping produce public sense in the community rather than pursuing private truth in individual solitude. His intelligence was, in the best sense, polemical rather than either technical or prophetic; his particular gift was the sensitive lucidity with which he reacted to the intellectual ebb and flow of his culture. From an early point, one can detect almost a contracyclical quality in his thought, as if he were impelled always to redress the balance against the dominating suppositions of the day—sometimes after he himself had given these suppositions their most clear and trenchant statement.

So, in 1911, for all the temptations of James and Santayana and Harvard philosophy, Lippmann must have felt some inadequacy in academic life. He worked afternoons in settlement houses; contact with Graham Wallas, at Harvard as visiting lecturer from the London School of Economics, enlarged his interest in social problems, even if Wallas himself was by then disenchanted with socialism; and his own dangerous susceptibility to syllogism doubtless beckoned him then, as it sometimes did later, toward deductive conclusions which very likely outstripped his practical beliefs. In any case, he called himself a socialist and became president of the Harvard Socialist Club; and, though his socialism never went very deep, it did go deep enough to involve him in his first experiment in political activism. For a few moments in college and after, socialism represented for him the transcendent faith through which the intellectual could crystallize the purposes and unify the energies of society. As he later ruefully remarked of this period, "The general scheme of the human future seemed fairly clear to me."[4]

His first job after finishing Harvard was to serve an apprenticeship in reporting to Lincoln Steffens on *Everybody's*. In 1911, George R. Lunn, running on the Socialist ticket, was elected mayor of Schenectady. Lunn soon invited the brilliant young Harvard socialist to join his staff, and Lippmann, with evident eagerness, seized the opportunity to serve the cause. The result was quickly disillusioning. "I have lived with politicians," Lippmann wrote sadly the next year. The good will of these municipal socialists was abundant, and their intentions were constructive. But the futilities of politics seemed unbearable. Petty vexations piled up into mountains; distracting details scattered the attention and broke up thinking; committee sessions wore out nerves by aimless drifting; constant speechmaking thrust men back on their weary stock of platitudes. "Misunderstanding and distortion dry up the imagination, make thought timid and expression flat, the at-

---

[4] Lippmann, *The Good Society* (Boston: Little, Brown, 1937), p. xi. Hereafter all citations will be to writings of Lippmann unless otherwise attributed.

mosphere of publicity requires a mask which soon become the reality." His socialist colleagues used to claim that they were fighting "The Beast" or "Special Privilege." "But to me it always seemed that we were like Peer Gynt at struggling against the formless Boyg—invisible yet everywhere."[5]

Politics was obviously something more than the painless application by young intellectuals of general principles to concrete circumstances. Lippmann forsook Schenectady after a few months and, reflecting on the difficulties he had encountered, retired to Maine and wrote a perceptive and thoughtful book entitled *A Preface to Politics*. Here, in reformulating the political problem, Lippmann redefined his conception of the role in politics of the man of ideas. The essential political conflict, he felt, was between routine and creativity. The real business of statesmanship was not the preservation of order, the guarding of privilege, the administration of existing machinery; it was the anticipation of social wants, the invention of new forms, the preparation for new growths. "The deliberate making of issues," he wrote, "is very nearly the core of the statesman's task. His greatest wisdom is required to select a policy that will fertilize the public mind."

But there were obstacles to the easy execution of this mission. One was the complexity of society. "It is a great question whether our intellects can grasp the subject. Are we perhaps like a child whose hand is too small to span an octave on the piano?" Yet, in the real world, Lippmann responded, action cannot always wait on thought; we must act on half-knowledge, illusion, and error, and trust to experience to convert mis-

[5] *A Preface to Politics* (New York: Kennerley, 1913), pp. 54–55, 183.

takes into wisdom. An equal problem, it seemed, was the character of the public itself. If one trouble was lack of facts about society, the reason that newspapers and magazines would not print them, Lippmann contended, was less the pressure of advertisers than the awful sensibilities of readers.

No financial power is one-tenth so corrupting, so insidious, so hostile to originality and frank statement as the fear of the public which reads the magazine. For one item suppressed out of respect for a railroad or a bank, nine are rejected because of the prejudices of the public. This will anger the farmers, that will arouse the Catholics, another will shock the summer girl. Anybody can take a fling at poor old Mr. Rockefeller, but the great mass of average citizens (to which none of us belongs) must be left in undisturbed possession of its prejudices. In that subservience, and not in the meddling of Mr. Morgan, is the reason why American journalism is so flaccid, so repetitious and so dull.

How could these obstacles be overcome? How, given the complexity of the material on the one hand and the "prejudices of the public" on the other, could one make the issues that would replace routine by creativity? Lippmann's answer was, in effect, to propose a partnership between the intellectual, who could master the material, and the statesman, who could master the public. The intellectual would no longer intervene directly, as in Schenectady. Rather, the statesman would act as the intermediary between the experts and his constituency. The statesman, wrote Lippmann, instancing Theodore Roosevelt and the conservation movement, "makes social movements conscious of themselves, expresses their needs, gathers their power and then thrusts them behind the inventor and the technician in the task of actual achievement." With such creative leadership, "there will be much less use for lawyers and a great deal more for scientists." And more use also, he implied, for philosophers, for those who sought to make society conscious of its purposes and problems: "Make a blind struggle luminous, drag an unconscious impulse into the open day, see that men are aware of their necessities, and the future is in a measure controlled."[6]

In *Drift and Mastery* in 1914, Lippmann further clarified his notion of the intellectual's role in society's struggle for coherence. Civilization, he wrote, was, in effect, the "substitution of conscious intention for unconscious striving"—the constant effort "to introduce plan where there has been clash, and purpose into the jungles of disordered growth." But this process of mastery could no longer be haphazard and spasmodic. Nor was an emotional faith, like socialism, adequate to bring about control. "What men need in their specialties in order to enable them to cooperate is not alone a binding passion, but a common discipline." And this discipline lay at hand: it was science.

> The discipline of science is the only one which gives any assurance that from the same set of facts men will come approximately to the same conclusion. And as the modern world can be civilized only by the effort of innumerable people we have a right to call science the discipline of democracy.

Drift and Mastery thus cast the intellectual as the articulator of the discipline of science in society's effort

[6] *A Preface to Politics*, pp. 26–27, 105–6, 196–97, 250, 301–2, 306–7, 315.

to control its own evolution. Lippmann did not mean by this, however, that the intellectual should detach himself from all purpose and striving. "If the student is merely disinterested," he wrote, "he is a pedant . . . The true scientist is inspired by a vision without being the victim of it." What was necessary, as Lippmann put it, was not just ideas but "passionate ideas."[7]

He soon had an opportunity to test out his new conception of the relationship between the intellectual and politics. His argument in *Drift and Mastery* was the elaboration of a viewpoint which Theodore Roosevelt, borrowing a phrase from Herbert Croly, had baptized the "New Nationalism" three years before. In the course of 1914, Croly invited Lippmann to join him on the staff of a projected magazine to be called the *New Republic*. Croly had already provided in *The Promise of American Life* the best historical and philosophical vindication of Roosevelt's general ideas and attitude; and the *New Republic* promised to be, along with Roosevelt's own *Outlook*, the chief organ of Rooseveltian Progressivism. In November 1914, T.R. displayed his own high regard for Croly and Lippmann in an *Outlook* article on *Drift and Mastery* and Croly's new book, *Progressive Democracy:* "No man who wishes seriously to study our present social, industrial, and political life with the view of guiding his thought and action so as to work for National betterment in the future can afford not to read these books through and through and to ponder and digest them."[8]

The experiment in collaboration between intellectual and statesman seemed ideally conceived. And for

[7] *Drift and Mastery* (New York: Holt, 1914), pp. 269, 281–82, 285, 307, 317.

[8] Theodore Roosevelt, "Two Noteworthy Books on Democracy," *Outlook*, November 18, 1914.

a time everything went along swimmingly. "Our general position at the outset delighted Roosevelt," Lippmann later wrote, "and we saw a good deal of him in the first few weeks."[9] T.R. called Lippmann "a personal friend of mine . . . I think, on the whole, the most brilliant young man of his age in all the United States. He is a great writer and economist. He has real international sense."[10] But events soon confronted Croly and Lippmann with the old choice between commitment and detachment—in this case between suppressing their opinion of a powerful friend in the hope of retaining their capacity to influence him, or publishing that opinion at the risk of estranging him. When Roosevelt launched a particularly crude attack on Wilson's Mexican policy, the *New Republic* preferred editorial integrity to personal loyalty, and condemned their patron. Roosevelt "reproached us bitterly," as Lippmann later recalled it, "and never forgave us." Lippmann added, "After that we never had any close personal association with any public man."[11]

This final statement undoubtedly expressed a moral which has ruled Lippmann ever since. A commentator could no more enjoy friendship with a statesman than a dramatic critic could with a leading lady. And this was true with T.R. despite an agreement on issues that persisted long after the personal coolness—which lasted, indeed, until, as Lippmann saw it, Roosevelt himself in 1916 deserted the New Nationalism and the philosophy of mastery in favor of a jumble of phrases about honor, patriotism, and righteousness. Up to this point, Lippmann had been critical of Wilson's New

[9] "Notes for a Biography," *New Republic*, July 16, 1930.
[10] Theodore Roosevelt, *Letters* (Cambridge: Harvard University Press, 1954), Elting E. Morison, ed., Vol. VIII, p. 872.
[11] "Notes for a Biography."

Freedom as the philosophy of drift, the vision of a nation of villagers. But gradually Wilson appeared to have apprehended the need for national purpose and control; the Democratic party, Lippmann concluded in 1916, was the "only party which at this moment is national in scope, liberal in purpose, and effective in action."[12]

If the experiments with Lunn and Roosevelt had destroyed for Lippmann the conception of the intellectual as close personal adviser, there still remained the essence of the role sketched in *Drift and Mastery*—the expert who could collaborate with the statesman in the task of social control. The *New Republic's* rapprochement with Wilson now afforded an opportunity to explore the implications of this role. In the winter of 1916, Lippmann had two or three interviews with Wilson; and soon both he and Croly began to hold regular fortnightly meetings with Colonel House. Lippmann subsequently minimized the significance of this relation; any resemblance between the policies of the administration and the line of the *New Republic*, he said, was partly the result of "a certain parallelism of reasoning," partly of sheer coincidence.[13] Nonetheless, the relationship grew; and, when America entered the war, Lippmann, to Croly's dismay, took leave from the magazine and entered the government service.

There then ensued Lippmann's longest and most significant venture in official life. He first succeeded Felix Frankfurter as special assistant to Secretary of War Newton D. Baker, working particularly on labor matters (here, on an interdepartmental committee, he met the Assistant Secretary of the Navy Franklin D.

[12] A. M. Schlesinger, Jr., *The Crisis of the Old Order* (Boston: Houghton Mifflin, 1957). p. 35.
[13] "Notes for a Biography."

Roosevelt). Then, when House set up the Inquiry, a collection of experts to begin planning for the peace, Lippmann became its secretary and the chief liaison between the Inquiry and the White House. House's experts did the preliminary work on Wilson's peace proposals; and subsequently Lippmann himself, along with Frank Cobb, wrote what came to be accepted as the official American interpretation of the Fourteen Points.

In due course, Lippmann was commissioned in Military Intelligence and sent to France to pursue what another generation would call psychological warfare against Germany. Wilson was a little unhappy when he heard of this mission. "I have a high opinion of Lippmann," he wrote the Acting Secretary of War, "but I am very jealous in the matter of propaganda . . . I want to keep the matter of publicity in my own hands."[14] But House continued to send Lippmann's reports to the President and eventually put Lippmann on his own staff in Paris.

Peace making, however, turned out to be easier on paper than around a conference table. Lippmann, discouraged, resigned to return to the *New Republic* before the deed was finally done. There, with some misgiving, he accepted Croly's decision to oppose the result. His disillusion over Versailles was not so violent as that of some contemporaries: "if I had to do it all over again," he said in 1930, "I would take the other side."[15] Yet, on balance, he plainly felt that something had gone badly wrong, that his work had miscarried. Still, this failure did not invalidate his conception of the intellectual as the indispensable expert. It only

[14] R. S. Baker, *Woodrow Wilson: Life and Letters* (New York: Doubleday, 1939), Vol. VIII, pp. 384–85.
[15] "Notes for a Biography."

challenged the way the intellectual's contribution was organized and the climate in which he worked. It was necessary now to go on beyond *Drift and Mastery* if the intellectual's role was to be adequately defined.

Why had Versailles failed? Lippmann's answer was that the people of Europe and America did not know the facts. Not knowing the facts, they were unable to protest the betrayal of ideals for which the war had been fought. Blocked by censorship and secrecy, they could not intervene to affect the negotiations at the time when intervention would have counted most and cost least: "In the last analysis," Lippmann wrote, "lack of information about the conference was the origin of its difficulties."[16] In *Liberty and the News* in 1920, he tried to draw out the implications of this proposition for the general theory of democracy.

Events in the United States meantime increased his concern about the adequacy of public information. The activities of Attorney General A. Mitchell Palmer dramatized the power of the state to manipulate and suppress opinion. ("The most exhilarating experience we had, as I now look back," he wrote later, "was the resistance of the *New Republic* in 1919 and 1920 to the Red hysteria."[17]) The confusion of misinformation in even the *New York Times* concerning the Soviet Union showed the editorial irresponsibility of the press. Above all, Lippmann's increasingly oppressive sense of the complexity of modern society convinced him that if, on top of everything else, people were denied the facts, the common method of science could not hope to work, and men were doomed to bafflement and subservience. "There can be no liberty for a

[16] *Liberty and the News* (New York: Macmillan, 1920), p. 66.
[17] "Notes for a Biography."

community which lacks the information by which to detect lies." It was necessary not only to have "a common intellectual method," but "a common area of valid fact" if the "unity of disciplined experiment" was to concert the hopes and energies of men. Freedom, in essence, meant the guarantee of the integrity of the sources of information. To assure the flow of uncontaminated fact, Lippmann proposed the establishment of technical research organizations which could help construct "a system of information increasingly independent of opinion." The intellectual, in short, should become the man, no longer of "passionate ideas," but of "neutral facts."[18]

Liberty and the News, for all its apprehensions about the actual workings of democracy, preserved the assumption that, given the neutral facts, the people as a whole could be relied on to act rationally. But Lippmann soon found he could not rest comfortable in this assumption. As he gazed out at America in the '20's, he wondered if better reporting would really solve the problem of public confusion and apathy. Was the "news" really enough? Should he not have insisted more on a distinction between "news" and "truth," the one registering an event, the other expressing a vital relationship? With such thoughts in mind, he turned anew to the whole question of the popular psychology. The result, published in 1922 under the title *Public Opinion,* carried his argument still another step away from his onetime faith in a rational society.

Public Opinion is still a remarkable book. The stupefying mass of writing, both learned and popular, which has appeared on this subject in the last quarter century has added surprisingly little to Lippmann's

[18] *Liberty and the News*, pp. 64, 67, 91–92, 96–97, 99.

analysis; and none of it has had anything like his fertility of insight or elegance of expression. For most people, Lippmann argued, the world they were supposed to deal with politically was "out of reach, out of sight, out of mind." The real environment was replaced by a "pseudo-environment," compounded of ignorance, distortion, tradition, emotion, stereotype, and manipulated consent.

> These limitations upon our access to that [real] environment combine with the obscurity and complexity of the facts themselves to thwart clearness and justice of perception, to substitute misleading fictions for workable ideas, and to deprive us of adequate checks upon those who consciously strive to mislead.

Public opinion, in consequence, became primarily "a moralized and codified version of the facts." Nor would liberation of the facts by itself effect a cure, since few people were prepared to absorb them or to assess them at their proper significance. What was necessary was some means of making the facts intelligible, and this less for the people at large than for the few who had to make great decisions. Most people Lippmann felt obligated to dismiss as "outsiders," without the time, or attention, or interest, or equipment for judgment. It was the men on the inside, charged with power and responsibility, who made the decisions of society. And the role of the intellectual, Lippmann now believed, was precisely to serve these insiders. In a more urgent version of his research proposal of 1920, he called for bodies of experts, immune from the temptations of power, inspired by a "selfless equanimity," dedicated to the task of inventing and organizing a machinery of knowledge. These experts, Lippmann insisted, must confine themselves to the production of data for policymakers; they must themselves stay rigorously out of policy. "The power of the expert," as he put it, "depends upon separating himself from those who make the decisions, upon not caring, in his expert self, what decision is made." "The perfectly sound ideal," he added, in an odd forecast of the presidential philosophy of the 1950's, "[is] an executive who sits before a flat-top desk, one sheet of typewritten paper before him, and decides on matters of policy presented in a form ready for his rejection or approval."[19]

Where the role of the intellectual had once been to declare the constitutional pattern of the universe to all mankind, now it was only to serve up neutral facts to the ruling elite. *Public Opinion* thus represented a further step in Lippmann's disengagement of the intellectual from policies and values. And, as he ruminated over his distinction between insiders and outsiders, he found the role of the broad public increasingly shadowy and impalpable—a conclusion proclaimed in the title of his next book, *The Phantom Public*, in 1925. His growing skepticism about absolutes was carrying him into new positions—not, it should be emphasized, to a lack of faith in democracy, but to a lack of belief in any ultimate rationality behind it. Up to this point, he had clung to the supposition that the universe contained a pattern of meaning. Now for the first time he seemed to doubt whether there was any ultimate perspective in terms of which everything else would come into focus.

The private citizen, Lippmann began, was like the deaf spectator in the back row: "he does not know what is happening, why it is happening, what ought to

[19] *Public Opinion* (Pelican ed.), pp. 20, 41, 56, 93, 228, 271, 280.

happen"; "he lives in a world which he cannot see, does not understand and is unable to direct." Public opinion, in consequence, could not hope to deal with the substance of political issues. All it could do was to intervene in times of crisis to support one set of individuals or proposals against another. "Public opinion in its highest ideal will defend those who are prepared to act on their reason against the interrupting forces of those who merely assert their will."

In short, "actual governing is made up of a multitude of arrangements on specific questions by particular individuals"; public opinion was at best sporadically mobilizable to settle particular controversies. Santayana's realm of essences, where all conflicts would be reconciled and harmonized, was receding from view, leaving behind the prickly and unfinished universe of William James, filled with an irreducible diversity of intractable and immiscible facts and ideas. "The attempt to escape from particular purpose into some universal purpose, from personality into something impersonal," Lippmann now scorned as a "flight from the human problem," though he added a little wistfully: "It is at the same time a demonstration of how we wish to see that problem solved. We seek an adjustment, as perfect as possible, as untroubled as it was before we were born." But man had moved beyond the womb into the stubborn and inherent pluralism of reality.

> Against this deep pluralism thinkers have argued in vain. They have invented social organisms and national souls, and oversouls, and collective souls; they have gone for hopeful analogies to the beehive and the anthill, to the solar system, to the human body; they have gone to Hegel for higher unities and

to Rousseau for a general will in an effort to find some basis of union.

All, all in vain. No such basis existed. Monism was a delusion. We could no longer expect, Lippmann wrote "to find a unity which absorbs diversity. For us, the conflicts and differences are so real that we cannot deny them, and, instead of looking for identity of purpose, we look simply for an accommodation of purposes."[20]

The Phantom Public was a brilliant and unrelenting exercise in skepticism. At last, Lippmann despaired of finding the unifying vision he had pursued so long. By now every universal pattern, every central perspective, seemed to have washed out from under him: first, socialism; then majority rule, derived from majority rationality; then the common method of science; then the common area of valid fact; then the provision of expert reports to insiders by disinterested social scientists. He had supposed that a fully informed people could govern modern society, but he had discovered, first, that the people were not fully informed, and second, that, even if the facts were fully available, only a small minority were capable of absorbing them. The substantive unification of experience seemed an unattainable ideal. The hope he offered in *The Phantom Public* was procedural—agreement in the rules of the game, "the maintenance of a regime of rule, contract and custom," and, within that, the piecemeal resolution of pressing problems through the wisdom of statesmen and the knowledge of experts.[21]

One other hope remained; and here again he

---

[20] *The Phantom Public* (New York: Macmillan, 1925), pp. 13–14, 39, 41, 69, 97–98, 170–71.
[21] *The Phantom Public*, p. 105.

showed the impact of William James. Lippmann retained an emphasis on one factor in the equation as unpredictable and yet decisive—the human will. Logical analysis, Lippmann now said, might clarify the will and the situation in which it operated; but it could not, in the present state of the art, anticipate what the will would make of future situations in which it might find itself. "Until that time comes,—if it comes," Lippmann wrote, after due quotations from James,

> — we shall lack the support and guidance of a philosophy. We shall live as we are now living without any sense of the whole, without any clear conception of our destiny, with only improvised ideas of what is the better and the worse.[22]

This conclusion paradoxically prepared him for a resumption of the search for unity from a new tack. If objective ground for unity in human experience had given way under stress, the human will itself still remained as a source of moral energy. Could not man by an act of will instill in his own life a sense of order and coherence to replace the ancestral creeds now dissolving in the acids of modernity? This possibility provided the theme in 1929 for *A Preface to Morals*. If whirl was king, the key to intelligibility, Lippmann contended, lay within. It lay in man's capacity for "insight into the value of disinterestedness." Disinterestedness was the means of re-educating the passions which created the disorders and frustrations of life; it would render a dogmatic morality unnecessary; it would enable man to be harmonious with himself and with reality. Moreover, as he sought to show in detail, the ideal of

[22] *American Inquisitors* (New York: Macmillan, 1928), pp. 116–17.

disinterestedness had become "inherent and inevitable in the modern world." The discipline of science was one aspect; the growing importance in politics of "technicians, experts, and neutral investigators" was another. What the prophets had seen as the essence of high religion, what psychologists delineated as a matured personality, what society required for its practical fulfillment were, said Lippmann, "all of a piece and . . . the basic elements of a modern morality." He sketched his portrait of the modern man:

> The mature man would take the world as it comes, and within himself remain quite unperturbed . . . Would he be hopeful? Not if to be hopeful was to expect the world to submit rather soon to his vanity. Would he be hopeless? Hope is an expectation of favors to come, and he would take his delights here and now. Since nothing gnawed at his vitals, neither doubt, nor ambition, nor frustration, nor fear, he would move easily through life. And so whether he saw the thing as comedy, or high tragedy, or plain farce, he would affirm that it is what it is, and that the wise man can enjoy it.[23]

The ideal of disinterestedness had been latent in his lifelong faith that human reason could relieve the turmoils and unify the energies of society. Now, as everything else had crumbled away, it had become itself the means of salvation, man's only rock against the indifferent storms of a pluralistic universe. But the disinterested man was due for a testing sooner perhaps than Lippmann supposed. Shortly after *A Preface to Morals* came out, the Wall Street crash ushered in the long de-

[23] *A Preface to Morals* (New York: Macmillan, 1929), pp. 204, 208, 209, 231, 239, 271–72, 323, 329–30.

pression. Abroad, totalitarian faiths won new converts and threatened new horrors. Did not now something begin to gnaw at the vitals of modern man? Could he move with such easy composure through a world now so demonstrably fearful and tragic?

Lippmann recognized the new pressures; but this recognition did not at first affect the ideal of disinterestedness. Speaking at the Columbia commencement of 1932, he mentioned the "special uneasiness" perturbing the scholar—"every student of economics and of politics, of law, of education, and of morals"—the feeling that he ought to be doing something about the world's troubles.

> The world needs ideas: how can he sit silently in his study and with a good conscience go on with his thinking when there is so much that urgently needs to be done?

Yet, said Lippmann, the scholar also heard another voice, telling him that to do his job "he must preserve a quiet indifference to the immediate and a serene attachment to the processes of inquiry and understanding." The second voice was evidently Lippmann's own. If the scholar tried to make contributions to practical affairs, Lippmann warned, he might well "have less to contribute than many who have studied his subject far less than he"; worse than that, he would suffer in his own estimate when he pronounced conclusions in which he only half believed. What disqualified the scholar most of all was his inability to understand the public opinion, with its transience, restlessness, and willfulness. "We must not expect society to be guided by its professors," Lippmann declared, "until, or perhaps I should say unless, the fluctuating opinions that now govern affairs are replaced by clear, by settled, moral values"—and this was the hope he had only recently dismissed as a fantasy of regression. What was most wrong with the world was that democracy had become the creature of the immediate moment. "With no authority above it, without religious, political, or moral convictions which control its opinions, it is without coherence and purpose. Democracy of this kind cannot last long . . . But in the meanwhile the scholar will defend himself against it. He will build a wall against chaos." His duty above all was to refuse to let himself be absorbed by distractions about which, as a scholar, he could do nothing.[24]

Lippmann in 1932, while yearning for a settled moral pattern, for an order of authority above democracy, was thus still in his mood of *The Phantom Public* and *A Preface to Morals;* he evidently did not believe that that higher moral order, however desirable it might be, really existed. This faith in detachment as the strategy of pluralism persisted into 1933. What brought it to an end—what seems suddenly to have revived Lippmann's belief in ultimate patterns—was the explosion of moral and intellectual energy accompanying the first years of the New Deal.

Lippmann, who had now known Franklin Roosevelt for fifteen years, had watched his astonishing rise with a mixture of admiration and doubt. When Roosevelt received the vice-presidential nomination in 1920, Lippmann had wired him with enthusiasm: WHEN CYNICS ASK WHAT IS THE USE WE CAN ANSWER THAT WHEN PARTIES CAN PICK A MAN LIKE FRANK ROOSEVELT THERE IS A DECENT FUTURE IN POLITICS. Roosevelt's speech nominating Smith in 1924 stirred Lippmann to write a note praising it as "a moving and

[24] "The Scholar in a Troubled World," *Atlantic*, August 1932.

distinguished thing. I am utterly hard-boiled about speeches, but yours seems to me perfect in temper and manner and most eloquent in its effect." Lippmann's early respect had declined sharply, however, during Roosevelt's governorship. "The trouble with Franklin D. Roosevelt," he wrote during the Walker affair, "is that his mind is not very clear, his purposes are not simple, and his methods are not direct." In January 1932, he was provoked to his celebrated evaluation of Roosevelt as "not the dangerous enemy of anything . . . too eager to please . . . a pleasant man who, without any important qualifications for the office, would very much like to be President."[25] Nonetheless, when Roosevelt took over, Lippmann was generous in his praise of the new national leadership. "At the end of February," he wrote in a summary of Roosevelt's first Hundred Days, "we were a congeries of disorderly panic-stricken mobs and factions. In the hundred days from March to June we became again an organized nation confident of our power to provide for our own security and to control our own destiny."[26]

If these were exciting days for Roosevelt, they were also exciting days for Lippmann. His vogue in 1933 was greater than ever before. James Truslow Adams called him "one of the most potent political forces in the nation . . . the only national leader who has appeared in these post-war years."[27] More than this, he was having an impact on presidential decisions perhaps even greater than he had had fifteen years earlier. Roosevelt seems to have been a faithful reader of Lippmann, though apparently no effort was made on either

[25] Schlesinger, *The Crisis of the Old Order*, pp. 96, 291, 362, 395.

[26] Schlesinger, *The Coming of the New Deal* (Boston: Houghton Mifflin, 1959), p. 22.

[27] J. T. Adams, "Walter Lippmann."

side to resume close personal relations, and several moments can be isolated where Lippmann, by analyzing complex problems with lucidity, precipitated in Roosevelt's mind a solution toward which the President had, in his own more intuitive way, been groping.

Lippmann was particularly influential on monetary issues. Thus, when Roosevelt was pondering the question of the gold standard in the spring of 1933, a Lippmann column arguing that "a decision to maintain the gold parity of currency condemns the nation which makes that decision to the intolerable strain of falling prices" convinced the President that the gold standard would have to go. As Raymond Moley was departing for London and the World Economic Conference, Roosevelt sent him off with a quotation from Lippmann to the effect that international cooperation was a good idea if it resulted in concerted action, but not as an end in itself—not if it merely produced a negative and impotent stability. Lippmann himself was in London when Roosevelt's message to the conference expressed his decision to give the American price level priority over the stability of the international exchanges. Not only did Lippmann defend the decision publicly, but he collaborated privately with Moley and John Maynard Keynes in drafting the official explanation of the American position. Later, Lippmann urged tolerance toward the gold-purchase program, and in the spring of 1934 his column provided the formula that broke the deadlock over the congressional demand for silver-purchase legislation.[28]

The excitement of watching intelligence at work in public decision seems to have begun to restore Lipp-

[28] Schlesinger, *The Coming of the New Deal*, pp. 199–200, 216, 224–25, 241, 251.

mann's faith in the rationality of society. Perhaps this experience could provide a pattern in which the disinterested man could find a larger solace than Lippmann had offered him in *A Preface to Morals.* "A planned society can exist," he wrote, "only where disinterested men have the confidence of the people"; and, while this state of beatitude was not imminent, it represented, Lippmann believed, the direction in which society had to move. The unifying vision, which he had renounced a few years before, was now reappearing on the horizon. The "ideal of a consciously controlled society" challenged man once again with a transcendent purpose.

> In our world, amid the wreckage of empires and the breakdown of established things, such a purpose has been born, and I say to you, my fellow students, that the purpose to make an ordered life on this planet can, if you embrace it, and let it embrace you, carry you through the years triumphantly.

This ideal expressed, he thought, the revival of a deep instinct of men "for the unity of civilization." Taken as the animating principle of men's lives, it would offer "composure, purpose and confidence amidst the vast hurlyburly of modern things."[29]

Lippmann developed and refined this theme in his remarkable Godkin Lectures of 1934, published under the title *The Method of Freedom.* In some respects, this remains Lippmann's most brilliant and prophetic work. Laissez faire, he argued, had failed; the self-regulating and self-adjusting character of the old order had been destroyed; under modern conditions the state

[29] *A New Social Order* (New York: John Day, 1933), pp. 16–17, 21–22, 24–25.

had no choice except to intervene. But it could intervene in two radically different ways. Here Lippmann distinguished between what he called the Directed Economy and the Compensated Economy. The Directed Economy was the centrally planned and physically regimented economy of the totalitarian state. The Compensated Economy, on the other hand, retained private initiative and decision so far as possible but committed the state to act when necessary to "redress the balance of private actions by compensating public actions"—by fiscal and monetary policy, by social insurance, by business regulation, by the establishment of minimum economic levels below which no member of the community should be allowed to fall.

Having stated the alternatives, Lippmann proceeded with precision to define the central political difficulty of the Compensated Economy.

> In substance, the state undertakes to counteract the mass errors of the individualist crowd by doing the opposite of what the crowd is doing: it saves when the crowd is spending too much; it borrows when the crowd is extravagant, and it spends when the crowd is afraid to spend . . . it becomes an employer when there is private unemployment, and it shuts down when there is work for all.

In short, the compensatory method required the state to act almost continually contrary to prevailing opinion. "Will a democracy authorize the government, which is its creature, to do the very opposite of what the majority at any time most wishes to do?" This was—and is—a searching question; it is no criticism of Lippmann to say that he failed in 1934 to answer it. In *The Method of Freedom,* he chose to speculate about institutional solutions to a problem which we would tend to regard today more a matter of education and leadership. But the book's whole argument implied a confidence in the human capacity to devise intelligent compensatory policies; it thereby enlarged and socialized the role of the intellectual.[30]

The next year, in *The New Imperative*, he reaffirmed his faith in the potentialities of rational planning. "If you wish to know why the political sciences are not [yet] a true discipline for the future guardians of our civilization, but are a haphazard collection of disconnected specialties," he explained, "this is the reason: it is disreputable to hold and to declare a positive and coherent conception of the function of the state in a modern economy." It was "obscurantism," he continued, to say that society could not be governed without sacrificing personal liberties to the authority of the state; the only result of such talk would be to stop men from working on the problem that historic necessity compelled them to face.

> We must answer the question that young men put to us. We must tell them that they will have to manage the social order. We must call them to the study, not warn them away from it, of how to achieve the healthy balance of a well ordered commonwealth.[31]

The sequel constitutes a puzzling passage in Lippmann's intellectual history. Toward the end of 1935, Lippmann began to lose his earlier confidence in Roosevelt's policies. For reasons not altogether clear, he began to see in the New Deal the unlovely lineaments of the Directed Economy. The paradox is that this im-

[30] *The Method of Freedom* (New York: Macmillan, 1934), pp. 18, 46, 59, 74.

[31] *The New Imperative* (New York: Macmillan, 1935), pp. 47, 51.

pression began to seize his mind just at the time that the New Deal itself was shifting from the very policies Lippmann had identified in *The Method of Freedom* as measures of direction (like NRA and AAA) to the compensatory policies of public spending, social minima, and business regulation.[32] Perhaps it was that New Deal planning had failed in Lippmann's view to achieve the necessary qualities of impersonality and disinterestedness. Whatever the cause, Lippmann grew increasingly alarmed over what he considered a passion for centralization accompanied by ominous symptoms of arrogance and vindictiveness.

In any case, in 1936, while retaining his revived faith in ultimate patterns, he abruptly recoiled from the expression of such patterns in social planning. "No greater delusion has ever cast its spell upon the human imagination," he wrote, "than that a group of mortal men can plan the future of a whole society and direct the affairs of a whole civilization." In sharp reassertion of his old demand for absolute disinterestedness, he harshly condemned those college professors who had become "entangled in the making of policy and the administration of government."

It is only knowledge freely acquired that is disinterested. When, therefore, men whose profession it is to teach and to investigate become the makers of policy, become members of an administration in power, become politicians and leaders of causes, they are committed. Nothing they say can be relied upon as disinterested. Nothing they teach can be trusted as scientific. It is impossible to mix the pursuit of knowledge and the exercise of political

[32] *The Method of Freedom*, p. 70.

power and those who have tried it turn out to be very bad politicians or they cease to be scholars.

"My own conviction," Lippmann concluded, "is that this choice has to be faced in American universities."[33] In a rare departure from his usual neutrality, he even called for the election to the Presidency of Alf M. Landon.

Still, if planning were wrong, Lippmann had nonetheless re-embarked on his long quest for a unifying vision. The old ideal of individual disinterestedness was no longer enough by itself. It required a broader and solider foundation; it demanded a higher and more objective authority. In his language of 1932, the fluctuating opinions that governed affairs had to be replaced by clear and settled moral values if society were to be guided by its intellectuals. The search for a common moral discipline now replaced the common scientific discipline he had invoked twenty years before. The result was his book of 1937, *The Good Society*.

The Good Society is a curious and valuable work. It is curious because in so many respects it reads like a polemic launched by someone else against *The Method of Freedom*. In the earlier book, Lippmann had warned against those who would not distinguish "between the traditional policies of free states in the Nineteenth Century and the essentials of free government itself."[34] Now, under the influence of Hayek and von Mises—and perhaps, too, of Roosevelt's attack on the Supreme Court—Lippmann three years later seemed to verge on that error himself. Yet *The Good Society* remains valuable because in so many respects it restated

[33] "The Deepest Issue of Our Time," *Vital Speeches*, July 1, 1936.
[34] *The Method of Freedom*, p. viii.

the insights of *The Method of Freedom* in a different context. Though many took it at the time as a campaign document against the New Deal, Lippmann meant it primarily as a critique of fascism and communism; today it reads in great part as the vindication of the New Deal's essential idea.

At the beginning of *The Good Society,* Lippmann's earlier distinction between the Directed and the Compensated Economies appeared to vanish in a scattershot indictment of "nearly every effort which lays claim to being enlightened, humane and progressive" as involving "the premise of authoritarian collectivism." This indictment was launched in the name of liberalism, and liberalism, to the unwary reader of Lippmann (there were plenty in 1937) appeared to be that same old idea of a self-adjusting, self-regulating economy whose obsolescence he had earlier demonstrated with such cogency. By proposing "graduated collectivism" as the intermediate stage on the road to perdition, by defining it as the resort to tariffs and bounties, price fixing and wage fixing, and other devices to supersede the sovereignty of the market, and by instancing the New Deal as a prime example, Lippmann further seemed to be rejecting the mixed economy in favor of the artificial resuscitation of classical liberalism. Yet the book contained, if it did not feature, unsparing criticism of latter-day liberals of the Spencer type; and actually, the Compensated Economy, having apparently been discarded at the start, was smuggled in later on in the book under the less provocative title of "The Agenda of Liberalism." This liberal agenda, with its plea for contracyclical spending, social insurance, antitrust action, collective bargaining, redistributed profits tax, adds up to a surprisingly accurate description of the policies of the New Deal of 1937—the

New Deal having, like Lippmann himself, for some time turned against the Directed Economy.[35]

Such implications of *The Good Society* were muted, however, because of the polemical orientation of the book—too many people read it as Lippmann's explanation of his vote for Landon. They were muted too because Lippmann, in his recoil against the illusion of the omniscient planner, seemed desperate to find an impersonal, automatic means by which society could regulate itself. He thus apotheosized the market and the law as self-operating techniques of equilibration which could avoid the pitfalls of intervention by limited and fallible mortals. But these solutions were, of course, far less self-operative than they seemed on the surface. As his own text made clear, the market and the law were not automatisms at all; they were pseudoautomatisms: the market required supplementation and control, the law amendment and revision. Neither expressed the uncontaminated disinterestedness which he sought in the govenment of society. Both emerged from the conflicts, passions, and weaknesses of men. Far from guaranteeing unity in society, they only pushed the problem back a further step—to man himself.

Lippmann did not thus state the dilemma. But he evidently felt it, for *The Good Society* concluded with testimony about his dim but powerful apprehension of some law higher than parliaments, majorities, or kings. At this point, he could only define that higher law in procedural transactions. Yet he was ready to declare his intuition of the existence of some transcendent ethic, founded not on the moral constitution of man, as in *A Preface to Morals*, but on the moral necessities

[35] *The Good Society*, pp. 4, 119, 173, chap. xi.

of the universe. The search to define this ethic became his next intellectual preoccupation.

Lippmann began writing *The Public Philosophy* in 1938; it was finally published sixteen years later. Its argument was in curious counterpoint with that of *The Phantom Public,* taking off from a major conclusion of the earlier work but using that conclusion to justify a diametrically opposite philosophical result. In *The Phantom Public,* it is to be recalled, Lippmann's note of hope against the irreducible pluralism of the world was "the maintenance of a regime of rule, contract and custom." In 1925, this was for Lippmann a procedural conception. But in the years thereafter, what began as a functional necessity was somehow hypostatized into a transcendental faith—and then employed to abolish the very pluralism which originally produced it. The invocation of due process grew into "a universal order on which all reasonable men were agreed," "a common conception of law and order which possesses a universal validity," natural law, the public philosophy. By this he meant the realm of essences ("I am using the ambiguous but irreplaceable word 'essence' as meaning the true and undistorted nature of things"), a world of "immaterial entities . . . not to be perceived by our senses," but nonetheless more real than anything else.

> It was not someone's fancy, someone's prejudice, someone's wish or rationalization, a psychological experience and no more. It is there objectively, not subjectively. It can be discovered. It has to be obeyed.

In the name of the public philosophy, Lippmann spurned his pluralism of the '20's. A "large plural society," he argued, could not be governed "without recognizing that, transcending its plural interests, there is a rational order with a superior common law." This was so because it *had* to be so:

> As the diversity of belief, opinion and interest became greater, the need for a common criterion and for common laws became more acute. . . . In this pluralized and fragmenting society a public philosophy with common and binding principles was more necessary than it had ever been.

And it was the responsibility of intellectuals to propagate the public philosophy. Even if they did, it might not be enough to save the West, Lippmann somberly wrote; but, "if the prevailing philosophers oppose this restoration and revival," the inexorable decline could not be arrested. In an unwontedly fierce statement from so normally courteous a man, Lippmann even suggested:

> There is no reason to think that this condition of mind can be changed until it can be proved to the modern skeptic that there are certain principles which, when they have been demonstrated, only the willfully irrational can deny, that there are certain obligations binding on all men who are committed to a free society, and that only the willfully subversive can reject them.[36]

No one likes to nominate himself as willfully irrational or willfully subversive. Yet for those brought up in the tradition of James, Lippmann's conception of natural law, for all its nobility, cannot help seem an ar-

[36] *The Public Philosophy* (Boston: Little, Brown, 1955), pp. 104, 110, 142.

tificial construct.[37] Was he not succumbing to the very danger he warned against so eloquently a quarter of a century before—the "attempts to escape from particular purpose into some universal purpose, from personality into something impersonal"? Was this not, after all, the "flight from the human problem," the search for "an adjustment, as perfect as possible, as untroubled as it was before we were born"? One wonders indeed whether so acute and honest a mind as Lippmann's can rest long in this solution. Are there perhaps signs that he is swinging back to a more vivid appreciation of the reality of pluralism? Certainly he was unsparing in his criticism when John Foster Dulles, almost as if in response to Lippmann's summons to the philosophers, sought to preach something sounding suspiciously like the public philosophy to our erring brothers overseas. In his most recent book, Lippmann appears to recede sharply from the notion that a single standard can comprehend the multifarious values and activities of the contemporary world. He condemns

> the fallacy of assuming that this is one world and that the social order to which one belongs must either perish or become the universal order of mankind.

[37] For searching philosophical criticism of Lippmann's argument for Natural Law, see Reinhold Niebuhr's essay in Marquis Childs and James Reston, eds., *Walter Lippmann and His Times* (New York: Harcourt, Brace, 1959), and also Morton White, *Social Thought in America* (rev. ed., Boston: Beacon, 1957), pp. 264–80. For an illuminating general discussion of the contrasting implications of the two theories (a) that all virtuous purposes are ultimately reconcilable (*The Public Philosophy*), and (b) that they are not (*The Phantom Public*), see Sir Isaiah Berlin's Oxford inaugural lecture, *Two Concepts of Liberty* (Oxford: Clarendon, 1959).

"The truth, as I see it," Lippmann now concludes, "is that there has never been one world, that there has never been a universal state or a universal religion."[38] One is tempted to ask: Has there ever been a public philosophy?

One can hardly criticize Walter Lippmann for having failed to clear up the problem of the One and the Many. Doubtless a few more years will go by before the great computers will end civilization's long suspense and break the problem down into its definitive mathematical solution. While the discussion lasts, one must be grateful for the urbanity and intelligence with which Lippmann through the years has pursued in his own mind the long dialogue set off by James and Santayana at Harvard half a century ago.

As Lippmann has followed out his explorations, he has envisaged a number of roles for the intellectual, though most often as the disinterested voice of some unifying vision, from socialism through science to the public philosophy. For a season in the '20's, the unifying vision disappeared from view; but the urgencies of a collapsing world brought it back. For Lippmann, the intellectual has been most characteristically engaged in ideas, disengaged from movements; he is something different from the man who makes decisions and does things; his responsibility remains always somehow to influence the actor and permeate the culture. One cannot be sure, though, whether he speaks for the public philosophy or for himself.

If Lippmann has not really solved the role of the intellectual in free society, it must be said that he has magnificently exemplified it. In *Public Opinion*, he re-

[38] *The Communist World and Ours* (Boston: Little, Brown, 1959), pp. 50–51.

counts the scene in Book V of *The Republic* when Socrates stalks out after warning Adeimanthis to attribute the uselessness of philosophers "to the fault of those who will not use them, and not to themselves." Lippmann comments: "Thus, in the first great encounter between reason and politics, the strategy of reason was to retire in anger."[39] As the veteran of many such encounters, Lippmann has rarely taken the easy course of withdrawal into irresponsibility. "We are challenged, every one of us," he wrote as a young man, "to think our way out of the terrors amidst which we live."[40] He has not flinched from that challenge. His manner of meeting it has been a credit to himself and often a salvation to his contemporaries.

He once spoke of the Compensated Economy; he is himself a wonderful example of the Compensated Mind, seeking through continuous intervention to restore our society to the paths of decency and rationality. When the crowd has boasted a common faith, as in the '20's, Lippmann has stressed pluralism; when the crowd appears to have no faith at all, as in the '50's, he stresses monism (except as against the too insistent faith of Mr. Dulles, when he again turns to pluralism); when the crowd is overcommitted to drift, he stresses mastery; when the crowd is overcommitted to mastery, he stresses drift. The classic clarity of his language, studded, it would seem, with lapidary absolutes, has obscured the almost tactile sensitivity of his mind. His commentary has probed the problems of society and the problems of philosophy with unfailing reason and grace. He has preserved a fine magnanimity of temper in rancorous times and against bitterly unfair innuen-

[39] *Public Opinion*, p. 311.
[40] *The Stakes of Diplomacy* (New York: Henry Holt, 1915), p. 10.

does and attack. His spirit has been both independent and compassionate.

Above all, Lippmann has insisted in the heat and clamors of the present on the indispensability of the long view. He once wrote,

> This is not the last crisis in human affairs. The world will go on somehow, and more crises will follow. It will go on best, however, if among us there are men who have stood apart, who refused to be anxious or too much concerned, who were cool and inquiring and had their eyes on a longer past and a longer future.
>
> By their example they can remind us that the passing moment is only a moment; by their loyalty they will have cherished those things which only the disinterested mind can use.[41]

If this is the intellectual's responsibility, then Walter Lippmann has discharged it superbly; and his age stands deeply in his debt.

[41] Lippmann, "The Scholar in a Troubled World."

11.

Bernard DeVoto and Public Affairs
(1960)

Bernard DeVoto was born in Ogden, Utah, in 1897 of a Mormon-Catholic marriage. These facts are crucial to an understanding of his subsequent career.

Birth made him a westerner. It gave him an identification with the experience of the frontier and a permanent concern with the process by which America became a continental nation. It also made him a Populist. I recognize that this term has gone out of fashion; but, as DeVoto used it, it was an honorable word. It meant a sense that the basic conflict in America was among sections rather than among classes. It meant a broad sympathy for the pioneer over the capitalist—for the men who opened up and settled a region as against those who came along later and drained it of its wealth. It meant an abiding, if sometimes sorely tried, faith in the good sense of plain Americans. It meant a conviction that people ought to leave the world a better place than they found it.

If environment thus made him a westerner and Populist, the Mormon-Catholic collision in his parentage made him a relativist and a skeptic. He was, so to speak, suspended in his own family between two revelations, authoritatively certified as divine but mutually contradictory. His boyhood intensified the puzzlement of this clash. His first education was in the pieties of a convent school; at the same time, he lived among people who though sworn to an incompatible creed were no less persuaded that theirs was the unique road to salvation. This experience bred in him a natural distrust of revelation in general. "I early acquired," he later wrote:

> a notion that all gospels were false, and all my experience since then has confirmed it. All my life people around me have been seeing a Light, that, with a vision certified as excellent by the best oculists, I have been unable to see. At first astonishing contradictions in the reports they gave me troubled my mind, but, you well understand, I came to conclude that absolutes were a mirage. And in my desert country, mirages are also commonplace.[1]

His upbringing thus defined the poles of activism and skepticism—of passion and detachment—between which he oscillated most of his life. From an early age he had a nonconformist's love of freedom, a Populist's rage at injustice, and, though he would have indignantly denied it, a crusader's desire to knock sense into people's heads and build a better world. And from an early age he also had a relativist's dislike of all forms of dogma and revelation and a pragmatist's distrust for all varieties of ideologist and prophet. These two divergent strains warred within him until in the last years of his life he fused them into an effective synthesis.

The inner tension is visible from his first days in college. As a freshman at the University of Utah, he was a crusader. He helped found a chapter of the Inter-collegiate Socialist Society, he backed faculty members under criticism for heterodox views, and, when the university disbanded the Society and fired the professors, he felt the Salt Lake City campus was no place for him. The next year he transferred to Harvard. Here

[1] *Minority Report* (Boston: Little, Brown, 1940), pp. 164–65.

evangelism gave way to empiricism, and he devoted himself to science—to positive knowledge, in other words, as the best answer to the pretensions of dogma and revelation.

His first ambition was to become a mineralogist. But, though he got through geology and chemistry well enough, he encountered difficulties with crystallography. He learned the structure of crystals from textbook models, but he was never able to match these ideal crystals with the "wrenched, distorted, displaced, reversed, bent, crushed, and completely transformed crystals of actual rock."[2] This experience only confirmed his doubts about the utility of theories and his preference for existence over essence. The defeat by crystallography did not, however, diminish his fascination with science, and he found a more congenial outlet in psychopathology. Soon he planned to go to medical school and become a doctor. Then the American entrance into the First World War interrupted his plans. When he returned to Harvard after two years in the Army, he believed himself too old and too broke for a medical career.[3] But the ideal of the doctor cast a spell over him for the rest of his life; on the whole, doctors seemed to him of all people to have best united disinterested analysis and beneficial result, to have best resolved his own tormenting antinomy of theory and experience.

The war had meanwhile offered a new challenge to his crusading impulse. He regarded Wilson's decision of 1917 as just and necessary; and he promptly volunteered for the Army. His skill as a marksman meant that he saw service as a rifle instructor in the United

[2] *Minority Report*, pp. 172–73.
[3] *Minority Report*, p. 173.

States rather than as a soldier in France, but he endured the dreary months without losing faith in the war's essential idealism. Still determined to make the world safe for democracy back in Ogden after the war, he joined the American Legion and tried to use it to help elect a liberal lawyer to the state legislature. In 1920 he campaigned for James M. Cox, Franklin D. Roosevelt, and the League of Nations.

The '20's were for DeVoto, as for most Americans, a vacation from public policy. He was busy establishing himself as a teacher of English at Northwestern: busy soon in marrying the prettiest freshman in his class; busy too in beginning his career as a writer. As a reformer, he wrote about education; as a skeptic, he sent his reforming pieces to the *American Mercury*. By 1927 he was doing well enough to abandon Evanston and attempt a life as a freelance writer. Attracted by the Harvard University Library, he moved back to Cambridge.

The DeVoto who came to Cambridge was still at heart the western radical. An impassioned essay in *Harper's* in 1934 called "The Plundered Province" brought up to date the Populist version of the history of the West. In language that would have delighted James B. Weaver, DeVoto described the procession of marauders who had pillaged his native land; the mines and the railroads; then the water companies, the road companies, the land companies, the grain-storage companies, the mortgage companies, the banks: "all of them looted the country in utter security with the Government itself guaranteeing them against retributive action by the despoiled." As a consequence, "the few alpine forests of the West were levelled, its minerals were mined and smelted, all its resources were drained off through the perfectly engineered gutters of a system designed to flow eastward. It may be empire-building.

The westerner may be excused if it has looked to him like simple plunder."

But this was not all. "Besides taking over the country, then, the East added direct usury." Through the entire West, said DeVoto, "no one has ever been able to borrow money or make a shipment or set a price except at the discretion of a board of directors in the East, whose only interest was to sequester Western property as an accessory of another section's finance." Of course, a part of the loot had flowed back to the West through the redistributive effect of federal taxation; but this was only a sort of bakshish; "the West has sometimes been tipped a fractional per cent of its annual tribute in the form of Government works or social supervision." Moreover, even this had been dispensed to the accompaniment of eastern complaints about the mendicant West and only as an expedient to buy off the farmers when they grew troublesome. And the result of eastern exploitation? The West, wrote DeVoto, "is the one section of the country in which bankruptcy, both actuarial and absolute, has been the determining condition from the start."[4]

"The Plundered Province" is notable as evidence of DeVoto's continuing populism. It is also notable as one of the few sustained pieces he wrote about the West during these first years in Cambridge. It did not precisely exhaust his radicalism: when he became editor of the *Harvard Graduates' Magazine* in 1930, he enlivened the first numbers of this previously sedate journal with attacks on the Watch and Ward Society for its censorship of books and on Harvard's new House system as a possible institutionalization of Ivy League snobbery. Yet his radicalism now observed distinct lim-

[4] *Forays and Rebuttals* (Boston: Little, Brown, 1936), pp. 53–57.

its—limits displayed, for example, in his attitude toward the Sacco-Vanzetti case.

Sacco and Vanzetti had gone to the electric chair in Charlestown in the very month in 1927 in which DeVoto arrived in Cambridge. DeVoto had no doubt about the reasons: "two humble Italians were executed because the ruling class did not like their political beliefs." But the totality of his reaction suggests the extent to which in this period radicalism was subdued by relativism. "Several inabilities," as he put it in 1932, "cut me off from my fraternal deplorers of this judicial murder." Most of all, "I was unable to feel surprise at the miscarriage of justice—unable to recall any system of society that had prevented it or to imagine any that would prevent it."[5] His best novel, *We Accept with Pleasure* (1934), effectively conveys this mixture of indignation and acquiescence. The vivid picture in the novel of Boston on the night of the execution testified to DeVoto's sense of the crime against justice. Yet the work left a final impression, in the words of Garrett Mattingly, of "the impermanence and futility of the emotions aroused, and the inexorable impersonality of the historical process at work."[6]

Increasingly, acquiescence seemed to be triumphing over indignation. By 1936 DeVoto, in the preface to his first collection of essays, *Forays and Rebuttals,* appeared ready to make an explicit farewell to liberal illusion. Ten years ago, he said, he had been all for reform, but,

> like all reformers, I outrageously oversimplified the problem. Today I know a good deal more . . . I

[5] Garrett Mattingly, *Bernard DeVoto: A Preliminary Appraisal* (Boston: Little, Brown, 1938), pp. 35–36.

[6] Mattingly, *DeVoto,* pp. 35–36.

know that most proposed reforms are undesirable, and that practically all of them are impossible of achievement and must produce conditions worse than the diseases they undertake to cure.[7]

He was speaking specifically of educational reform, but his remarks had a wider application. After 1932 his essays, in Mr. Mattingly's succinct description, were "full of ridicule of planned societies and Marxist dialectics, and usually assume the complete futility of trying to reform anything."[8]

How is one to account for this apparent swing to the political right, especially at a time when in the nation liberalism, after years of being in the wilderness, had gained exuberant control of political power? Actually, of course, these two phenomena, far from being contradictory, were intimately related. DeVoto's nonconformist instincts always led him to run against the popular grain. The passion to correct the fashionable errors of the day led him inevitably during the zenith of the New Deal to concentrate on the excesses of liberalism. More than that, he was beginning to develop a theory of liberalism in which he identified the reforming mind not at all with pragmatism and experiment, but with *a priori* ideology.

He reached this identification by analogies from the literary scene. As editor of the *Saturday Review of Literature* in the mid-'30's, he made it his office to champion pluralism and relativism against all absolutes. The "literary mind" became his particular target. It was characterized, he believed, by an incorrigible preference for generalizations over facts. Erecting "articulated structures of abstractions as a rampart against

[7] *Forays*, p. ix.
[8] Mattingly, *DeVoto*, p. 55.

experience" might provide comfort and reassurance; but "the theory killeth."[9]

He objected, for example, to literary historians who, as he saw it, were drawing the past in terms of their own preconceptions.

> All these literary efforts display a hunger for unity. They are efforts to impose order and simplicity upon an obstinate multiplicity, and their authors are incorrigible monists . . . There is an eternal, fundamental and irreconcilable difference between fantasy, any kind of fantasy, and fact. The fantasies of the literary historian are frequently beautiful and nearly always praiseworthy, but they are a form of protective or wishful thinking, a form of illusion and even of delusion, and they must be constantly denounced as such.[10]

The amalgamation of the literary mind with the reforming mind was not difficult.

> My sense of propriety becomes active [DeVoto wrote in 1937] when they take over that twelve-inch rod, which does not exist, apply it as a measuring rod to things that do exist—and then as a result of those measurements order me to believe and behave in specified ways, order a novelist or a poet to write books in specified ways or else, and order society to reconstruct itself according to syllogisms . . . Idealism, whether moral or metaphysical or literary, may be defined as a cross-lots path to the psychopathic ward, Berchtesgaden, and St. Bartholomew's Eve. Absolutes mean absolutism.[11]

[9] *Minority Report,* p. 161.
[10] *Forays,* pp. 168, 177–78.
[11] *Minority Report,* p. 184.

Marxism, of course, was the supreme example of this in politics; and he wrote brilliantly and devastatingly about the delusions of the Communists, the fellow travelers and the Popular Fronters. But reform in general seemed to him dangerously susceptible to the intoxication of abstractions.

All this was crystallized in his mind by a new friendship in Cambridge. He had come to know L. J. Henderson, a formidable member of the Harvard faculty, noted for his pink whiskers and his powerful intelligence. Henderson had been trained as a doctor and had made his reputation as a biological chemist; he thus satisfied DeVoto's admiration for the medical scientist. In more recent years his interest had begun to shift from science to society. Henderson was a type unusual in America; he was an exceedingly intelligent and articulate conservative; and his innate conservatism had been reinforced by his immersion in the works of the Italian sociologist Vilfredo Pareto. When Henderson introduced DeVoto to Pareto, DeVoto found what seemed for a moment a perfect ally in his battle against the intellectuals, whether literary or political, who were bemused by abstractions. In a piece in the *Saturday Review of Literature* in 1933, DeVoto seemed almost to herald Pareto as the prophet of a new revelation. Under the spell of Pareto he could write, for example, in 1934, "Socially, it is much better for any writer (or any realtor, farmer, or stevedore) to increase his sense of personal integrity by identifying himself with a group than it is for him to suffer impairment in that sentiment by remaining just an individual."[12]

But DeVoto was far too intractable an individualist

[12] *Forays,* p. 320.

to stay very long in so self-abnegating a mood. By 1937 he wrote disarmingly, "I am not much of a Paretian." He asked people to forget his *Saturday Review* piece of 1933—"one of my unfortunate attempts to annoy certain literary people"—and concluded of the experience, "Though I learned much from Pareto, I was never a member of the movement but only a kind of cooperating press agent."[13] This is fair enough. After all, DeVoto learned a good deal from Pareto, as well as from Henderson, and there was much anyone could profitably learn from both. For DeVoto the effect was to strengthen his skepticism at the expense of his radicalism and to exaggerate for a season his disdain for reform.

All this shaped his reaction to the New Deal. His first attitude was one of wary approval. The main New Deal policies did little to offend his sense of propriety. His knowledge of the frontier, for example, divested him of any illusions about the sanctity of American individualism. "The very conditions of frontier life in the desert imposed cooperation,"[14] he wrote; and again, "To the dismay of bond-holders and cartoonists, the West is integrated collectively. It will stay that way while climate is climate. That also may be a portent for the nation whose dream has receded."[15] He was also grateful to the New Deal for the absence of social disorder. "Considering the gravity of the situation, the appeal to violence has been shockingly small—and un-American. During the worst of 1932 one saw miserable 'Hoovervilles' built sometimes literally in the shadow of elevators and mills bursting with grain and flour that could not be sold—and none

[13] *Minority Report*, pp. 167, 180.
[14] *Forays*, pp. 42–43.
[15] *Forays*, p. 64.

of the wretched seized the food. To a historian it is all but incredible."[16]

He praised TVA, SEC, and New Deal policies in agriculture, labor, conservation, and relief. No one paid a more stirring tribute to the Writers' Project established under the Works Progress Administration and its splendid series of state guides.[17] He voted for Roosevelt in 1932 and again in 1936. But he objected, with increasing vehemence, to what he regarded as the seizure of the New Deal by the ideologists—by those who felt they knew better than the ordinary man what was good for him. His objections finally boiled over in 1937 when Roosevelt followed the attempt to enlarge the Supreme Court by proposals for the reorganization of the executive branch of the government.

DeVoto obviously did not regard "Desertion from the New Deal" as a definitive statement; he never republished it, for example, in his collections of essays. But it registered sharply his mood of the day. He had been willing to go along with the New Deal for a long time, he wrote, despite the "hooey and hosannas," the "fruitless experiments and ghastly waste," the "immensely multiplied bureaucracy . . . dreadful increase of expenditure . . . centralization of demagogic control." All these things constituted a steep price, but they were all in the legitimate bill, "and we were willing to pay it . . . We stood, and we found an Administration that stood, for human interests above property interests. We accepted the implications, all of them, and we wanted everything done that could be done." But these latest proposals were too much. Oddly enough, it was Roosevelt's relatively innocuous bills

[16] "Notes on the American Way," *Harper's,* May 1938.
[17] "The Writers' Project," *Harper's,* January 1942.

for government reorganization that forced DeVoto over the brink. These bills, DeVoto declared, "proved what the Supreme Court bill had intimated: that the first Roosevelt Administration had been abandoned, that the President now thought he could do the impossible, and that he wasn't concerned about what happens when you try to do the impossible and fail." These bills, he added, "assume that our present form of government is ineffective and played out . . . that we are on the brink of dissolution and armed revolt . . . that you can change social energies with a wave of a hand and regenerate the human race with tricks and some centralization." The New Deal had "sold out to the millennial vision"; "the liberal government dies of an overdose of idealism, arrogance, and miracles." Far from being the Kerensky of the American Revolution, Roosevelt had become its Trotsky, sacrificing everything on the altar of ideology.[18] Nor was this a passing mood. Six months later DeVoto described the New Deal as "clearly designed not to regulate the system of profits . . . but to transform it." He denounced deficit spending, derided the notion of a hundred billion dollar national income, and predicted inflation.[19] Writing in 1938, Garrett Mattingly could say, "Although Mr. Edmund Wilson was too intelligent, too sensitive to nuances, to class DeVoto as a right-winger, *Forays and Rebuttals* [a collection of DeVoto's magazine pieces] gives him some excuse to do so."[20]

Edmund Wilson was right: it was not that simple. Responding to Wilson's challenge, DeVoto said, "I am, if you must have words, a pluralist, a relativist, an em-

[18] "Desertion from the New Deal," *Harper's*, October 1937.
[19] "The Game and the Candle," *Harper's*, March 1938.
[20] Mattingly, *DeVoto*, p. 55.

piricist . . . We must avoid certainty, unity, vision and the loaded dice."[21] Such attitudes made him seem conservative only when he was confronting the liberals; when he started to confront the conservatives, these same attitudes made him recoil to the left. In 1940 he voted again, not without misgivings, for Roosevelt and the New Deal. The misgivings were due to Roosevelt's methods—his weakness for tricks and ruses, his unwillingness to take the people into his confidence. "There is no way of unifying a nation," DeVoto warned, "by stealth, cunning, or sleight of hand . . . You assume that it is adult, intelligent, and courageous. You move openly and in the light of day, and you tell the truth." But he voted for Roosevelt nonetheless, because he approved the historic function of the Democratic party—"the fact that it has periodically been used by the forces in American democracy which permit the accomplishment of revolutionary ends peacefully and within the framework of our political institutions." In 1800, 1828, 1884, 1912, and 1932, he said, "the Democratic Party came to power charged with the duty of repairing situations and arresting trends which had carried the nation dangerously out of equilibrium . . . Five times a campaign charged it with what amounted to a revolution. Each time it accomplished the revolution. Each time its success proved the ability of the American system to rectify abuses in an orderly, peaceable, and democratic manner."[22] This statement more or less summed up his eventual position on the New Deal. He wrote in his 25th Anniversary Report in 1943, "Politically, I am a New Dealer on Election Day and a critic of the New

[21] *Minority Report,* pp. 165, 168.
[22] "The Mugwump on November 6th," *Harper's,* January 1941.

Deal at other times. My social ideas are a good deal left of the New Deal." And shortly before his death in 1955:

> I doubt if anyone was over a 100 per cent New Dealer—obviously Mr. Roosevelt wasn't—but, though many New Deal intellectuals had a much higher proof than mine, on the whole I had to go along. I got to that position by studying history, and the study of history has held me to the working principles of American liberalism.[23]

Even as he was pondering the choice in 1940, new forces were beginning to dissolve his apparent conservatism of the mid-'30's. The retreat of the New Deal and the revival of genuine conservatism was unquestionably one factor; as always, DeVoto reoriented himself to oppose new tides of superficial fashion. Another factor was the resurgence of his interest in the West. During most of the '30's, he had been preoccupied with literature; but history was reasserting itself in his inner imagination; and by the end of the decade, his great trilogy of westward expansion was beginning to take shape in his mind. In 1940, preparing to write *The Year of Decision,* he made a long automobile trip through the West. I had the good fortune to be his companion during a part of this journey. I learned a great deal from him, and I saw renew within him the concern with land and water and resources which had more or less lain dormant since "The Plundered Province" in 1934.

As the conservationist hope now began to possess him, there began to emerge in his mind a new and more appealing image of the liberal reformer. In the

[23] *The Easy Chair* (Boston: Houghton Mifflin, 1955), p. 9.

stress of the '30's, he had tended to see the reformer only as a doctrinaire obsessed with ideology. Yet a theoretical alternative remained: in 1937 he had allowed that "liberal" might refer to "people who try to apply logical and experimental knowledge to social problems" (while adding that this was quite separate from the usage of the day).[24] Now conservation offered the liberal an opportunity to appear in a more benign light. DeVoto began to see the reformer increasingly as sober, sensible, and pragmatic. He saw him particularly, indeed, in the model of John Wesley Powell, the great director of the Geological Survey and the founder of modern conservation, whom DeVoto rediscovered with passion at the end of the decade. In his book of 1944, *The Literary Fallacy*, DeVoto invoked Powell as the means of rebuking the abstractionism of "the literary mind."

Powell had "a vision of society," said DeVoto, but he was no visionary. His vision was not composed out of abstract logic and beautiful thought; it was based on knowledge, rigorously determined, rigorously applied. Such a vision might legitimately serve as a basis for reform. Powell thus "conceived that society itself must be responsible for the preservation and development of their [natural] wealth" and fought "heroically" for this conception "against the forces of private exploitation, confused state and national interests, scandal, libel, and the ruthless drive of industry and finance."[25]

This was a significant tribute, for it was, after all, a tribute to a liberal activist, not to a hero out of Pareto or Henderson. As DeVoto's friend Wallace Stegner put it in his life of Powell (for which DeVoto wrote the in-

[24] *Minority Report*, p. 111.
[25] *The Literary Fallacy* (Boston: Little, Brown, 1944), pp. 128, 134–35.

troduction), Powell had "repudiated that reading of Darwinism which made man the pawn of evolutionary forces. In his view, man escaped the prison in which all other life was held, because he could apply intelligence and will to his environment and bend it."[26] There now surged within DeVoto a new determination to help fulfill John Wesley Powell's vision—in his words of 1944, "to make the land live rather than die, to build a society that may have decent security and dignity in accord with the conditions set by nature, to correct folly and restore social health."[27] The return to the West thus helped liberate him from the social quietism which had weighed upon him in the '30's.

Another factor, perhaps even more important, speeded the renewal of his radical idealism. This was the oncoming of the Second World War. Nothing does greater credit to DeVoto's intelligence than the clarity with which he saw the meaning of fascism. His character and concerns—his absorbing interest in the American past, his refusal ever to travel outside the American continent, his impatience with European examples and analogies—might well have predisposed him toward isolationism. But he had no doubt from the start either about American stakes in the war or about American responsibilities to the world. He had never surrendered to revisionist interpretations of the First World War, and he believed that German aggression offered a greater threat in 1939 than in 1914. Shortly after war broke out in 1939 he wrote, "We are in the war to stay. Whether formally remote or raising such armies as I was discharged from twenty-one years ago, we shall finish it—America will wage the war in one way or an-

[26] Wallace Stegner, *Beyond the Hundredth Meridian* (Boston: Houghton Mifflin, 1954), p. vii.
[27] "The Easy Chair," *Harper's*, February 1944.

other and take the responsibility of fitting together what fragments of the world are left when it is finished."[28] The onset of war released the idealism which DeVoto had suppressed during the '30's. What of the young man who faced military service? "He will not grow up in the America he was born in," DeVoto wrote, "but neither did I or anyone else who has ever lived here; and if he cannot have the hope perhaps he can have the will to do more than I did in the shaping of his own America."[29]

War overshadowed our trip to the West in 1940. I can remember hot arguments in the editorial chambers of the then isolationist *Post-Dispatch* in St. Louis, as we tried to convince Fitzpatrick, Irving Dilliard, and the others that they should pay more attention to the Nazi rush across the Low Countries. Benny used to say afterward that the *Post-Dispatch* published an editorial, reprinted up and down the Mississippi Valley, warning the West against panic-spreaders and warmongers from the East. I remember too when we drew up at the side of the road at sunset outside Trinidad, Colorado, to hear Roosevelt's Fireside Chat of May 26, 1940, on national defense. The red light was fading on the Spanish Peaks; soon dusk fell, and everything was dark and silent and limitless. As Benny told the story in a subsequent Easy Chair: "Some Mexicans came out of a little adobe hut, bowing, smiling, apologetic, and asked if they might listen too. When it was finished one of our guests said, 'I guess maybe America declare war pretty soon now.' We waved goodbye and drove on to Trinidad. I guess maybe." He wrote from New Mexico in June:

[28] *Minority Report,* p. 132.
[29] *Minority Report,* pp. 134–35.

We have come twenty-five hundred miles, from Cambridge to Santa Fé. It is a dreamlike time for traveling across America, with the fears loosed from the cave and the whole country roused to dread; and yet as we moved westward we found it progressively less roused, so that we have been bearers of evil tidings, the wave following behind us down the sun's path.[30]

In that eerie twilight period between the invasion of Poland and Pearl Harbor, DeVoto never faltered in the trenchancy of his perceptions. "What ought they to say?" he wrote of the presidential candidates in November 1940. "Simple, elementary, readily understandable things . . . Just that the world is on fire. That America will be burned up unless you come awake and do something." When isolationists accused DeVoto of hysteria, he was able to turn back the charge: "Hysteria, remember, is the mind's retreat from what it dare not face. That's what happened to you, that's why your home town is serene. Of course you're quiet: anyone is quiet who is scared stiff. There is such a thing as coma."[31] His piece of May 1941, "What to Tell the Young," provoked the heaviest mail he ever received in his life from a single article, heavier than in the worst days of the McCarthy fight. He asked the young men's question: "Would you send me out to die?" and answered: "When the time comes, yes . . . The chance for anyone is precarious but he must take it . . . What happens if he does not take the chance? In what terms will there be ambition, career, or individual significance if the United States goes down?"[32] When the young wrote

[30] "Letter from Santa Fé," *Harper's,* August 1940.
[31] "All Quiet along the Huron," *Harper's,* November 1940.
[32] "What to Tell the Young," *Harper's,* May 1941.

back to say that they would be glad to fight if only they had a faith to defend, DeVoto was moved to wrath:

> You haven't got any faith, any belief? What you mean is that, in spite of all the chaos and waste of these years, even those of you who have had to work in a rich man's club have fed on fat so thick, have found life in America so soft, so promising, and so firmly established on the democratic assumptions that you have never been forced to take thought of it.
>
> You are forced to take thought of it now. The simple thing on which everything rests is endangered. It is not an ordinance of Almighty God; it is only the labor of Americans. It can survive or it can go under; it can be forfeited or it can be fought for. Maintaining it long enough for you to voice your ignorance of it while you share and inherit it has sometimes required Americans to die for it who were quite as valuable to America as you are. What are you going to do about it?[33]

For DeVoto, the Civil War was the paradigm of all wars. It was the war he knew best, which preoccupied him most, and from which he drew images and arguments and parallels most freely. The impact of the Second World War on him can be measured by the change it wrought in the way he conceived the Civil War. In 1937, during his retreat from idealism, he had come almost to accept the revisionist view of the Civil War as a needless conflict brought about by "the humanitarians, the pure in heart, the idealists, and the dreamers." Nearly everyone lost the war, he said, "especially the American Republic." "So maybe the craven thing in

[33] "Either-Or," *Harper's,* August 1941.

1860 would have turned out to be the best thing by 1937"; "maybe the best thing to have done was to hold on somehow, to give here and take there, to compromise when possible and yield when compromise failed, to do the next thing no matter how little of the long view or the austere vision it had—but to insist on the established forms, maintain the accustomed mechanism, allay as much passion as might be and reduce as much friction, give the thing space to writhe in, and above all gain time."[34] This was a good piece of Paretianism, and in 1937 this might have seemed a tolerable formula. But when Neville Chamberlain applied it at Munich in 1938, it began to lose its allure. By 1941 DeVoto had come to the position which he so brilliantly expounded in his destruction of the revisionist position after the war—that "the war had to be fought for many sufficient reasons . . . and the victory of the North was good for the modern world." Slavery, after all, was an evil; the South, in defending slavery, had "set itself square against the current of the democracy"; and the experience taught the nation "that some questions can be settled forever by war and that it is best to have them settled in your interest."[35]

Between them, the West and the war, aided by the fading away of the New Deal, emancipated DeVoto from Pareto and Henderson and permitted his radical idealism to come again to the fore. But his idealism now operated freely within the context of relativism and skepticism, and indeed derived added force from that context. One began to feel that the two strains in DeVoto were no longer in conflict with each other: his empiricism was no longer hamstringing his populism;

[34] *Minority Report,* pp. 29–30.
[35] "Easy Steps for Little Feet," *Harper's,* March 1941.

the two were working together to fulfill chosen purposes. John Wesley Powell helped point the way to reconciliation; so too in retrospect did Franklin Roosevelt, in whom DeVoto now began to recognize much the same union of pragmatism and idealism which was coming into balance in himself. In 1944 DeVoto voted a fourth time for Roosevelt. A year later, when the war came to its final end, he noted with regret that on the day of final victory, "No one, so far as I am aware, spoke from Hyde Park to remind you that the man buried there had not lived to see this day and that his voice could not commemorate it by any miracle of radio."[36]

He thus entered the postwar world with idealism and skepticism, radicalism and relativism, in fruitful equilibrium. The nation's drift to the right after the war, working on DeVoto's natural contracyclical impulses, sharpened the edge of his radicalism. The hothouse attempt to construct a New Conservatism roused him to derision: "I feel no impulse to regress to Burke, Hobbes, Mandeville, or personal revelation."[37] The man for whom he felt the closest moral and intellectual sympathy was Elmer Davis, who combined, as he did, skepticism and radicalism in pungent union. His accustomed position as scourge of the fashionable cliches now put him on the left rather than on the right, as he had seemed to be in the 1930's. One felt that his new position was more congenial to his temperament and his convictions: he seemed never freer than in this last period and never more productive.

He defined his political position in 1950: "I am a Mugwump, 60 per cent New Dealer, 90 per cent Pop-

[36] "The Knowledge of Triumph," *Harper's*, October 1945.
[37] *Easy Chair*, p. 9.

ulist dirt-road historian."[38] From this perspective he spoke out vigorously against the tendencies toward smugness and conformity in the postwar world. In 1946 he turned sharply against the Truman Administration, pronouncing it "Republican in everything except the label." He found it hard for the moment "to determine which party Mr. Truman himself belongs to, but, when you cast the average of his policies, provided that is the right word, he seems to be playing about a yard back of the line on the Republican team, in the slot between tackle and end." Given this situation, DeVoto himself, like many Massachusetts liberals, cast his ballot for Henry Cabot Lodge, Jr., for senator against David I. Walsh. "I'm voting Republican," he said; adding quickly, "For this date and train only. It comes hard." He concluded about the election, "'Business' has been given and has accepted its chance to run the United States. A lot of us think this is the last chance that Business will ever get and from where I sit it looks as if it has fumbled the ball on fourth down."[39] By the fall of 1948, DeVoto looked more genially on Truman and cast a relatively enthusiastic vote for his re-election.

But politics constituted only a minor part of DeVoto's postwar commentary. In a society growing steadily more conservative, he found himself forced, in order to maintain the social equilibrium, to become himself steadily more radical. An essay of 1952, called "The Third Floor," took off from the fact that old houses in Boston and Cambridge often had unheated third floors for the Irish servants who presumably did not need to be warm in winter. The people who had lived in comfort on the first and second floors, DeVoto

[38] *Easy Chair,* p. 192.
[39] "The Easy Chair," *Harper's,* December 1946.

reported, were now expressing indignation over the new affluence descending on the once poor and submissive people upstairs. Social Security, as DeVoto put it in a paraphrase of the standard conservative complaint, "has killed self-reliance and initiative. It has poisoned us; the United States is 'apparently so prosperous but is so rotten at the core. The five-day week and forty-hour week will cause our downfall' . . . now everyone is recklessly spending money." DeVoto went on to condemn "the idea that it is reckless to spend money you have earned but admirable to spend money someone else has earned, that a gentlewoman may properly tour the Orient on an inherited income but a waitress is bringing about our downfall if she buys a radio."[40]

But he was by no means uncritical of what his friend J. K. Galbraith would call the "affluent society." De-Voto long preceded contemporary critics of planned obsolescence and the style racket in his attack on the designed waste of postwar manufacturing: the tires that wore out after two thousand miles, the meat knives that could hardly cut butter, the appliances which cost more in maintenance than in original purchase. In the '30's, he had thought it important to defend the profit motive against what he regarded as the planning mania in Washington; the quest for profit at least kept things close to practical experience. But now that the acquisitive impulse was no longer contained by a liberal government, DeVoto was quick to denounce its excesses. Perhaps nothing was more symptomatic than his willingness now to criticize the profession which had so long been his ideal of humane and disinterested wisdom—the doctors. He still in-

[40] *Easy Chair,* pp. 34–35, 37.

sisted that "the medical researcher and experimenter, while working at his trade, is just about the most admirable of human beings," but as an interest group, the profession seemed to him "biased, obscurantist, and reactionary to an astonishing degree." He contrasted the open mind the doctor showed in his laboratory with the "scarcity of objective thought, ignorance of economic and social developments, neophobia, docile acceptance of the fuehrer principle" he showed as a member of the American Medical Association and argued strongly for a national health program free of AMA interference or supervision.[41]

As against the affluent society, its avalanche of gadgets and gimmicks, its conviction that anything which made a profit justified itself and anything which didn't invited suspicion, DeVoto sought always to urge the indispensable importance of the free individual. And this meant for him, more forcibly than ever before, *all* individuals. The problems of the South, he wrote before the war had ended, including "the Negro problem (and Miss Lillian Smith of Clayton, Georgia, has pointedly reminded us all that we had better say the white problem)," were not the "private business" of southerners. "They are our business too. They are national problems. Everything that happens to you because of them happens to us as well." He recalled the 1850's—"racial myth, biological and ethnological dogma not only of white supremacy but of Southern superiority, suppression of civil rights . . . mobbing and lynching of people who dared to invoke the right to inquire, quarantine of the Southern mind." These were alarming enough in the 1850's, he said, and now that we have them in sharp contemporary perspective, they

[41] *Easy Chair,* pp. 92–93, 101.

could be alarming again.[42] And he was appalled by the spread of southern folkways northward. Traveling across Wisconsin by train a year later, he heard middle westerners talking about "niggers" raping "eight or ten white women a day in Chicago." "For half an hour," DeVoto wrote, "I listened to a conversation which I would have said could not take place in Wisconsin in any circumstance whatever . . . I think it was the most shocking experience I have ever had in a railroad car."[43] It would not have shocked L. J. Henderson, but DeVoto had moved far beyond the acquiescences of the '30's.

His most spectacular defense of the individual came, however, in the field of civil liberties rather than civil rights. Freedom of utterance and expression had, of course, been a long-time concern. Before the war he had often denounced the censors and the patrioteers. The flag wavers, he wrote in 1934, reminded him of vaudeville managers trying to save weak acts during the First World War: "A team of ham acrobats or a group of badly trained seals were coached to come into their finale brandishing the Stars and Stripes."[44] The function of political patriotism, he thought, was to disguise bad arguments, and he was merciless in exploring the implications, especially when he came to the Dies Committee in the late '30's.

He had lively memories of A. Mitchell Palmer and the Red Scare of 1920, and he was alert for signs of a postwar reaction against individual freedom. When Homer Rainey was driven from the presidency of the University of Texas in 1945, DeVoto was quick to respond. "Here," he wrote, "is a naked form of the old

[42] "The Easy Chair," *Harper's*, November 1944.
[43] "The Easy Chair," *Harper's*, January 1946.
[44] *Forays*, p. 159.

terror: thinking is dangerous. Here are subversive, clear-minded men winning the support of honest, troubled men to another panic-stricken attack on education in the belief that education, which might be the interpreter and enlightened guide of change, is the begetter of change." This attack on academic freedom seemed to him "the first of a new model. As the waves of reaction gather strength in the years immediately ahead of the United States, the same attack will be made repeatedly, in many colleges, always by the same kind of men representing the same interests and forces, employing the same or equivalent means. What has happened to the University of Texas has happened to us all."[45]

The erosion of the Bill of Rights became almost his major theme in the late '40's. "The enemy is still the same," he wrote: "absolutism, authoritarianism, dictatorship, tyranny, whatever threatens freedom."[46] Long before Senator McCarthy first unfurled his fluctuating list of Communists in the State Department, DeVoto was in the forefront of the fight to defend privacy against the snoopers. His famous column "Due Notice to the FBI" was published four months before McCarthy made his speech at Wheeling. Here DeVoto sounded a splendid protest against the spreading impression that "the interrogation of private citizens about other citizens is natural and justified." A single decade, he wrote, "has come close to making us a nation of common informers." All this, he said, has gone too far.

We are dividing into the hunted and the hunters. There is loose in the United States today the same

<hr />

[45] "The Dark Age in Texas," *Harper's,* August 1945.
[46] *Easy Chair,* pp. 188–89.

evil that once split Salem Village between the be-witched and the accused and stole men's reason quite away. We are informers to the secret police. Honest men are spying on their neighbors for patri-otism's sake. We may be sure that for every honest man two dishonest ones are spying for personal ad-vancement today and ten will be spying for pay next year.

DeVoto served public notice: he would no longer dis-cuss any individual with any government representa-tive. "I like a country," he wrote, "where it's nobody's damned business what magazines anyone reads, what he thinks, whom he has cocktails with . . . We had that kind of country only a little while ago and I'm for get-ting it back." When J. Edgar Hoover replied that he would not "dignify Mr. DeVoto's half-truths, inaccura-cies, distortions, and misstatements with a denial or an explanation," DeVoto wondered whether an American citizen was not entitled to something better than this from the head of the Federal Bureau of Investigation. "Not dignifying," he said, "makes a neater game than answering criticism. It is also a form of loud-mouthed personal abuse, which has other names as well, by a man of great power and high public office."[47]

The rise of McCarthy only stimulated DeVoto to further defiance. Nothing outraged him more in the early '50's than the respect accorded to the ex-Com-munist as an authority on loyalty and on history. "Be-fore you can add a column of figures correctly," said DeVoto in a sardonic formulation of the McCarthy ar-gument, "you must first add them wrong. He who would use his mind must first lose it. Various ex-com-munist intellectuals are offering themselves on just that

[47] *Easy Chair,* pp. 172–76, 350.

basis as authorities about what had happened and guides to what must be done. Understand, I am right now *because* I tried earlier to lead you astray. My intelligence has been vindicated *in that* it made an all-out commitment to error."[48]

No one, except DeVoto's friend Elmer Davis, wrote more effectively against what DeVoto called "the sickness of our time, the craziness of our time, the craziness of everyone."[49] Inevitably his defense of freedom guaranteed him the denunciation of McCarthy and his followers. In a nation-wide telecast in the 1952 campaign, indeed, McCarthy, to DeVoto's chagrin, angrily denounced him as "Richard" DeVoto. Little was more ironic than the attempt to portray DeVoto, who had been a scathing critic of the Communists twenty years before McCarthy had ever raised the issue, as a Communist sympathizer.

The fight for the Bill of Rights marked one great expression of DeVoto's postwar radical idealism. But perhaps an even more significant contribution—and one which gave full expression to his love for the West and for the land, the rivers, and the mountains of America—lay in his battles in defense of the nation's resources. Even despite the war, the West had been at the center of DeVoto's consciousness ever since his trip of 1940. The publication of *The Year of Decision: 1846* in 1943 was followed by *Across the Wide Missouri* in 1947, *The Course of Empire* in 1952, and his edition of *The Journals of Lewis and Clark* in 1953. Even his single novel of the period was entitled *Mountain Time*. And his concern with the West was as much contemporary as it was historical.

[48] *Easy Chair,* p. 178.
[49] *Easy Chair,* p. 228.

In 1946 he made an extended trip through the West. He now began to see "the plundered province" in a deeper perspective than he had in 1934; and, when he returned, he set forth a new thesis—a thesis summarized in the title of a piece for *Harper's,* "The West against Itself." The New Deal and the war, he felt, had given the West a new opportunity for economic independence by laying the basis for an industrial economy. The decision for the West was whether it would seize this opportunity; and what DeVoto now particularly noted was the role the West was playing—and had always played—in its own spoliation. The rich men of the West, he observed, were in overwhelming majority allied with the system of absentee exploitation which had drained the West's resources and wealth eastward. The West's "historic willingness to hold itself cheap and its eagerness to sell out" were the product of the West's own weaknesses. The West had certainly been raped by the East, DeVoto said, but its posture had always invited rape. "Thus the basic problems are internal." If the East had not destroyed the resources of the West, the West would do so by itself. And his trip provided him new evidence of western schizophrenia. "There is intended," he wrote in *Harper's* in December 1946, "an assault on the public resources of the West which is altogether Western and so open that it cannot possibly be called a conspiracy. It is an assault which in a single generation could destroy the West and return it to the processes of geology."[50]

With that passage, DeVoto signaled the beginning of a long and remarkable campaign to save the West from itself. He later said that the controversy over the

[50] "The Anxious West," *Harper's,* December 1946.

public lands was the only one he ever deliberately precipitated.[51] The particular issue was an assault by the
organized stockmen against the Forest Service and ultimately against the whole idea of a national domain.
Cattlemen and sheepmen had long enjoyed the privilege of grazing their stock on certain public lands for
the payment of a minimal fee and the observance of
certain standards. The first objective of their new campaign was to transform this privilege into a vested right
subject only to such regulation as they might impose
on themselves. Beyond this, they planned a transfer of
public lands in general from federal protection to the
states. State governments, of course, could be coerced
as the federal government could not be; and state ownership would be a preliminary to turning the public
lands over to private ownership at forced sale and at
bargain prices (the price most commonly suggested
was ten cents an acre). The Forest Service, in this
stockmen's paradise, would be confined to rehabilitating land which lumbermen and stockmen had made
unproductive under compulsion to transfer it to private ownership as soon as it had been made productive
again. The ultimate goal was "to liquidate all public
ownership of grazing land and forest land in the
United States. And the wording of the resolution in
which the U.S. Chamber of Commerce came to the
support of the program *excepted no government land
whatever.*"[52]

The stakes in the public lands could hardly be
greater: an estimated 4 billion barrels of oil, enough oil
shale to produce 130 billion barrels of crude oil, 111
trillion cubic feet of gas, 324 billion tons of coal, not to

[51] *Easy Chair,* p. 7.
[52] *Easy Chair,* pp. 246–55.

speak of timber, grass, electric power, water and minerals, the total value well over a trillion dollars—quite a lot to go on the cheap from the people to the oil companies, the timber companies, the mining companies, and the investment trusts. The result might be the biggest landgrab in American history and an incomparable steal by private interests. More than that, by removing these great tracts from federal control, this program would encourage overgrazing and other abuses of the land, damage the watersheds, lower the water table, and accelerate the whole terrible process of erosion.

At some point along the way, one is compelled to suppose, a steal of this proportion and with such catastrophic consequence would have been halted. That it was halted so rapidly and that the nation was spared so much needless destruction was the single-handed work of DeVoto. He was the first conservationist in nearly half a century (except Franklin D. Roosevelt) to command a national audience. His *Harper's* pieces alerted conservationists through the country, and the ensuing revolt of public opinion cut off the stockmen's legislative program of 1947 before it could get under way. In the 1948 election one senator (D'Ewart) and one congressman (Barrett of Wyoming) identified with the landgrab were retired to private life.

This was only the beginning of a fight which continued for the rest of DeVoto's days. He covered every sector of the battle front with meticulous and passionate exactitude. Thrown back in one place, the stockmen counterattacked in another; and the change of administration in Washington in 1953 meant that, for the first time since Herbert Hoover had proposed that the unreserved public lands be turned over to the states, the stockmen and their associates had allies in the Executive Branch. DeVoto's last big piece on the subject, published in 1954, bore the somber title "Conservation: Down and on the Way Out." "In a year and a half," he wrote, "the businessmen in office have reversed the conservation policy by which the United States has been working for more than seventy years to substitute wise use of its natural resources in place of reckless destruction for the profit of special corporate interests. They have reversed most of the policy, weakened all of it, opened the way to complete destruction. Every move in regard to conservation that the Administration has made has been against the public interest—which is to say against the future."[53] No man did more to rouse public opinion against this reversal than DeVoto. He was, in the phrase of his friend and ally Senator Richard Neuberger of Oregon, "the most illustrious conservationist who has lived in modern times."[54]

It was the conservation fight which brought DeVoto into practical politics. During the '30's, his acquaintance with public officials and with politicians had been limited and accidental. But the future of the public lands was to be decided, of course, in the Congress; and in the course of his campaign DeVoto worked closely with senators and congressmen who shared his concern. Men like Neuberger, Lee Metcalf of Montana, Paul Douglas of Illinois, Clinton P. Anderson of New Mexico became his friends. And he came to know well, too, many men in the government service. In 1949 Oscar Chapman, as Secretary of the Interior, appointed him a member of the National Parks Advisory Board. In the Forest Service itself, DeVoto had a score of staunch and faithful co-workers.

[53] Easy Chair, p. 345.
[54] New York Times, September 25, 1960.

The culmination of his interest in politics came when Adlai Stevenson emerged as the leader of the Democratic party. The two men established a deep and lasting sympathy. Stevenson renewed DeVoto's faith in politics as a means of greatly serving the national welfare; DeVoto strengthened Stevenson's concern with the future of land and water and natural resources in America. DeVoto was far too good a writer to be useful as a draftsman of campaign speeches; but his spirit pervaded Stevenson's utterances on conservation in the 1952 campaign and even more in the years following. In 1954 the two men spent three or four days together in the Northwest inspecting the wilderness and contemplating the national ruin which lay ahead if the give-away programs should ever succeed.

The fight for conservation, the fight for civil freedom, the fight for Adlai Stevenson—in this succession of battles DeVoto's radical idealism came to its fine maturity. He never became the kind of *a priori* liberal he had detested in the '30's; his skepticism, the hard, rough edge of his mind, persisted to the end. But in these last years he applied his skepticism unsparingly to the pretensions of power and in so doing helped keep open essential options for his fellow countrymen. His broader view of democracy remained tempered and sardonic. This was perhaps the fundamental reason for his closeness to Adlai Stevenson—an intimacy he would not have achieved, or perhaps cared to achieve, with less reflective and complex political leaders, even those he came to admire, like Franklin Roosevelt and Wendell Willkie.

He had given his own sense of democracy poignant expression twenty years before his death. He was speaking at the University of Missouri on the writer who lay closest to his heart and in whose work he had been immersed so much of his life—Mark Twain. "In our day," DeVoto mused, "has perished the New Jerusalem of the democratic hope." Democracy, once so ecstatic in its visions, had begun to recognize the limits of the human predicament. "It was learning to come to terms not only with realities but with self-knowledge. Neither man nor society, it was coming slowly to perceive, had in itself the seeds of perfection." Mark Twain had been among the first to understand these things—to understand that democracy could rise no higher than its source and that its source was the human race, for which old Mark, as DeVoto noted, was willing to find the conclusive adjective.

"He had been called a pessimist," DeVoto wrote of Mark Twain. "Pessimism is only the name that men of weak nerves give to wisdom. Say rather that, when he looked at the human race, he saw no ranked battalions of the angels . . . Say that with a desire however warm and with the tenderness of a lover, he nevertheless understood that the heart of man is wayward, a dark forest. Say that it is not repudiation he comes to at last, but reconciliation—an assertion that democracy is not a pathway to the stars but only the articles of war under which the race fights an endless battle with itself."[55]

This was, as DeVoto saw it, the meaning of democracy. And fighting such a battle, DeVoto might have added, vindicates democracy by producing men of compassion, of courage and of faith. These men justify the battle and renew the strength and decency of a civilization. Bernard DeVoto was such a man.

[55] *Forays*, pp. 370–71.

12.
Whittaker Chambers and His *Witness*
(1952)

Whittaker Chambers has written one of the really significant American autobiographies.[1] When some future Plutarch writes his American Lives, he will find in Chambers penetrating and terrible insights into America in the early 20th century. Nor need he search long for the parallel life; just as Henry L. Stimson's *On Active Service* is the powerful counterstatement to Henry Adams' *Education,* so Whittaker Chambers' *Witness* is the counterstatement to that book so influential twenty years ago, *The Autobiography of Lincoln Steffens.*

Together Adams and Stimson portrayed the life of the aristocracy in America, one in terms of frustration, the other in terms of fulfillment. Together Steffens and Chambers portray an aspect of the political history of the American middle class—Steffens driven by optimism to turn from freedom to communism, Chambers driven by pessimism to turn from communism to freedom. A symbolic historical meeting even took place between them. "My hat came off while I was reading today a story of yours," Steffens wrote to Chambers on June 18, 1933. "How you can write! . . . Whenever I hear people talking about 'proletarian art and literature,' I'm going to ask them to shut their minds and look at you." Chambers later went to see Steffens at the Hotel Commodore in New York, when Steffens wanted him to write a biography of Edward Filene

---

[1] *Witness* (New York: Random House, 1952).

(not, surely, as Chambers now recalls, of William Filene). After they parted, with Chambers half-way down the red-carpeted corridor to the elevator, Steffens opened the door and called after him, "Keep a warm spot in your heart, Whittaker." The memory surged back into Chambers' mind when he went again, years later, to the Commodore—this time to confront Alger Hiss.

In the end, worlds divided Steffens and Chambers. The one, as he said so often, had been over into the future, and it worked. And the other said, on breaking with the Communist party: "I know that I am leaving the winning side for the losing side, but it is better to die on the losing side than to live under Communism." ("Almost nothing that I have observed, or that has happened to me since," Chambers writes in 1952, "has made me think that I was wrong about that forecast.")

In part, *Witness* is an extraordinary personal document—a powerful and compassionate story of a middle-class family broken on the shoals of life in middle-class America, until the surviving son rejects his class and enlists in the ranks of the proletarian revolution. But, like the other great autobiographies, *Witness* is much more than a personal document. It is also a political document and a philosophical document. Its weight and urgency as a personal document are likely to win acceptance for its politics and its philosophy. But the politics and the philosophy, in my judgment, raise basic issues which deserve independent and critical examination.

Chambers' picture of the world he grew up in is precise, poignant, and wonderfully evocative. He reproduces with painful and unsparing intensity the agony of his family life, the burden of disappointment and failure which lay over both his father and his mother, the madness of his grandmother, the suicide of his brother, the hurt and hardships which accompanied a sensitive boy growing up in a family steadily falling to pieces. "We are hopeless," his brother said. "We are gentle people. We are too gentle to face the world." The whole wretched life could produce only a single conclusion: Chambers and his family felt themselves outcasts, with no friends, no social ties, no church, no community. "We could scarcely be more foreign in China than in our alienation from the life around us." In this mood Chambers in 1925 joined the Communist party.

"In the West," Chambers writes, "all intellectuals become Communists because they are seeking the answer to one of two problems: the problem of war or the problem of economic crises." Yet in 1925 neither war nor economic crisis was an urgent problem. Many people joined the Communist party in the '30's in response to depression or to fascism; but joining in 1925, at the height of prosperity and peace, was another matter. Chambers' own accounting for this fact, even now, is perplexing. He felt, he said, that the world was dying, that it was without faith, hope, or character, that only surgery could now save the wreckage of mankind, and that the Communist party was history's surgeon. But one cannot escape the conclusion that the tragedy of his family, rather than the crisis of history, shaped Whittaker Chambers' decision. "Compared to us," he conceded, "the life around us was orderly and happy. We were not happy."

In another part of the book Chambers makes a profounder analysis of the appeal of communism. The conviction which unites and explains all Communists, he suggests, is the simple belief that it is necessary to change the world. To this the Communists add the corollary belief that man's liberated mind, by the force of rational intelligence, *can* change the world. This assumption and this hope underlie Communist fanaticism, whether the world to be changed is the rural stagnation and squalor of Asia, the misery and insecurity of industrial Europe, or the intolerable tensions of a divided home. In this deeper sense Chambers' choice in 1925 could thus seem "a choice between a world that is dying and a world that is coming to birth."

Once in the party Chambers served it for a season, drifted away, returned, and then joined its underground apparatus. He gives a detailed and vivid picture of the life of the party—its satisfactions and its corruptions—and he adds a calm, factual account of the workings of the Communist conspiracy. Then the familiar tale unwinds with the implacability of a Greek tragedy: the Washington network; Alger Hiss; the gradual break with communism; the flight from Communist retaliation; the reconquest of identity; *Time* Magazine; the Un-American Activities Committee; the trials; the final retirement and vindication. The suspense and excitement of the story remain. Chambers tells it, too, on the whole, without undue bitterness. One could hardly blame him for being bitter, when one recalls the ugly and vicious stories invented and repeated by respectable lawyers and college professors—stories which purported to "explain" everything, but which, when the time came, the Hiss defense never cared to bring up in court. The anti-Chambers whispering campaign was one of the most repellent of modern history. But Chambers, on the whole, except for one or two singularly unjustified cracks at that excellent paper, the Washington *Post*, keeps his temper.

No brief recapitulation can do justice to the impact

of the Chambers book. The book is well—often brilliantly—written. But it is written with intensity—with
an un-American, I was about to say, or at least un-
Anglo-Saxon intensity; and the intensity sometimes
leads to grotesque stylistic effects. "This case," he will
write, "has turned a finger of fierce light into the suddenly opened and reeking body of our time." But if the
style is often overwrought and improbable, so too are
the events which the book describes. Chambers is a figure out of Dostoyevsky, not out of William Dean How-
ells, and the intensity of the prose suggests the extent
to which the more smiling aspects of life are no longer
necessarily the more American. On the whole, for all
its excesses, the prose succeeds in bathing with baleful
light the struggle of the spirit with which the author is
so intensely concerned.

Those who resist this intensity—in many cases, because they refuse to believe in the reality of the Chambers nightmare—will continue to sneer at the book.
There is an opposite danger, too: that those who succumb to the fierce emotions and hypnotic spell of the
book will succumb also to Mr. Chambers' political and
philosophical conclusions. These conclusions are
deeply felt and persuasively formulated. They issue
powerfully from the terrible experience with which the
book is concerned. But to this reviewer these conclusions raise far more questions than they answer; and
their origin, far from validating the conclusions, suggests perhaps the hazard of founding dogmatic generalizations on experience so narrow and fragmentary.

Mr. Chambers' political conclusion is that Communist penetration inside the United States Government
enabled the Soviet Government not only to influence
"the staggering sum of day-by-day decisions," but "to
use the American State and Treasury Departments as a

terrible engine of its revolutionary purposes." These Communist activities, he declares, "affected the future of every American now alive" and "decisively changed" the history of the world. Mr. Chambers would add that the New Deal—in fact any political effort dedicated to social welfare or to the use of the government for the general welfare—inevitably plays into the hands of the Communists. "When I took up my little sling," he writes, "and aimed at Communism I also hit something else. What I hit was the forces of that great Socialist revolution, which in the name of liberalism, spasmodically, incompletely, somewhat formlessly, but always in the same direction, has been inching its ice cap over the nation for two decades."

First, let us consider the specific role and influence of the Communists within the American government. Mr. Chambers bases his case for their effectiveness on three kinds of evidence: on the facts of Communist espionage; on the nature of the jobs held by Communists; and on three foreign policy issues—the loss of China, the Morgenthau Plan, and Yalta.

The question of espionage is a serious one. But it is hard to contend that any historical calamities followed upon this espionage; and Chambers does not make this contention. His own conclusion, after reading the documents he got from Hiss, Harry White, and Julian Wadleigh, was that "political espionage was a magnificent waste of time and effort." This does not excuse the spies, but it does bear on any judgment as to whether Communist subversive activity changed the course of history. Atomic espionage, of course, is quite another matter; this, however, was not conducted in Washington and makes up no part of the Chambers indictment.

The espionage mission, though, is directly relevant

to the question of policy influence. For, in any well-conducted intelligence service, the functions of espionage and policy influence are kept sharply apart. The reason for this is obvious. The job of the spy is to procure intelligence. He cannot jeopardize this role by taking positions on policy questions which might attract interest and rouse suspicion. That is why actual members of the Soviet espionage apparatus were almost certainly under orders *not* to contend for pro-Soviet positions in policy discussions. A floater like Harry White might do this; but not an agent like Alger Hiss.

This fact reduces the importance of the actual positions which the Communists held. "I can imagine no better way," Chambers writes, "to convey the secret power of the Communist Party in the domestic policies of the United States Government" than to list the posts held by the members of his underground group. I can imagine a number of better ways. One of them would be to name one specific policy which would not have been undertaken had it not been for the secret Communist influence. Chambers makes a good deal of the fact that Hiss was counsel for the Nye Committee. But the moving spirits in the Nye Committee were Senator Nye, John T. Flynn, and Stephen Raushenbush. The Nye Committee would have reached its conclusions about the munitions industry just the same had Alger Hiss never existed. The fact that Lee Pressman, Nathan Witt, and John Abt held a variety of government jobs is no proof at all that they affected government policy. All it suggests is that they pretended to *accept* government policy; they had to if they wanted to keep the jobs. The only proof of their influence would be evidence that their presence *transformed* government policy. Mr. Chambers presents no such evidence in the domestic field. So far as I can see, a case can be made out for Communist influence on domestic policy in only one agency—the National Labor Relations Board, when Witt was the Board's secretary; and his influence hardly changed the course of history. Moreover, it was a situation fully understood by the White House. Roosevelt spent a good deal of time in 1940 in cleaning the Communists out of the NLRB.

The same considerations hold for foreign policy. The Morgenthau Plan was a bad plan; and Harry White certainly played an important role in its formulation. But to assume that without Communist influence there would have been no demand in 1944 for a hard peace is fantasy. Is Sir Robert Vansittart to be considered a tool of the Communists? James B. Conant backed the Morgenthau Plan; Bertram D. Wolfe wrote at the time that Stalin "would fear a greatly weakened Germany as much as a revolutionary Germany." Were Conant and Wolfe under Stalinist influence? Lauchlin Currie, on the other hand, fought the Morgenthau Plan—which complicates the whole Elizabeth Bentley theory of Communist influence in Washington. And the Soviet Union itself opposed the Morgenthau conception. If anything is obvious out of this confusion, it is that, after four years of bitter war against Nazism, one would naturally expect a series of harsh and punitive proposals, especially in view of the belief that leniency in 1919 had contributed to the rise of Hitler. Our absorption with the Communist conspiracy must not permit us to forget that such great upheavals as depression and war may sometimes have influence on human behavior.

The fall of China provides no more clear a case for the Chambers contention. It is absurd to assume that all those who saw no future in Chiang Kai-shek and some hope in Chinese communism were members or dupes of a Stalinist conspiracy. Many people of diverse political views detected virtue in the Chinese Communists. George Sokolsky wrote "The morally best elements of the nationalist movement in China are now in the Communist ranks. . . . And Chiang may yet fail, and the Soviet China may yet come into existence. But will it matter much? Will China be altogether altered? Will China take on a Russian façade? It is doubtful." Freda Utley declared that Chinese Communism had abandoned dictatorial aspirations; "its aim has genuinely become social and political reform along capitalist and democratic lines." Mistakes are inevitable in the analysis of an infinitely complicated situation. Why always equate human error with Communist conspiracy?—especially when the only course which would have averted the collapse of Chiang Kai-shek—the commitment of an American army to the mainland of China—is something which no one was ready to advocate in 1947, and few are willing to advocate today.

As for Yalta, Alger Hiss had nothing to do with the Far Eastern discussions, and knew nothing of their existence. Indeed, his chief role in the conference was to *oppose* the Russian demand for extra votes—an action compatible with the theory of Hiss as an agent, but hardly compatible with the theory of Hiss as a pro-Soviet influence in the State Department.

All the events which Mr. Chambers attributes to Communist influence are fully explainable on other grounds. Under the pressure of his own natural absorption with the Communist conspiracy, he commits the fallacy of excess interpretation and thereby does the Communists altogether too much credit. The one striking fact about the Communists in the '30's and '40's was not their success but their failure. The climate could hardly have been more propitious for them—first a depression, with fifteen million Americans out of work, then a war, in which the Soviet Union was a valuable and respected ally, and all the time a negligent and gullible nation. Yet the Communists bungled nearly every opportunity.

Why did communism fail? The answer to this question bears on Mr. Chambers' second political contention—that the support of social reform inevitably plays into the hands of communism. For the reason communism failed was surely the fact that the New Deal showed that reform and recovery were possible within the framework of free institutions. At the time that Whittaker Chambers and Alger Hiss, Louis Budenz and Lee Pressman, and all the intellectuals of the *Modern Quarterly* and the *New Masses,* were certain that capitalism and democracy were absolutely finished, Franklin Roosevelt and the New Dealers, instead of beating their breasts and prophesying doom, took off their shirts and buckled down to the job of saving capitalism and democracy. By so doing, they restored the faith of the American people in the vitality of free government. By so doing they prevented American communism from ever being anything more than a sordid sideshow for political *voyeurs.* It should be a political truism that communism is the response not to the potency but to the impotence of democratic government. That is why communism is strong today in France and in Italy, but weak in the very nations whose affirmative social policy Mr. Chambers regards with such abhorrence.

Mr. Chambers has some shrewd and intelligent things to say about "the Popular Front mind" and its influence among the intellectuals. But he errs when he identifies the Popular Front mind, which was a psychosis of the New York intellectual, with the New Deal mind, which was essentially concerned with trying to hold the American system together against economic crisis. The New Deal mind had its Popular Front version; there is, alas, something to Mr. Chambers' statement that "every move against the Communists was felt by the liberals as a move against themselves." But this was a consequence, not of the corruption of the New Deal, but of its innocence. Preoccupied with the day-to-day necessities of keeping the nation afloat, the New Dealers had little time for the intricacies of Soviet conspiracy; nor did anyone demonstrate to them why they should take time away from pressing tasks for remote fantasies. Mr. Chambers is highly sardonic on the subject of Adolf Berle; but he forgets that he gave Mr. Berle everything but the evidence. He does state with candor that "once I had put documentary evidence in the Justice Department's hands, Hiss *was* promptly indicted; Thomas F. Murphy *was* chosen by the Government to try the case; Hiss *was* convicted and his appeal opposed and denied." But surely these facts are relevant to his larger judgment.

Nor does Mr. Chambers' contention that the New Dealers were psychologically disabled from opposing communism have more than a fragment of validity; indeed, it is opposed by a good deal of the material in his own work. When Mr. Chambers describes the class lines opened up by the Hiss case, he writes, "It was, not invariably, but in general, the 'best people' who were for Alger Hiss and who were prepared to go to almost any length to protect and defend him." It would be news to Franklin Roosevelt that these same "best people" were among his own ardent supporters. Was John Foster Dulles, who got Hiss his Carnegie job, a passionate New Dealer? Were the unidentified steel magnates, department store owners, and Republican politicians, to whom Mr. Chambers alludes with natural resentment, zealous liberals? As for his own sympathizers, Mr. Chambers sums it up this way: "The inclusive fact about them is that, in contrast to the pro-Hiss rally, most of them, regardless of what they had made of themselves, came from the wrong side of the railroad tracks." These, after all, were the people who voted four times for the New Deal.

The politics of the Hiss case, in short, seem far more complicated, even by Mr. Chambers' own account, than some of his formulations suggest. For my own money Theodore Roosevelt was right, and not a Marxist dupe, when he said: "The more we condemn unadulterated Marxian Socialism, the stouter should be our insistence on thorough-going social reforms." For my own money the reformed Communist is too often like the reformed drunkard, preaching hoarsely that there is no middle ground between total abstinence and delirium tremens. But the normal man can take government, like liquor, in moderation and benefit from it. Communism was the overwhelming experience of Mr. Chambers' life. It was not the overwhelming experience of America in this generation; and not everything is to be explained in terms of it.

But Mr. Chambers goes beyond politics to larger questions of philosophy and religion. Here he makes his most eloquent and deeply felt testimony, and it is impossible to deny its earnestness and power. Communism, he says, is dominated by the vision of man's mind displacing God as the creative intelligence of the world: this is the ultimate sin of pride and the ultimate act of corruption. From this he concludes that the final division between the Communists and the anti-Communists turns on the issue of belief in God.

At every point [he writes], religion and politics interlace, and must do so more acutely as the conflict between the two great camps of men—those who reject and those who worship God—becomes irrepressible. Those camps are not only outside, but also within nations.

I sympathize basically with this analysis of communism. I concluded my book *The Age of Jackson* with Pascal's aphorism: "He who would act the angel acts the brute"; and I think that Whittaker Chambers, who reviewed *The Age of Jackson* for *Time,* knows how I stand on this matter. But Mr. Chambers, I believe, while he has the beast by the tail, does not name it correctly. The essential issue is not belief in God. It is rather the sense of human limitation, of human fallibility, of what he himself calls the "mortal incompleteness" of man. And the tragedy of religion is that belief in God is by no means a guarantee of humility.

The whole record of history, indeed, gives proof that a belief in God has created human vanity as overweening and human arrogance as intolerable as the vanity and arrogance of the Communists. Mr. Chambers mentions Dostoyevsky. But has he ever pondered the significance of the Grand Inquisitor? Was it just accident that Dostoyevsky chose the officer of a church as his symbol of the conviction and corruption of infallibility? Mr. Chambers admires Reinhold Niebuhr; but he seems to have forgotten Niebuhr's repeated warnings that no human being—nor human church— is safe from the flux and relativity of human existence, and that religion confronts fallible and prideful man with some of his gravest temptations. Mr. Chambers himself hears voices; so did Joan of Arc; but so did Hitler.

To divide the world between those who reject God and those who worship God would put some curious people in Mr. Chambers' camp. "It is not at all chance," he writes, "that both the Chamberses and the Hisses, arriving over very different routes, should at last have found their way into the community of Quakers." So? Then Quakerism, far from chastening the spirit of the Hisses and of Noel Field, only strengthened their Communist dedication. Many Fascists and Communists have found a belief in their own infallibility entirely compatible with a belief in God; while many people who have not believed in God have had a profound sense of humility and contrition. It would be a narrow view which would welcome such believers as General Franco and the Grand Inquisitor and Ivan the Terrible into the community of freedom, but would bar many decent, humble people who have no pretensions to certainty about the absolute. I know that it is fashionable to say today, as Mr. Chambers suggests, or as Mr. Justice Douglas (a New Dealer!) put it the other week, that "we are a religious people whose institutions presuppose a Supreme Being." But it is notable that the word God does not appear in the Constitution of the United States; and history would support the opposing contention of Mr. Justice Jackson—"The day that this country ceases to be free for irreligion, it will cease to be free for religion."

It is also fashionable today, as part of the demand for absolute, immutable, external standards, to blame the ills of the world on pragmatism. Relativism, it is said, inevitably leads to totalitarianism, while absolute values provide the only basis for resisting totalitarianism. But logic in these matters is easy. It can be argued quite as logically that only those who believe in absolute values can achieve the conviction of infallibility which permits tyranny and murder; and that, if there is anything from which the pragmatist flinches, it is the hypostatization of his own tentative, fragmentary, and incomplete views into dogmatic fanaticism. The fact is that here logic is no guide. We are reduced to observation and experience. Some pragmatists have a sense of human limitation; some do not. So, too, some believers have a sense of human limitation; some do not. To argue in the face of experience that belief infallibly creates humility and pragmatism infallibly creates totalitarianism is to revive the logic of Torquemada.

Peter Viereck cried "Enough of Toughmindedness!" a few weeks ago on these pages. But he seems to have forgotten what William James meant by the word "tough-minded." James did not mean a callous indifference to human suffering. He meant the fidelity to concrete facts which issues in pluralism and skepticism. And by "tender-minded" he meant the fidelity to abstract principle which issues in monism and dogmatism. Only the tender-minded, for whom human life is less important than absolute dogma, can easily destroy life in the name of dogma; and it is the Communists who are the tender-minded, if the hardhearted, of our day. Our world is more threatened, in my judgment, by the tender-mindedness of absolutism than by the tough-mindedness of pragmatism.

When Mr. Chambers demands belief in God as the first credential, he is surely skating near the edge of an arrogance of his own. He has forgotten the Grand Inquisitor; he has forgotten his reading in Dr. Niebuhr. For Niebuhr's conception of history involves no herding of mankind into worshipers and rejectors. His conception allows, as Mr. Chambers' does not, for the fanatical believer. It allows nonworshipers or rejectors to be tentative and experimental in history and humble and contrite before the mystery which lies beyond history. It is aware that the vanity of belief may be as corrupting as the vanity of atheism. Mr. Chambers' conception of the fellowship of the righteous seems at times almost as exclusive as that of the Communist fellowship he has foresworn.

Witness is the impressive and searching record of one man's experience. It is an invaluable account of the Communist conspiracy in the United States. In the long run, I suspect and hope, Mr. Chambers' dogmas in politics and philosophy will recede, like the dogmas of Henry Adams and Lincoln Steffens. What will remain is a personal testament of enduring interest.

13.
The Oppenheimer Case
(1954)

It is not likely that a great many people will bother to read *In the Matter of J. Robert Oppenheimer: Transcript of Hearing before Personnel Security Board* (United States Atomic Energy Commission), though it is available for $2.75 from the Superintendent of Documents. Its 992 pages are in the finest of the Government Printing Office's fine print; its form is meandering and discursive; its points are often confused and obscure. Yet it is a work of the greatest fascination and the highest significance. It offers an unequaled picture of the paradoxes of national security. It provides, in addition, the first authentic series of glimpses into the new, post-atomic, scientific-military world which in the past dozen years has risen behind and beyond and above lay American society.

Without our fully realizing it or their fully desiring it, this new community of weapons scientists has become in many ways the arbiter of our destinies. One regrets that no American novelist seems to have been attracted by this phenomenon; we do not even have the picture which C. P. Snow and Nigel Balchin have provided of its British counterpart. This lack of a sense of human background makes the impression which emerges from the Oppenheimer record all the more strange and shadowed. The record is not only fragmentary in its portrayal of the new technocracy; but too much of what is portrayed is unintelligible to the layman, because of both the difficulty of the scientific ideas and the excisions of the security officer.

Yet an impression does emerge—a singular, tantalizing, incomplete impression of this new world where science and policy intersect at the point of maximum destruction; where the life and death of civilization may hang on incomprehensible equations fed into giant calculating machines; where yet the old human emotions—love, loyalty, envy, hate—are still alive and powerful. It is a world of machines and processes—cyclotrons and reactors, heavy water piles and neutron diffusion. But it is also a world of men. What sort of men are these who inhabit this world, where so little can be freely communicated save images of destruction and death?

Their names have been known long enough—Oppenheimer, Rabi, Fermi, Teller, Bethe, Bacher, Zacharias, and the rest; but they have been words in headlines, faces flashing by in newsreels, the agents of catastrophic but vague experiments in distant places, shadowy magicians of the atomic age. One merit of the Oppenheimer transcript is that it presents these men to us in action, and not so much as scientists, impersonal and unchallengeable, but as human beings, involved in the inquiry into the loyalty and security of the one among them who more than any other was considered by the public to be their archetype and their leader. Inquisition both reveals and diminishes them. At the same time, it admits sharp light (too much, according to some specialists in security) into those debates in the back rooms which may already, by now, have shaped the future or nonfuture of civilization.

The scientists, it must be said, have long resented the secrecy in which they must live; that is one of the counts the state has against them. One feels almost, at moments, that the final struggle of our time will be between the scientists and the security officers—between those whose business it is to discover and propagate truth and those whose business it is to conceal it. But science, now that it has invaded the world of policy and power, cannot hope to escape the burden of security. These scientists are not fools. They know that their secrets in the hands of others—in the hands of the Communists—might be fatal; so the tension between dissemination and suppression is deep in themselves. They form a compact, taut community—brilliant men working under indescribable pressure on unimaginable weapons, cut off by "security" from the rest of society, thrust in terribly upon themselves and their science. Los Alamos during the war only carried this isolation to its logical extreme—the troop patrols around the perimeter, the monitored phone calls, the censored mail, the surveillance of personnel away from the base. But all scientists working in the higher reaches of the weapons field continue to dwell in Los Alamoses of their own construction.

For such men, science and life must become in the end almost indistinguishable. Each is joined indissolubly with his colleagues in the excitement and beauty of the scientific passion. Each may be divided irrevocably from them as technical divergences turn, under the pressure, into intolerable differences of personality and philosophy. The line between fusion and fission is close, for humans as well as for atoms. So Oppenheimer, who loathed the thermonuclear bomb as a dreadful weapon, could exult, "From a technical point of view it was a sweet and lovely and beautiful job." So Teller, who admired Oppenheimer and helped drive him from public service, could say with sincere regret, "There is no person whose friendship I'd value more than Oppie's if the circumstances of our deep technical disagreements would permit it."

These were the men now presenting their testimony to the AEC's Personnel Security Board—to Gordon Gray, former Secretary of the Army, president of the University of North Carolina, brisk, competent, unassuming, and businesslike; to Dr. Ward V. Evans, the aging chemist from Loyola, with his seemingly aimless but sometimes piercing questions and his sociable inquiries about old friends or students the witnesses might have encountered; to Thomas A. Morgan, former president of the Sperry Corporation, silent and enigmatic.

Witnesses friendly to Oppenheimer sought to prepare the Board for the queer inhabitants of this post-atomic scientific world. One such witness was General Groves, the wartime commander of the Manhattan District. Before the Board, he was an odd and not unimpressive mixture of candor and arrogance, essentially banal and unimaginative in his judgments, but still trailing the glory of the great war experience which for a moment had brought out the strength within him and in which he had played so honorable, if at times so reluctant, a role. He spoke of the scientists as one might of one's children—they were men "who would become violently excited about the most minor thing. . . . They were tense and nervous and they had to be soothed all the time." He understood that scientists could have little sympathy with security requirements. "I never held this against them," said General Groves, "because I knew that their whole lives from the time they entered college almost had been based on the dissemination of knowledge." They had fought the General incessantly, forcing him into the position of having to accept things they knew he disapproved. Yet "they were the kind of men that made the project a success. If I had a group of yes men we never would have gotten anywhere."

John Lansdale, Jr., said much the same thing—Lansdale who had been a lieutenant colonel and security officer at Los Alamos and is now a lawyer in Cleveland; in 1944 exercised over the commissioning of Communists by the Army, in 1954 exercised over other matters ("I think that the hysteria of the times over communism is extremely dangerous"). Like Groves, Lansdale had been much exasperated by the scientists. In crisp and effective testimony, he described as "almost maddening" the tendency of the "more brilliant people to extend in their own mind their competence and independence of decision in fields in which they had no competence." Yet Lansdale, again like Groves, was prepared to accept arrogance as the price of genius and to take calculated risks. Both had agreed in rejecting the original recommendations of security officials that J. Robert Oppenheimer be barred from atomic work. Both believed that he should be placed in charge of Los Alamos in 1943. Neither, in the spring of 1954, saw any reason to regret this decision.

Oppenheimer was, of course, the first of the scientists to appear. Not always his own best witness, he gave precise, fluent, impatient testimony, filled with the wonder and disgust which might afflict a man of reason compelled to contemplate his own past imbecilities. The AEC counsel, Roger Robb, vigorous and bludgeoning, intent not to comprehend but to indict, took full advantage of Oppenheimer's predicament. Most of the hammering came over the indication to Oppenheimer in 1943 by his friend Haakon Chevalier that, if he wanted to transmit secrets to Soviet scientists, channels were available; Oppenheimer's attempt to tip off the Manhattan District security officers to espionage possibilities without implicating his friend had resulted in a miserable botch of falsehoods, though the prosecution questioned whether he had uttered them in 1943 or was uttering them in 1954. Robb, pitiless, pressed every advantage, extorted every concession: "You lied to him?" "Yes." ". . . So you lied to him, too?" "That is right." ". . . This also was a lie?" "Yes, sir." ". . . Was that part of what you call a cock and bull story, too?" "It certainly was." ". . . According to your testimony now you told not one lie to Colonel Pash, but a whole fabrication and tissue of lies?" "Right." Why, oh why? "Because I was an idiot" was all Oppenheimer could say, perhaps despairing to convince anybody, perhaps despairing to convince himself. "This whole thing is a piece of idiocy. I am afraid I can't explain why there was a consul, why there was a microfilm, why there were three people on the project, why two of them were at Los Alamos. . . . I wish I could explain to you better why I falsified and fabricated."

Out of such perplexity, hard questions emerge. Could Oppenheimer have been telling the truth to Colonel Pash in 1943? Could he be lying now? Could he still be shielding atomic scientists involved in an espionage ring? Practical judgment on this had to rest on analysis, not of this episode alone, but of Oppenheimer's total career.

On the basis of the written record, it is hard to tell how effective Oppenheimer was before the Board; apparently not enough. Yet the Berkeley scientists, when they came to testify, argued that Oppenheimer's powers of persuasion surpassed all normal bounds—that, as Dr. Wendell Mitchell Latimer, professor of chemistry at the University of California, put it, "He is one of the most amazing men that the country has ever produced in his ability to influence people. It is just astounding the influence that he has upon a group. It is an amazing thing." No one could resist this influence, said Professor Latimer, not even General Groves; "not even General Groves, but the other members of the committee, Conant and the other members, they were under the influence of Dr. Oppenheimer, and that is some influence, I assure you"; only geographical remoteness, added Professor Latimer, had saved himself; "I might have been [under Oppenheimer's influence] if I had been in closer contact."

Another Berkeley scientist, Dr. Luis Walter Alvarez, professor of physics, reported, "Every time I have found a person who felt this way [that is, against the thermonuclear bomb] I have seen Dr. Oppenheimer's influence on that person's mind . . . one of the most persuasive men that has ever lived." The Gray Board, however, found in Oppenheimer not the qualities of Svengali but rather those of Trilby and criticized him for showing an undue "susceptibility to influence."

Yet Oppenheimer's persuasiveness had certainly worked in the past. Groves and Lansdale had known of the Chevalier episode in 1943 and had not withdrawn Oppenheimer's security clearance; David Lilienthal and the AEC had known about it in 1947, when Oppenheimer's clearance was confirmed; Gordon Dean, Lilienthal's successor as AEC chairman, had known about it. Indeed, Lilienthal and Dean headed a remarkable group of public officials not scientists themselves but men who had exercised grave responsibilities in the weapons field, who now appeared to testify for Oppenheimer. The testimony of both Lilienthal and Dean revealed traces of past friction with Oppenheimer; but both men—Lilienthal, precise and cautious, carefully referring to documents and memoranda; Dean, vivid, lucid, definite, pointed—swore their utter confidence in Oppenheimer's loyalty and his reliability. Other such men appeared: George F. Kennan; John J. McCloy; General Frederick Osborn; Sumner T. Pike—one after another praising the man and pledging their reputation to his probity. Even Bernard Baruch offered an affidavit on Oppenheimer's behalf.

And then the scientists: Dr. Vannevar Bush, dean of the American scientific community, said of Oppenheimer: "More than any other scientist that I know of he was responsible for our having an atomic bomb on time," and affirmed his entire faith in his character. Dr. Hans Bethe said, "I believe that Oppenheimer had absolutely unique qualifications for this job [Los Alamos] and that the success is due mostly to him." Dr. James B. Conant said, "He is one of the 3 or 4 men whose combination of professional knowledge, hard work, and loyal devotion made possible the development of the bomb." Dr. Norman Ramsey said, "He did a superb technical job, and one which also made all of us acquire the greatest of respect and admiration for . . . his loyalty and his integrity." Dr. I. I. Rabi said, "Oppenheimer set up this school of theoretical physics which was a tremendous contribution. In fact, I don't know how we could have carried out the scientific part of the war without the contributions of the people who worked with Oppenheimer." Dr. L. A. DuBridge, president of the California Institute of Technology, said, "I feel that there is no one who has exhibited his loyalty to this country more spectacularly than Dr. Oppenheimer. He was a natural and respected and at all times a loved leader." And Bacher, Bradbury, Compton, Fermi, Fish, Lauritsen, Von Neumann, Whitman, and Zacharias spoke to the same effect—all eminent scientists who had played the most essential roles in the American weapons program.

Yet from the start another note sounded: other men—other eminent scientists—had different things to say. The discordant theme had its origin in three places—in Dr. Edward Teller; in the scientists clustered around Professor Ernest Lawrence at Berkeley (whom Teller has since joined); and in the Strategic Air Command and especially in the former Air Force scientist, David Griggs.

Teller had received his first mention in Oppenheimer's own testimony. He appeared there as a brilliant and stormy figure, dissatisfied with the progress of research at Los Alamos, anxious that Fermi or Bethe or Oppenheimer himself take charge of the thermonuclear work. Then Gordon Dean described Teller as "a very, very able man . . . a genius . . . a very good friend of mine . . . a very difficult man to work with." Dean added: "You can't break up a whole Los Alamos laboratory for one man, no matter how good he is." Said Hans Bethe, "He did not want to work on the agreed line of research. . . . He always suggested new things, new deviations." Said Sumner Pike, "Dr. Teller was never one to keep his candles hidden under bushels . . . a very useful and a very fine man, but . . . lopsided." Dr. Bradbury, present head of Los Alamos, told of the circumstances which led to Teller's final departure from Los Alamos. And yet Professor Latimer of the Berkeley group, when asked whether Teller was a hard man to work with, replied vigorously, "I can hardly think of a statement that is further from the truth. . . . In any friendly climate, Dr. Teller is a perfect colleague, scientifically and personally."

It was Teller who believed in the thermonuclear bomb, worked for it from 1944 on, strove singlemindedly on its behalf, resented any diversion from it, and, in 1951, produced the invention which made it possible. But the great battle over the thermonuclear bomb—over Super, as it was termed in the scientific-military world—had been fought two years earlier. The Soviet achievement of an atomic explosion in September 1949 had detonated the American thermonuclear effort. Simultaneously Professor Lawrence and his Berkeley colleagues and the generals of the Strategic Air Command saw in Super the only means of recapturing American weapons superiority; and Teller now had the chance to make his dream come true.

The Gray Board made a great deal of Oppenheimer's opposition to Super; the Atomic Energy Commission, in the end, excluded it as a factor in the case. But, whether a formal factor in the final decision, it was certainly the primary factor in setting in motion the train of events which brought Robert Oppenheimer to Room 2022, Building T-3, of the Atomic Energy Commission, on April 12, 1954. For the opposition to Super fixed in Teller's mind the belief that Oppenheimer was acting "in a way which for me was exceedingly hard to understand"; after the Super debate Teller concluded that the vital interests of this country should be "in hands which I understand better, and therefore trust more." The opposition to Super persuaded Ernest Lawrence and the Berkeley group that there was a doubtful if not sinister pattern in Oppenheimer's behavior. And the opposition to Super launched David Griggs of the Air Force on his campaign to save the Strategic Air Command from Oppenheimer's ideas and influence.

From a dramatic viewpoint, Teller's eventual appearance before the Board, after all the buildup, must have been something of an anticlimax. A Hungarian by birth, a student in Germany, a teacher in England, a reasarch fellow in Denmark, a professor at American universities since 1935, Teller seemed troubled, earnest, and, in obvious intent, fair-minded, torn between his concern for the United States and his desire not to do an injustice to Oppenheimer. He said of Oppenheimer at the start, "I have always assumed, and I now assume, that he is loyal to the United States. I believe this, and I shall believe it until I see very conclusive proof to the opposite." In his testimony, he tried hard to draw a just balance sheet on Oppenheimer's activities. Gordon Gray, seeking something more clearcut, finally put the direct question: would it endanger the common defense and security to grant clearance to Oppenheimer? Teller replied that, so far as loyalty was concerned, he saw no reason to deny clearance; but "if it is a question of wisdom and judgment as demonstrated by actions since 1945, then I would say one would be wiser not to grant clearance. I must say that I am myself a little bit confused on this issue." He did, indeed, seem confused about the nature of the security problem, since the giving of bad advice has not usually been considered to make a man a security risk. But Gordon Gray replied: "I think that you have answered my question."

The Berkeley group—Alvarez, Latimer, Pitzer; Lawrence himself was prevented by illness from testifying—added to this only the emphasis on Oppenheimer as the great persuader. The more intense attack on him came from a man who had only been a minor and transient figure in the early testimony—from David Griggs, formerly Chief Scientist of the Department of the Air Force.

The broad Air Force view had been first presented by General R. C. Wilson, en route from command of the Air War College at Maxwell Field to the Third Air Force in England. But General Wilson had begun by saying firmly that he wanted the record to show "that I am appearing here by military orders, and not on my own volition," and that he had no question concerning Oppenheimer's loyalty. He did feel, he conceded under questioning, that Oppenheimer's advice on strategic questions had threatened to jeopardize the national defense. But by this, it became clear, General Wilson simply meant that Oppenheimer's strategic views were opposed to the theory of the Strategic Air Command—the theory that the central reliance of our national defense should be on SAC and the hydrogen bomb. "I am first of all a big bomb man," General Wilson explained.

The General remained a reluctant and reserved witness, testifying only because he had been ordered to do so by the Chief of Staff of the Air Force. David Griggs was less inhibited. A geophysicist, now at the University of California at Los Angeles, Griggs had served as Chief Scientist of the Air Force from September 1951 to July 1952.

His testimony was nervous, detailed, and copious. He announced his suspicions of Oppenheimer's loyalty and further alleged the existence of a scientists' conspiracy, headed by Zacharias, Oppenheimer, Rabi, and Lauritsen, which operated, he said, under the name of ZORC, and which was pledged to the destruction of the Strategic Air Command. His words, as he candidly warned the Board, throbbed with strong emotion. He even produced a memorandum describing an occasion when he told Oppenheimer face to face that he could not be sure whether or not Oppenheimer was pro-Russian. Oppenheimer "then asked if I had 'impugned his loyalty.' I replied I had. He then said he thought I was paranoid. After a few more pleasantries our conversation came to an end."

Those who used to know Griggs when he was around Harvard in the late '30's remember him as a man of violent feelings, working out aggressions against a world which he conceived to have injured him. He told now of watching Zacharias write the initials ZORC on a blackboard before fifty or a hundred people in a meeting in Cambridge in September 1952; yet Zacharias and other participants at the meeting deny that such an episode ever took place; Zacharias, indeed, swore that he had never heard of the initials until he read them many months later in an article in *Fortune*. Similarly Griggs imputed to Zacharias, as the proponent of continental defense, the statement that it was necessary to give up American strategic air power, at a time when a strengthening of the Strategic Air Command was an essential part of Zacharias's theory of continental defense. And he similarly charged Thomas K. Finletter, then Secretary of the Air Force, with making remarks about Oppenheimer's loyalty which Finletter has since said he never made.

Griggs strongly favored the thermonuclear bomb, and it is certainly true that Oppenheimer opposed it. It is even true that Oppenheimer opposed it—and the strategy of making atomic retaliation the main reliance of our defense—with passion and anger. Oppenheimer thus seems to have believed, and perhaps even to have repeated, stories about Finletter as a bomb-brandishing imperialist which were patently false and vicious. Yet many other responsible people opposed the bomb, too—some, like Conant, before Oppenheimer had crystallized his own opinion. One ground for opposition was the reasonable belief that the cost of the thermonuclear effort in terms of plutonium bombs might well result in the weakening of American defense.

Oppenheimer's own reasons were more complicated than that—so complicated, indeed, that the problem of his motives thoroughly fascinated the Gray Board, which concluded that he had not been "entirely candid" in his statements on the issue. There are real puzzles here. Oppenheimer, for example, expressed in 1949 a moral distaste for Super which he did not seem to feel for the atomic bomb; yet in 1945 he had supported the research which led to Super, and in 1951, after Teller's brilliant invention, he seemed, according to some witnesses, wholly sympathetic to the thermonuclear project; others thought he was still dragging his feet. To complicate the affair, the thermonuclear bomb, as it was finally built, was, because of Teller's invention, a quite different matter from the bomb which had been discussed in 1949. By Teller's own testimony, Oppenheimer said that if the new style of bomb had been suggested earlier, he would never have opposed the project. Oppenheimer's record of vacillation here is manifest, though it would, of course, be a hopeless government in which officials did not feel free to change their minds or to express their dissenting opinions. Vannevar Bush stated the issue with eloquence when he discussed before the Gray Board the original bill of particulars against Oppenheimer. The AEC letter, Bush said,

> is quite capable of being interpreted as placing a man on trial because he held opinions, and had the temerity to express them. . . .
>
> I think this board or no board should ever sit on a question in this country of whether a man should serve his country or not because he expressed strong

opinions. If you want to try that case, you can try me. I have expressed strong opinions many times, and I intend to do so. They have been unpopular opinions at times. When a man is pilloried for doing that, this country is in a severe state.

In the end, the H-bomb problem settled itself. Truman, Acheson, McMahon, Finletter, Louis Johnson, Teller, Griggs and the other supporters of the thermonuclear effort were vindicated. And, in the end, Oppenheimer's opposition to the effort was not to be formally held against him by Lewis Strauss and the AEC. Yet few who read the record are likely to doubt that, if Oppenheimer had not opposed Super in 1949, he would not have had to stand trial in 1954.

If the thermonuclear debate was eliminated, what was left in the record to cast doubt on Oppenheimer's loyalty or security? One would presume something fairly weighty; for the Gray Board by a 2–1 vote and the Atomic Energy Commission by a 4–1 vote concluded that Robert Oppenheimer was a security risk, not to be trusted with secret information without danger to the United States. The AEC majority, which had the final say, rested its decision on two main allegations: "imprudent and dangerous associations" and "substantial defects of character."

On the question of associations, the AEC majority reproached Oppenheimer not only with his early and admitted Communist relationships, but with "persistent and continuing association with Communists" in the years since the war. In terms of the record, this last phrase is perplexing; and the AEC itself only specified one association—that with Chevalier—to support the "persistent and continuing" charge. As for Chevalier, whom the AEC assumed without proof to have been still a Communist in 1953, Oppenheimer dined with him one night in Paris that year, and on the next day drove with him to meet with André Malraux. Malraux, of course, is not only the pre-eminent literary man of France but is also an intimate political adviser of General de Gaulle and a passionate anti-Communist. It seems unlikely that any friend of Malraux would be an active Communist today. (But Gordon Gray and Thomas Morgan, in discussing this incident, could only refer vaguely to the distinguished writer and notable anti-Communist as "a Dr. Malraux.")

Beyond the Chevalier incident, the record reveals no other post-1946 associations with Communists or even ex-Communists on Oppenheimer's part, save for occasional chats with his brother, a chance meeting in 1949 with two Fifth Amendment physicists while leaving the barbershop in Princeton, a scolding of the Harvard ex-Communist, Dr. Wendell Furry, for having employed the Fifth Amendment, and perhaps brushes with persons at scientific conventions. Did these brief and random meetings over a decade really constitute a sinister and deliberate pattern of association with Communists? If so, one wonders what will now happen to Vannevar Bush, Bethe, Fermi, Rabi, and the other scientists who will doubtless continue to associate with Oppenheimer—and thus will have far more of a record of "persistent and continuing" association with a certified security risk than Oppenheimer himself has had since the war.

On this whole problem of associations, George Kennan reasonably remarked to Gordon Gray, "I suppose most of us have had friends or associates whom we have come to regard as misguided with the course of time, and I don't like to think that people in senior capacity in the Government should not be permitted or conceded maturity of judgment to know when they can see such a person or when they can't." Kennan added, "I myself say it is a personal view on the part of Christian charity to try to be at least as decent as you can to them." But neither the Gray Board nor the AEC majority were prepared to accord to high government officials the exercise of maturity, or to indulge them in impulses of charity. The higher the government official, contended the AEC, the less latitude should be permitted him.

Oppenheimer's truly damaging pattern of association took place, of course, before the war and might be presumed to have been offset by his war and postwar record. That record, as unfolded in the hearings, was, after 1943, a not unimpressive one. Before 1943, he was, like so many scientists (and like some of his colleagues who retain clearance today), a political sentimentalist, soft-headed and unsuspecting. But as early as 1943 he could tell the Los Alamos security officer that present membership in the Communist party was in his judgment incompatible with loyalty to the atomic bomb project. After the war he ignored even liberal opinion in the scientific community to testify in favor of the May-Johnson bill, fearing lest the disintegration of Los Alamos might weaken American defense. He resigned from the Independent Citizens Committee of the Arts, Sciences and Professions in 1946, when its pro-Communist tendencies became apparent to him. He helped formulate the principles in the Baruch plan which the Communists found least acceptable; and when General Osborn took over the job of negotiating for atomic control in the United Nations, Oppenheimer flew from San Francisco to urge him to discontinue negotiations because of the hopeless attitude of the Communists. When his counsel was sought by scientists in trouble for past political associations, he told them not to plead the Fifth Amendment; and in 1949 he freely testified before the House Un-American Activities Committee concerning the Communist relationships of at least one atomic scientist. As hostile witnesses testified, he was more responsible than anyone else for educating the Army and even the Air Force to the potentialities of tactical atomic weapons and for integrating such weapons into military plans; and, as they also testified, he played a substantial role in the fight for adequate air defense against possible Soviet attack. No one before the Board charged him with a "soft" or pro-Communist utterance in the last half-dozen years. In writing, in speech, and in conduct, Oppenheimer would seem to have acted like an impassioned and even obsessed anti-Communist through most of the last decade; Dr. Rabi even told the Board that Oppenheimer had seriously discussed the advisability of preventive war.

The problem of "substantial defects of character" is even harder to pin down. The AEC majority assembled half a dozen apparent ambiguities and equivocations, purporting to demonstrate Oppenheimer's basic unreliability. Some of these had to do with lapses of memory. Nor, judging by the hearing, was Oppenheimer the only scientist liable to such lapses. Indeed, noting the fallible memory exhibited by one scientist after another, one began to wonder whether there was something about the scientific focus which, in the purity of its concentration, left human relationships in a vague and easily forgotten penumbra. In one such incident, Oppenheimer denied having received a letter from Dr. Seaborg though the government had the letter in its possession, having taken it from Oppenheimer's files. Obviously, if Oppenheimer had recalled the existence of the letter, he would have gained no advantage by denying it, for he would have known that the government had it. With the exception of the Chevalier episode, the six examples cited by the AEC majority were about of this weight. On the basis of this, would Oppenheimer's character as disclosed in the hearing seem more defective, say, than Griggs's? At least Oppenheimer's demonstrated lies were in the past and were freely conceded. Yet, despite the misrepresentations in Griggs's testimony, it can be assumed that Lewis Strauss had made no move to withdraw Griggs's Q clearance.

The whole concept of "defects of character" seems a hazardous one. The American government from 1789 on has always had a large share of people—including some of the ablest men in it—who had, by AEC standards, "substantial defects of character." Yet even if characters become so deplorable that one fears contamination from them, one still shudders to have the concept of "security risk" so tortured that it becomes a synonym for a character less righteous than one's own. By the Lewis Strauss interpretation of "security risk" Alexander Hamilton and Grover Cleveland would have been fired out of government service as adulterers, U. S. Grant as a drunkard, and so on. Would such exclusions have improved the safety of the republic? Bureaucratic infighting in the government has always been bitter and acrimonious; it is likely to be, when dedicated men strongly believe that the safety of the republic depends on their policies; and each side characteristically regards the other as deficient in morality. But when the winning side starts trying to outlaw the losers as "security risks," as happened in the China service and is now beginning to happen in the scientific-military world, one wonders what sort of people our future governments will attract.

The culmination of the AEC case against Oppenheimer's character had to do with something else: it had to do with Oppenheimer's attitude toward the security system—as the AEC majority put it, his "persistent and willful disregard for the obligations of security." But once again the AEC was astonishingly weak in bringing forward concrete evidence. The decision mentioned only the Chevalier case—which was, after all, eleven years old—and referred, without specification, to "other instances."

It is true that there had been ambiguous incidents during the war, and the Chevalier episode was certainly much more than that. But, as General Groves testified, all the scientists chafed under security restrictions; and, as others testified, Oppenheimer was far more security-conscious than most. General Groves told how he had once warned Niels Bohr not to talk about certain things at Los Alamos; "he got out there and within 5 minutes after his arrival he was saying everything he promised he would not say." Groves had a similar experience with Ernest Lawrence; and he also reported that Lawrence had bucked when Groves told him to get rid of a security risk in the Berkeley laboratory. Colonel Lansdale recalled that Lawrence "yelled and screamed louder than anybody else about us taking Lomanitz [a Communist for whose draft deferment Oppenheimer made perfunctory intercession] away from him." Yet, in 1954, only illness prevented Lawrence from bearing testimony against Oppenheimer. Similarly, as much substantial testimony was brought forward in the hearing to show that David Griggs had tried to retard and sabotage the project for continental defense as was brought forward to show that Oppenheimer had tried to retard and sabotage the hydrogen bomb project.

The AEC majority had begun by defining the issue as whether Oppenheimer should continue to have access to "some of the most vital secrets in the possession of the United States." This definition suggested that a security risk was a person who could not be trusted with vital secrets because, deliberately or inadvertently, he might allow them to reach the enemy. Yet no serious person faintly contended that Oppenheimer's defects of character and association, over a period of a dozen years, had been responsible for the loss of a single secret. Colonel Pash, a hostile witness, swore that he had no information "of any leakage of restricted data through Dr. Oppenheimer to any unauthorized person."

Nowhere was Oppenheimer charged with doing concrete injury to the national security through mishandling of secrets. His essential crime, as the Gray Board finally suggested, was lack of "enthusiastic support of the security system"; as Commissioner Murray argued at length in an AEC concurring opinion, "loyalty" should mean not just loyalty to the nation but "obedience to the requirements of [the security] system." Oppenheimer thus became a security risk, not because anything he had done had harmed national security, but because he had declined at times in the past to collaborate with professional security officers. Yet even here the AEC majority cited no specific instance of such non-collaboration later than 1943!

When Groves kept Oppenheimer at Los Alamos in 1943, he overrode the recommendations of the professional security officers. Possibly if the Gray Board and Lewis Strauss's AEC had been in existence then they would have kept Oppenheimer well out of the Manhattan District. Yet it seems hard to believe that our national security over the past dozen years would have been greater today if Oppenheimer had been barred from atomic work. And, unless one would argue this, it would seem even harder to argue that our national security is now to be greatly strengthened by barring an older, wiser, and more chastened Oppenheimer in 1954.

The Gray Board was prepared to excuse Groves's 1943 decision on the ground that there might then have been an "overriding need" for Oppenheimer's services; such a need, the Board contended, no longer exists in 1954. Conceivably our weapons program will not suffer unduly from the elimination of Oppenheimer: physicists are said to age fast (though Oppenheimer is only four years older than Teller) and a new generation has come along to take up the research burden. But is it not an error to construe the Oppenheimer decision as having no greater effect than subtracting a single overage scientist from government weapons work? Will the new generation of physicists now flock so eagerly into the government laboratories? And what will the consequences be for American security if they don't? It is of importance that the two official protests against the purge of Dr. Oppenheimer—by Dr. Evans of the Gray Board and by Dr. Smyth of the AEC—came from the only scientists to take part in the review of the case. Dr. Smyth, pointing to the role of "powerful personal enemies" in bringing the action against Oppenheimer, could only conclude with a despairing appeal to thoughtful citizens to read the record.

The AEC made its decision at just the point when we have begun to realize that the Soviet Union is fast cutting down our lead in the weapons race (or at least so the man in charge of these things at the Pentagon,

Donald Quarles, has said; his boss, Charles E. Wilson, has denied it). This is surely a race which may mean life or death for us all. At just this point, one would think, the government might be doing what it could to enlist the ardor and devotion of the scientific community in our weapons program. Instead, one of our great scientists has been struck from the program, not because of any specific harm he has brought—or is considered to be likely to bring—to national security, but because his character and his associations are disapproved by professional security officers. In so doing, the administration has evidently spread consternation through the scientific community and has made it harder than ever for our allies to trust our judgment and accept our leadership. In the name of a wholly ritualistic conception of "security," the administration may have done irreparable injury to the substance of America's national interest. "Our internal security system has run wild," Dr. Vannevar Bush has said. "It is imperative to our real security that the trend be reversed."

John J. McCloy, speaking before the Gray Board, pointed to what he called the "relative character of security." Security had two aspects, he proposed: the negative aspect of preventing the loss of secrets, and the affirmative aspect of making sure that we have a continuous supply of secrets to be protected. The fervor which stimulates thinking, the freedom which gives it scope—these, McCloy contended, were just as much a part of the security problem as the blocking of espionage. "If anything is done which would in any way repress or dampen that fervor, that verve, that enthusiasm, or the feeling generally that the place where you can get the greatest opportunity for the expansion of your mind and your experiments in this field is the

United States, to that extent the security of the United States is impaired. . . . If the impression is prevalent that scientists as a whole have to work under such great restrictions and perhaps great suspicions in the United States, we may lose the next step in this field, which I think would be very dangerous for us."

McCloy made this point with great earnestness; but the Board (except perhaps Dr. Evans) did not react. "I don't want to cut you off at all," said Gordon Gray, cutting him off, "but you were getting back about something of the Nazis during the war." And, in his own report, Gray emphatically rejected McCloy's notion of the relative character of security. National security, said the majority of the Gray Board in solemn language, "in times of peril must be absolute."

Absolute security? Might this not be the most subversive idea of all? Dr. Evans in his dissent demurred: "All people are somewhat of a security risk." George Kennan has elsewhere observed that "absolute security" is an unattainable and self-devouring end—that its frenzied pursuit must incline toward absolute tyranny. The problem of security, as Kennan sees it, is not to seek "a total absence of danger but to balance peril against peril and to find the tolerable degree of each."

Is absolute security possible short of an absolute state? Robert Oppenheimer was doubtless at moments a cocky, irritating, even arrogant man. But surely no arrogance of Oppenheimer equals the arrogance of those who, in the frightening words of the Gray Board, affirm that "it has been demonstrated that the Government can search . . . the soul of an individual whose relationship to his Government is in question."

The government which claims to do this would hardly seem a government for Americans.

Part IV

Politics and Culture

14.
The Highbrow in American Politics
(1953)

Amid the other legacies it bequeathed to the American people, the campaign of 1952 has bequeathed a particular perplexity to the philologists. In September of that year, Mr. Stewart Alsop, the well-known syndicated columnist, was traveling through Connecticut with Governor Stevenson. In order to get a Republican estimate of the local situation, he phoned his brother, Mr. John Alsop of Avon, a prominent younger figure in Connecticut politics. In the course of the conversation, Stewart Alsop pointed out that certain intellectuals, who had backed General Eisenhower up to the convention, were now deserting him. This comment somewhat irritated John Alsop; so, dredging a term up from his subconscious, he dismissed these defections as the "egghead" vote.

John Alsop did not invent the term "egghead"; but no one had ever before applied it to the nation's intellectuals. "I suppose if one were to analyze the term," John Alsop wrote later, "one would say that it is a visual figure of speech, tending to depict a large, oval head, smooth, faceless, unemotional, but a little bit haughty and condescending." It should be emphasized that for the Alsops, graduates of Yale and anti-anti-intellectuals, "egghead" was still an amiable epithet; and it was in this sense that the word made its debut in the language.

On September 26, after a visit to Springfield, Stewart Alsop used the word publicly in a column, applying it both to those intellectuals who were swinging to Governor Stevenson and to the young men who were active in the Stevenson headquarters in Springfield. At this stage, "egghead" had rather an Ivy League connotation—an A.B. degree, button-down collars, tweeds and flannels, perhaps pipes and crew haircuts, with a lively but amateur interest in the political life and a belief that reading books was not necessarily un-American. Governor Stevenson himself was amused by the word and used it while speaking to an egghead audience at the University of Wisconsin. In the next weeks the term caught on with a rapidity which suggested that it filled some precise need in American discourse or perhaps touched some sensitive nerve in the social organism.

Certainly there was rough justice in the application. While Governor Stevenson had no more eggheads about him than Franklin D. Roosevelt used to have, he diluted them less with the professional politicians, the admirals, the old Harvard cronies and the other nonintellectual types who moved in the Roosevelt entourage. Moreover, while Roosevelt had an active and detailed interest in issues of public policy, his reactions to art or literature were perfunctory and conventional. Stevenson, with his literate and well-stocked mind, his urbane and apt allusions and quotations, gave the impression of being a man of far broader and more humane culture.

To the intellectuals of the country, he seemed one of their own; and they responded to him as they had never responded to Roosevelt. Or, at least, so I have been repeatedly told since the campaign; and, when I have wondered whether this was simply the application of the rule that people in love find all their previous affairs tawdry and superficial, I have been told, No—that there was a sense of kinship and sympathy with Stevenson which had never been felt with the more remote, abstract, contrived Roosevelt. As Eudora Welty well stated the Stevenson appeal, "The voice of the passionate intelligence speaks to the whole range of the mind—in politics as well as in poetry." And, as she went on, in a post-election message to Governor Stevenson, "This writer knows of people here and there like herself, previously political ignoramuses (we now feel a fellowship)—well-intentioned ever, but not ever in the sense of being personally involved, concerned deeply by a political campaign until this year. Then, with your appearance on the national scene, we found out how deeply concerned we could be."

Certainly, as the campaign progressed, writers and artists began to discover a wholly unexpected intensity of commitment. Men like Richard Rodgers and Howard Lindsay, who had been for Eisenhower in February, found themselves swept away by the Stevenson movement in October. Others, who had exhausted themselves through the years in a series of political disappointments and felt that they could never respond again, found welling up within new reserves of political emotion and energy. Still others, who had never before strayed from the strict sectarianism of third-party politics, now voted with enthusiasm for a major party candidate.

No doubt, intellectuals being intellectuals, the involvement had unexpected manifestations. One activist of the *Scrutiny* circle proposed after the election that such people as F. R. Leavis, Djuna Barnes, and Cecil Beaton make up a package of their books, appropriately inscribed to the Governor, in order to help relieve in some amiable way the painful tension of defeat. But this very gesture from the aesthetic camp, surely unprecedented in the history of American presidential politics, reveals the special feeling evoked by the Stevenson candidacy among even the most anti-political of the intellectuals.

Writers have been involved in politics enough—perhaps too much—in the recent past. But the Stevenson involvement was qualitatively different from the others—from the sordid liaisons of Popular Front days, for example, or from the hearty propaganda of the Writers' War Board. Those involvements had primarily served political ends. The Stevenson involvement, retaining an innocence, even perhaps a purity, of its own, primarily served humane and artistic ends. The intellectuals desired Stevenson's victory, not to attain public objectives or even to affect public policy, but to affirm an interior sense of admiration and of belief.

This passion of the intellectuals for Stevenson, while not to be a major factor in the outcome, could not escape due notice in the heat of the campaign. The Republicans became considerably irritated by what appeared to be a closing of the literary and academic ranks behind the Democratic candidate. Anti-intellectualism is always epidemic in the business community; and the campaign of Senator McCarthy and his associates, as well, doubtless, as past excesses of the intellectuals themselves, had spread the infection through much of the country. In the last weeks of the campaign, the Republicans made a calculated effort to rouse and exploit this accumulating exasperation.

It was in the course of this effort that the word "egghead" entered a new phase of its evolution. What had started out as an affable and friendly term now began to acquire uglier connotations. Senator McCarthy, while avoiding the word, devoted two nationwide broadcasts to attacks on the Stevenson advisers, a sinister crew of people which included two Pulitzer Prize historians, one of them a former editor of the *Saturday Review of Literature,* as well as a Bollingen Prize poet and former Librarian of Congress. Others seized with relish on the new word itself. "There has come a wonderful new expression," exulted Louis Bromfield, a McCarthy admirer, on October 26, "to define a certain shady element of our American population. Who conceived the expression, I do not know. . . . It seems to have arisen spontaneously from the people themselves."

Mr. Bromfield went on to offer a voluble and excited definition—"a person of intellectual pretensions, often a professor or the protégé of a professor . . . superficial in approach to any problem . . . feminine . . . supercilious . . . surfeited with conceit . . . a doctrinaire supporter of middle-European socialism . . . a self-conscious prig . . . a bleeding heart"—166 hot words pouring out in a confused stream an interesting collection of Mr. Bromfield's own resentments and rancors. If Stevenson were to be elected, he sternly concluded, "the eggheads will come back into power and off again we will go on the scenic railway of muddled economics, Socialism, Communism, crookedness and psychopathic instability."

It was this approach which set the tone for much of the postelection discussion. The returns were hardly in before *Time* Magazine, recounting the tribulations of the Eisenhower crusade, observed that it had survived "the egghead rebellion, the desertion . . . by scores of intellectuals, journalists, Hollywoodians and other opinion makers." From this fact *Time* drew ominous conclusions. "The final victory discloses an alarming fact, long suspected: there is a wide and unhealthy gap between the American intellectuals and the people."

This theory of the gap instantly commended itself to

all those seeking to discipline the intellectuals. It soon received a more comprehensive exposition under formidable religious auspices. In an article late in November in the Protestant weekly the *Christian Century,* the Reverend Dr. Robert A. Fitch, a graduate of Yale, Union Theological Seminary, Columbia, and the Sorbonne, a member of the American Philosophical Association, and currently dean of the Pacific School of Religion, addressed himself to the subject of the "Intelligentsia in Defeat."

For the Reverend Dr. Fitch, the election marked, above all, the long awaited punishment of the American intelligentsia. In Governor Stevenson he saw "the perfect incarnation of the liberal logos." The Democratic candidate, in Dr. Fitch's view, was characterized by his passion for truth; and, while Dr. Fitch made clear that he had nothing against truth, "more vulgar politics might argue that the real objective is not truth but right action; and that, while it should be an ingredient in all right action, truth must mingle with other necessities that determine a course of conduct."

It was no doubt this theory of the limited role of truth in politics which would permit Dr. Fitch to spread his ecclesiastical mantle over Senator McCarthy. The one issue which really concerned the intelligentsia, Dr. Fitch continued, was civil liberties, which, he added disagreeably, was their class issue— much presumably as the wool tariff would be the class issue for the owners of sheep. "With this lofty passion," Dr. Fitch said, in an appropriate vein of sarcasm, "the intelligentsia recognized only one real incarnate devil in the campaign, and - that was Senator McCarthy." But was not Senator McCarthy, Dr. Fitch asked, really justified? It is true that the character of the treason of the intellectuals "was not altogether [sic] of a sort that can be recognized in a court of law." It consisted rather "in the gross of a whole tradition of scholarship and of philosophy which dealt in too cavalier a fashion with the irreducible articles of the American faith," Dr. Fitch said, trailing off in a sputter about "positivism . . . nihilism . . . ethical relativism," Seen this way, Dr. Fitch declared, McCarthy was but "the spokesman for the suspicions of inarticulate people that somehow and somewhere in their country a great betrayal was going on." (One hardly knows how to interpret the news that the Union Theological Seminary has recently engaged Dr. Fitch to take the place of Dr. Reinhold Niebuhr during Dr. Niebuhr's current illness.)

Nor was the theory that Senator McCarthy had become the appointed instrument of divine wrath to chastise the intellectuals confined to such emblems of the Protestant clergy as Dr. Fitch. Rabbi Benjamin Schultz, at a luncheon for the Senator at the Hotel Astor in New York, declared that the great tragedy of our times is the "dichotomy between the people and the so-called intellectuals." But do not despair. "Thank God, the people have arisen to protest through the person of Joseph R. McCarthy." And what was intoned by Protestants and Jews also commanded the assent of Catholics.

What these expressions signaled was a rise to climax of the hatred of the intellectuals which had long been stewing and stirring in various sections of American society. The dominant sentiment of the '20's, our last interlude of business rule, it had been driven underground by the depression and the New Deal to find only sporadic vent through the years in congressional investigations and in the gutter press. Now it burst forth in full violence. By early November the word "egghead" seemed almost to detonate the pent-up ferocity of twenty years of impotence. On November 4 the Republican victory licensed those feelings and, in a sense, established them in power.

The new President, of course, was no particular enemy of the intellectuals. He had himself been a university president, of a sort; and even before his inauguration, he had appointed three other captains of education to key positions in his administration (though, perhaps significantly, no university professors). But other members of his party were less admiring of the life of the mind. A number of Republican senators and congressmen, flushed with political victory, now sought to convert the Democratic defeat into an egghead rout by tracking the intellectual down to his final stronghold, the university.

These men did not underestimate what they described as their courage in thus pressing the hunt. "This will be the most unpopular, the most unpleasant task any one can do," Senator McCarthy bravely explained, "that is, exposing Communists and Communist thinkers—I'd rather use the words 'Communist thinkers' than 'Communists'—in your educational institutions, because the minute you do that all hell breaks loose. From coast to coast you hear the screaming of interference with academic freedom." But, fortified by a series of decorations tardily conferred by the United States Marine Corps, the junior Senator from Wisconsin has announced himself ready to lead the assault—if Congressman Velde and Senator Jenner and the other aspirants for the honor will let him. In any case, the bullies are forming their pack. And, as usual, a few intellectuals who would like to have been bullies are running out in front, snuffling along the ground to uncover the trail, ready to rush back to their new masters, wagging their tails, whenever they find an egghead track. Mr. James Burnham and the *Freeman* (or ex-*Freeman*) set are convenient examples.

Today, as a consequence of the election, the American intellectual finds himself in a situation he has not known for a generation. The *Partisan Review's* symposium in reconciliation, "America and the Intellectuals," celebrated the end, and not the beginning of an epoch. For twenty years, the government of the United States, while often one which the intellectual has found confused or mistaken, has nevertheless been one which has basically understood, respected and protected intellectual purposes. Now business is in power again; and with it will no doubt come the vulgarization which has been the almost invariable consequence of business supremacy. American writers have already been denounced for not providing favorable portraits of businessmen in their novels, as Communist writers are berated for not doing justice to the new Soviet man. And, while no modern equivalent of Bruce Barton's *The Man Nobody Knows* has yet been produced, Harry A. Bullis, chairman of the board of General Mills, a director of the National Conference of Christians and Jews, a Legionnaire, a Republican, and a Methodist, has already written an article entitled "God Is My Senior Partner" (with full immunity from suspicions of blasphemy; think what would happen to an intellectual who wrote an article entitled "God Is My Literary Agent"!).

A position of alienation is, of course, normal and essential for an artist. Indeed, no other position is possible; for no society can ever satisfy all the subtle scruples and needs of the individual sensibility. The artist must be a lonely man. (When Simonov writes, "If you ask me what the Soviet system has done for the writer

I should answer that, first of all, it has erased from his inner self all sense of loneliness, and given him the feeling of complete and absolute 'belonging' to society,'' he gives the whole Soviet show away.) But there is a difference between the normal alienation of any artist in society and the organized official hostility which puts the artist on the run and obsesses him with the necessities of self-defense.

In the '20's, this situation was manageable. The social pressures were heavy, but escape was easy. Satire was an available weapon: Mencken, Lewis, Lardner, and their imitators could cope with society by ridiculing it. Or, if this form of intellectual escape was unsatisfying, then physical escape was easily possible, and a literary generation fled to Paris. And, in any case, there was an abundance of outlets; it was possible for persons with modest sums of money to start new publications and, in one way or another, gain circulation for even the most vapid and eccentric writing.

In the generation since, the horizon has closed in. The cold war and the Soviet threat have necessarily narrowed alternatives; and the indulgence of freedom must inevitably take second place in the real world to the harsh requirements of survival. And the intellectuals themselves, in many cases, have forfeited sympathy or respect because of the arrogance and egotism they displayed when they were riding high—an arrogance too often accompanied by political imbecility, if not by political guilt. Yet the demagogues of the right, trying to pluck power out of anxiety, have narrowed the alternatives far beyond the point of necessity. And, though the intellectuals may have deserved much in the way of correction, they did not deserve as the instrument of chastisement a blatant liar whose own awakening to the Communist threat was delayed until February 9, 1950—a date by which time all but the most obtuse intellectuals had long since tumbled to the facts of life.

The new atmosphere is no longer conducive to the old escapes. To satirize the American businessman today, for example, is to invite suspicion and attack; what was once satiric is now (in the business community, at least) subversive. When Robert E. Sherwood presented the not unfamiliar dramatic type of the hard-fisted local banker in *The Best Years of Our Lives,* he was attacked as providing propaganda for the Communists. James Thurber said last summer that it would no longer be possible to write a satiric comedy so "free and exuberant" as *The Male Animal.* And he is clearly right: the businessman who was the comic trustee in 1940 would be the university president today, and hardly a fit subject for humor. The most brilliant and daring of our comic strip cartoonists, Al Capp, finally had to marry off his two leading characters, because, no longer feeling himself free to "kid hell out of everything," he felt he had no choice but to convert knockabout satire into a fairy story. "For the first 14 years [of the strip] I reveled in the freedom to laugh at America. But now America has changed. The humorist feels the change more, perhaps, than anyone. Now there are things about America we can't kid."

And the range of outlets has narrowed drastically too. The cost of entry into the magazine field is almost prohibitive today. For a generation freedom of expression in America has survived in part because one group in the country controlled the government and another group controlled the mass media. Now the same group controls both, and we are confronted with the possibility of a communications monopoly unprecedented in our history. The effect of this potential monopoly will be grave enough in the political field, where the Democratic party and the liberals will be badly handicapped in their attempts to combat the right-wing Republican effort to smear the Democratic party as incurably devoted to disloyalty and treason; but its effect there may well be less grave than its effect on the general level of culture. The mass communications, as Gilbert Seldes has pointed out, are dominated by the concept of the "great audience." By concentrating on the lowest common denominator, they may in time create the very uniform unleavened mass which is already the postulate of their activities.

The intellectual in 1953 thus faces an incalculable but depressing combination of factors. He is dismissed as an "egghead," governed by a party which has little use for him and little understanding of what he is about. He is the natural and obvious scapegoat for the country's new rulers; he invited the Japanese attack on Pearl Harbor, lost China, invented the graduated income tax, and piled up the national debt; anti-intellectualism has long been the anti-Semitism of the businessman. Escape into satire only worsens the intellectual's position in the United States. Escape into foreign lands only deepens his predicament and his melancholy: after all, Jean-Paul Sartre is both far more irritating and a far greater enemy of freedom than Herbert Brownell. Publication, in general, will be far more difficult than ever before; the problem of the mass media ever more pressing; the attack on cultural diversity ever more methodical and effective.

This is far deeper than a political problem; but, like all problems in this age, it has a political cast. The intellectual should take heed from the "egghead" episode. He is on the run today in American society; and he cannot hope to escape by silence or by retiring to cultivate his garden or—certainly—by sidling up to his pursuer and offering his services. In a sense, the Reverend Dr. Fitch was right; civil liberties are the class issue of the intelligentsia; and nothing has been more pathetic than the scurrying to cover of certain intellectuals when called upon to stand up for the freedom of expression. And this freedom too, in the long run, affords the only basis on which the problems of mass culture can be answered. Tocqueville commented a century ago that many people considered equality of conditions as one evil and political freedom as a second. "When they are obliged to yield to the former, they strive at least to escape from the latter. But I contend, that in order to combat the evils which equality may produce, there is only one effectual remedy—namely, political freedom."

Not all intellectuals may be willing or able to understand the complexities of the dollar gap or the price-support program. But they should at least, like the trade unionist or the cattleman or the oil magnate, be willing to understand their own class interests. Most of them rightly recognized that one candidate in the 1952 campaign spoke with wisdom and courage and understanding on the issue of the free mind, while the other showed only a blank indifference. Defeat does not foreclose the issue: the blankness of Republican victory may yet be inscribed by Senator McCarthy—or, perhaps, by James B. Conant. The fight continues and must enlist our best efforts.

Much as the highbrow in his present mood may dislike politics, he cannot escape or reject it. We hear that the new intellectual is entering into a phase of contemplation and withdrawal. But, if he decides to flee it all and become a Yogi, he will have no one else to blame if Senator McCarthy becomes the Commissar.

15.

Time and the Intellectuals
(1956)

For some years *Time,* with its other heavy responsibilities, has been keeping a sharp eye on the American intellectual. This preoccupation seems to have begun in 1952. Shortly after the election *Time* declared that the Eisenhower victory confirmed the suspicion its editors had harbored so long: that there was "a wide and unhealthy gap" between the American intellectuals and the people. The existence of this gap evidently preyed on the minds of *Time*'s editors. The next year, on *Time*'s 30th anniversary, they consequently chose, among all possible subjects, to reflect on "intellectuality, its condition and prospects, because this subject cuts across all the others."

At this point, *Time*'s analysis was illuminated by a recently published book, Eric Voegelin's *The New Science of Politics.* Inspired by Voegelin's account of Joachim of Flora and his influence, *Time* boldly traced the contemporary world crisis to a conspiracy of Gnostics, plotting darkly through modern history and reaching the climax of their subversive activities in the 20th century. "Gnosticism," wrote *Time,* "seeping down from the intellectuals to politicians to the people, had become a mass movement affecting the basis of Western life. . . . Gnosticism is the source of 20th Century intellectual confusion, the 'pattern' in the chaos." The essential Gnostic heresy was to believe that salvation could be achieved on earth. As for Gnostic operators, they were positivists, yet believers in verbal magic; they were foes of "the idea of an objective, unchanging moral law," yet unrepentant moralists; some posed as Christians, but what *Time* called "gnostic activists" became openly anti-Christian. Still, if the Gnostic wore a thousand faces, all concealed the treacherous smile of the intellectual, who therefore became the cause of our current troubles.

After this fruitful beginning, the Gnostic conspiracy mysteriously disappeared from the pages of *Time*. In 1954, *Time* took a somewhat more benevolent attitude toward the intellectual. In a cover story on David Riesman, it said that intellectuals had "understandably" failed to keep up with the evolution of American society. Riesman seemed to *Time* among those intellectuals at last beginning to "update the future." But Riesman was too ambiguous a figure for a clear-cut *Time* conclusion, and, after an excellent summary of his views, the story warily refrained from judgment.

The intellectual report of 1955—a cover story on Herman Wouk—was less restrained. Wouk, after all, had written in *The Caine Mutiny* the great anti-intellectual novel, dedicated to the thesis that Keefer, the rootless critic, was a far greater threat to society than Queeg, the mad and cowardly embodiment of authority. "His chief significance," *Time* said of Wouk, "is that he spearheads a mutiny against the literary stereotypes of rebellion. . . . He is one of the few living US writers who carries no chip on his shoulder [except perhaps when intellectuals are concerned] and who gives the US straight A's in his fictional report cards." In the "clear-eyed" and wholesome novels of Wouk, *Time* found a heartening reaction against three lamentable decades "dominated by skeptical criticism, sexual emancipation, social protest and psychoanalytic sermonizing."

A few weeks ago, in its issue of June 11, 1956, *Time* delivered this year's communiqué on the intellectuals. Whether because of the Wouk Mutiny, or for other reasons, it found the situation much improved. The intellectual, so long the victim of self-pity, has finally begun to grow up. "In 1956, it would seem, the intellectual has ceased weeping. . . . Many have come at last to realize that they are true and proud participants in the American Dream." The hero of this verdict, evidently the Herman Wouk of the nonfiction set, turned out to be Jacques Barzun of Columbia University.

What *Time* particularly admired in Jacques Barzun was his forthright castigation of those intellectuals who continue to grumble about America. The article began with an approving quotation from Barzun on the subject of crape-hangers: "They forget that the true creator's role, even in its bitterest attack, is to make us understand or endure life better. Our intellectuals do neither when they entice us to more self-contempt." In Barzun's supposed contention that adjustment should be the highest intellectual aspiration, *Time* saw the arrival of the "Man of Affirmation," belatedly and mercifully replacing the bad old "Man of Protest." With Barzun, the "wide and unhealthy gap" of 1952 is apparently being closed.

It is, of course, unfair to acquiesce in *Time*'s decision to pin this solemn responsibility on Jacques Barzun, who is an historian of distinction, an admirable teacher, and a gentleman of urbanity and charm. It is an old principle of common law that no man can be held accountable for what a *Time* cover story may choose to say about him. Indeed, *Time,* in clasping Barzun to its bosom, may have got more than it bargained for. The editor responsible for the Barzun cover must have neglected to clear with the moral philosophy desk, because Barzun, a shameless relativist, pragmatist, pluralist, romanticist, and radical empiricist, is precisely the sort of man whom *Time,* in other moods, has condemned as a skeptic about moral absolutes, an enemy of natural law, and a subverter of the young. Professor Barzun may even be a secret Gnostic.

But, leaving Barzun aside, one may still find it worthwhile to examine the image of the American intellectual as finally approved by *Time.* The intellectual should be primarily a Yea-sayer; and, in *Time'*s view, he must especially say Yea to America, which means Mr. Luce's America. This distinction is important, for those who say Yea to Emerson's America or Jackson's America or Lincoln's America might conceivably wish to say Nay to *Time'*s America. I would not venture here to define *Time'*s America with precision. The official Time, Inc., version of the American Dream, in which intellectuals are to become such true and proud participants, was presumably rendered by Russell Davenport and the Editors of *Fortune* in *U. S. A.: The Permanent Revolution.* Certainly from this and other sources, the ambience of Mr. Luce's view becomes plain enough. *Time'*s demand is essentially for benign approval of an America in which the business community wields the political power (as it was a demand for waspish Nay-saying to an America in which the non-business sections of society held, or shared, this power).

Those intellectuals who have faith in *Time'*s America and are ready to denounce their colleagues for criticizing it are, in *Time'*s valuable phrase, Men of Affirmation. The Men of Protest are a disgruntled collection of snobs, grouches and expatriates, grumbling and griping in the outer darkness. The tableau is vivid enough. Yet one wonders how fair it is to assume that the Men of Protest are un-American; or, to put it differently, to assume that those who question *Time*'s America may not be loyal to Americas of their own. Most Men of Protest protest in the name of something they affirm; and what they protest in the name of may very likely be their own versions of the American Dream. Their reading of this Dream may sometimes be even more pure and exacting than that of *Time,* which explains possibly why their stance inclines to be one of criticism rather than of complaisance. It is surely ungenerous to suppose that therefore they believe in America the less. As one of the Men of Protest of the last generation (now, alas, transformed into a Man of Affirmation) once movingly put it, "America our nation has been beaten by strangers who have turned our language inside out who have taken the clean words our fathers spoke and made them slimy and foul." In writing this, was Dos Passos rejecting America? Or was he not rejecting those who, as he thought, were betraying America?

The question is: Is the American Dream something we have already achieved? Or is it something different from and better than what we have? If the former, the intellectual should be a Man of Affirmation; if the latter, he might well be a Man of Protest. But the suggestion that we have already achieved the American Dream—that therefore the Queegs are by definition better than the Keefers—sounds very much like the Gnostic heresy. One wonders whether *Time* itself can have been infiltrated by the conspiracy.

Actually the categories of Affirmation and Protest are hardly so clear-cut as *Time* suggests. Thus *Time* rates Jefferson, Franklin, and Emerson as Men of Affirmation and yearns for their equivalents today. But one hardly feels that, if *Time* had been going in the early 19th century, it would have applauded these prophets of revolution, deism, and pantheism. It would more likely have found them as wicked in their intellectual influence as it finds Oliver Wendell Holmes today. (And fifty years from now, *Time* may well be using Holmes to beat the young intellectuals of the 21st century.) If the radicalism of one age is the conservatism of the next, then plainly one generation's Man of Protest is likely to be the next generation's Man of Affirmation. It is perhaps revealing that *Time* cherishes Men of Protest only when they are dead.

The basic fallacy in the *Time* article is the attempt to assign a single role to the intellectual. Mr. Luce himself has changed from a Man of Protest to a Man of Affirmation within the memory of living men; others now deplored by Mr. Luce passed him on the same road traveling in the opposite direction. But do they not all have their value—Mr. Luce as a knocker in the '30's and as a booster in the '50's? Others as Yea-sayers then and Nay-sayers now? The contribution of the intellectuals surely comes as they stir a ferment along an entire front, not as they reinforce single salients, whether of assent or of rebellion. To demand that all intellectuals in 1956 be Herman Wouks or Jacques Barzuns (by which I mean here the *Time*-images of Wouk and Barzun) and to chastise those who decline to give Mr. Luce's America "straight A's" in their report cards is to miscontrue the pluralism which is the essence of free society. It is particularly to misconstrue the historical role of the American intellectuals.

Intellectuals have played many honorable roles in American history. They have also played some sorry roles; and no intellectual, resenting current attacks, can overlook the extent to which sentimentality, stupidity and even corruption in the intellectual community have given the anti-intellectuals their most effective ammunition. But on the honorable side one can distinguish the Intellectual as Prophet, the setter of goals, the peerer beyond distant horizons, the interpreter of the future to the present—Emerson, say, or Dewey. Then there is the Intellectual as Analyst, the diagnostician of man and society in their concrete and secular preoccupations, the astute commentator and thoughtful critic—Sumner or Veblen. Then there is the Intellectual as Activist, the participant in events, the man who feels that the ultimate responsibility in having ideas lies in applying them to actuality—from Jefferson and Hamilton to the Kennans, Oppenheimers, and Frankfurters of today. And there is the Intellectual as Gadfly, buzzing in everybody's ear, harassing the comfortable and stinging the complacent, the chronic critic and perpetual irritant—in short, Mencken.

We need all these varieties of intellectuals today; and we impoverish ourselves when we try to shame any into silence. If Mr. Luce looks out on contemporary American society and really thinks all beyond criticism (except the critics), let him freely say so. But if Mr. George Kennan can think of few countries in the world "where the artist, the writer, the composer or the thinker is held in such general low esteem as he is here in our country," that does not necessarily make him morally inferior to Mr. Herman Wouk, or less an American patriot.

Indeed, I have the personal conviction that, of the varieties of intellectuals, the sort America most needs at this moment is precisely the opposite of *Time*'s Man of Affirmation. What we need now, I suggest, is the Intellectual as Gadfly. The condition of our society is surely nearer to complacency than to skepticism, to self-righteousness than to self-doubt. We have been told too long that there are things beyond criticism and that the proper moral posture is one of reverence. What we require now is a return to a more careless and free-swinging American attitude—the attitude of the skeptical, irreverent, unimpressed man of the frontier, for whom nothing was sacred. What would Mark Twain make of our current accumulation of pieties? One begins to feel that in the cloying atmosphere of 1956 any assertion of individuality, no matter how crude or vulgar, tends to be liberating; in this mood, I begin to detect a growing mellowness in myself even about Westbrook Pegler. No matter how offensive he generally is, Pegler speaks for himself, and, if he is loud, he is also, occasionally, funny. We need more people who don't give a damn and can awaken responses in us.

In a time when a society is threatened by sharp internal conflict, there is a powerful case for the unifying voice and the healing personality. But in a time when society is threatened by homogenization, there is a powerful case for the grouch and the grumbler, the sourpuss and the curmudgeon, the nonconstructive critic, the voice of dissent and the voice of protest. I have a feeling that the existence of dissent is almost becoming more important than its character, so that the Peglers and any writers of comparable individuality and vitality on the far left (I regret that none come to mind) may have for the moment a positive value, in spite of the nonsense they disseminate.

If this is so, then among recent acts of piety toward the American intellectual, it may seem in time that Henry R. Luce has done far less by embalming Jacques Barzun on a *Time* cover than Miss Marilyn Monroe did by announcing her engagement to Arthur Miller the day after he risked a contempt citation before the House Un-American Activities Committee.

16.
The Crisis of American Masculinity
(1958)

What has happened to the American male? For a long time, he seemed utterly confident in his manhood, sure of his masculine role in society, easy and definite in his sense of sexual identity. The frontiersmen of James Fenimore Cooper, for example, never had any concern about masculinity; they were men, and it did not occur to them to think twice about it. Even well into the 20th century, the heroes of Dreiser, of Fitzgerald, of Hemingway remain men. But one begins to detect a new theme emerging in some of these authors, especially in Hemingway: the theme of the male hero increasingly preoccupied with proving his virility to himself. And by mid-century, the male role had plainly lost its rugged clarity of outline. Today men are more and more conscious of maleness not as a fact but as a problem. The ways by which American men affirm their masculinity are uncertain and obscure. There are multiplying signs, indeed, that something has gone badly wrong with the American male's conception of himself.

On the most superficial level, the roles of male and female are increasingly merged in the American household. The American man is found as never before as a substitute for wife and mother—changing diapers, washing dishes, cooking meals, and performing a whole series of what once were considered female duties. The American woman meanwhile takes over more and more of the big decisions, controlling them indirectly when she cannot do so directly. Outside the home, one sees a similar blurring of function. While men design dresses and brew up cosmetics, women become doctors, lawyers, bank cashiers, and executives. "Women now fill many 'masculine' roles," writes the psychologist Dr. Bruno Bettelheim, "and expect their husbands to assume many of the tasks once reserved for their own sex." Women seem an expanding, aggressive force, seizing new domains like a conquering army, while men, more and more on the defensive, are hardly able to hold their own and gratefully accept assignments from their new rulers. A recent book bears the stark and melancholy title *The Decline of the American Male*.

Some of this evidence, it should be quickly said, has been pushed too far. The willingness of a man to help his wife around the house may as well be evidence of confidence in masculinity as the opposite; such a man obviously does not have to cling to masculine symbols in order to keep demonstrating his maleness to himself. But there is more impressive evidence than the helpful husband that this is an age of sexual ambiguity. It appears no accident, for example, that the changing of sex—the Christine Jorgensen phenomenon—so fascinates our newspaper editors and readers; or that homosexuality, that incarnation of sexual ambiguity, should be enjoying a cultural boom new in our history. Such developments surely express a deeper tension about the problem of sexual identity.

Consider the theater, that faithful mirror of a society's preoccupations. There have been, of course, popular overt inquiries into sexual ambiguities, like *Compulsion* or *Tea and Sympathy*. But in a sense these plays prove the case too easily. Let us take rather two uncommonly successful plays by the most discussed young playwrights of the United States and Great Britain—Tennessee Williams' *Cat on a Hot Tin Roof* and John Osborne's *Look Back in Anger*. Both deal with the young male in a singular state of confusion and desperation. In *Cat on a Hot Tin Roof*, Brick Pollitt, the professional football player, refuses to sleep with his wife because of guilty memories of his relations with a dead teammate. In *Look Back in Anger*, Jimmy Porter, the embittered young intellectual who can sustain a relationship with his wife only by pretending they are furry animals together, explodes with hatred of women and finds his moments of happiness roughhousing around the stage with a male pal.

Brick Pollitt and Jimmy Porter are all too characteristic modern heroes. They are, in a sense, castrated; one is stymied by fear of homosexuality, the other is an unconscious homosexual. Neither is capable of dealing with the woman in his life: Brick surrenders to a strong woman, Jimmy destroys a weak one. Both reject the normal female desire for full and reciprocal love as an unconscionable demand and an intolerable burden. Now not many American males have been reduced to quite the Pollitt-Porter condition. Still the intentness with which audiences have watched these plays suggests that exposed nerves are being plucked—that the Pollitt-Porter dilemma expresses in vivid and heightened form something that many spectators themselves feel or fear.

Or consider the movies. In some ways, the most brilliant and influential American film since the war is *High Noon*. That remarkable movie, which invested the Western with the classic economy of myth, can be viewed in several ways: as an existentialist drama, for example, or as a parable of McCarthyism. It can also be viewed as a mordant comment on the effort of the

American woman to emasculate the American man. The sheriff plainly did not suffer from Brick Pollitt's disease. But a large part of the story dealt with the attempt of his girl to persuade him not to use force—to deny him the use of his pistol. The pistol is an obvious masculine symbol, and, in the end, it was the girl herself, in the modern American manner, who used the pistol and killed the villain. (In this connection, one can pause and note why the Gary Coopers, Cary Grants, Clark Gables, and Spencer Tracys continue to play romantic leads opposite girls young enough to be their daughters; it is obviously because so few of the younger male stars can project a convincing sense of masculinity.)

Psychoanalysis backs up the theater and the movies in emphasizing the obsession of the American male with his manhood. "Every psychoanalyst knows," writes one of them, "how many emotional difficulties are due to those fears and insecurities of neurotic men who are unconsciously doubting their masculinity." "In our civilization," Dr. Theodor Reik says, "men are afraid that they will not be men enough." Reik adds significantly: "And women are afraid that they might be considered only women." Why is it that women worry, not over whether they can fill the feminine role, but whether filling that role is enough, while men worry whether they can fill the masculine role at all? How to account for this rising tide of male anxiety? What has unmanned the American man?

There is currently a fashionable answer to this question. Male anxiety, many observers have declared, is simply the result of female aggression: what has unmanned the American man is the American woman. The present male confusion and desperation, it is contended, are the inevitable consequence of the threatened feminization of American society. The victory of women is the culmination of a long process of masculine retreat, beginning when Puritanism made men feel guilty about sex and the frontier gave women the added value of scarcity. Fleeing from the reality of femininity, the American man, while denying the American woman juridical equality, transformed her into an ideal of remote and transcendent purity with overriding authority over the family, the home, the school, and culture. This habit of obeisance left the male psychologically disarmed and vulnerable when the goddess stepped off the pedestal and demanded in addition equal economic, political, and legal rights. In the last part of the 19th century, women won their battle for equality. They gained the right of entry into one occupation after another previously reserved for males. Today they hold the key positions of personal power in our society and use this power relentlessly to consolidate their mastery. As mothers, they undermine masculinity through the use of love as a technique of reward and punishment. As teachers, they prepare male children for their role of submission in an increasingly feminine world. As wives, they complete the work of subjugation. Their strategy of conquest is deliberately to emasculate men—to turn them into Brick Pollitts and Jimmy Porters.

Or so a standard indictment runs; and no doubt there is something in it. American women have unquestionably gained through the years a place in our society which American men have not been psychologically prepared to accept. Whether because of Puritanism or the frontier, there has been something immature in the traditional American male attitude toward women—a sense of alarm at times amounting to panic. Almost none of the classic American novels, for example, presents the theme of mature and passionate love. Our 19th-century novelists saw women either as unassailable virgins or abandoned temptresses—never simply as women. One looks in vain through *Moby Dick* and *The Adventures of Huckleberry Finn,* through Cooper and Poe and Whitman, for an adult portrayal of relations between men and women. "Where," Leslie Fiedler has asked, "is the American *Madame Bovary, Anna Karenina, Wuthering Heights,* or *Vanity Fair?*"

Yet the implication of the argument that the American man has been unmanned by the emancipation of the American woman is that the American man was incapable of growing up. For the 19th-century sense of masculinity was based on the psychological idealization and the legal subjection of women; masculinity so spuriously derived could never—and should never—have endured. The male had to learn to live at some point with the free and equal female. Current attempts to blame "the decline of the American male" on the aggressiveness of the American female amount to a confession that, under conditions of free competition, the female was bound to win. Simple observation refutes this supposition. In a world of equal rights, some women rise; so too do some men; and no pat generalization is possible about the sexual future of society. Women have gained power in certain ways; in others, they have made little progress. It is safe to predict, for example, that we will have a Roman Catholic, perhaps even a Jew, for President before we have a woman. Those amiable prophets of an impending American matriarchy (all men, by the way) are too pessimistic.

Something more fundamental is involved in the unmanning of American men than simply the onward rush of American women. Why is the American man so unsure today about his masculine identity? The basic answer to this is plainly because he is so unsure about his identity in general. Nothing is harder in the whole human condition than to achieve a full sense of identity—than to know who you are, where you are going, and what you mean to live and die for. From the most primitive myths to the most contemporary novels—from Oedipus making the horrified discovery that he had married his mother, to Leopold Bloom and Stephen Dedalus searching their souls in Joyce's Dublin and the haunted characters of Kafka trying to make desperate sense out of an incomprehensible universe—the search for identity has been the most compelling human problem. That search has always been ridden with trouble and terror. And it can be plausibly argued that the conditions of modern life make the quest for identity more difficult than it has ever been before.

The pre-democratic world was characteristically a world of status in which people were provided with ready-made identities. But modern Western society—free, equalitarian, democratic—has swept away all the old niches in which people for so many centuries found safe refuge. Only a few people at any time in human history have enjoyed the challenge of "making" themselves; most have fled from the unendurable burden of freedom into the womblike security of the group. The new age of social mobility may be fine for those strong enough to discover and develop their own roles. But for the timid and the frightened, who constitute the majority in any age, the great vacant spaces of equalitarian society can become a nightmare filled with nameless horrors. Thus mass democracy, in the very act of offering the individual new freedom and opportunity, offers new moral authority to the group and thereby sets off a new assault on individual identity. Over a century ago Alexis de Tocqueville, the perceptive Frenchman who ruminated on the contradictions of equality as he toured the United States in the 1830's, pointed to the "tyranny of the majority" as a central problem of democracy. John Stuart Mill, lamenting the decline of individualism in Great Britain, wrote: "That so few now dare to be eccentric marks the chief danger of the time." How much greater that danger seems a century later!

For our own time has aggravated the assault on identity by adding economic and technological pressures to the political and social pressures of the 19th century. Modern science has brought about the growing centralization of the economy. We work and think and live and even dream in larger and larger units. William H. Whyte, Jr., has described the rise of "the organization man," working by day in immense business concerns, sleeping by night in immense suburban developments, deriving his fantasy life from mass-produced entertainments, spending his existence not as an individual but as a member of a group and coming in the end to feel guilty and lost when he deviates from his fellows. Adjustment rather than achievement becomes the social ideal. Men no longer fulfill an inner sense of what they *must* be; indeed, with the cult of the group, that inner sense itself begins to evaporate. Identity consists not of self-realization but of smooth absorption into the group. Nor is this just a matter of passive acquiescence. The group is aggressive, imperialistic, even vengeful, forever developing new weapons with which to overwhelm and crush the recalcitrant individual. Not content with disciplining the conscious mind, the group today is even experimenting with means of violating the subconscious. The subliminal invasion represents the climax of the assault on individual identity.

It may seem a long way from the loss of the sense of self to the question of masculinity. But if people do not know *who* they are, it is hardly surprising that they are no longer sure what sex they are. Nigel Dennis' exuberant novel *Cards of Identity* consists of a series of brilliant variations on the quest for identity in contemporary life. It reaches one of its climaxes in the tale of a person who was brought up by enlightened parents to believe that there was no such thing as pure male or female—everyone had elements of both—and who accepted this proposition so rigorously that he (she) could not decide what his (her) own sex was. "In what identity do you intend to face the future?" someone asks. "It seems that nowadays," comes the plaintive reply, "one must choose between being a woman who behaves like a man, and a man who behaves like a woman. In short, I must choose to be one in order to behave like the other." If most of us have not yet quite reached that condition of sexual chaos, yet the loss of a sense of identity is obviously a fundamental step in the decay of masculinity. And the gratification with which some American males contemplate their own decline should not obscure the fact that women, for all their recent legal and economic triumphs, are suffering from a loss of identity too. It is not accidental that the authors of one recent book described modern woman as the "lost sex."

If this is true, then the key to the recovery of masculinity does not lie in any wistful hope of humiliating the aggressive female and restoring the old masculine supremacy. Masculine supremacy, like white supremacy, was the neurosis of an immature society. It is good for men as well as for women that women have been set free. In any case, the process is irreversible; that particular genie can never be put back into the bottle. The key to the recovery of masculinity lies rather in the problem of identity. When a person begins to find out *who* he is, he is likely to find out rather soon what sex he is.

For men to become men again, in short, their first task is to recover a sense of individual spontaneity. And to do this a man must visualize himself as an individual apart from the group, whatever it is, which defines his values and commands his loyalty. There is no reason to suppose that the group is always wrong: to oppose the group automatically is nearly as conformist as to surrender to it automatically. But there is every necessity to recognize that the group is one thing and the individual—oneself—is another. One of the most sinister of present-day doctrines is that of *togetherness*. The recovery of identity means, first of all, a new belief in apartness. It means a determination to resist the overpowering conspiracy of blandness, which seeks to conceal all tension and conflict in American life under a blanket of locker-room affability. And the rebirth of spontaneity depends, at bottom, on changes of attitude *within* people—changes which can perhaps be described, without undue solemnity, as moral changes. These changes will no doubt come about in as many ways as there are individuals involved. But there are some general suggestions that can be made about the techniques of liberation. I should like to mention three such techniques: satire, art, and politics.

Satire means essentially the belief that nothing is sacred—that there is no person or institution or idea which cannot but benefit from the exposure of comedy. Our nation in the past has reveled in satire; it is, after all, the nation of Abraham Lincoln, of Mark Twain, of Finley Peter Dunne, of H. L. Mencken, of Ring Lardner. Indeed, the whole spirit of democracy is that of satire; as Montaigne succinctly summed up the democratic faith: "Sit he on never so high a throne, a man still sits on his own bottom." Yet today American society can only be described as a pompous society, at least in its official manifestations. Early in 1958 Mort Sahl, the night-club comedian, made headlines in New York because he dared make a joke about J. Edgar Hoover! It was not an especially good joke, but the fact that he made it at all was an encouraging sign. One begins to feel that the American people can only stand so much reverence—that in the end our native skepticism will break through, sweep aside the stuffed shirts and the stuffed heads and insist that platitudes are platitudinous and the great are made, among other things, to be laughed at. Irony is good for our rulers; and it is even better for ourselves because it is a means of dissolving the pomposity of society and giving the individual a chance to emerge.

If irony is one source of spontaneity, art is another. Very little can so refresh our vision and develop our vision and develop our values as the liberating experience of art. The mass media have cast a spell on us: the popular addiction to prefabricated emotional clichés threatens to erode our capacity for fresh and direct aesthetic experience. Individual identity vanishes in the welter of machine-made reactions. But thoughtful exposure to music, to painting, to poetry, to the beauties of nature, can do much to restore the inwardness, and thereby the identity, of man. There is thus great hope in the immense cultural underground of our age—the paper-bound books, the long-playing records, the drama societies, the art festivals, the new interest in painting and sculpture. All this represents a disdain for existing values and goals, a reaching out for something

more exacting and more personal, an intensified quest-
ing for identity.

And politics in a true sense can be a means of liberation—not the banal politics of rhetoric and self-congratulation, which aims at burying all real issues under
a mass of piety and platitude; but the politics of responsibility, which tries to define the real issues and
present them to the people for decision. Our national
politics have become boring in recent years because
our leaders have offered neither candid and clear-cut
formulations of the problems nor the facts necessary
for intelligent choice. A virile political life will be definite and hard-hitting, respecting debate and dissent,
seeking clarity and decision.

As the American male develops himself by developing his comic sense, his aesthetic sense, and his moral
and political sense, the lineaments of personality will
at last begin to emerge. The achievement of identity,
the conquest of a sense of self—these will do infinitely
more to restore American masculinity than all the hor-
mones in the test tubes of our scientists. "Whoso
would be a *man*" said Emerson, "must be a nonconformist"; and, if it is the present writer who adds the
italics, nonetheless one feels that no injustice is done to
Emerson's intention. How can masculinity, femininity,
or anything else survive in a homogenized society,
which seeks steadily and benignly to eradicate all differences between the individuals who compose it? If
we want to have *men* again in our theaters and our
films and our novels—not to speak of in our class-
rooms, our business offices, and our homes—we must
first have a society which encourages each of its members to have a distinct identity.

17.

Look Back in Amazement
(1957)

The success—first in London, now in New York—of John Osborne's *Look Back in Anger* is a phenomenon which deserves more extended analysis than it has been getting.

Look Back in Anger is about a bright young man from the working class named Jimmy Porter. As a beneficiary of the welfare state, Jimmy received his education at a provincial university. Thereafter he tried his hand variously at journalism, at advertising, at selling vacuum cleaners. At the age of twenty-five, he is now the proprietor of a sweet stand in which he was installed by the mother of his closest friend, another young working-class intellectual named Hugh Tanner. At some point along the way, he has met Alison Redfern, a pretty upper-middle-class girl. She is attracted by his fierceness; he by the howl of outrage that went up from her family when she showed interest in him. They marry, breaking Jimmy's friendship with Hugh Tanner. As the play opens, they have been married for four years. By now, Jimmy has acquired a new male pal, Cliff Lewis. The Porter marriage has degenerated into cold war, with Cliff serving somewhat despairingly as a stabilizing force between Jimmy and Alison.

The first act catches the three on a dreary Midland Sunday afternoon, Jimmy and Cliff deep in the Sunday papers, Alison ironing. Bored and restless, Jimmy fills the empty stretches of the day with aimless, compulsive abuse of Alison for her obnoxious social origins.

In the second act Alison produces Helena, an upper-middle-class girl friend; is told with contempt by Jimmy that his highest hope is "to stand up in your tears, and splash about in them, and sing. I want to be there when you grovel"; and returns to her family to have a baby. The third act opens with the same tableau as the first, Sunday papers and all, only with Helena at the ironing board instead of Alison. It ends with the return of Alison, haggard and broken from the loss of her baby, and her groveling capitulation to Jimmy.

To get the idea, it is only necessary to see the first act, which is written with considerable vividness and passion. Mr. Osborne, alas, uses up all his ideas and themes in that act: thereafter he has nothing to offer in dramatic invention or character development—nothing except more of the same, until the hysteria, self-pity, and sadism of Jimmy Porter become boring in the extreme. Or, at least, boring to this observer; one is compelled to admit that audiences, both in London and in New York, sit hypnotized by the spectacle of Jimmy Porter. Jimmy's anger obviously strikes an exposed nerve. And this leads to the mystery of the play: why is Jimmy Porter angry?

The usual answer is that Jimmy Porter is angry because he is a man of talent denied by his society a decent job to do or even a decent cause to believe in. As T. C. Worsley put it in the *New Statesman and Nation*, "Jimmy Porter, the protagonist, is a brilliant young intellectual adrift." The welfare state first educated him and then betrayed him by failing to provide him the opportunities to which his genius entitles him. It offers him not a reason to live nor even a reason to die. "There aren't any good, brave causes left," Jimmy cries. "If the big bang does come, and we all get killed off, it won't be in aid of the old-fashioned grand design. . . . [It will be] about as pointless and inglorious as stepping in front of a bus." So, condemned to keeping a sweet-shop, he naturally and rather heroically rails against the mediocrity of the age and against the unfairness of the class system, both conveniently embodied for him in the person of his wife.

There are several troubles with this explanation. For one thing, Jimmy is obviously not a brilliant young intellectual. He is an egomaniac bore, lazy and self-pitying, with a certain gift of gab—the familiar type of demi-intellectual, who, instead of doing something, spends his time and energy bewailing the unjust world which prevents him from doing things. It is no surprise that he failed in journalism or even in selling vacuum cleaners (though one wonders a little why he did not succeed in advertising). Far from being a man of talent held down by a rigid caste society, Jimmy is a man of negligible talent in an England where class lines have never counted for less. It is revealing to contrast Mr. Osborne's passion for his hero with the attitude toward their characters of, say, H. G. Wells or Arnold Bennett, who emerged from equally unpromising social origins at a time when the class system in England was infinitely tougher to buck. It is impossible to imagine Wells or Bennett reveling in the kind of self-pity which Mr. Osborne mistakes for splendid defiance. For them, Jimmy Porter would have been not a major tragic hero but minor comic relief.

Jimmy Porter may think he is a genius unappreciated by obtuse society; but he is wrong; British society has never been more eager to take up the Jimmy Porters (as the success of the play shows). Social injustice is his rationalization; it is not the real source of his anger. I believe that one must therefore dismiss the sociological explanation. This brings us to a psychological explanation developed by Mr. Geoffrey Gorer, and, I think, a little closer to the mark. According to Mr. Gorer, Jimmy is angry because of hypergamy, a term used by anthropologists to designate the phenomenon of marrying into a superior caste. Overeducated by the welfare state, the Jimmy Porters are split personalities: during their childhood, when the main lines of their character are formed, they grow up in working-class families; during their adolescence and youth, they superimpose upper-class interests, values and accents on their working-class basis. They inevitably seek their wives in the upper classes, but their childhood expectations doom them to frustration in marriage. "The upper middle-classes and the working-classes have very different models of ideal masculine and feminine, husbandly and wifely behavior, and each is seen as destructive to integrity and self-respect by the member of the other sex and class." Thus Jimmy thinks he is being "destroyed" by Alison, or would be "destroyed" by her if he didn't go back to his working-class environment or reduce both of them to mutual misery and recrimination.

This explanation is good so far as it goes. But I wonder if it goes far enough. Mr. Gorer is, of course, absolutely right when he points to Jimmy's fear of being destroyed by Alison. But, as one reads the play, one wonders whether Jimmy hates just upper-class women, or whether he does not hate women in general. Listen to him on the subject, and meditate on his imagery:

> When you see a woman in front of her bedroom mirror you realize what a refined sort of a butcher she is. Did you ever see some dirty old Arab, sticking his fingers into some mess of lamb fat and gristle? Well, she's just like that. . . . I had a flat underneath a couple of girls once. You heard every

damned thing those bastards did, all day and night. The most simple, everyday actions were a sort of assault course on your sensibilities. . . . Slamming their doors, stamping their high heels, banging their irons and saucepans—the eternal flaming racket of the female.

Or, again, on love:

She just devours me whole every time, as if I were some over-large rabbit. That's me. That bulge around her navel. . . . She'll go on sleeping and devouring until there's nothing left of me.

Or take the conclusion of Jimmy's whine about the absence of causes, which has misled some of the critics into thinking that he is a leftover hero from the Spanish Civil War.

No, there's nothing left for it, me boy, but to let yourself be butchered by the women.

Indeed, the only way in which Jimmy and Alison can sustain a relationship at all is by pretending to be not men and women but bears and squirrels. This whimsy produces some of the most bloodcurdling passages to be found in 20th-century drama—passages which I was confident would have been laughed off the New York stage (but I obviously underestimated the power of Mr. Osborne's deeper fantasy):

JIMMY: You're very beautiful, A beautiful, great-eyed squirrel. (*She nods brightly, relieved.*) Hoarding, nut-munching squirrel. (*She mimes this delightedly.*) With highly polished, gleaming fur, and an ostrich feather of a tail.
ALISON: Wheeeeeee! . . . You're a jolly super bear, too. A really soooooooper, marvellous bear.

JIMMY: Bears and squirrels *are* marvellous.

ALISON: Marvellous *and* beautiful. (*She jumps up and down excitedly, making little paw gestures.*) Ooooooh!

If you think A. A. Milne has taken over the angry young men, you have seen nothing yet.

JIMMY (*pointing at Cliff*): He gets more like a little mouse every day, doesn't he? He really looks like one. Look at those ears, and that face, and the little short legs.

ALISON: That's because he *is* a mouse.

CLIFF: Eek! eek! I'm a mouse.

JIMMY: A randy little mouse.

CLIFF (*dancing around the table, and squeaking*): I'm a mouse, I'm a mouse, I'm a randy little mouse.

And the play's incredible dénouement:

JIMMY: We'll be together in our bear's cave, and our squirrel's drey, and we'll live on honey and nuts—lots and lots of nuts. And we'll sing about ourselves—about warm trees and snug caves, and lying in the sun. And you'll keep those big eyes on my fur, and help me keep my claws in order, because I'm a bit of a soppy, scruffy sort of a bear. [Etc., etc.]

As one might expect from a man who hates women and who can tolerate his wife only by imagining himself a bear and her a squirrel, all Jimmy's vital relationships are with men. He is furious at Alison because she refuses to go to the funeral of Hugh Tanner's mother. Of Alison's friends, the only one, Jimmy tells Alison, who is worth tuppence is a homosexual, "a sort of female Emily Brontë." He spends much of the play roughhousing with Cliff: they wrestle, dance, grapple,

Look Back in Amazement 309

roll on the floor, twist each other's ears and exchange repulsive tendernesses (CLIFF: "Let me get on with it, you big, horrible man"; or JIMMY: "You're such a scruffy little beast"). "Sometimes," Jimmy muses, "I almost envy old Gide and the Greek Chorus boys." And the meaning of some of his badinage with Cliff is hardly veiled:

> JIMMY: You spend good money on a new pair of trousers, and then sprawl about in them like a savage. . . . Take 'em off. And I'll kick your behind for you.

Or again:

> CLIFF: You're a stinking old bear, you hear me?
> JIMMY: Let go of my foot, you whimsy little half-wit. You're making my stomach heave. I'm resting! If you don't let go, I'll cut off your nasty, great, slimy tail!

One need wonder no longer why Jimmy Porter is angry. He is not angry because he is a suppressed or neglected genius. He is not even angry because he is married to an upper-class girl. He is angry because he is married at all. He bears every mark of a homosexual who has not quite achieved the final moment of self-recognition.

If Mr. Gorer were right, and hypergamy were what *Look Back in Anger* is about, one could understand its vogue in a Britain shuddering before an impending class upheaval, but hardly its vogue in New York, where marrying upwards is stale business. But the play plucks at a deeper nerve, in New York as in London. Its contrived mixture of hysteria, sadism, and self-pity fascinates audiences already fascinated before they enter the theater by the homosexual anxiety, that increasingly prevalent obsession of our theater, if not of our age. One must, in the end, disagree with Mr. John Raymond, who has committed himself to the following singular sentiment: "It has been Mr. Osborne's privilege and good fortune to write the play of his generation." A fairer assessment of *Look Back in Anger* would be to say that it would make a good footnote to the Wolfenden Report.

18.
Notes on a National Cultural Policy
(1960)

Too much discussion of the problems of mass culture takes the form of handwringing. The point to be understood, I would think, is that these problems, while complicated and often discouraging, are by no means insuperable, unless we ourselves make them so. Things can be done in all sorts of ways to counteract the more depressing tendencies in our mass civilization. I would like in this brief note to call particular attention to possibilities in the field of public policy.

Let me begin with something both important and specific—that is, the problem of television. There are now over 50 million television sets in the country, covering almost 90 per cent of American households. From its inception, television has been in a downward spiral as an artistic medium; but it has taken recent disclosures of fraud in quiz programs to awaken the nation to the potentialities locked up in the tiny screen. The question is: What, if anything, can be done to improve the honesty and the quality of our television programing?

The first point is that television is an area in which there can be no question concerning the direct interest of the national government. No one has a divine right to a television channel. The air belongs to the public; and private operators can use the air only under public license. Why therefore should the national government stand helplessly by while private individuals, making vast sums of money out of public licenses, employ public facilities to debase the public taste? Obviously there seems no reason in law or prudence why this should be so. Government has not only the power but the obligation to help establish standards in media, like television and radio, which exist by public sufferance.

It has this obligation, among other reasons, because there seems no other way to rescue television from the downward spiral of competitive debasement. There are responsible and enlightened men managing television networks and stations; but they are trapped in a competitive situation. The man who gives his audience soap opera and give-away shows will make more money for his stockholders than the man who gives his audience news and Shakespeare. In consequence, the tendency is almost irresistible for television programs to vie with each other, not in elevating the taste of their audiences, but in catering to the worst side of the existing taste. As *Fortune* recently summed up the situation, it seems "that television has reached a kind of ceiling, that mediocrity is increasing, and that only *through some drastic change in the medium's evolution* will the excitement and aspiration of, say, 1954 return to our TV screens" (my italics). *Fortune*'s analysis was, as usual, better than its solution, which was Pay TV. Pay-as-you-see TV would be no more exempt from the passion to maximize its audiences than is free TV; and, in due course, it would doubtless undergo the same evolution. (See *Fortune,* December 1958.)

Still "some drastic change in the medium's evolution" remains necessary. But what? Actually there is nothing new about the situation of responsible TV people; they are in precisely the position that responsible businessmen were in twenty-five years ago when they wanted, for example, to treat their workers better but could not afford to do so because of the "competitive situation." Thus many employers disliked sweat-shops and child labor but knew that raising wages and improving working conditions would increase their costs and thereby handicap them as against their more callous competitors. Private initiative was impotent to deal with this situation: gentlemen's agreements within an industry always broke down under pressure. There was only one answer—public action to establish and enforce standards through the industry. Finally the Wages and Hours Act required all employers in inter-state commerce to meet certain specifications and thus abolished the economic risks of decency.

What television needs is some comparable means of equalizing the alleged competitive disadvantages of en-lightened programing. Fortunately the machinery for this is already at hand. According to the Communica-tions Act of 1934, the Federal Communications Com-mission is to grant licenses to serve the "public con-venience, interest, or necessity." A television channel is an immensely lucrative thing; and those lucky enough to secure an FCC license ought to be regarded not as owners of private property with which they can do anything they want but as trustees of public property under the obligation to prove their continuing right to the public trust.

It is up to the FCC, in short, to spell out the equiva-lent of minimum wages and maximum hours for tele-vision. What would this imply? It would surely imply the following:

1. A licensing system which would cover networks as well as individual stations.
2. The writing into each license of a series of stipu-lations which the grantee pledges himself to fulfill in order to retain the license.

3. A major stipulation would be the assumption by the networks and stations of full control over their programing—which means that sponsors and advertising agencies would no longer influence the content of programs. Other media live off advertisements without letting advertising agencies and sponsors dictate and censor content as they do in television. So long as television permits this, it will be fourth-rate. We should go over to the British and Canadian systems, in which the advertiser purchases time on the air as he purchases space in a newspaper, and has to leave editorial matters alone.

4. Other stipulations might include the allocation of stated portions of broadcast time to cultural and educational programs, to programs dealing with public issues, to local live programs; the limitation of advertising (the House of Commons has currently under consideration a bill prohibiting advertising on British TV for more than six minutes in any hour); the allocation of free time during presidential campaigns to all parties polling more than 10 per cent of the vote in the previous election.

5. Licenses should come up for annual renewal; and stations which have not met their obligations should expect to have their licenses revoked (the FCC has not refused a request for license renewal since 1932).

6. All this implies, of course, a revitalization of the FCC, which once had chairmen and commissioners of the caliber of Paul Porter, James Lawrence Fly, and Clifford Durr, but has become in recent years the preserve of complaisant political hacks.

Back in 1946, the FCC proposed in its famous Blue Book doing much this sort of thing for radio; but the industry issued the standard lamentations about governmental control, the public remained indifferent, and nothing came of it. One can expect to hear the same wail of "censorship" raised now against proposals for the establishment of federal standards. The fact is that we already have censorship of the worst kind in television. As John Crosby has written, "So long as the advertiser has direct personal control over programs, or direct ownership of programs, it's silly to talk about [government] censorship. The censorship is already stifling. The government should step in not to censor broadcasting but to free it."

The setting of federal standards does not mean government domination of the medium, any more than the Wages and Hours Act meant (as businessmen cried at the time) government domination of business. But the rejection of the Blue Book in 1946 emphasizes the difficulty of the problem. The FCC, even reconstituted as it would have to be in another administration, could not tighten up federal standards by itself. If the FCC proposes to buck the industry, it will require organized public support; it is perhaps a mistake that public energy which might have gone into establishing general standards was diverted into setting up separate facilities for educational television. And the FCC would also probably require some form of administration supplementation—perhaps a National Citizens' Advisory Board, of the kind proposed some years ago by William Benton,[1] or a National Broadcasting Authority, financed by rentals on the licenses, of the sort recently suggested by John Fischer in *Harper's*.[2]

[1] William Benton, in his testimony before the Senate Interstate Commerce Committee, printed in the May 31, 1951, issue of the *Congressional Record* (A3313-7).

[2] John Fischer, "Television and Its Critics," *Harper's Magazine*, 219 (July 1959): 10–14.

The measures proposed above represent a minimum program. Walter Lippmann and others have recently argued for the establishment of a public network to be "run as a public service with its criterion not what will be most popular but what is good." Lippmann does not suppose that such a network would attract the largest mass audience. "But if it enlisted the great talents which are available in the industry, but are now throttled and frustrated, it might well attract an audience which made up in influence what it lacked in numbers. The force of a good example is a great force, and should not be underrated." Proposals of this sort still horrify many Americans, though fewer now than in the days when Charles Van Doren was a community hero. But clearly, if television cannot clean its own house and develop a sense of responsibility commensurate with its influence, we are bound to come to a government network. If, as Dr. Frank Stanton of the Columbia Broadcasting System insists (his italics), *The strongest sustained attention of Americans is now, daily and nightly, bestowed on television as it is bestowed on nothing else*[3] then television is surely a proper subject for public concern. If the industry will not undertake to do itself what is necessary to stop the drift into hopeless mediocrity (and, far from showing any signs of so doing, its leaders deny the reality of the problem and even justify the present state of things by pompous talk about "cultural democracy"), then it must expect public intervention.

The case for government concern over television is indisputable because government must control the air. The case for government concern over other arts rests

[3] Frank Stanton, "The Role of Television in Our Society," an address of May 26, 1955.

on a less clear-cut juridical basis. Yet, one hundred and thirty-five years ago, John Quincy Adams clearly stated that a government's right and duty to improve the condition of the citizens applied no less to "moral, political, intellectual improvement" than to internal improvements and public works.

The American government has acknowledged this responsibility variously and intermittently since its foundation. But the problem of government encouragement of the arts is not a simple one; and it has never been satisfactorily solved. In order to bring some coherence into its solution, Congressman Frank Thompson, Jr., of New Jersey has been agitating for some time for the establishment of a Federal Advisory Council on the Arts, to be set up within the Department of Health, Education, and Welfare and charged with assisting the growth of the fine arts in the United States. "A major duty of the Council," the bill (H.R. 7656) reads, "shall be to recommend ways to maintain and increase the cultural resources of the United States."

There is no automatic virtue in councils. Congressman Thompson and Senator Fulbright, for example, got through Congress a year ago an act establishing a National Cultural Center in Washington. After a protracted delay, President Eisenhower named the thirty-four members of the new Center's board of trustees. Of the whole group, only a handful had shown any evidence of knowing or caring anything about the arts; the typical members include such cultural leaders as the former football coach at West Point, the President's minister (balanced, of course, by Catholic and Jewish clerics), his television adviser, representatives of labor, etc. A Federal Advisory Council on the Arts, appointed on such principles, would be worse than useless. But in due course some President will seek out genuine leaders of the arts and ask them to think through the issues of the government relationship.

Let no one mistake it: there are no easy answers here. But also there has been, in this country at least, very little hard thought. Government is finding itself more and more involved in matters of cultural standards and endeavor. The Commission of Fine Arts, the Committee on Government and Art, the National Cultural Center, the Mellon Gallery, the poet at the Library of Congress, the art exhibits under State Department sponsorship, the cultural exchange programs—these represent only a sampling of federal activity in the arts. If we are going to have so much activity anyway, if we are, in addition, worried about the impact of mass culture, there are strong arguments for an affirmative governmental policy to help raise standards. Nor is there reason to suppose that this would necessarily end up in giving governmental sanction to the personal preferences of congressmen and Presidents—e.g., making Howard Chandler Christy and Norman Rockwell the models for American art. Congressmen have learned to defer to experts in other fields, and will learn to defer to experts in this (one doubts, in any case, whether the artistic taste of politicians is as banal as some assume; certainly the taste of the two most recent governors of New York is better than that of most professors).

Certain steps are obvious. Whereas many civilized countries subsidize the arts, we tend to tax them. Let us begin by reducing federal taxes on music and the theater. Then we ought to set up a Federal Advisory Council on the Arts composed not of presidential chums and other hacks but of professional and creative artists and of responsible executives (museum directors, presidents of conservatories, opera managers, etc.). This council ought to study American precedents in the field and, even more important, current experiments in government support of the arts in Europe. A program of subsidies for local museums and galleries, for example, would be an obvious possibility.

There is a considerable challenge to social and administrative invention here. As the problems of our affluent society become more qualitative and less quantitative, we must expect culture to emerge as a matter of national concern and to respond to a national purpose. Yet the role of the state can at best be marginal. In the end the vitality of a culture will depend on the creativity of the individual and the sensibility of the audience, and these conditions depend on factors of which the state itself is only a surface expression.

Part V

Observations and Entertainments

19.
Varieties of Communist Experience
(1960)

I have recently returned from a month's trip to the Soviet Union, Poland, and Yugoslavia. So superficial an inspection could hardly be expected to yield profound conclusions. Still, a swift and concentrated tour in lands previously known only through the eyes of others offers certain advantages. Old assumptions and expectations dissolve in a flood of new and concrete impressions; the easy abstractions which rule our thought trip up over the complexities of experience. For this traveler, one impression above all was paramount. We have often tended to suppose that communism, as the most explicit and comprehensive of the ideologies of our day, would stamp the nations under its sway into a fairly uniform mold. The very phrase "the Communist world" conveys the customary notion of essential homogeneity. But what strikes the casual observer—or at least this one—is precisely the heterogeneity of Communist practice. This phenomenon, I think, is worth examination, because it seems likely that such heterogeneity holds out the best, if not the only, hope, for eventual world peace.

Communism is not a monolith; it is a spectrum. At one end of the spectrum lies China—messianic, austere, passionately ideological, deeply fanatical, and inaccessible to the American observer. (Though the State Department has now relented, Peking has not—the problem today is, not American passports, but Chinese visas.) At the other end of the spectrum lie Poland and

Yugoslavia—countries whose species of communism confound the clichés which have dominated Western thought in the last decade. In between lies the Soviet Union, the most powerful Communist nation of them all, a singular mixture of excessive confidence and excessive insecurity, of extraordinary efficiency and exasperating inefficiency, of venturesome innovation and rigid ideology.

Power, of course, settles heavily on the Sino-Russian side of the spectrum. By themselves Poland and Yugoslavia can make little difference to the international balance of force. Yet conceivably, if the Polish and Yugoslav experiences express a possible direction in which communism might evolve, then what is going on in these smaller countries may be of incalculable significance. It is not too much to suggest that the future may depend on whether the Soviet Union remains within the orbit of ideology or begins to move imperceptibly toward a more genial and pragmatic form of communism.

The one safe generalization about the Soviet Union is that it is in flux. The changes which have taken place since the death of Stalin continue to be a source of local wonder and delight. Soviet citizens talk freely about the "bad times," by which they mean the period from 1948 or so to 1953. When one asks what these years were like, they reply that no one dared speak his private thoughts, no one trusted anyone else, no one was safe from arbitrary and unpredictable terror. This relative candor about the last days of Stalin is curiously devoid of bitterness toward "the Old Man" himself; he is either seen as a great builder who went wrong in his last years or else as an aged leader deceived and betrayed by unscrupulous subordinates, like Beria. Still, the frankness about the "distortions" which took place under his sponsorship is of enormous significance. The revulsion against the "cult of personality" and against the omnipotent secret police is deeply felt and genuine. People say over and over with fervent conviction, "We will never go through anything like that again!" (When one asks how they can be sure that the cult of personality will not revive, whether any structural changes have taken place to prevent the emergence of a new tyrant, they only say, "Because we have been through this once, we will not permit it to happen again"—a proposition rather more convincing to the speaker than to the beholder.)

The implication of the talk about the "bad times" is that times are much better now. This cannot be gainsaid. There has been a vast increase in personal security. One hears little now about sudden midnight arrests. The secret police have been sharply reduced in power. The streets of Moscow are filled with people trickling back from exile and hard labor in Siberia. The labor camps themselves have apparently undergone a drastic change in character. More than this, Khrushchev, after eliminating Malenkov in the post-Stalin struggle, took over the Malenkov program (as Stalin once took over the economic program of Trotsky), and in the last two years has been making a prodigious effort to raise standards of life and comfort. The traveler cannot help being impressed by the variety and abundance (if not necessarily by the quality) of consumer goods in the department stores of the large cities.

At no time since the Revolution have ordinary Soviet citizens felt themselves both so free and so affluent. Quite naturally, they exult in a tremendous debt to the man who made these gains possible. Certainly Khrushchev himself rejoices in their gratitude. Still, to be fair, there is little evidence yet of the emergence of a new personality cult. One sees few pictures of Khrushchev around and no statues, and one does not constantly feel a Big Brotherly presence as one did in prewar Germany or Italy or in Stalinist Russia. Khrushchev is a rare bird among dictators: he wants very much to be liked. He cares about popular moods, he basks in the affection of crowds, and he whistle-stops around his country as if engaged in a perpetual campaign for re-election.

Watching these developments, some observers have expressed the hope that the combination of personal security, consumer goods, and a dictator who wants to be popular would bring about a relaxation of the grimly ideological character of Soviet society. It has been reasonably argued that political dogmatism cannot survive an increase in free discussion and that administrative totalitarianism will melt away under the diversifications inherent in a consumer economy. All this may be so. There is little evidence for it yet in contemporary Russia.

Nearly all the changes which have taken place since the death of Stalin have been in what the Western liberal must call the right direction. Despite these changes, the Soviet Union remains a theological society. Khrushchev has not liberalized the regime. What he has done is to begin to normalize it. This is not unimportant: the Soviet citizen is acquiring for the first time a sense of what is normal—what is his "right"— in the way both of personal security and of material comfort, and he is not likely to relinquish these norms willingly short of the threat of war against his country. Still, this is quite a different thing from liberalizing Soviet society—from making it less dogmatic and totalitarian, more pragmatic and tolerant.

The heart of Soviet dogmatism is the principle of infallibility, applied to leader, to party, and to theory of history. The gains under Khrushchev, far from weakening that principle, may very likely have strengthened it. Thus personal security and consumer goods, by satisfying the urgent demands of the managerial and technical groups, may actually reduce strivings toward intellectual and political liberty and increase political passivity. In the last days of Stalin, Soviet citizens questioned (in the privacy of their minds) the notion that their leadership could do no wrong. But today, when leadership is beginning to produce a multitude of pleasurable results, the results themselves—from improving the style of women's shoes to hitting the moon—only verify the infallibility both of the leader and of the ideology behind him.

At least it is difficult to explain otherwise the characteristic state of mind in the Soviet elite—the stupefying mixture of confidence, ignorance, imperviousness, and incuriosity. Nothing is more dismaying to the visitor than this almost total lack of curiosity (except about new productive methods or techniques). The members of the elite are absolutely confident that they know far more about Britain than Mr. Macmillan or Mr. Gaitskell, far more about France than General de Gaulle, far more about the United States than President Eisenhower or Governor Stevenson. Both this confidence and the accompanying ignorance much disturbed Hugh Gaitskell and Aneurin Bevan on their recent visit to Moscow. A newspaperman who accompanied them has written:

> One of the highest personalities of the régime was entirely ignorant of the existence of the National Health Service in Britain. Another, who accompanied us to an anti-colonial ballet at the Bolshoi, re-

fused to believe that a play opposing racial discrimination could be put on in the United States or that anti-colonial propaganda was legal in Great Britain. . . . The unemployed are believed to be queueing up before all the work-exchanges of Paris and London. . . . On a lower level, things are even worse. Our guide at Leningrad refused to believe that I could welcome Soviet visitors at my home in Paris, or that the best Western writers weren't Communists, or that abstract painting was not an American invention and sign of capitalist decadence, etc. And what was concerned here was not just a natural difference of opinion but incomprehension concerning even what we were talking about.

What seem ascertainable facts to the Westerner are believed in the Soviet Union only when they conform to the official stereotypes. If a statement fits the stereotype, one's Soviet friend beams with triumph; things that don't fit are rejected out of hand with smiles of pitying condescension. Nothing is more futile, by the way, than to hope to encourage the Soviet citizen to candor about his country by admitting faults in one's own. The visitor receives no credit for such admissions; it is rather assumed that the defects are so patent and overwhelming that "even you are forced to admit them." As for foreign comments on life and conditions in the Soviet Union: anything which falls short of fulsome praise is likely to be resented as needling and hostile.

Paddy Chayefsky, the playwright, a member of our party, remarked, "The Soviet Union is like a husband and wife who keep telling everyone all the time how happy they are."

When pressed hard about any point, Soviet citizens seek refuge in talk about their terrible suffering during the Second World War. No one can underestimate the extent of this wartime suffering. Yet most people in the Soviet Union seem to have argued themselves into the conviction that they were the only victims of Nazi terror. Indeed, forgetting their alliance of 1939–41 (and to bring that up in the Soviet Union is accounted the worst of taste), they talk a good deal of the time as if they were alone in resisting Hitler. The fearful ravages of war, carefully renewed in memory by novels and movies, have become the universal alibi, the all-conquering justification of every excess, error, or atrocity committed since. Bevan thus observed to a Ukrainian farmer that he was getting more gallons a year per cow in Britain than Ukrainian cows seemed able to produce. "But you weren't overrun by Hitler," came the inevitable reply. Bevan said: "Those were not the cows that were overrun by Hitler."

One has only to add that, within the elite, manners tend to be pompous and hectoring, and the conception of discussion is hopeless. I had to listen to Yury Zhukov, the Soviet Minister in charge of cultural exchanges, denounce the Russian Research Center at Harvard for its tendentious and distorted researches in Soviet affairs—tendentious and distorted, it appeared, because they refused to accept official Soviet documents as the last word. The afternoon before, I had spent some time with the Professor of American History in a leading Soviet university and the head of the American section in a leading historical institute. The conversation (conducted through an interpreter) revealed surprising ignorance about American history and historians. (The two Soviet Americanists, for example, had not heard of Richard Hofstadter or Oscar Handlin.) But what does ignorance matter if you already possess the key to the universe?

This state of mind has one particularly unpleasant consequence. I have traveled in many countries of the world; but I have never been lied to as casually, contemptuously, and persistently as in the Soviet Union. One expects to be lied to on large issues—that Soviet writers are free to write as they please, or that the South Koreans invaded North Korea. These are high-policy lies and comparable lies would doubtless be told foreigners in the United States. But one is lied to equally on petty issues, where what is at stake is not some question of national policy but rather the relationship of one person to another.

An episode is worth recounting. Paddy Chayefsky's parents came from a village in the Ukraine; and it had been his hope that he might be able to revisit the ancestral home. He communicated this hope to the Soviet Embassy in Washington and again to the Writers' Union in Moscow. In due course, a trip was laid on to Kiev, where the rest of the group would meet local writers and see the town while Mr. Chayefsky would go by automobile to his village. Then, the day before we were due to go, the trip was canceled. The reason provided by the Writers' Union? "No hotel rooms are available in Kiev."

The reason did not seem convincing. Mr. Chayefsky pointed out that a Soviet writer, eager to visit a place near Montgomery, Alabama, would be a bit suspicious if he were told that the trip was out because there were no hotel rooms in Montgomery. He then walked over to Intourist, where he was informed that there were plenty of rooms available in Kiev. Being a man of determination, Mr. Chayefsky booked passage for New York and announced that he would leave the next day unless the Kiev trip was reinstated by five o'clock that afternoon. A few moments before his deadline, hotel rooms were found.

So we went to Kiev. For Mr. Chayefsky to make his pilgrimage and rejoin the rest of the party on what we were told was "the last plane that evening to Moscow," it was necessary for him to leave the hotel at eight in the morning. He then could drive five hours to the village, stay an hour, and drive back to Kiev in time for the evening plane. But no car appeared at eight, or at nine, or at ten, or at eleven. In Kiev, a city of nearly a million, the Ukrainian Writers' Union seemed unable to find a car and driver for the American writer who wished to see where his parents were born. Around noon a car at last arrived. It was pointed out to Mr. Chayefsky that, if he went now, he could not catch up with the rest of the party that evening. But Mr. Chayefsky's curiosity and determination were at a high point, and he insisted on going. Just before his departure, a new and later Kiev-Moscow plane was discovered; if he hurried, he was now told, he still could get back to Moscow that night.

He left, drove five hours, and reached the village. The villagers had never seen an American before. They greeted him with enthusiasm; people who remembered his parents appeared; preparations had already been made for a banquet. Then, after seven minutes, Mr. Chayefsky's escort reminded him that, if he wanted to make the late plane, he would have to depart. They drove furiously back to Kiev, rushed to the airport— and found that there was no late Moscow passenger plane!

Why this fantastic effort to prevent Mr. Chayefsky from seeing his ancestral home? It was partly, no doubt, the feeling that this was a poor village, and that the American writer wanted to see it only to gather material about "negative" aspects of Soviet life. It was partly, too, the deeply ingrained habits of falsification and contempt.

These have been general considerations; our particular concern on this trip was Soviet literary life. Edward Weeks, Alfred Kazin, Paddy Chayefsky, and I made up the first American writers' delegation to visit the Soviet Union under the Lacy-Zarubin cultural exchange agreement. Seeing writers may not tell one much about the power structure of a country; but it does tell a good deal about the intellectual atmosphere. A good deal—not everything. The presence of a delegation inevitably injects a certain artificiality into a gathering. Frank and confidential interchange is most unlikely, especially with one or two literary bureaucrats on hand. Freedom of comment has unquestionably improved since the death of Stalin, but it is still reserved for chat within the family. Most of the time the Soviet writers, with the exception of one or two who are sufficiently established to be permitted a certain latitude, or sufficiently brave or cynical not to give a damn, hand the foreigners a set of weary official responses. Do these people always believe what they say? It is entirely possible that men who seem rigid and impervious when foreigners voice doubts are actually voicing the same doubts themselves in private. Delegations do not have much chance to probe beneath the surface of Soviet culture; and one feels that beneath the surface there is a good deal stirring.

Still, the official atmosphere is what matters for the moment, and delegations get a sizable dose of this. It is clear, of course, that writers are conceived of by the state—and for the most part conceive of themselves—as instruments in the general task of uplifting Soviet society. In part, this is the expression of a natural patriotic desire to take part in a vast national effort; in part, it is the arrangement of the state to keep so potentially subversive a section of the population under discipline. "Writers are a type of artillery," Khrushchev told the Writers' Congress in May. "They clear the way for our forward movement and help our party in the Communist education of the workers. . . . You must brainwash people with your works."

This is the official literary mission. The editor of *Oktyabr,* a leading cultural magazine, opened a meeting with our group by a rambling stump speech, delivered to the accompaniment of approving chuckles from his claque, about an incident in London when someone had said to him, "You want to conquer us." The editor replied, according to his own account: "Why the hell should we want to conquer you? We have more natural resources than any country in the world. We have more gold than any country in the world. We have more diamonds than any country in the world. Etc., etc. Why in hell should we want you? Of course, if you want a fight, we will be glad to take you on and beat you up. But we don't need you and don't want you. All we want is peace." This seemed a strange introduction to a literary discussion; it is regrettably symptomatic. (Alfred Kazin appropriately responded that, since the United States was a richer nation than the Soviet Union, it must therefore be, according to the editor's own argument, even more peace-loving.) Similarly, the editor of *Inostrannaya Literatura* launched into a diatribe on, of all things, science fiction, seeking to show that Soviet science fiction revealed a serene, constructive, and optimistic nation, while American science fiction showed a nation afraid of the future—all this, the editor added, because of the need to keep the people tense and frightened in order to get them to pay the taxes required to maintain the defense spending required to maintain the capitalist economy. Yet these editors were accounted among the more free-spirited in the Soviet literary world.

The style in which they discussed such matters was as discouraging as the substance. Indeed, there is little better test of the literary sensibility of a society than its taste in rhetoric. Soviet rhetoric is brutal, strident, and banal. It was disconcerting to watch the old formulas of denunciation come tumbling out when otherwise intelligent men ventured into general political or even literary discussion. And where else in the civilized world could the following verse be printed in a serious literary publication?

> Ye poets
> > sing out the grand story
> The song
> > of our young workers' dreams.
> Of inspired ones
> > who win a new glory,
> Of Communist
> > labour teams!
>
> The secrets of science
> > we'll master.
> The problems
> > of technique we'll beat;
> Advancing,
> > with speed ever faster,
> The universe
> > lies at our feet.
>
> Our enemies
> > pale from frustration!

How vain now
  their blustering seems!
So forward
  ye pride of our nation—
Ye Communist
  labour teams!

Conceivably, the poem sounds better in Russian than it does in English (but it couldn't sound very much better); in any case, no malice attaches to the translation which was done in Moscow and published in a recent issue of *Soviet Literature,* an English-language publication supposedly devoted to the most exportable Soviet writing.

The obsession with political purpose and effect has created a cult of the mass. The most sophisticated writer in the Soviet Union told us that he learned far more from the thousands of untutored letters sent him about his books than from the most thoughtful literary criticism. A poet said he had received 40,000 letters about a single poem. Can such things be true? If the poet (as he claimed) read all these letters, it would have taken him (allowing two minutes per letter and an eight-hour working day) five-and-a-half months; one wonders when he would have had time to write his poetry. Still, the claim suggests the extent to which the cult of the mass has put a premium on the quantitative approach to literature. Writers fulfill quotas like factory workers. Notes like the following abound in the Soviet literary press:

> Between the 3rd and 4th Congress of the Ukrainian Writers' Union (1954–59) the Ukrainian writers published 65 new novels, 118 short stories, 193 collections of tales and articles, 295 volumes of verse, and 268 books for children. About 70 new plays

were produced. . . . Last year alone over a thousand fiction titles with a total print of over 40 million were published in the Ukraine.

The sense of political mission brings with it an intense preoccupation with literary dogma. "Socialist realism" is still a major issue for the ordinary Soviet writer. At a recent conference on the Problems of Socialist Realism (organized by the Union of Soviet Writers and the Gorky Institute of World Literature), the speaker rather oddly stressed that, "despite the claims to the contrary made by foreign revisionists, the method of socialist realism not only exists, but is steadily developing and becoming richer."

> The attempts of some bourgeois ideologists to pretend that socialist realism was "decreed" by the State and "foisted on" Soviet writers was nothing short of ridiculous; in fact the history of literature and art had shown that the way had been prepared for this creative method by all the preceding artistic development of mankind and was a new natural stage of this development.

In practice, "socialist realism" tends to become a flexible conception. One doubts whether it really exists at all; an old and cynical writer told us that socialist realism was nothing more than what the people approved. Yet the preoccupation survives; the doctrine worries Soviet writers. And along with it are the other staples of Soviet literary control: the "positive hero," the compulsory optimism, the happy ending. In his Writers' Congress speech, Khrushchev ranged himself with the "positive" writers, the so-called "embellishers."

> Who are the non-embellishers? Some of them say that the principal task of literature consists of root-

ing out all the faults and failings possible, ignoring at the same time the great conquests of Soviet society. So listen, dear friends, if it is anyone who reveals and lays bare failings and faults, and whose hand will not falter in so doing, it will be the Party and its Central Committee (*stormy applause*).

In other parts of his speech, Khrushchev expressed a genial tolerance toward writing and a hope that writers could hereafter solve their own problems (i.e., substitute self-censorship for state censorship); but his central argument left no doubt about the limited role permitted to writers in Soviet society.

The Soviet conception of the writer as a gunner, an engineer of the soul, a mass educator—as almost anything except a writer—has to be understood if we are to understand what the Soviet Union means by "cultural exchange." It does not mean free trade in ideas. It means rather a series of reciprocal trade agreements, in which usable ideas of one country are bartered for usable ideas of another. The editor of *Oktyabr* explained to us that any impression of Soviet indifference to Western ideas was all wrong. "We are eager to take everything constructive and good you have to offer," he said, and went on to instance agronomy, metallurgy, and engineering as fields in which the West had something to contribute. The implication, in a statement addressed to the American writers' delegation, was plain enough: the Soviet Union had nothing to learn from literary critics, editors, or historians. So the visiting scientist or engineer is assured of a warm welcome and an interested hearing; even the visiting economist finds a ready audience for a discussion of technical problems of economic management; but the Soviet elite is not much interested in the visiting humanist, who, after all, has no techniques to communicate—has, indeed, nothing to lose but his ideas.

The hard fact is that the last thing the Soviet Union cares about is a free exchange of ideas. Nothing is more puzzling, for example, given the blazing self-confidence of the Soviet regime, than the distress, even fear, with which Soviet citizens confront the thought of the sale within the U.S.S.R. of foreign books, magazines, and newspapers. The foreigner in Moscow, going slowly mad as he tries to figure out what is happening in the world from the pages of the London *Daily Worker* and *L'Humanité*, soon begins to inquire why he cannot buy *The Times* or the *Daily Telegraph* of London, or the *New York Times* or *Herald Tribune*. Embassies, government offices, and a few libraries receive copies of foreign magazines and newspapers; but, for all practical purposes, the ordinary foreign visitor or Soviet citizen has no access to non-Communist publications. Why should this be? We used to tell Soviet writers that we would be glad to take them to bookshops in Washington, New York, and London where they could buy *Pravda, Izvestia,* and Soviet magazines and books. Why, we would ask, could they not take us to similar places in Moscow? This appeal left them singularly unmoved. So far as one can tell, the present one-way passage strikes most of them as perfectly right and natural.

Pressing the question further produced curious results. A couple of eminent writers, separately explaining why Moscow could not put the London or New York *Times* on sale, cited what they represented as typical Western kiosks, one in Nice, the other on Broadway. From the lurid and somewhat lip-smacking descriptions, one learned that these stands offered nothing but sex and pornography.

"That is what you want to do with us," we were told in grandiloquent tones. "You want to make us accept your Western obscenity and filth. But we say to you that we will not accept it. We will not corrupt our people the way the capitalists have corrupted yours." To this, one replies that the Soviet Union can keep out all the pornography it wants, but that neither *Times* is usually regarded as primarily a medium for pornography. One says plaintively: Let us please talk about serious magazines and books and newspapers. Why can't such be sold? The reply comes in increasingly angry and incoherent tones.

"We have told you that we do not want your filth. You want to force your Western ideas upon us. We are going to keep them out. You had better understand that. . . . Etc., etc."

The other argument invoked to defend the ban on foreign publications is that "the time is not ripe," the Soviet people are still like a growing child, and a child has to have its reading selected for it until it reaches maturity. This suggests that admitting the *New York Times* is felt likely in some way to endanger the stability of the regime. When one replies that the theory of the 42-year-old infant is not convincing and that the Soviet regime is surely so well established that it has little to fear from permitting a few hundred copies of the *New York Times* to be sold each day, one only elicits new bursts of incoherence and anger.

How is one to interpret this? Do people become angry because they realize how stupid and feeble their arguments sound? Or do they really feel that Western newspapers and magazines constitute a threat to the regime? I doubt whether it is either of these things. What they do feel, I believe, is a sense of infallibility about their own ideas and a despair at the incomprehension of Westerners or a rage at their Machi-avellism.

"Our people do not want to eat bad food poisoned with the venom of bourgeois ideas," as Khrushchev put it the other day. ". . . Let us take from each other only what is best, exchange what is best, and you eat your rotten goods yourselves."

So long as the Soviet Union remains a theological society, based on the principle of infallibility, it will not permit the circulation of Western skepticism and heresy—and it will remain proud in its prohibition.

This state of mind is the psychological expression of what one feels most vividly of all in the Soviet Union—a capacious, unlimited, and arrogant sense of power. It is impressive and scary to see what energy a great nation can generate when it allocates its talent and resources according to an intelligent system of priorities, sternly enforced not just by ruthless coercion (as under Stalin) but by ruthless enthusiasm. In this respect, the unwary visitor must take care to keep his eye on the ball. The American tourist who cried out in the lobby of the Hotel Ukrainia, "These people can't even get me a ticket to Odessa! How can anyone suppose that they could send a rocket to the moon?" misconstrues the sit-uation. He innocently supposes that service to the con-sumer is the ultimate test of economic and administra-tive efficiency. Khrushchev operates under no such illusion. The Soviet leadership thinks it important to send a rocket to the moon and not very important to supply tourists with tickets to Odessa, so they appor-tion their talent and resources accordingly. The able men work on rockets, the dopes on tickets. And one cannot but feel that, if they ever thought tickets to Odessa important, a shift in talent and resources would make Intourist the best travel agency in the world. Our own beloved country meanders along on the opposite theory: we allow the market to determine our national priorities, which means that we allocate a major share of our talent and resources to consumer services and too often leave the sending of rockets to the moon to men who might be better employed selling tickets to Odessa. If three quarters of the national energy now dedicated to creating and satisfying consumer wants were dedicated instead to building national power, we would not have to worry about the Soviet campaign to "overtake and surpass" the United States.

A mere four years ago, John Foster Dulles assured the House Appropriations Committee that the Soviet Union was "on the point of collapsing." Today, the Soviet Union has already won the race to the moon; Khrushchev has completed a triumphal tour of the United States; and the American Secretary of Defense has conceded[1] the Soviet Union a 3–1 advantage in the weapon of the future, the intercontinental ballistic missile, by the early 1960's. In every field of national power the Soviet Union radiates purpose, progress, and success; and it is this discharge of directed national energy which underlies the explosion of Soviet self-esteem. No wonder Russians feel on top of things: experience seems every day to confirm their faith that their ideology has conferred on them a unique mastery of the dynamics of history.

In 1930 Stalin wrote a famous article for *Pravda*. People intoxicated with one gain after another, he said, "become dizzy with success, they lose all sense of proportion, they lose the faculty of understanding realities." Khrushchev's Russia is dizzy with a success of which Stalin's Russia could only have dreamed.

[1] Mistakenly, it has subsequently turned out (1962).

The full theological commitment of the Soviet Union is not to be understood until one has visited Poland and Yugoslavia. Passing from Moscow to Warsaw, one has the illusion of entering a free country. This is, of course, just an illusion. Both Poland and Yugoslavia are Communist dictatorships with wide and vital areas (especially in politics and economics) where the regime enforces conformity quite as vigorously as in the Soviet Union itself. Yet, for all this, one feels oneself in qualitatively different cultures. At first, there are only the familiar and comforting signs of Western decadence—pretty girls, slim waists, tipping, hula hoops, shoeshine boys, sociologists, neckties, advertising posters, kissing in parks. But these clearly are expressions of what is basically a quite different attitude toward communism itself.

One enters the hotel in Warsaw; on the newsstands are the London and New York *Times*, the *New Statesman, Life*. Here communism is hardly a decade old, not forty-two years, but the authorities are prepared to run the terrible risk of importing a few foreign publications. One evening a friend took me to a reading-room-cum-coffee-shop in the outskirts of Warsaw. Like everything else (or nearly everything else), this was set up and run by the state. There, hanging on the racks for any Polish citizen to read, were not only the usual repertoire of East European papers but also a representation of the wicked capitalist press, including ample copies of Mr. Luce's favorite picture magazine. In the great bookstore in the Palace of Culture (the repellent Russian-built skyscraper which was Stalin's gift to the Polish people), one can find nearly all the Anglo-American books one wants, short of the most passionate anti-Communist works.

In the Soviet Union, communism means more than

a set of political and economic dogmas: it also means a set of equally rigid moral, aesthetic, literary, and metaphysical dogmas, covering every aspect of human existence. A good Soviet Communist not only favors communism as a form of political and economic organization; he also abominates abstract art, detests modern music, scorns Proust, and hates religion. The day after I arrived in Poland, an exhibition of contemporary Polish art opened in Warsaw. It consisted almost entirely of abstractions. A Polish Communist told me that a Soviet Communist had recently visited his apartment, noted an abstraction on the wall, and exclaimed with shock and astonishment, "But I thought you were a *good* Communist!" A week later the International Festival of Contemporary Music, complete with dodecaphonic quartets by Schönberg and even more esoteric pieces by Boulez, opened in Warsaw. A leading Communist cultural weekly in Warsaw was serializing excerpts from the *Remembrance of Things Past*. When one asked Polish writers about "socialist realism" they laughed derisively, and replied that no one had talked about *that* in Poland for five years. The introduction to an English-language book on Maja Berezowska, a favorite Polish artist (whose drawings could easily appear on the pages of the American *Playboy*), even declares, "Maja Berezowska's world of drawings is free from the crude passions of our time. It steers clear of all troubles and fears that harass contemporary man living in an era of wars and upheavals." (These words, I should perhaps add, were *not* written in condemnation of Berezowska.) And the churches, of course, are open: friars in medieval garb walk cheerfully around the streets; religious objects are freely on sale in the shops.

Yugoslavia is much the same, with variations. A

Polish joke describes the variations without too much exaggeration: "What is the difference between Poland and Yugoslavia? In Yugoslavia, you can abuse the Soviet Union to your heart's content, but you can't say anything against your own government. In Poland, it's just the opposite." (I remarked to a Pole about the number of jokes I had heard since arriving in Warsaw. "Of course we have a lot of jokes in Poland," he replied. "After all, we have to make jokes for the entire Communist world.") There appears to be more intellectual freedom (or, at least, variety) in Poland than in Yugoslavia. Yugoslavia, on the other hand, appears to have more economic freedom (or, at least, decentralization) than Poland. A visitor cannot hope to tell how much is sham and how much reality in Yugoslav institutions like the workers' councils; one doubts whether a high-technology society can really be run by such means; but there can be no question that "the free-market socialism" of the Yugoslavs is a reality, and that the Yugoslav planners have devised with skill a system of harnessing the incentives of the market to their central controls.

Coming straight from a theological society, one is doubtless tempted to exaggerate the pragmatism and tolerance of Polish and Yugoslav communism. A. M. Rosenthal, the able Warsaw correspondent of the *New York Times,* insists rightly on the importance of the distinction between "freedom of conversation" and "freedom of speech"; the Poles have the first, but not the second. The two non-Communist parties play no serious role in Polish politics. In Yugoslavia, the one-party system is firmly entrenched; Milovan Djilas lingers in prison, as a reminder of the sharp local limits on freedom of opinion.

No one can regard Poland and Yugoslavia as libertarian societies in the Western sense. But they are quite as clearly not totalitarian societies in the Soviet sense. "Freedom of conversation" is not everything, but it is a good deal better than nothing. For the Yugoslavs and even more perhaps for the Poles, communism is essentially a system of economic and political organization. A good Communist must wholeheartedly accept the proletarian dictatorship, the one-party state, the centrally-planned economy, and the abolition of profit in private property. But that is about all. Beyond that, a good Communist can like or dislike abstract art, as he chooses. He can admire Sholokhov or he can admire Proust. He can think about literature in aesthetic terms and about economics in empirical terms, and he doesn't care much one way or the other if his fellow-countrymen choose to go to church.

With such people, communication suddenly becomes possible again. Even when one agrees with a Soviet Communist, one feels it as an accidental convergence over an infinitely wide abyss; when one disagrees with the Polish or Yugoslav Communist (as one generally does), one somehow disagrees in the same language. In the Soviet Union, dogma provides the exact answer to everything. Poles and Yugoslavs are more ready to admit that they don't know all the answers and that existing formulas don't solve all conceivable problems. The Soviet Union dwells by the mystique of a single truth. In Poland—and to some, though a lesser, degree in Yugoslavia—one feels that the Marxist truth coexists with other truths. In Polish universities, the Marxist historian lives side by side with the Catholic historian and the bourgeois-progressive historian. The Soviet Union is still a totalitarian society—far more amiable than in the days of Stalin, but no less dogmatic and ideological. Poland and Yugoslavia are semipluralistic societies. The Polish and Yugoslav Communists take open pride in the fact that their communism is far more free, pragmatic, and humane (i.e., less Communistic) than communism anywhere else.

Poland and Yugoslavia forced this observer to concede the feasibility of what I had always previously supposed to be impossible—"liberal communism." Both countries combine a Communist political and economic structure with a considerable measure of intellectual, cultural, and religious freedom. The question remains whether these countries represent a fortuitous concatenation of circumstances not likely to be reproduced elsewhere—or whether a nonfanatical, nontotalitarian communism of the Polish-Yugoslav sort could possibly be the direction in which even the Soviet Union itself might be moving.

Poland and Yugoslavia gained their present positions by quite separate roads. Yugoslavia achieved its own liberation during the war. Tito had his own army and his own secret police and was consequently in a position to defy Stalin when Soviet demands became too exorbitant. Having suffered from the heavy hand, Yugoslavs undertook after 1948 what they proudly describe today as "the first experiment in de-Stalinization." Djilas subsequently carried the logic of Titoism to a point unacceptable to Tito, but this should not obscure the fact that Tito himself carried it to a point unacceptable to Stalin. In Yugoslavia today, Tito seems oddly to have receded from the picture. He remains first in war and first in peace, like George Washington; but he spends more and more time in Brioni, less and less in Belgrade; and the Yugoslavs do not ceaselessly speculate about his moods and whims, as the Russians do about Khrushchev and the Poles about Gomulka. One feels that some sort of constitutional order is evolving in Yugoslavia, and that the present mixture of freedom and dictatorship can survive a good deal, including even the death of Tito.

Poland won its autonomy in another way. Occupation by the Red Army restricted its range of political alternatives in the years after the war. But Stalinism produced a reaction as definite in Poland as in Yugoslavia: the word "revolution" in Poland today refers not to the imposition of communism in 1945 but to the revolt against Stalinism in 1956. That revolt brought the astute figure of Gomulka to the top; and Poland today is the expression of Gomulka's two remarkable deals— one with the Soviet Union, the other with the Polish people. These details were the almost inevitable result of Poland's geographical and cultural location. On the one hand, geography committed Poland to the East: even anti-Communist Poles were forced to accept the imperatives of Poland's strategic situation. On the other, culture committed Poland to the West; its tradition was one of feeling and spontaneity; even pro-Communist Poles were forced to accept the imperatives of Poland's cultural inheritance. This balance of imperatives defined Gomulka's task—and opportunity. With regard to the Soviet Union, Gomulka traded the independence of Polish foreign policy for a measure of latitude at home, especially in policy toward the intellectuals, the Catholic Church, and the peasants. Within Poland, Gomulka offered the people areas of relative freedom in exchange for their acquiescence in Communist rule and a pro-Soviet foreign policy. This equilibrium of unwritten treaties provides the basis for Polish autonomy—conceivably a basis less shaky than it sounds.

Obviously Poland and Yugoslavia have attained their forms of liberal communism in quite special ways. Will they remain unique? Or (as the Poles think and the Yugoslavs hope) may the Soviet Union itself evolve in a liberal and pluralistic direction?

I have described the Soviet Union as essentially a theological society manned by a collection of true believers. I have suggested that the unquestionable progress in the last half-dozen years toward greater personal security and greater personal comfort may even have strengthened rather than weakened the dogmatic and ideological character of Soviet society. Yet are there no fissures in the Soviet structure? Are there no grounds to substantiate the Polish conviction that "the eventual logic of de-Stalinization is de-totalitarianization"?

The most significant remark made to me in the Soviet Union came from one of the wiliest and most experienced of Soviet writers. He said, "In the U.S.S.R., the grandfathers and the grandsons have more in common than either has with the fathers." By this he meant that those who grew up *before* the Revolution and those who grew up *after* the Second World War have a mutual rapport, a common sympathy and understanding, as against those who grew up between the wars.

The older Western assumption had been that the children in a totalitarian society, having been exposed to systematic indoctrination from the cradle, would form the most orthodox, rigid, and hopeless group in that society. One remembers the character of Gletkin in *Darkness at Noon*—the complete Soviet man, steel-willed, fanatical, and indestructible, who took over from the older interrogator and finally broke Rubashov down. As time went on, we supposed, the Soviet Union would consist completely of row after row of Gletkins. Now Koestler's sketch was essentially right for the generation between the wars. The present So-

viet elite consists of middle-aged editions of this monolithic Soviet man. But what none of us allowed for is
the now evident fact that the sons and daughters of
Gletkin are turning against their father. The monolithic
style of life bores them, estranges them, leaves them
disturbed and rebellious. They are reaching out for
beauty and gaiety, for speed and risk, for autonomy,
privacy, and self-expression. Instead of the revolution
devouring its children, perhaps the children may end
by devouring the revolution.

The character of this revolt needs to be defined with
precision. It certainly is not a revolt against Communism. Soviet youth today are Communists—in somewhat the sense that the youth of Europe and America
today are Christians. Communism is for them the
framework of life and belief. But it does not seem for
them, as it did for their fathers, a living and militant
faith to which every decision must be sternly referred.
Communism controls their day-to-day activity hardly
more than Christianity controls the day-to-day activity
of Western youth. As against the bleak and sterile dogmatism of their fathers, they—or at least a significant
minority among them—appear to be reaching out for
concreteness, variety, spontaneity. These rebels accept
the political and economic forms of life as permanent.
Their own political ideas are confused and sentimental. But they chafe under the moral and aesthetic dogmatism of the all-out Communist ideology. In one way
or another, they want to break the mold.

"Young people are curious," Khrushchev himself
admitted during his American tour.

Many of our young people hear about religion, about
God, about the saints, about church ceremonies, and
they have a curiosity about it. Even if each one of

them goes to church only once, they're so numerous that the doors of our churches would never close. The feeling of curiosity is very important.

It is indeed very important, and it is characteristic of Khrushchev as a dictator that he both perceives the mood and concedes its significance. Again and again, one notes the contrast between the complacent certitude of the middle-aged and the open-minded enthusiasm of the young. When an established scholar pompously scolded Alfred Kazin for not having written the right things about Theodore Dreiser, a student approached Kazin after the meeting and said in English, pointing to the older man, "I hope you don't think we are all as illiberal as he is." When Leonard Bernstein and the New York Philharmonic gave Stravinsky's *Sacre du Printemps* its first Moscow performance in a generation, the stalls (filled with the New Class) were restrained and perfunctory in their response, but the galleries (filled with younger people) gave Stravinsky as well as Bernstein a wild and continuing ovation. At the American Exhibition, young artists clustered with excitement around the abstractions, while Khrushchev, with customary delicacy, said they looked to him as if they had been painted by a little boy urinating in the sand.

Youth and old age—against middle age. No one knows what is going on beneath the surface in Soviet culture; but every once in a while something rises into sight which suggests ferment underneath. Thus the veteran critic K. Paustovsky, a "grandfather," wrote in *Literaturnaya Gazeta* last May a scathing critique of official Soviet notions of literature. He scornfully attacked the convention of "the sickeningly sweet happy endings."

We are lucky that Leo Tolstoy managed to write *Anna Karenina* before this tradition appeared. He did not have to "take a bow" to anyone, even the publisher; he could allow Anna to break up her family and pass out of life from purely private, and, consequently, impermissible considerations.

Compare this with the contemporary Soviet insistence on "positive" achievements—

> . . . taken with such obstinate persistence, that one would think one should have to drive home to every Soviet reader the advantages and superiority of our system to the capitalist system in the 42nd year of our revolution, mind you!—and as if we, ourselves, feel doubtful about it and are astonished, taking it as an illogical miracle.

Soviet literature is afraid to write of suffering and sadness "as if all our life must go on under a sky of sweets and sugar." As for the degradation of the Russian language, so scintillating, melodious, and picturesque—

> Are we jealously preserving this language? No! On the contrary, it is being increasingly soiled, twisted, and reduced to a garble. We are threatened with the danger that pellucid Russian will be replaced by an impoverished and lifeless language of bureaucratic red tape. Why have we allowed this nauseating language to creep into literature? Why do we admit to literature and even to membership in the Writers' Union people who don't know Russian and care not a fig for it?

Paustovsky's conclusion was concise and arresting: "It is, perhaps, that we shout so much and so loudly about truth in literature exactly because we lack it."

We were unable to persuade any Soviet writer (except Ehrenburg) to discuss with us the issues raised by Paustovsky. But clearly Soviet writers must discuss these issues among themselves. And evidently Paustovsky speaks not only for those who, like himself, can remember the European culture of prerevolutionary Russia but also for men and women in their twenties yearning for forms of expression and creation which would express, not official ideology, but personal experience.

The restlessness among the youth represents, I think, a great hope in the Soviet Union for evolution in a pragmatic and pluralistic direction. And, though consumer goods *per se* will work no miracles, one cannot help feeling that the movement toward a consumer society will in the long run begin to erode the dogmatic monolith. There can be no question that Khrushchev has committed his country to the consumer-goods merry-go-round. The critical question is whether the present Soviet capacity to build national power at a high rate through the efficient concentration of talent and resources can survive the transformation into a consumer society—or whether the consumer-goods passion may not upset the system of priorities and sap the single-minded intensity with which the Soviet economy dedicates itself to the building of national power. One detects already a new deference to consumer motives. Two-tone Soviet cars crowd Moscow streets. Television aerials soar over Moscow apartment houses. Russian girls queue up for Italian-style Czech shoes. The director of Moscow television, commenting on the possible exchange of programs between Britain and the Soviet Union, observes (with almost the sense of priorities of an American network official), "Perhaps football matches between the Russian and English teams at Moscow Sports Stadium could be shown. If there were a summit conference that too would be of interest. . . ." In the end, the commitment to the consumer-goods merry-go-round may fix the Soviet Union, as it has already fixed the United States.

All these represent possibilities, not predictions. The Poles keep up their own spirits by pretending that the Polish example is having "great impact on the Soviet Union." One is sorry to report that, in our visit to the Soviet Union, we never heard anybody mention anything going on in Poland. Still, the one thing above all indispensable for the victory of the Polish-Yugoslav tendency is the relaxation of international tensions. The stepping-up of the cold war might snuff out the inchoate burgeonings in the Soviet Union, jeopardize the incipient liberalism of Poland, and probably freeze the state of affairs in Yugoslavia.

Khrushchev said many disingenuous things in the United States; but almost the least disingenuous was the one for which he was most widely attacked—that is, his speech before the United Nations. Obviously Khrushchev would prefer disarmament on terms which would weaken his side least and the other side most; so, it must be admitted, would we. Yet his desire for a *détente* may well be genuine. It seems to me a grave error to suppose that there is no "real difference" between Stalin's Russia and the Russia of Khrushchev. Stalin *required* international tension: only an overhanging external threat could reconcile his people to his savage interior tyranny. Khrushchev, by diminishing the interior tyranny, diminishes at the same time the need for external crisis. To try to deal with Khrushchev with policies developed in the age of Stalin—which, until very recently, has been the West's idea—appears to me wrong. I would guess that

Khrushchev deeply wants a *détente* if only because of his superb confidence that the Communists will win the peaceful competition hands down in every area of human activity. No one in the West should seek a *détente* which would endanger any vital Western interest. But surely one of the strongest arguments for a *détente* is precisely the fact that relaxation might give the forces of pluralism and tolerance a chance to dissolve the ideological dogmatism of Soviet society.

The great value of a few weeks behind the Iron Curtain is to remind oneself of the treachery of abstractions. Both the Communists and ourselves have divided the world too glibly between the "democratic" or "capitalist" and the "socialist" or "Communist" camps. We have all assumed that these platonic essences are more "real" than their confused and imperfect approximations in the concrete experience of contemporary societies. We have thus accepted the mystique of either/or; and, in endowing essence with greater actuality than existence, we have committed what A. N. Whitehead used to call the "fallacy of misplaced concreteness." The great need of our times is liberation from the fanaticism of abstractions and a new concern for the empirical realities of life.

We are intermittently aware of the fact that the platonic essence of "capitalism" does not correspond to the many mutations of a ceaselessly changing economic system. Only just recently, Henry Cabot Lodge, addressing both Mr. Khrushchev and the New York Economic Club, casually discarded official American dogmas about the sacred and irrevocable character of free private enterprise. The difference between the early capitalism analyzed by Marx (and, Mr. Lodge implied, analyzed with some justice) and "our modern system of economic humanism" is as great "as the difference between black and white." He went on to announce, in defiance of a generation of Republican oratory, the Americans lived in a "welfare State" and that business prospered "at the same time that the Federal Government, in ways large and small, pervades our lives." Most of us agree with Mr. Lodge that capitalism is not a fixed orthodoxy or a single structure; it is a name which covers a variety of political and economic institutions.

We must equally begin to take note of the gap between the abstract model of totalitarianism and the fumbling and fallible reality. After the war, in a world shocked by the horror of Nazi concentration camps and fearful of the fanaticism of Stalinist communism, it was easy to accept the image of totalitarianism as an all-encompassing, all-devouring, *pure* expression of absolute power. George Orwell and Hannah Arendt developed this image in memorable literary terms, and for a moment we all succumbed to the notion that movement into totalitarianism from ordinary society involved a change of phase and a transvaluation of all ordinary human motives.

Yet human nature is too obstinate, various, and elusive to be efficiently mastered by any technique thus far devised short of physical obliteration. Of course, this is an available technique; and madmen like Hitler and the senile Stalin attempted precisely that. But they could never kill enough people to make their nightmare societies safe, and in the end they died themselves. The dictator who stops short of murdering all oppositionists, corruptionists, and apathetics must permit them to live; and, as soon as he permits them to live, he terminates the purity of his totalitarian experiment and admits dangerous strains of normality into his society. Normality seems a weak and sketchy emotion, but, given time, it can split a monolith as ivy can split a block of granite. We supposed for a moment during the war that Nazi Germany was the climax of totalitarian purity; we discovered afterwards that it was honeycombed with intrigue like a Byzantine court and that it actually mobilized less of its economic potential than Great Britain. We supposed for a moment after the war that Soviet Russia was even more pure and absolute a totalitarianism than Nazi Germany; but since the death of Stalin it has been divesting itself of much of the irrationality which we considered its essence; and we are discovering now that its power, while frightening enough, is not supernatural, and that human motives somehow survive and even prosper. And Poland and Yugoslavia confuse analysis further by presenting examples of what appear to be functioning, nontotalitarian, semiliberal Communist societies.

We must transfer our attention from essence to existence. Life is far more complicated than our categories. In this century, for example, "capitalism" has survived only by strong injections of "collectivism," and "collectivism" has survived only by strong injections of "capitalism." We must reject the mystique of either/or, and begin to lead the world back to intellectual sanity. We Westerners have a predominantly pragmatic and pluralistic tradition; we become dogmatists and monists only in times of crisis and hysteria. When we abandon the empirical approach to life, how can we hope to restrain others from turning into raving ideologues?

The question of the future is whether sensible Western policy can contribute to an evolution in the Soviet Union along lines already traced in Poland and Yugoslavia, or whether the tradition of infallibility is so profound and terrible in Russia that the Soviet leadership can never emerge from ideological madness. The Soviet Union is presently "dizzy with success." But given time, given peace and growth in the West, the forces of human normality, weak but irresistible, will perhaps begin to have their effect. Even in the Soviet Union, one finds still hanging in Tolstoy's country estate, in the calm and lovely Yasnaya Polyana, a picture of William Lloyd Garrison, the American abolitionist, inscribed in flowing hand: *"Liberty for each, for all, and for ever!"*

20.
Invasion of Europe, Family Style
(1957)

From the days of the Goths and the Huns, the battered continent of Europe has been subjected to a good many invasions. The earlier barbarian efforts were often attended by pillage and rapine. In more recent years, however, the invasions have sometimes (not, alas, always) taken technically more peaceful forms. In the 18th century, Europe suffered the Grand Tour, a leisurely inspection conducted by infuriatingly supercilious Englishmen. In the 19th century, it endured the organized mass tour, a form of torture for tourist and touree alike to which Mark Twain left an eloquent memorial in *Innocents Abroad*. In the early 20th century, it had to confront the Lost Generation, which for a decade filled the cafés of Paris and the beaches of Majorca with cries of creative joy and agony. But since the Second World War, it has had to face up to a new and more ominous challenge: invasion by families. And notably by American families.

It is natural enough that this invasion should at last take place. Intrepid householders—gallant and lonely pioneers—have dragged families along for a considerable time; but it has taken the spread of the automobile, the hard-surface road, and the filling station to make family travel finally possible on a large scale. The plain fact is that there is no reasonable way to take a large family around Europe except by motorcar. The nervous wear and tear of making train or plane reservations for a party of, say, six would demoralize a veteran of the Korean armistice negotiations (not to mention the cumulative cost of tickets, which is staggering, even if it is decreed that all children under 12 must travel third class or wash dishes in the restaurant car). Since the American family was mechanized earlier than any other, and since the American inherits an instinct for mobility from a life of driving thirty miles for a movie and fifty for a drink, it is natural enough, too, that the American family should be at the vanguard of this new blitzkrieg.

This summer there are probably more American families in Europe than ever before. Bemused Europeans, even in remotest villages, begin to find them a familiar sight, debouching en masse from their Detroit station wagons or Volkswagen microbuses in a litter of maps, guide books, and newspapers, tumbling out in unpredictable numbers like clowns from a circus car. First the father, grim and harried, bearing on inadequate shoulders the heavy burden of strategic and logistical planning, always persuaded that there will be no room at the inn; then the mother, absent and unconcerned, her mind on higher things like the beautiful town square or the fine Palladian church; then a scramble of children, speculating about baseball standings or demanding Coca-Cola. Europe, with all its wide experience, has never seen anything quite like this—anything quite so innocent or quite so devastating. But the' great old continent, having taken so much in its stride, seems prepared to accept and absorb even this.

The penetrating reader will have concluded by now that this battle report is not based entirely on research in libraries. The author is in midstream, so to speak, on a tour of Europe with an infinitely patient wife and four spirited children, all six traveling in the usual Volkswagen. It is his purpose to reassure those who are considering a similar expedition in this or another summer and to encourage those who have already embarked on safaris of their own. The message is: it can be done—and it's worth doing.

There are ghastly moments in this form of travel, as indeed there are in any form. Six people of varying degrees of equability and temper are shut up for long periods in a moving vehicle—and often (especially in Europe in recent weeks) at a high temperature. Let me warn all heads of families to make sure that the car is large enough so that there is a minimum of physical contact. Moreover, it is apparently a principle of the common law that every child has a natural right to a window. But even when these conditions are satisfied, one still has the occasional impression that Laocoön and his troupe are traveling in the back seat.

The exotic scene outside provokes an endless series of comments, reactions, and questions. Particularly if the father has the misfortune to be an historian by profession, he is expected to have an endless fund of knowledge about all regions, periods, and personalities; in vain does one protest that one's *expertise* expires beyond the three-mile limit. In the end, one thinks fondly of Ring Lardner's classic rendition of a father's response after hours of remorseless interrogation by the younger members of his family—" 'Shut up,' he explained." But the alternative to Q. and A. is to play car games; and most car games, whether they involve constructing the alphabet out of signs on the road or counting gas stations or whatever, are guaranteed to drive the adult players in a very short time to imbecility.

Moreover, sightseeing itself can be an unexpected drain on energy. Some places, like Venice, for example, or Pompeii, are made to order for family visits. Here the sights occur in natural settings; there is plenty of stimulus to the imagination; you can get the point without detailed technical knowledge; and there are lots of places to rest. But an unvaried diet of galleries and churches can break down the morale of the most tractable child (and the most hopeful parent). And let the parent not deceive himself about his own responsibility in sightseeing. He had better review those old lecture notes from Fine Arts 23 if he wants to satisfy his children about the difference between the Sienese and Florentine schools or the evolution of the baroque. The discipline thus imposed on the parent is useful. He regards with appreciation more fervent and grateful than ever a gallery arranged along rational lines like the Uffizi in Florence. He detests more profoundly than ever a gallery arranged on the logic of a junk shop, like the Pitti.

But the point about sightseeing is that everyone's absorptive capacity is limited (even, perhaps, that of parents). At times, one is tempted to growl at children, "Well, if baseball is all you care about, it would have been easier to have got you a season ticket to Fenway Park." This is no doubt a powerful line, but it should not be used every day. The most willing child succumbs in time to museum ataxia. Why not? Think of yourself at the age of 10 or 14! The answer is neither indignation nor grief. It is never to stray too far from a beach, which remains the best outlet for excess energy and excess boredom.

And there are compensations. One gratifying feature of traveling with a large number of children is the amount of sympathy one gets along the way for courage and self-sacrifice in the face of presumably appalling difficulties. In fact, family travel has many advantages quite apart from the pleasure of getting to know one's family.

First of all, Europeans seem to like children. Our youngest, a smiling little boy of 8, has been so spoiled by the hotel porters who have patted his head and the museum guards who have waved him through without a ticket that his older brother and sisters felt themselves compelled to take stern measures to set him right. But the father discovers with some relief that this enthusiasm for little boys induces a greater tolerance for the little boy's father as he fumbles with language or currency. Similarly, our oldest girl, a pretty young lady of fourteen, has aroused an intensity of interest new in her experience. She has been admired, ogled, followed, and even pinched—experiences for which she was not prepared by life in Cambridge, Mass. But this unconcealed delight in her charms, while a nuisance to her, can sometimes get things for her distrait parents which it seems unlikely they could get for themselves.

For another thing, family travel represents the only known way to solve the European hotel dilemma. By the European hotel dilemma I mean, of course, the problem of the bedroom/bathroom ratio. European hotels, most of them built, it would seem, before the democratization of plumbing, still tend to offer many fewer baths than rooms. This is a constant irritation, to the individual traveler. For the chief of an expedition, however, it could not be better. It means that he asks for three double rooms, one with private bath. He thereby gains the amenities of life for his family, saves money, and does not violate the ratio.

In the same way, family travel makes it possible to conquer the European meal problem. Food is wonderful in Europe, but one tends to be served a good deal more than the normal American is prepared to eat. We all love Italian cooking, for example. But what person, used to a drugstore lunch or a sandwich at the desk, can put away at midday a heaping plate of *pasta* followed by a generous meat course followed by a large salad followed by a sweet, all washed down with liters of wine? Americans who try to adjust themselves to an Italian diet are likely to end up at Montecatini Terme, drinking odorous waters for their liver. With a family, there is no problem at all. You simply order three or four meals and six plates. Everyone is happy. The children are well fed; the waiter is pleased at a decent display of economy; the management admires you for having gone Italian; and the strain at once on the budget and the stomach is relieved.

One continental lunch or dinner a day is enough for anyone except a coal miner (even discounting the continental breakfast, the only feature of European life thus far which has driven my own children to overt complaint). Family travel has an easy answer to this: revive the picnic. Instead of stuffing yourself at huge expense in restaurants, why not eat pleasantly in the open? Every market is filled with tasty cold meats; butter, mayonnaise, and honey come unexpectedly and conveniently out of tubes; wine is available at the price one pays for soda pop in the United States; and it is difficult anywhere to find better bread, strawberries, and cherries. What better dispensation than to sit in a mass of wild flowers in a sun-drenched Alpine meadow, cooled by breezes fresh off the snow, watching lush green valleys unroll for miles and, in the distance, glistening white mountains. Who would spare a thought for Howard Johnson now?

I could list other incidental advantages of travel. It even helps smooth over the problems of family management. For years, it seems, one's children try to rene-gotiate their allowances, demanding escalator clauses or cost-of-living bonuses. And, indeed, such sums as fifty cents or a dollar a week come to have the sound of sweated wages, fit only for peons. How much more impressive these sums appear in foreign currency! Six hundred and twenty lira a week is princely; one thousand (to which excess one is tempted to go) seems a fortune. The only drawback is contemplating the problems of contraction in scale as one returns to hard-currency countries.

Families, of course, differ widely among themselves. One notes several varieties of traveling families. Most admirable is the rugged family. This one lives in pup tents and sleeping bags and disdains the whole idea of making advance reservations or going to bed between sheets. It lives cheaper, gets to know the country better, has more picturesque experiences, and is bitten by a wilder variety of insect.

At the opposite extreme, there is the apprehensive family. This one lives only at the Hotel Splendido or at a carefully vetted pension. It never dares venture outside the hotel dining room and insists, even there, on bottled water. It keeps to the main thoroughfare and is in bed every night by nine. This tour is more expensive, more antiseptic, and conceivably less rewarding than any other.

In between there is the *moyen sensuel* family, which rocks along on the momentum of its own inconsistencies. Heaven alone knows where it gets its hotels and restaurants—from guidebooks or great aunts or chance acquaintances along the way. Somehow it all works out. And the traveling family now enjoys a vast freemasonry. Words of commendation or warning travel fast along mysterious routes. As tramps are supposedly told by cryptic symbols at the gatepost of the inclination of the people within, so families single out the places entitled to the magic password, "They are nice to children." They had better be—family travel is obviously the wave of the future.

THE
BITTER
HERITAGE

●●●

Vietnam and
American Democracy
1941–1968

REVISED EDITION

For those fighting in Vietnam

As Lord Milner put it some time later on, 'in a certain sense the war would never be ended'; it would just fade away. The guerrilla phase would be ended by the armies; and after that, brigandage in the mountains and the back-veldts would be put down by armed police.

This was an error destined to cost us dear. . . . The flames of partisan warfare broke out again and again in regions completely pacified. . . . This long-drawn struggle bred shocking evils. . . .

Never, never, never believe any war will be smooth and easy. . . . The Statesman who yields to war fever must realize that once the signal is given he is no longer the master of policy but the slave of unforeseeable and uncontrollable events. Antiquated War Offices, weak, incompetent or arrogant Commanders, untrustworthy allies, hostile neutrals, malignant Fortune, ugly surprises, awful miscalculations—all take their seats at the Council Board. . . . Always remember, however sure you are that you can easily win, that there would not be a war if the other man did not think he also had a chance.

—Winston S. Churchill,
A Roving Commission: My Early Life

Contents

Remarks on United States Foreign Policy
Arthur M. Schlesinger, Jr.
March 8, 1967

The situation in Vietnam presents us with our most urgent problem today in the field of foreign affairs. But
the Vietnam problem is only the most vivid expression
of a deeper crisis in American foreign policy. The roots
of this deeper crisis lie not in the malevolence of men
but in the obsolescence of ideas.

For we live in a time when the velocity of history is
greater than ever before. The world has changed more
in the last hundred years than it did in the thousand
years preceding. The transformations wrought by science and technology have acquired a cumulative momentum and an exponential effect. One consequence is
that perceptions of reality become obsolete with new
and disconcerting rapidity. This would be all right, if
the way we perceive reality changed as reality itself
changes. But, as we all know, it doesn't. Our perceptions of reality are crystallized in a collection of stereotypes; and people become so fond of the stereotypes, so
much at home with them, that they stop looking at actuality. In this way they protect themselves from the
most painful of human necessities, which is, of course,
the taking of thought.

The rapidity with which reality outstrips our perceptions of reality is an underlying source of our troubles
with foreign policy. I do not suggest that, if our perceptions were kept up to date, this would solve all our
problems, because many of the great problems of the
world are in their nature insoluble. But I am sure that
we cannot make much sense at all in the world as long

as we continue to base policy on anachronism. We must be forever vigilant to prevent transient strategies from turning into cherished and permanent verities.

Thus the ideas which dominate our foreign policy today were largely shaped by a very different world—a world threatened by massive, unitary, centralized movements of military aggression and social fanaticism: Adolf Hitler and Nazism in the thirties, Josef Stalin and Communism in the forties and early fifties. These ideas were admirably suited for this world and admirably achieved their objectives. They reflected a great and challenging time in world history, and the men who grew up in that time and acquired those ideas quite naturally find it hard to relinquish them. Yet the world itself has changed drastically—and this fact surely demands the review, if not the revision, of the presuppositions of our policy.

The most drastic change of all has taken place, as this essay points out, within the Communist empire itself. Twenty years ago Communism was still relatively monolithic in ideology and in discipline. Communist parties and governments everywhere took their orders from Moscow. A new Communist state meant the automatic extension of Russian national power; and, given the character of Soviet purpose, this in turn meant an increased threat to the security and freedom of the democracies. Communism, in short, was a unified and expanding international movement capable of the gravest possible challenge to the democratic world.

But that was 1947. It was true through the years of the Korean War. But it is now 1967, and Communism today is in a very different situation. For the quarrel between Moscow and Peking means the irrevocable end of the unity of Communist discipline and ideology.

It means the disappearance of any sole and single center of authority in the Communist empire. It has consequently set all Communist states free to respond to national interests and to pursue national policies. It has thereby transformed the character of the Communist problem. In this new polycentrist world, divergent nationalist forces are producing a wide diversity of behavior among the Communist states. Communism is no longer a unified, coordinated, centralized world conspiracy. This is the new reality which wise policy must surely begin to take into account.

The administration has partly recognized this evolution of affairs so far as Eastern Europe is concerned. President Johnson's emphasis on "bridge-building," as in his excellent speech last October, expresses a shrewd understanding of the advantages to the United States in encouraging diversity within the European Communist bloc and in enlarging the ties between the Eastern European states and the West. But we have not yet begun to apply this understanding to the problems of Western Europe. For in Western Europe we still seem committed to policies which were superbly brave and right in the world of twenty years ago but are much less germane to the world today.

So long as we insist on regarding NATO, for example, as first of all a means of deterring a Soviet invasion of Western Europe, we doom it to irrelevance. Thus the Chairman of the Joint Chiefs of Staff said only the other day, "The threat is, if anything, greater than it was in the day [our troops] were put there." If this assertion represents the administration's perception of European reality, one can only admire so stern and determined a fidelity to the truths of yesteryear. For, whatever the danger twenty years ago when Western Europe was politically demoralized and economically prostrate, the notion that an invasion of Western Europe ranks very high on Moscow's list of priorities today obviously requires an extraordinary *tour de force* of the imagination.

And, in the Far East, the administration seems determined to perceive Communism as it was a generation ago. It evidently regards East Asian Communism as a homogeneous and disciplined movement of international aggression, posing a threat to the United States comparable to that posed by Hitler in the thirties or Stalin in the forties. "The contest in Vietnam," the President has said, "is part of a wider pattern of aggressive purposes." The Secretary of State's constant reliance on the Munich analogy makes it clear that he sees the United States as challenged, not by ragged bands of guerrillas in black pajamas without heavy artillery or air power, but by a heavily armed, highly wound-up, overwhelmingly strong military power committed to the course of instant expansion.

For the evidence fails to sustain the thesis that the war in Vietnam is Mao's war or that the Viet Cong are only the spearhead of a Chinese program of aggression. Indeed, most of the evidence suggests that Asian Communism is as fragmented as—perhaps even more fragmented than—European Communism. The proposition that we are fighting in Asia to restrain Chinese aggression—that we must fight in Vietnam today or else we will be fighting in Hawaii tomorrow—is a product not of contemporary evidence but of mechanical historical analogy. It represents the triumph of stereotype over reality. For the evidence strongly suggests that we confront in Vietnam, not a fateful test of wills with China, but a nasty local war, mounted by Communists who want to take over Vietnam, not for Peking but for themselves—and who, if they succeeded, might be no more enslaved by Peking than North Korea is today.

This is, of course, a very different situation from the one described to us by the administration. It is a more manageable situation—and also a situation calling far less for the sacrifice of American lives. And, if this is the real situation, the argument for bringing the war to an end and stopping the killing seems very strong indeed. Hence the great present concern with the problem of negotiation.

One can have no question about the genuineness of President Johnson's wish for a negotiated settlement in Vietnam. But the administration has made it clear, I would judge, that, while negotiation remains its ultimate objective, it does not consider negotiation advantageous at this time (April 1967). Why else, unless it thought this, would Washington have hardened the American terms at the very time that Hanoi apparently allowed Moscow to soften the North Vietnamese terms?

In April 1965 Hanoi laid down its Four Points as a basis for negotiation. These points were not very helpful. They included such hopeless stipulations as the withdrawal of United States forces from South Vietnam (though it was not always clear whether this meant withdrawal in advance of negotiations) and the final settlement of the internal affairs of South Vietnam "in accordance with the program" of the Viet Cong. These points, especially if the first implied prior withdrawal, were clearly and rightly unacceptable to the United States.

The American position as it evolved in response was that the United States was prepared to suspend the bombing of North Vietnam for "nothing more," as *Time* magazine has put it, "than an agreement to begin negotiations." Thus the Secretary of State said on February 16, 1966, "Some governments said Hanoi would talk if we would stop bombing North Vietnam. We tried that twice . . . but it made no difference. Hanoi would not come to the conference table." On March 13, 1966, the Vice President said that, if Hanoi had shown any interest in negotiation during the recent bombing pause, this "obviously would have kept the bombing pause going."

Now, a year later, both Kosygin and U Thant said that North Vietnam was prepared to meet these terms. If the United States unconditionally stopped the bombing of North Vietnam, these authorities claimed, negotiation could begin. There was no mention of the Four Points. In other words, as Mr. Lippmann has put it, they "brought us the assurance that our 1966 terms—suspension for an unconditional parley—would now be accepted by Hanoi." One cannot be sure, of course, that Moscow could have delivered Hanoi to the conference table on these terms. Ho Chi Minh's passion for negotiation is, to put it mildly, reserved and equivocal; and his tone is abominable. But this is no argument against making the attempt. The whole Soviet initiative was unprecedented, and, if it had been taken up, the responsibility for producing Hanoi would have fallen on Moscow. If we really wanted negotiation, we had a good chance of having it in 1967 on the same terms that we sought it in 1966.

But these terms were evidently now unacceptable to us. For Washington has considerably stiffened its position and now demands from Hanoi things it did not demand a year ago. Publicly we have only asked for the prior assurance of some unspecified act of reciprocal de-escalation—"just almost any step," the President said—in return for the cessation of the bombing.

But privately President Johnson in his letter of February 2 to Ho Chi Minh was far more specific and drastic. He then said he would stop the bombing of North Vietnam only "as soon as I am assured that infiltration into South Vietnam by land and by sea has been stopped." This meant, in the view of Mr. Reston of *The New York Times,* "that the North Vietnamese [had to] act *first* to stop the infiltration . . . before the United States stops the bombing." It meant that Ho Chi Minh could no longer supply his forces in South Vietnam while the United States retained the right to supply American forces. President Johnson's offer to desist at the same time from "further augmentation of United States forces in South Vietnam" could hardly have been deeply moving to those in Hanoi who reflected that there were already 420,000 American troops in South Vietnam as against 50,000 Vietnamese regulars and that, under the President's terms, the American troops would be free, in the words of Mr. Reston, "to hunt and destroy an enemy cut off from his supplies in the North." Could anyone have honestly supposed that such a proposition would be faintly interesting to Hanoi?

Not only did President Johnson thus harden the American position beyond anything disclosed to the American people (his letter to Ho Chi Minh was released by Hanoi); but he described the North Vietnamese proposal as one requiring that we cease " 'unconditionally' and *permanently* [emphasis added] our bombing operations against your country." The repeated American insistence that Hanoi demands a "permanent" cessation of bombing reinforces the impression of our reluctance to negotiate at this time. For neither Kosygin nor Podgorny said anything about "permanent" cessation. Ho Chi Minh's reply to President Johnson said that "if the U.S. Government really wants these talks, it must first of all stop uncondition- ally its bombing raids and all other acts of war against the Democratic Republic of Vietnam." He did not use the word *permanent*. The very idea that one state could expect another to pledge never, never, never, in whatever contingency and in all perpetuity, to refrain from bombing another state is self-evidently absurd. It would represent a derogation of sovereignty that no nation would ever accept. No doubt the word "perma- nent" sounded at some point in the medley of voices out of Hanoi. But a resourceful diplomacy, thus faced with conflicting proposals, would surely have done as we did when confronted by two contradictory propos- als from Khrushchev during the Cuban missile crisis: it would have responded to the one that suited our inter- ests best. Had we followed in October 1962 the prac- tice of ignoring the acceptable and fastening on the un- acceptable proposal, we might well have stumbled into the Third World War.

If we had really wanted negotiation in February 1967, we would have ended the bombing as the Rus- sians suggested and let the burden of delivering Hanoi to the conference table fall to Moscow. On the other hand, if we could not figure out how negotiation at this point could yield satisfactory results, we would do exactly as we did—ignore the Soviet initiative, claim that we knew Hanoi's mind better than Kosygin and Podgorny did, acknowledge only the most extreme and extravagant proposals from North Vietnam and put forward proposals of our own that we could be absolutely certain Hanoi would not accept. The ac- tions of the administration lead irresistibly to the con- clusion that it does not consider this a favorable time to negotiate, and that it cannot summon up the energy or imagination to seek a solution in unfavorable circumstances.

One regrets that high officials have seen fit to accompany this by rather far-fetched misrepresentations of other people's ideas. Thus the Secretary of State said, "Proposals substantially similar to those put forward by Senator Kennedy were explored prior, during, and since the Tet truce—all without result." Yet the Secretary of State, who is an intelligent man, must surely know that the administration proposal, insisting as it did on prior action by Hanoi, was very different from Senator Kennedy's proposal. How could he possibly describe two proposals—one for the conditional and the other for the unconditional cessation of bombing—as "substantially similar"? And how for that matter could the President of the United States imply that the cessation of the bombing of the north would leave our soldiers defenseless in the south? "If they are going to lob their mortar shells into the backs of our soldiers," he said, ". . . you must, if you are at all fair to those who are defending you there, permit them to respond." I know of no proposals that American troops should stop defending themselves or even any for the cessation of bombing in the south. Such misstatements advance neither the clarity of the debate nor the credibility of the administration.

Still, I do not suggest that the administration's evident desire to postpone negotiations is without rational justification. The reasoning behind it, I imagine, runs something like this. The administration apparently regards the recent signals from Hanoi as a response to the bombing of the north and, in consequence, a vindication of the bombing policy. At the same time, it evidently does not see how, given the present military balance, a negotiation can lead to a desirable outcome. It looks forward, moreover, to the stabilization of the political situation in South Vietnam through the formation of a civilian government (though, if Marshal Ky should end up as head of this government, it seems doubtful how much more stable the situation would be). Therefore, it reasons, if we bomb a few months more, Hanoi will be even more anxious to end the war than it is today; Saigon will be in better shape; and at that point we can negotiate under much more advantageous conditions.

This analysis is not illogical, and it may well be right. But it is not so self-evidently right as to be immune to question. For one thing, its basic assumption is that the peace signals are as a response to bombing. Yet it is entirely possible—I should say, even probable—that the signals from Hanoi are a response, not to our air war in the north, but to our ground war in the south. Hanoi and the Viet Cong may well have come to the conclusion that they can hope neither for a military victory in the south nor an American withdrawal, and that they therefore must begin to shift from the idea of a short-run military victory to that of a long-run political victory. Furthermore, the turmoil in China has doubtless conferred a greater freedom of action on Hanoi. These reasons are quite sufficient to explain Hanoi's renewed interest in negotiations, without supposing that it is all a result of bombing.

Moreover, the theory that we can obtain more favorable terms by intensifying the war is based on an old fallacy—that, while we escalate, the other side will sit still, and that escalation will consequently bring us a clear margin of superiority. This has been the reasoning behind every previous step of escalation; and it has always proved wrong. The other side, instead of sitting still, had escalated too. Instead of achieving a margin of superiority, all we have done is to raise the stalemate to a more bloody and more explosive level. The Russians, for example, cannot be expected to do nothing while we widen the war in North Vietnam. They are already increasing their shipments of anti-aircraft missiles and guns and other arms and supplies. Our bombing will further harden the resolve of the North Vietnamese themselves. If past experience has any relevance, the consequence in six months of this new exercise in escalation will be, not at all the victory the generals keep promising us, but a new and even more perilous stalemate.

The problem is that there is never a right time for negotiation. In the past some in Hanoi have no doubt construed our own calls for negotiation as a sign of weakness and have, in consequence, argued for stiffening their own position. So some in Washington today construe Hanoi's signals as a sign of weakness, contend that the enemy is on the run and call for an intensification of military pressure. By this logic we cannot negotiate when we are behind because we are weak; and we can't negotiate either when we are ahead because, if we keep on doing what we have been doing, we will be even farther ahead at some later point.

The time has surely come to break the hopeless logic which can never find the right moment for negotiation. Too much is imperiled by the continuation of the war: the lives of American soldiers, as well as of the Vietnamese; the confidence and support of our allies; our position in Europe and Latin America; our relationship with the Soviet Union; not to mention the vast needs of our national society—our cities, our schools, our poor, our minorities, our old and our young.

The urgent need is to explore every opportunity to slow down the war. The bombing of North Vietnam has failed to halt the infiltration or to break the will of the people of North Vietnam or to bring Hanoi to the conference table. Moreover, if we bombed North Vietnam back to the stone age tomorrow, the war would continue in South Vietnam. The cruel fact is that we can never win a guerrilla war in South Vietnam by the aerial obliteration of North Vietnam. Instead, therefore, of seeking excuses to avoid negotiation, instead of upping our ante and insisting on the worst possible interpretations of our adversaries' position, it would be interesting for us to appear for a moment before the world as the champion, not of bombing and destruction, but of vision and peace.

There is a deeper question involved here—and that has to do with the character of America's role in the world. There is abroad in the land the notion that foreign policy is not, as we have traditionally supposed, about the accommodation of conflicting national entities, but about questions of right and wrong. This, oddly enough, is a view of foreign policy shared by the Secretary of State and the New Left. And one detects in some of our official pronouncements the implication that the United States, as a result of its inherent moral superiority, is the world's judge, jury and executioner; and that, where things are wrong, it is the American mission to set them right. This seems a distorted, even dangerous, view of the American role in the world. For, while the men who founded this republic did believe that America had a mission to mankind, they conceived this mission as one to be spread by example and persuasion, not by force. John Quincy Adams well stated the classical American creed when he noted that the United States would always view with sympathy any foreign group struggling for independence: "But she goes not abroad in search of monsters to destroy.

She is the well-wisher to the freedom and independence of all. She is the champion and vindicator only
of her own."

I fear a current tendency to go abroad in search of
monsters to destroy. Yet this enterprise ignores the limitations on our own knowledge and on our own power.
President Kennedy put the matter well some years ago:
"We must face the fact that the United States is neither
omnipotent nor omniscient—that we are only 6 per
cent of the world's population—that we cannot impose
our will on the other 94 per cent of mankind—that we
cannot right every wrong or reverse each adversary—
and that therefore there cannot be an American solution to every world problem."

The world is filled with contradiction and evil and
will continue to be so for a long time. We cannot hope
to resolve every contradiction and overcome all the
evils and produce an American solution to every problem—especially if we try to do so on the basis of
stereotypes which express the reality of another generation. It is bad enough to be a messiah; it is even worse
to be a messiah spouting clichés. And, if we insist on
casting ourselves as the world's savior, the effect on
ourselves will be as fatal as on the rest of mankind. For
no one can play God with impunity. "He who would
act the angel," said Pascal, "acts the brute"—a warning alike to men and nations.

1.

How We Got There

Why we are in Vietnam is today a question of mainly historical interest. We *are* there, for better or for worse, and we must deal with the situation that exists. Our national security may not have compelled us to draw a line across Southeast Asia where we did, but, having drawn it, we cannot lightly abandon it. Our stake in South Vietnam may have been self-created, but it has none the less become real. Our precipitate withdrawal now would have ominous reverberations throughout Asia. The magnitude of our national concern is measured by our commitment of over 400,000 troops, young men of exceptional skill and gallantry, engaged in cruel and difficult warfare. This is a larger force than we had in Korea fifteen years ago—larger indeed than we have had in any war in our history, except for the Civil War and the two World Wars. More American soldiers already have died in combat in Vietnam than in the Revolutionary War, the War of 1812, the Mexican War or the Spanish-American War.

We must, I say, deal with the situation that exists. We cannot undo the events which have brought us to this tragic climax. Still, a glance at the past may at least remind us of illusions which will otherwise continue to mislead us in the future. For our experience with Vietnam is older than we generally recognize. This is not the first time, for example, that Vietnam has involved us in war. In 1941 Franklin Roosevelt regarded the Japanese movement into Indochina as a threat to vital American interests. He saw it as a threat because the occupation of Vietnam would give Japan a base for larger aggression against all Southeast Asia and also, more specifically, because it would jeopardize the supply of natural rubber upon which the American defense industry depended. In consequence, the Japanese demands on Indochina in July 1941 led directly to the American decision to freeze Japanese assets in the United States; and this action, in turn, led directly to the Japanese decision to attack the American fleet at Pearl Harbor.

Vietnam thus precipitated American entry into the Second World War; nor did this faraway land thereafter disappear from the mind of the American President. Convinced that the war would set off a worldwide revolt against European colonialism, Roosevelt judged Indochina one of the weakest links in the chain of western empire. In March 1943 he therefore proposed to the British Foreign Minister, Anthony Eden, that Indochina, instead of being restored to the French after the war, should be placed under an international trusteeship and prepared for independence. He discussed this idea with Chiang Kai-shek at the Cairo Conference and with Stalin at Teheran, When the State Department suggested to the President in early 1944 that the French army would undoubtedly return to Indochina in the natural course of military events, Roosevelt told Under Secretary Stettinius that "no French troops whatever should be used in operations in Indo-China." He told Secretary Hull: "France has had the country—thirty million inhabitants—for nearly one hundred years, and the people are worse off than they were at the beginning. . . . France has milked it for one hundred years. The people of Indochina are entitled to something better than that." Indochina was much on his mind when he went to Yalta in February 1945. "For two whole years," he then said—

> I have been terribly worried about Indochina. . . . I suggested . . . to Chiang, that Indochina be set up under a trusteeship—have a Frenchman, one or two Indochinese, and a Chinese and a Russian, because they are on the coast, and maybe a Filipino and an American, to educate them for self-government. . . .
> Stalin liked the idea, China liked the idea. The British didn't like it. It might bust up their empire, because if the Indochinese were to work together and eventually get their independence, the Burmese might do the same thing.

Roosevelt's proposal had a certain eccentricity of detail; but it was founded in realism and wisdom, and, if its essence had been carried out, the world might have been spared much bloodshed and agony. Alas, the idea died with him a few months later. The State Department soon expressed the belief that there could be no trusteeship in Indochina "except under the French Government," adding vaguely that it was President Truman's purpose "at some appropriate time" to ask France for "some positive indication of its intention in regard to the establishment of basic liberties and an increasing measure of self-government in Indochina."

Five months after Roosevelt's death, Ho Chi Minh, a Vietnamese Communist who had served the Comintern for twenty years and had more recently emerged as a leader of the anti-Japanese resistance movement (in which capacity he had worked closely with the American Office of Strategic Services), proclaimed the Declaration of Independence of the Democratic Republic of Vietnam. This document, curiously, was modeled on the American Declaration of 1776 and actually began with the exceedingly non-Marxist quotation: "All men are created equal. They are endowed by their Creator with certain unalienable rights, among these are Life, Liberty and the pursuit of Happiness." The French responded by a determined attempt to reestablish colonial rule. For the next eight years this effort, occasionally interrupted by spasms of negotiation, brought the French and such Vietnamese as they could persuade to go along with them into increasingly savage conflict with the Viet Minh under Ho Chi Minh—who, in consequence, emerged increasingly the hero of Vietnamese nationalism in its war for independence.

The American government at first paid little attention to the fighting in Vietnam. But the fall of mainland China to the Chinese Communists in 1949 and the invasion of South Korea by the North Korean Communists in 1950 produced new anxieties about communist expansion in Asia. In this light the French appeared to be holding the southern line against Asian communism; the State Department, condemning Ho as "an agent of world communism," pronounced the French role in Indochina "an integral part of the worldwide resistance by the Free Nations to Communist attempts at conquest and subversion"; and, once the Paris government had satisfied the American anticolonial conscience by making token concessions to its client regime in Saigon under Emperor Bao Dai, the Truman administration was prepared to send the French military and economic equipment. The Eisenhower administration enlarged this policy. By 1954, according to French figures, the United States was paying 78.25 per cent (490 billion old francs) of the

French cost of the war; the French were paying 21.75 per cent (136 billion old francs).

Our growing involvement in Indochina was taking place for reasons less specific than those which had moved Roosevelt a dozen years earlier. The wartime development of synthetic rubber had long since ended American dependence on Asian rubber plantations. Nor did an internal revolt of a band of Vietnamese nationalists, even if led by Communists, threaten all Southeast Asia as had the external conquest of the country a decade before by a powerful militarist state dedicated to the establishment of the Greater East Asia Co-prosperity Sphere. Secretary of State Dulles tried to supply this deficiency by invoking the specter of China. "There is a risk," he said in September 1953, "that, as in Korea, Red China might send its own army into Indochina. The Chinese Communist regime should realize that such a second aggression could not occur without grave consequences, which might not be confined to Indochina." But the prospect of a Viet Minh victory even without Chinese intervention was soon deemed almost as alarming. "You have a row of dominoes set up," President Eisenhower explained at a press conference early in 1954, "you knock over the first one, and what will happen to the last one is that it will go over very quickly." So the domino theory entered the political vocabulary. Even though the biggest domino of all, China, had fallen five years earlier without starting the chain reaction, the possible fall of the less consequential Indochinese domino was suddenly invested with the most fateful consequences.

The commander of the French force beleaguered in the fortress of Dien Bien Phu now began to plead for American military relief. Within the American government Admiral Radford, then chairman of the Joint

Chiefs of Staff, proposed an air strike from the Philippines. A few days later Vice President Nixon even suggested the possibility of "putting our boys in." However, President Eisenhower, doubtful about unilateral military intervention, decided to seek British collaboration. "If . . . Indochina passes into the hands of the Communists," he wrote Prime Minister Winston Churchill on April 4, 1954, "the ultimate effect on our and your global strategic position . . . could be disastrous. . . . We failed to halt Hirohito, Mussolini and Hitler by not acting in unity and in time. That marked the begining of many years of stark tragedy and desperate peril. May it not be that our nations have learned something from that lesson?" Then Dulles pressed on Anthony Eden, once again Foreign Secretary, the case for joint intervention. "I am fairly hardened to crises," Eden wrote later, "but I went to bed that night a troubled man, I did not believe that anything less than intervention on a Korean scale, if that, would have any effect in Indochina." Churchill thus summed up the American proposal: "What we are being asked to do is to assist in misleading the Congress into approving a military operation which would be in itself ineffective, and might well bring the world to the verge of a major war."

The campaign for intervention also caused concern in Washington. The Army Chief of Staff, General Matthew B. Ridgway, who had commanded the United Nations army in Korea, and the Chief of Plans, General James M. Gavin, both questioned the theory that bombing could reverse the tide of war, and both regarded the commitment of the American Army to war on the Asian mainland as strategically indefensible. "In Korea," as Ridgway later wrote, "we had learned that air and naval power alone cannot win a war and that inadequate ground forces cannot win one either. It was incredible to me that we had forgotten that bitter lesson so soon—that we were on the verge of making that same tragic error."

And in the United States Congress a number of senators expressed their doubts about the direction of American policy. Senator John F. Kennedy of Massachusetts had visited Indochina in 1951. "We have allied ourselves," he had said on his return, "to the desperate effort of a French regime to hang on to the remnants of empire. . . . To check the southern drive of communism makes sense but not only through reliance on the force of arms. The task is rather to build a strong native non-communist sentiment within these areas and rely on that as a spearhead of defense rather than upon the legions of General de Lattre. To do this apart from and in defiance of innately nationalistic aims spells foredoomed failure. . . . Without the support of the native population, there is no hope of success in any of the countries of Southeast Asia."

Now Kennedy rose in the Senate to say that, if the American people were to go to war for the fourth time in the century, "particularly a war which we now realize would threaten the survival of civilization," they had a right to inquire in detail into the nature of the struggle and the possible alternatives. He recapitulated the Washington litany about Indochina—Secretary of State Dean Acheson in 1952 ("the military situation appears to be developing favorably"), Assistant Secretary of State for the Far East Walter Robertson in 1953 ("in Indochina we believe the tide is now turning"), Secretary of Defense Charles Wilson (French victory is "both possible and probable") and Admiral Radford ("the French are going to win") in 1954—and contrasted the gush of official optimism with the grim actuality. "I am frankly of the belief," Kennedy said, "that no amount of American military assistance in Indochina can conquer . . . 'an enemy of the people' which has the sympathy and covert support of the people. . . . For the United States to intervene unilaterally and to send troops into the most difficult terrain in the world, with the Chinese able to pour in unlimited manpower, would mean that we would face a situation whch would be far more difficult than even that we encountered in Korea. It seems to me it would be a hopeless situation." He asked serious consideration of the question "whether all or part of Indochina is absolutely essential to the security of Asia and the free world."

The Democratic leader in the Senate, Lyndon B. Johnson of Texas, was even harsher about the Eisenhower policy. "The United States," Johnson said,

> is in clear danger of being left naked and alone in a hostile world. . . . American foreign policy has never in its history suffered such a stunning reversal. . . . What is American policy on Indochina? All of us have listened to the dismal series of reversals and confusions and alarms and excursions which have emerged from Washington over the past few weeks. . . . We have been caught bluffing by our enemies. Our friends and allies are frightened and wondering, as we do, where we are headed. . . . This picture of our country needlessly weakened in the world today is so painful that we should turn our eyes from abroad and look homeward.

The Eisenhower administration had not hit upon the latter-day doctrine that no one should criticize American policy in Vietnam lest such criticism encourage the enemy—the doctrine by which President Johnson a dozen years later sought to deter the Senator Johnsons of his own day; and the nervous Nellies of 1954 had their effect. The opposition of the congressional leaders, of Generals Ridgway and Gavin and of the British eventually forced the administration to drop the plan of military intervention. Could this plan have worked? Obviously air strikes alone would not have defeated the Viet Minh, and the Army was unquestionably right in supposing that intervention would soon have meant ground forces. If American combat troops had entered Vietnam in 1954 instead of 1965, they could certainly have beaten the Viet Minh in pitched battle; but they could hardly have crushed the guerrilla uprising or the nationalist emotions which sustained it. In retrospect, intervention in 1954 would only have dragged the United States into a conflict which would have seemed to most of Indochina—and most of Asia—a war not against communism but against national independence, a war not for freedom but for France.

But Eisenhower eventually decided against intervention, the French abandoned the fight after the surrender of Dien Bien Phu and negotiations in Geneva, in which the United States declined to take part, resulted in the *de facto* partition of Vietnam at the 17th parallel and the independence of Laos and Cambodia. Two months after Geneva, Dulles, in a conference at Manila, organized the Southeast Asia Treaty Organization (SEATO) including Pakistan, Thailand, the Philippines, Australia, New Zealand, France and Great Britain as well as the United States. A special protocol added South Vietnam, Laos and Cambodia to the area to be protected by the new organization. A few weeks later, Eisenhower, in response to a request from Prime Minister Ngo Dinh Diem of South Vietnam for "economic assistance," pledged American support "to assist the Government of Viet-Nam in developing and maintaining a strong, viable state, capable of resisting attempted subversion or aggression through military means." The United States, Eisenhower continued, expected that this aid would be met "by performance on the part of the Government of Viet-Nam in undertaking needed reforms."

In subsequent years both the SEATO treaty and the 1954 Eisenhower letter to Diem have been cited as not only justifying but *requiring* every action the United States has taken since in Vietnam, including sending in several hundred thousand combat troops eleven years later. Thus during the Senate Foreign Relations Committee hearings on Vietnam in January 1966, Senator Fulbright asked, "Does the Southeast Treaty, Southeast Asia Treaty Organization, commit us to do what we are now doing in Vietnam?" and the Secretary of State replied, "Yes, sir, I have no doubt that it does."

But the proposition that SEATO makes American military intervention mandatory in case of armed attack on South Vietnam finds no warrant in the treaty itself or its legislative history; even the Secretary of State did not advance this audacious idea until January 1966, and, according to Senator Morse, he had twice previously told the Foreign Relations Committee in executive session "that we were not acting in Vietnam under SEATO."[1] In the original SEATO hearings in November 1954, Secretary Dulles assured the Senate Foreign Relations Committee that, "if there is a revolutionary movement in Vietnam or in Thailand, we

[1] The transcript of the hearings of August 6, 1964, before the Senate Foreign Relations Committee, belatedly released in November 1966, discloses that the Secretary of State then testified: "We are not acting specifically under the SEATO Treaty."

would consult together as to what to do about it . . . but we have no undertaking to put it down; all we have is an undertaking to consult." He added that "the agreement of each of the parties to act to meet the common danger 'in accordance with its constitutional processes' leaves to the judgment of each country the type of action to be taken in the event an armed attack occurs." In the Senate debate on the treaty, Senator H. Alexander Smith, who had been a delegate to the Manila conference, explicitly dismissed the view that the treaty was "a compulsory arrangement for our military participation in case of any attack," adding, "We have no purpose of following any such policy as that of having our forces involved in a ground war. . . . We are not committed to the principle of NATO, namely, that an attack on one is an attack on all, calling for immediate military action without further consideration by Congress." No president of the United States before President Johnson interpreted the SEATO treaty as *compelling* American military intervention, and no other signatory so interprets the treaty today. In short, the Secretary of State's proposition that SEATO *commits* the United States to military intervention can only be regarded as an exercise in historical and legal distortion. Similarly the Eisenhower letter to Diem, as President Eisenhower pointed out himself on August 17, 1965, contemplated only economic and political support for the Saigon government. It was not a warrant for military intervention; indeed, at the end of his presidency, fewer than eight hundred American military personnel were stationed in South Vietnam.

On the other hand, the Eisenhower letter and, to a lesser degree, the special protocol to the SEATO treaty, did draw a line across Southeast Asia. Though these documents did not in any legal way compel American military intervention in South Vietnam, they did in a political way involve the United States in holding that line. That line could have been drawn elsewhere—along the Mekong River, for example, and the northern border of Thailand. No vital strategic interest required that it be drawn where it was.[2] But it *was* drawn in South Vietnam, for better or worse; a vital American interest was thus created where none had existed before; and a series of decisions followed in train which ended by carrying the United States into the fourth largest war of its history.

[2] This was recognized by the Eisenhower administration at the time. Thus in Secretary of State Dulles's press conference on May 11, 1954:

Q: Do you think, Mr. Secretary, that the Southeast Asia area can be held without Indochina?
Mr. Dulles: I do.

2.
What We Did There

The object of American policy in South Vietnam, as Eisenhower had written Diem, was to "discourage any who might wish to impose a foreign ideology on your free people." It was not clear that the people were so free or the ideology so foreign as Eisenhower supposed, but his language defined the mood in which Washington began the Vietnam adventure. That mood was essentially moralistic. The commitment to South Vietnam, like the parallel attempt to make the languid country of Laos a bastion of western power, followed directly from the Dulles conception of the world as irrevocably split into two unified and hostile blocs. In such a world, the threat of communism was indivisible,[1] the obligation to oppose that threat unlimited

---

[1] In fairness to Eisenhower and Dulles, it must be said that most public men of the day shared this theory of the homogeneity of communist power—and, of course, communism was much more homogeneous then than later. The one conspicuous exception was that premature polycentrist General Douglas MacArthur who, in the hearings after his dismissal in 1951, described Moscow as only "one of the loci" of the communist conspiracy and added, "The degree of control and influence that the Kremlin may have in China is quite problematical." This view differed sharply from the contemporary description of China by Assistant Secretary of State Dean Rusk (May 18, 1951): "The Peiping regime may be a colonial Russian government—a Slavic Manchukuo on a larger scale. It is not the government of China. It does not pass the first test. It is not Chinese." MacArthur's insight, however, was evidently employed to sustain the argument that it would be possible to attack China without provoking a Russian reaction. It did not inform MacArthur's general views of communism.

(up to the point, at least, of military action) and any yearning for neutrality in the struggle, in Dulles's word, "immoral."

For this reason, Washington supported Saigon in its determination to ignore the provision in the Geneva Agreements for all-Vietnam elections in 1956. However, the question of the 1956 election was agitated in later years far beyond its importance. For, even if President Eisenhower in his memoirs was ready to concede Ho Chi Minh 80 per cent of the vote, Ho himself never displayed any interest in permitting free elections on *his* side of the 17th parallel. So the *de facto* partition lengthened into a political division, and the Saigon and Hanoi governments both set to work to build the strength of their respective states.

On the other side of the parallel, the United States went ahead on the assumption that economic and political support alone would be sufficient to assure the survival of South Vietnam as an independent state. This was by no means an unreasonable judgment at the time. Few of those later critical of Eisenhower's letter to Diem opposed economic aid to South Vietnam in 1954. In the next five years Washington sent in $2.3 billion of aid—three-fifths economic, the rest military. For a time the policy seemed to be working: rice and sugar production rose; so did textile production; school rooms and medical dispensaries were built; there was a token land reform program; and American advisers helped create a South Vietnamese army.

Under the surface, however, things were less idyllic. All too little of the economic assistance went to the countryside, where most of the South Vietnamese lived. Our military assistance concentrated on building an army organized, not to fight guerrillas, but to repel a formal, Korean-style invasion from across the northern border. And the stipulation in Eisenhower's 1954 letter conditioning aid on the performance of "needed reforms" was largely forgotten. While American insistence did produce a little in the way of land reform (at least on paper), Ngo Dinh Diem was in the main able to pursue authoritarian political objectives without effective, or even visible, American objection.

Diem represented the older generation of Vietnamese nationalists—upper class, French speaking, Catholic. He had fought long and honorably for national independence, but he was not interested in disturbing the hierarchical structure of classical Vietnamese society. He subdued the religious sects, cleaned up Saigon, sought to restore the ancient Annamese morality and showed himself a man of rectitude and will, devoted and incorruptible. But he could hardly have had less sympathy with the popular aspirations for self-government stirred by the struggle for independence. A profound traditionalist, he considered it the obligation of the masses to respect and obey their leaders. He operated a family despotism in the oriental manner, abolishing elected village government in 1956, centering power in his own hands and those of his brothers, treating opposition as disloyalty and scorning the values and institutions of western democracy. "If we open the window," his sister-in-law, the lovely and serpentine Madame Nhu, once said, "not only sunlight but many bad things will fly in."

So the window was kept tightly shut. Diem's authoritarianism, which increasingly involved manhunts, political reeducation camps and the "regroupment" of population, caused spreading discontent and then armed resistance on the countryside. It is not easy to disentangle the events of these murky years; but few scholars believe that the growing resistance was at the start organized or directed by Hanoi. Indeed, there is some indication that the Communists at first hung back, evidently regarding the South Vietnamese guerrillas—soon to be called the Viet Cong—as putschists and infantile leftists (precisely as the Cuban Communist Party regarded Fidel Castro and the 26th of July movement at the same time in Cuba). The civil insurrection in South Vietnam began to gather force by 1958; it was not until September 1960 that the Communist Party of North Vietnam bestowed its formal blessing and called for the liberation of the south from American imperialism. Ho Chi Minh was now supplying the Viet Cong with training, equipment, strategic advice and even men—perhaps two thousand a year by 1960.[2] Nearly all the guerrillas who came from North Vietnam until we started bombing the north in 1965, however, were South Vietnamese who had gone north in 1954; most of the Viet Cong in any case continued to be recruited in South Vietnam; and most Viet Cong arms and equipment were captured from Diem's army.[3]

The Viet Cong unquestionably expressed a strain of genuine, if fanatic, idealism. They sang:

[2] All Vietnamese statistics are unreliable and must be regarded with inflexible mistrust. See below, Chapter 5.

[3] The Pentagon informed I. F. Stone that in the years 1962–1964 the South Vietnamese army lost 27,400 weapons of all sorts to the Viet Cong. During the same period 15,100 weapons were captured from the Viet Cong. The International Control Commission reported only 179 enemy-produced weapons in the eighteen-month period from June 1962 to January 1964. Assuming that half the 15,100 weapons were captured in these eighteen months, one must conclude that the Viet Cong before 1965 fought primarily with captured weapons.

We are peasants in soldier's clothing
Waging the struggle for a class oppressed for
  thousands of years.
Our suffering is the suffering of the people.

Nationalists fought side by side with Communists.
Many whom Diem had denied a role in political life
joined the resistance. From 1959 through 1962, according to Douglas Pike, the most careful student of
the Viet Cong, the guerrilla effort changed "from a
loose, disparate collection of dissident groups, often
with nothing more in common than hostility for the
Diem government, into a tightly knit movement." And
behind this process was a central animating purpose—

> not simply population control but to restructure the
> social order of the village and train the villagers to
> control themselves. This was the NLF's one undevi-
> ating thrust from the start. Not the killing of ARVN
> soldiers, not the occupation of real estate, not the
> preparation for some great pitched battle at an Ar-
> mageddon or a Dien Bien Phu, but organization in
> depth of the rural population through the instru-
> ment of self-control.[4]

It is important not to become romantic about the
Viet Cong. They did not simply represent a movement
of rural organization and uplift. They extended their
power as much by the fear they incited as by the hope
they inspired. And the systematic murder of village
headmen—half a dozen a day by 1960—could be an
effective weapon, especially when the people of the
countryside had been given little reason to prefer the

[4] See Douglas Pike, *Vietcong* (Cambridge, 1966). The NLF—National Liberation Front—is the political apparatus of the Viet Cong.
ARVN is the Army of the Republic of [South] Vietnam.

government in Saigon to their own survival. It was warfare in the shadows, ambush and assassination and torture, leaving behind a trail of burned villages, shattered families and weeping women.

By the end of 1960 the guerrilla attacks in Vietnam were increasing in boldness and scope. The success of the Communist guerrillas to the southeast in Laos— the Pathet Lao—had opened up a new corridor of assistance from North Vietnam. The South Vietnamese army, trained by the U.S. Military Assistance Advisory Group to fight quite another sort of war, was ineffective. There were now perhaps 15,000 Viet Cong in South Vietnam, overrunning half the country by day and a good deal more by night. In Saigon opposition grew to Diem, his autocratic methods and his conduct of the war. Discontent centered in the army, where American training, if it had not prepared the young Vietnamese officers for guerrilla warfare, had at least given them a sense of modern methods. In November 1960 a military coup almost overthrew the regime. Diem rode this out. Once back in control, he cracked down on all varieties or potentialities of opposition. He imprisoned or exiled a number of younger officials and, to guard against future coups, began a process of splitting the army and pitting one general against another. Trusting no one, he based himself more and more narrowly on his family, especially on his able and aggressive younger brother, Ngo Dinh Nhu.

In January 1961 the Vietnam mess fell to a new American president. Kennedy, who had long believed that the main communist reliance in the coming period would be on neither nuclear nor conventional but guerrilla war, saw the answer to the Viet Cong insurgency in counter-insurgency. For Kennedy counter-insurgency meant a good deal more than teaching soldiers to black their faces and strangle enemies in the night. Guerrilla warfare, he well understood, was essentially political warfare. Effective counter-insurgency, for example, depended on swift and accurate intelligence from the countryside. The Viet Cong could never be defeated unless the Saigon regime could enlist the support of the peasants. Magsaysay's campaign against the Hukbalahaps in the Philippines suggested the model: tough military action against the enemy, generous provisions for amnesty, real and sweeping social reform.

The first effort of the Kennedy years was to persuade the Diem regime to move along these lines. Success in this effort would have been unlikely in any case, given Diem's conviction that the Americans were impatient, naive and childlike, to be humored but never to be heeded. And it became all the more unlikely when the senior American diplomatic and military officials in Saigon decided that Diem was the key to stability and that the only policy was to win Diem's confidence by assuring him of Washington's unconditional support. Once he believed that Washington was with him, they thought, it might be possible to steer him gently and gradually toward reform, but attempts to bring pressure on Diem, in the view of Ambassador Nolting and General Harkins, would be self-defeating. American newspapermen in Saigon, less moved by the South Vietnamese leader, called this the policy of "sink or swim with Ngo Dinh Diem." Diem and Nhu no doubt swam, but the hope of effective reform sank.

The next question was whether Washington should increase its military assistance. Vice President Lyndon B. Johnson, who visited Saigon in May 1961, reported to Kennedy: "The basic decision in Southeast Asia is here. We must decide whether to help these countries to the best of our ability or throw in the towel and pull back our defenses to San Francisco. . . . More important, we would say to the world in this case that we don't live up to our treaties and don't stand by our friends. This is not my concept. I recommend that we move forward promptly with a major effort to help these countries defend themselves." However, American aid to enable a country to defend itself was—in Johnson's mind in 1961—very different from direct American defense of the country. "American combat troop involvement," he said, "is not only not required, it is not desirable." He went on: "Possibly Americans fail to appreciate fully the subtlety that recently colonial peoples would not look with favor upon governments which invited or accept the return this soon of Western troops. To the extent that fear of ground-troop involvement dominates our political responses to Asia in Congress or elsewhere, it seems most desirable to me to allay those paralyzing fears."

The situation in South Vietnam grew worse over the summer; and in October 1961 Kennedy sent General Maxwell Taylor and Walt W. Rostow, then (and in 1966 again) a White House aide, on a mission to Saigon. The Taylor-Rostow report recommended an enlargement of the American role, essentially through the penetration of the South Vietnamese army and government by American 'advisers,' attached to Vietnamese military units or government offices and designed to improve the level of local performance. Taylor and Rostow also recommended that an American military task force—perhaps 10,000 men—go to Vietnam, commissioned to conduct combat operations for self-defense and perimeter security and, if the Vietnamese army were hard pressed, to act as an emergency reserve. The report concluded by saying that this program would work only if infiltration from the north were stopped and that therefore, should this infiltration continue, the United States should consider a contingency policy of retaliation against the north, graduated to match the intensity of Hanoi's aid to the Viet Cong.

Kennedy rejected both the northern strategy and the use of combat soldiers. "They want a force of American troops," he remarked privately. "They say it's necessary in order to restore confidence and maintain morale. But it will be just like Berlin. The troops will march in; the bands will play; the crowds will cheer; and in four days everyone will have forgotten. Then we will be told we have to send in more troops. It's like taking a drink. The effect wears off, and you have to take another."

Yet he felt obliged to offer a small drink himself, and he increased the number of military advisers. More drinks were still to come. At the end of 1961, there were 1364 American military personnel in South Vietnam; at the end of 1962, 9865; at the time of Kennedy's death in November 1963, about 15,500. This was the policy of 'one more step'—each new step always promising the success which the previous last step had also promised but had unaccountably failed to deliver. Once, early in the Kennedy administration, the then Chairman of the Joint Chiefs of Staff outlined to the National Security Council the processes by which each American action in Southeast Asia, if it provoked a communist counteraction, could in turn provoke an even more drastic American response. He concluded, "If we are given the right to use nuclear weapons, we can guarantee victory." Kennedy sat glumly rubbing his upper molar, saying nothing. After a moment someone spoke up: "Mr. President, perhaps you would have the General explain to us what he means by victory." Kennedy grunted and dismissed the meeting. Later he said, "Since he couldn't think of any further escalation, he would have to promise us victory."

With the Taylor-Rostow mission, the Vietnam problem passed in effect from the Department of State to the Department of Defense, and, in spite of Kennedy's early insight into the political character of the problem in Vietnam, the projected American solution in 1961–1963 was increasingly framed in military terms. Why did Kennedy permit this to happen? One reason was that Vietnam was still in these years a low-level crisis. It was far less urgent than Cuba, or Berlin, or Latin America, or nuclear testing, or preserving the European alliance, or fighting for civil rights in the United States; far less urgent than the neighboring Asian crisis in Laos. Another reason was that the strategy of unconditional support of Diem combined with the military adviser system seemed to be working—or so at least the senior American officials in Saigon assured the President. Their dispatches conveyed the picture of a regime led by a doubtless difficult but unquestionably statesmanlike and, in any case, irreplaceable figure making steady progress in winning over the peasants, pacifying the countryside and restoring the stability of government. If there was no surge of social reform, at least the "strategic hamlet" program—the relocation of peasants into fortified villages, surrounded by barbed wire fences and ditches filled with bamboo spikes—was giving the countryside protection and a new sense of security and cutting off the Viet Cong from their primary sources of food, intelligence and recruits. Ngo Dinh Nhu made the strategic hamlet program his personal project and published glowing reports of spectacular success. One might have wondered whether Nhu was just the man to mobilize the idealism of the villages; but Ambassador Nolting and General Harkins listened uncritically to his claims and passed them back to Washington as facts, where they were read with elation.

Washington officials on hasty visits confirmed the picture. "Every quantitative measurement we have," Secretary of Defense McNamara said on his first trip to Vietnam in 1962, "shows we're winning this war." General Taylor, when he returned for a fresh look a year after his first mission, detected "a great national movement" rising to destroy the Viet Cong. It was hard to doubt a widespread and substantial improvement in the military situation. The President, who had other matters on his mind, accepted the cheerful reports from men in whom he had great confidence. His 1963 State of the Union message summed up the mood at the turn of the year: "The spearpoint of aggression has been blunted in South Vietnam."

The optimism continued well into 1963. In March the Secretary of State said that the war was "turning an important corner. . . . Government forces clearly have the initiative in most areas of the country." A month later he discerned a "steady movement toward a constitutional system resting upon popular consent," declared that "the 'strategic hamlet' program is producing excellent results," added that "morale in the countryside has begun to rise," assured his listeners that "to the Vietnamese peasant" the Viet Cong "look less and less like winners" and concluded, "The Vietnamese are on their way to success" (meaning presumably the South Vietnamese). In May the Defense Department announced, "The corner has definitely been turned toward victory in Vietnam." General Harkins predicted that the war would be won "within a year." "South Vietnam," said Ambassador Nolting in June, "is on its way to victory over communist guerrillas." "I can safely say," General Harkins unsafely said in October, "the end of the war is in sight."

There was another view of the situation—a view transmitted not in top secret cables but in dispatches to American newspapers and magazines.[5] The American reporters in Vietnam saw Diem not as a selfless national leader but as an oriental despot, hypnotized by his own endless monologues and contemptuous of democracy and the west. They detested the Nhus. They considered the strategic hamlet program a fake and a failure; and their visits to dismal stockades where peasants had been herded, sometimes at bayonet point, to engage in forced labor confirmed their worst misgivings. They stopped believing Diem's communiqués; and, when Harkins and Nolting kept insisting they were true, they stopped believing Harkins and Nolting. Their picture of South Vietnam differed from the official reports by about 180 degrees.

In response, the officials assailed the journalists. Admiral Felt, the commander of the Pacific fleet, reproached the man from the Associated Press: "Why don't you get on the team?" In reports to Washington the officials even gave the astonishing impression that there would be no trouble in Vietnam if only the newspaper fellows would follow the line. "The U.S. Embassy," wrote David Halberstam of the *New York Times*, who later won a Pulitzer Prize for his work in Vietnam, "turned into the adjunct of a dictatorship. In trying to protect Diem from criticism, the Ambassador

[5] This should console those who feel they are deprived of something if denied access to top secret dispatches.

became Diem's agent." One experience after another made the newspapermen more certain that the Embassy was lying to them. They did not recognize the deeper pathos, which was that the officials really believed their own reports. They were deceiving not only the American government and people but themselves.

Then in May 1963 Diem forbade the Buddhists to display their flags on Buddha's 2587th birthday, Diem's troops fired into a crowd of Buddhists in Hue, and the situation suddenly fell apart. The Buddhist trouble was as much social as religious in its impulse. It was at bottom an uprising, wholly unforeseen by American diplomats, of the new generation of nationalists, drawn largely from the middle and lower classes, speaking Vietnamese rather than French, professing Buddhism rather than Catholicism, xenophobic and hysterical, in revolt against traditional Vietnamese society. Diem and the Nhus retaliated with equal hysteria. The result was to expose the optimism that had been flowing so long and so imperturbably out of American officials in Saigon and to strengthen those few officials in Washington—notably Averell Harriman, Under Secretary of State, and Roger Hilsman, Assistant Secretary for Far Eastern Affairs, who for some time had been questioning the orthodox picture. The appointment of Henry Cabot Lodge as Ambassador to Saigon reinforced the skeptics.

The Buddhist troubles finally made Vietnam a matter of top priority, even in the months of Bull Connor and his police dogs in Birmingham, of the American University speech and the test ban treaty, of the fight for tax reduction and the civil rights bill. "In my opinion," Kennedy said, "for us to withdraw from that effort would mean a collapse not only of South Vietnam but Southeast Asia. So we are going to stay there." But he could not forget the French experience of a decade earlier; if the war were ever converted into a white man's war, the Americans would lose as the French had lost. "In the final analysis," he said on September 3, "it is their war. They are the ones who have to win it or lose it. We can help them, we can give them equipment, we can send our men out there as advisers, but they have to win it, the people of Vietnam."

Finally the South Vietnamese army brought off its coup, killed Diem and Nhu, and the war entered a new phase. Three weeks later Kennedy too was dead, and a new President inherited the trouble. Vietnam was still not a top problem. In his first State of the Union message, President Johnson hardly mentioned Vietnam.[6] In his 1965 message, Vietnam received hardly more than 100 words. Even his 1966 message took thirty-five minutes before there was any extended discussion of Vietnam. It is important to remember how long it was before Vietnam emerged as the all-consuming and all-dominating issue it is today.

It did, however, play a role in the 1964 election, largely because of Senator Goldwater's advocacy of an aggressive northern strategy. President Johnson replied:

> Some others are eager to enlarge the conflict. They call upon us to supply American boys to do the job that Asian boys should do. They ask us to take reck-

[6] The two references in the message of January 8, 1964, were speech-writer's reflexes: "Today Americans of all races stand side by side in Berlin and in Vietnam" (in a passage on civil rights) and "In 1964 we will be better prepared than ever before to defend the cause of freedom—whether it is threatened by outright aggression or by the infiltration practiced by those in Hanoi and Havana" (in a passage on national security policy).

less actions which might risk the lives of millions and engulf much of Asia.

(August 12)

I have had advice to load our planes with bombs and to drop them on certain areas that I think would enlarge the war and result in committing a good many American boys to fighting a war that I think ought to be fought by the boys of Asia to help protect their own land. And for that reason I haven't chosen to enlarge the war.

(August 29)

There are those that say you ought to go north and drop bombs, to try to wipe out the supply lines, and they think that would escalate the war. We don't want our American boys to do the fighting for Asian boys. We don't want to get involved in a nation with 700 million people and get tied down in a land war in Asia.

(September 25)

We are not going north and we are not going south; we are going to continue to try to get them to save their own freedom with their own men, with our leadership and our officer direction, and such equipment as we can furnish them.

(September 28)

We are not going to send American boys nine or ten thousand miles away from home to do what Asian boys ought to be doing for themselves.

(October 21)

3.
Where We Are Now

Campaign speeches are not sacred covenants with the people; they are expressions of intent and hope, and there is no reason to question the honesty of President Johnson's 1964 statements.[1] What the President apparently did not allow for was a continued decay in the military situation. Things became so desperate in the early months of 1965—or so we were later told—that only the February decision to start bombing the north, followed by the commitment of American combat forces the next month, averted total collapse. If the situation was really all that grave, the administration did not confide this fact at the time to the American people; in retrospect, one simply does not know whether this story is actuality or myth. If actuality, it might surely have called Washington's attention to the political weaknesses of the Saigon regime; for the South Vietnamese Army at this point still outnumbered the Viet Cong by at least six to one, and its capitulation would have been more an expression of political demoralization than of military inferiority.

In any case, the President now felt he had no alternative but to begin to supply American boys to do the job that he had thought a few months before Asian

[1] However, Charles Roberts, the White House correspondent of *Newsweek*, wrote in his book, *LBJ's Inner Circle*, "The President . . . told me in May 1965 that he had made the decision to bomb [North Vietnam] . . . four months before Pleiku." This would place the decision in October 1964. But the President's wording may have been loose or his memory faulty; for I know of no other indication that the decision was in fact taken that early.

boys should do. The number of American troops doubled, and doubled again; by August 1965 there were 125,000. The bombing steadily grew, except for a meaningless six-day pause in May. As we increased our activity, Hanoi reciprocated. According to our estimates, the enemy amounted to 90,000 in March 1964; 100,000 in January 1965; and, after the active American entry into the war, 135,000 by April and 170,000 by August. In December 1965 the United States instituted a second bombing pause. After thirty-seven days, the process of escalation resumed. By the end of 1966 the number of American troops was rising toward 400,000. As for the bombing of the north, there were 1935 missions in February 1966, 5183 in April, 7357 in June, 9765 in July, 12,673 in September.

And so the policy of 'one more step' lured the United States deeper and deeper into the morass. In retrospect, Vietnam is a triumph of the politics of inadvertence. We have achieved our present entanglement, not after due and deliberate consideration, but through a series of small decisions. It is not only idle but unfair to seek out guilty men. President Eisenhower, after rejecting American military intervention in 1954, set in motion the policy of support for Saigon which resulted, two Presidents later, in American military intervention in 1965. Each step in the deepening of the American commitment was reasonably regarded at the time as the last that would be necessary. Yet, in retrospect, each step led only to the next, until we find ourselves entrapped today in that nightmare of American strategists, a land war in Asia—a war which no President, including President Johnson, desired or intended. The Vietnam story is a tragedy without villains. No thoughtful American can withhold sympathy as President Johnson ponders the gloomy choices which lie ahead.

Yet each President, in the words of Andrew Jackson, remains "accountable at the bar of public opinion for every act of his administration." President Johnson has made his ultimate objective very clear: he does not seek, he has said, total military victory or the unconditional surrender of North Vietnam,[2] but a negotiated settlement. He has also made very clear his judgment that the way to achieve a political solution is by intensifying military pressure until a battered and reeling Hanoi agrees to negotiate—or, at least, pulls out its forces and allows the war to fade away. By continually increasing what the Pentagon calls the "quotient of pain," we can, according to the administration theory, force Hanoi at each stage of widening the war to reconsider whether the war is worth the price.

This has been the persistent administration course since February 1965. New experiments in escalation are first denied, then disowned, then discounted and finally undertaken. Thus in the early winter of 1965 the Secretary of Defense told Congress that bombing the petroleum facilities near Haiphong was of "no fundamental consequence"; in the spring the Secretary of the Air Force explained why we were not going to bomb Hanoi and Haiphong; on June 26, the Under Secretary of State denied that any decision had been taken to bomb the oil storage depots; on June 29, the bombing began. For a moment Washington put out stories suggesting that this was going to be some sort of turning point in the war. High officials cited unidentified intelligence dispatches reporting the decline of morale in North Vietnam. But in the months since it has become

[2] One must discount flourishes like the presidential exhortation to the combat commanders in the officers' club at Camranh Bay: "Come home with that coonskin on the wall."

evident that, once again, the newest step in escalation made no more difference than the previous steps.

So, once again, the demand arises for 'just one *more* step.' As past medicine fails, all we can apparently think to do is to double the dose. Plenty of room remains for widening the war: the harbors of North Vietnam, the irrigation dikes, the steel plants, the factories, the power grid, the crops, the civilian population, the Chinese border. The fact that we excluded such steps yesterday is, alas, no guarantee that we will not pursue them tomorrow. And if bombing will not bring Ho Chi Minh to his knees or stop his support of the Viet Cong in South Vietnam, there is always the resort of invasion. General Ky has already told us that we must invade North Vietnam to win the war. In an August press conference, the Secretary of State twice refused to rule out this possibility. And beyond invasion lies the field of nuclear weapons—weapons which General Eisenhower, who declined the conventional bombing of Dien Bien Phu in 1954, would not exclude in 1966.

The theory, of course, is that widening the war will shorten it. This theory appears to be based on three convictions: first, that the war will be decided in North Vietnam; second, that the risk of Chinese or Soviet entry is negligible; and third, that military 'victory' in some sense is possible—not perhaps total victory over North Vietnam but suppression of resistance in South Vietnam. Perhaps these premises are correct, and in another year or two we may all be saluting the wisdom and statesmanship of the American government. In so enigmatic a situation, no one can be confident about his doubt and disagreement. Nonetheless, to many Americans these propositions constitute a terribly shaky basis for action which has already carried the United States into a ground war in Asia and which may well carry the world to the brink of the third world war.

The illusion that the war in South Vietnam can be decided in North Vietnam is evidently a result of listening too long to our own propaganda. "The war," the Secretary of State has solemnly assured us, "is clearly an 'armed attack,' cynically and systematically mounted by the Hanoi regime against the people of South Vietnam." Our government has insisted so often that the war in South Vietnam is, in President Johnson's phrase, "a vicious and illegal aggression across this little nation's frontier," that it has come to believe itself that the war was started in Hanoi and can only be stopped there.

Yet the best evidence remains that the war began as an insurrection within South Vietnam which, as it has gathered momentum, has attracted increasing support and direction from the north. In August 1966, four correspondents who had been covering the Vietnam war—Malcolm Browne of the Associated Press (whose book on Vietnam, *The New Face of War,* had won the Pulitzer Prize), Jack Foisie of the *Los Angeles Times* (who is the Secretary of State's brother-in-law), Charles Mohr of the *New York Times* and Dean Brelis of the National Broadcasting Company—discussed this point:

> BROWNE: Of course, it is a civil war, by the Webster definition of the thing.
> NIVEN (moderator) : So you all agree?
> FOISIE: I think it is.
> BRELIS: Yes, I agree.
> MOHR: Yes, a special kind of civil war.

Even today the North Vietnamese regulars in South Vietnam amount to only a small fraction of the total enemy force (and to an even smaller fraction of the American army in South Vietnam). We could follow the genial prescription of General LeMay and bomb North Vietnam back to the Stone Age—and the war would still go on in South Vietnam. To reduce this war to the simplification of a wicked regime molesting its neighbors, and to suppose that it can be ended by punishing the wicked regime, is surely to misconceive not only the political but even the military character of the problem.

As for the assurances that China will not enter, these will be less than totally satisfying to those whose memory stretches back to the Korean War. General MacArthur, another one of those military experts on oriental psychology, when asked by President Truman on Wake Island in October 1950 what the chances were of Chinese intervention, replied, "Very little. . . . Now that we have bases for our Air Force in Korea, if the Chinese tried to get down to Pyongyang, there would be the greatest slaughter." Such reasoning lay behind the decision (the Assistant Secretary of State for Far Eastern Affairs at that time is Secretary of State today) to send American troops across the 38th parallel despite warnings from Peking that this would provoke a Chinese response. In a few weeks, China was actively in the war, and, while there was the greatest slaughter, it was not notably of the Chinese.

There seems little question that the Chinese have no great passion to enter the war in Vietnam. They do not want to put their nuclear plants in hazard; and, in any case, their foreign policy has typically been a compound of polemical ferocity and practical prudence. But it is essential, if we seek to assess Chinese policy realistically, to make the big effort and try to grasp the problem as it appears to them. Liddell Hart once wrote, in a passage cherished by John F. Kennedy,

"Never corner an opponent, and always assist him to save his face. Put yourself in his shoes—so as to see things through his eyes. Avoid self-righteousness like the devil—nothing is so self-blinding." Such precepts are infuriating to the moralists of diplomacy, who believe that foreign policy is essentially about questions of right and wrong. They are, however, indispensable to statesmen.

What, therefore, is the view from Peking? It is obviously of a gigantic American effort at the encirclement and strangulation of China. That is not, of course, our view of what we are doing; nor is it in fact what we are doing. But it really should not astonish us that a crew of dogmatic Marxist-Leninists should so interpret the extraordinary deployment of American armies, navies and military bases thousands of miles from the United States and mobilized—on the word of American leaders—against no one but themselves. Imagine our own feelings if the Chinese had 400,000 troops in southern Mexico, engaged in putting down what we had hoped to be a pro-American rebellion; if massive Chinese military bases were being built there; if Chinese planes were bombing northern Mexico every day; if a great Chinese fleet controlled the waters along our Pacific coast; and if Peking was denouncing the United States as the world's greatest threat to peace. The question, which so engages on our own sense of righteousness, of who the 'aggressor' is, depends a good deal on who looks through what glass and how darkly. The leaders in Peking are fully as devoted students of Munich as the American Secretary of State.[3] They are sure that we

[3] General Lo Jui-ching, in his introduction to Marshal Lin Piao's 1965 manifesto, invokes the Munich analogy three times; see the recent book by Brigadier General Samuel B. Griffith II, *Peking and People's Wars* (New York, 1966).

are out to bury them; they believe too that appeasement invites further aggression; and, however deep
their reluctance, at some point concern for national
survival will make them fight. "To save our neighbors," as Peking announced on November 4, 1950, "is
to save ourselves."

When will that point be reached this time? Probably
when the Chinese are confronted by a direct threat to
their frontier, either through bombing or through an
American decision to cross the 17th parallel and invade North Vietnam. If a Communist regime barely established in Peking could take a decision to intervene
against the only atomic power in the world in 1950,
why does anyone suppose that a much stronger regime
would flinch from that decision in 1966? Indeed, given
the present discord in Peking, war may seem the best
way to renew revolutionary discipline, stop the brawl-
ing and unite the nation.

It is true that the Chinese entry into the Korean War
had the support of the Soviet Union; but it would be
risky today to rely on the Russo-Chinese split to save
us from everything, including Soviet aid to China in
case of war with the United States or even direct Soviet
entry into the war in Vietnam. For the Soviet Union is
already extensively involved in Vietnam—more so in a
sense than the Chinese—and it is foolish to suppose
that, given Moscow's competition with Peking for the
leadership of the Communist world, Russia could afford to stand by and allow Communist North Vietnam
or Communist China to be destroyed by the American
imperialists.

And if China does enter? Once again, the bombing
illusion, the bane of American popular thought on military matters; I suppose we will be exhorted to blast
China back to the Stone Age too. But, as General Ridg-

way pointed out a decade ago, the Chinese "are not yet sufficiently 'advanced' to be truly vulnerable to the nuclear bomb. . . . Their civilization is not based on a complex nerve fabric, a web of interrelated and interdependent functions and services, as is ours. Theirs is a simpler and more primitive society that would be extremely difficult to destroy, just as the turtle and the crocodile are harder to kill than the higher animals." General Ridgway also questioned the morality of nuclear bombing—all the more relevant too, if we seem to reserve our most ghastly weapon for yellow people. China can be defeated only on the ground—and the Chinese will have a good many more foot soldiers than the United States to throw into any conflict.[4]

This consideration relates to the third premise: that military 'victory' is in some sense possible. The Joint Chiefs of Staff, of course, by definition argue for military solutions. They are the most fervent apostles of 'one more step.' That is their business, and no one should be surprised that generals behave like generals. The fault lies not with those who give this advice but those who take it. There is nothing infallible about the Chiefs, as anyone who recalls their counsel at the time of the Bay of Pigs and again during the Cuban missile crisis well knows. Their recommendations, even on strictly military questions, deserve the most hard and skeptical analysis.

What, for example, is the exact purpose of bombing the north? It is difficult to find out. According to Gen-

[4] One should perhaps record General LeMay's solution to this problem as an indication of the infinite capacity of the military mind for self-deception. "We need never invade with our own land forces. Air, naval and logistic support to Chiang Kai-shek on Formosa and General Chung Hee Park in South Korea should provide more than enough force to bring an unstable Red China to her knees."

eral Taylor, "The objective of our air campaign is to change the will of the enemy leadership." Secretary McNamara, on the other hand, has said, "We never believed that bombing would destroy North Vietnam's will." He told the Chamber of Commerce in May 1966 that, since North Vietnam was largely agricultural, with only 15 per cent of its gross national product coming from industry, it was "impossible" to bring the nation's economy "to a halt" through bombing. Whatever the theory, the results would appear to support Secretary McNamara. "There is no indication," General Westmoreland said in August 1966, "that the resolve of the leadership in Hanoi has been reduced." In other words, bombing has had precisely the effect that the analyses of the United States Strategic Bombing Survey after the Second World War would have forecast. Under Secretary of State George Ball was a director of that Survey; this may well be why he has been reported to be so unenthusiastic about the air assault on the north.

And, far from stopping infiltration across the 17th parallel, bombing, if our own reports are to be believed, has stimulated it. The first result was to bring North Vietnamese forces south of the border. "In 1965," according to General Westmoreland, "[the enemy] began to move regular North Vietnamese Army units into [South] Vietnam." "It is perfectly clear," Secretary McNamara has said, "that the North Vietnamese have continued to increase their support of the Viet Cong despite the increase in our effort. . . . What has happened is that the North Vietnamese have continually increased the amount of resources, men and material that they have been willing to devote to their objective." In May 1966, after fourteen months of bombing, Secretary McNamara said that the infiltration rate was "perhaps three times the level of last year"; in June he said that Communist supply deliveries had risen by 150 per cent and troop infiltration by 120 per cent over the previous year; and each month we are told, the rates continue to rise. Talk about bombing the "Ho Chi Minh Trail," for example, is misleading; it is not a broad highway accessible to aircraft but a maze of threads through the jungle; and, even if our planes were to knock out the North Vietnamese trucks, bearers could if necessary carry the amount needed to maintain Viet Cong operations at their present level. (No one knows what this amount is; Secretary McNamara has estimated it as twelve to thirty tons a day in 1965.) Bombing undoubtedly makes infiltration more difficult, but its effects are transient, and it will not bring infiltration to an end.

Moreover, far from discouraging external assistance to North Vietnam, our bombing has made Russian and Chinese aid to Hanoi a matter of Communist competition and honor. Russian exports to North Vietnam, for example, increased sharply (from 42.9 million rubles in 1964 to 67.4 million rubles in 1965) after we began to bomb the north. Richard N. Goodwin, a former special assistant to Presidents Kennedy and Johnson has said, "The increase in Soviet and Chinese aid, since the bombing, is far greater, in economic terms, than the loss through bombing. Except in human life, the North Vietnamese are showing a profit."

U.S. News & World Report remarked in its issue of August 22, 1966: "It's clear now to military men: bombing will not win in Vietnam." This is a dispiriting item. Why had our military leaders not long ago freed themselves from the illusion of the omnipotence of air power, so cherished by civilians who think wars can be won on the cheap? The Korean War, as General Ridgway has reminded us, "taught that it is impossible to interdict the supply route of an Asian army by air-power alone. We had complete air mastery over North Korea, and we clobbered Chinese supply columns un-mercifully. . . . But we did not halt their offensive nor materially diminish its strength." If air power was not decisive in Korea, where the warfare was conventional and the terrain relatively open and compact, how could anyone suppose that it would be decisive against guerrillas threading their way through the hills and jungles of Vietnam?

No doubt killing a lot of North Vietnamese may give some Americans inner psychic satisfaction. But the hard question is whether it will help 'win' the war. The evidence thus far is that bombing the north, in-stead of demoralizing North Vietnam, stopping the in-filtration and the foreign aid, driving a wedge between Hanoi and Peking and hurrying Hanoi to the confer-ence table, has stimulated infiltration and assistance, hardened the will of the regime, convinced it that its life is at stake, brought it closer to China and solidified the people of North Vietnam in its support. Mean-while it has had little effect on the real war—which, after all, is taking place not in the north but in the south.

Victory through bombing—the dream of an antisep-tic war and a painless triumph—is a cruel form of self-deception. Those who think total military victory the proper goal must have the moral and intellectual hon-esty (as, for example, Hanson Baldwin has) to face the probability that it can come only in South Vietnam and only through ground warfare. The bombing illusion applies, of course, to South as well as to North Viet-nam. Tactical bombing—bombing in direct support of ground operations—has its place; but the notion that strategic bombing can stop guerrillas runs contrary to experience. And we have it, on the authority of the Secretary of State, that despite the entry of North Vietnamese regulars the war in South Vietnam (as of early 1966) "continues to be basically a guerrilla operation."

Sir Robert Thompson, who planned the successful British effort against the Malayan guerrillas and later served as head of the British advisory mission in Saigon, has emphasized that in guerrilla warfare the defending force must operate "in the same element" as their adversaries. Counter-insurgency, he writes, "is like trying to deal with a tomcat in an alley. It is no good inserting a large, fierce dog. The dog may not find the tomcat; if he does, the tomcat will escape up a tree; and the dog will then chase the female cats. The answer is to put in a fiercer tomcat."

Alas, we have no fiercer tomcat. Kennedy's counter-insurgency effort in Vietnam has languished. Today we fight one war, with our B-52's and our naval guns and our napalm, and the Viet Cong are fighting another, with their machine guns and ambushes and forays in the dark. Our men in Saigon claim that Viet Cong morale is sinking under the pounding. A brilliant and informed columnist writes (in October 1966), "Within six, eight, ten or twelve months—before the end of 1967 at any rate—the chances are good that the Vietnamese war will look successful. We are much closer to the end of . . . the 'military war' than most people . . . dare to hope." We all pray that Mr. Alsop will be right. But that corner in Vietnam has been turned too often before.

"If we can get the Viet Cong to stand up and fight, we will blast him," General Westmoreland has plaintively said; and when they occasionally rise to the surface and try to fight our kind of war, we do blast them.

But the fact that they then slide back into the shadows does not mean that we are on the verge of some final military triumph. It means simply that we are driving them underground—where they renew themselves and where our large, fierce dog cannot follow. "When we have beaten the Army of North Vietnam and the main-force battalions of the Viet Cong," Ambassador Lodge said in November 1966, "we have simply won the opportunity to get at the heart of the matter, which is more than 150,000 terrorist guerrillas highly organized throughout the country and looking exactly like civilians." Or, as General Moshe Dayan, who led the Israeli Army in the 1956 campaign against Egypt, put it after a visit to Vietnam: "The Viet Cong army can, if it refrains from pitting regular units against regular units in frontal engagements and organizes guerrilla warfare, prevent the Americans and the Saigon government from pacifying the country. The Viet Cong cannot drive out the Americans, but they can, by adopting appropriate methods of warfare, avoid being driven out themselves."

As for the alleged collapse of guerrilla morale, there has thus far been no convincing evidence that the Viet Cong lack the political and emotional commitment to keep fighting underground for a very long time. Neil Sheehan of the *New York Times* wrote in his valedictory piece about Vietnam: "We are continually chagrined to discover that idealism and dedication are largely the prerogative of the enemy. . . . I can only conclude that Vietnamese will die more willingly for a regime which, though Communist, is at least genuinely Vietnamese and offers them some hope of improving their lives, than for one which is committed to the galling status quo and is the creation of Washington." Ellen Hammer in her book of 1954, *The Struggle for*

Indochina, reminds us of the ancient boast of the Vietnamese nationalists: "We have fought for a thousand years. And we will fight another thousand if need be."

Nor can we easily match the continuing infiltration by enlarging our own forces—from 300,000, for example, to 500,000 or 750,000. The ratio of superiority preferred by the Pentagon in guerrilla war is 10 to 1, which means that every time we send in 100,000 more men the enemy has only to send in 10,000 or so, and we are all even again. Reinforcement has not created a margin of American superiority; all it has done is to lift the stalemate to a higher and more explosive level. Indeed, there is reason to suppose that, in its own manner, the enemy can match our every step of escalation up to the point of nuclear war. And, should we attempt to root out the guerrillas in every village and cave, it would require almost a million American soldiers and a war of many years. Such an effort would hopelessly Americanize the war, transforming it from a conflict between nationalist and Communist Vietnamese into the white man's war which President Kennedy feared. It would hopelessly militarize the problem, diverting all thought and energy from the search for a political solution. The sheer weight of the American military presence would overwhelm the social structure of Vietnam, corrupt its way of life,[5] smother its national iden-

[5] "Corruption Is Taking Up to 40% of U.S. Assistance in Vietnam"—headline in *New York Times,* November 13, 1966. The piece begins "among the traditional by products of war are theft, bribery, black marketing, currency manipulation and waste. In the Vietnamese conflict these corrosive influences . . . have developed on a scale far vaster than should be expected for the size of the war." American officials, in challenging the 40 per cent estimate, concede "corruption and thievery to the extent that $35 million to $40 million worth of American commodities would be lost in Vietnam in the current fiscal year."

tity and produce in reaction an increasingly dangerous mood of anti-Americanism.

Meanwhile, as the number of our planes, our cannon and our ships increase, they will inevitably be thrown into battle. Already our bombers roam over the hapless country, dumping more tonnage of explosives each month than we were dropping per month on all Europe and Africa during the Second World War— more in a year than we dropped in the entire Pacific during the Second World War. Just the other day our bombs killed or injured more than one hundred civilians in a hamlet in the Mekong Delta—all on the suspicion that two Viet Cong platoons, numbering perhaps sixty men, were there. Even if the Viet Cong had still been around, which they weren't, would the military gain have out-weighed the human and political loss? General Dayan describes a small action where, "along the 200-yard-wide strip between jungle and fence the American support units laid down no less than 21,000 shells—more than the total volume of artillery fire expended by the Israeli Army during the Suez Campaign and the War of Independence together!"[6] General Johnson, the Army Chief of Staff,

[6] Nor does all our devastation land on verified military targets. According to Neil Sheehan, "Hamlets are also habitually bombed and shelled at the request of a South Vietnamese province or district chief who has been told by some paid informer that Communist troops are present there. Information from informers is notoriously unreliable, the peasants are often not responsible for the presence of the Communists and, since ground units do not exploit the bombings and shellings, these attacks seem to have negligible military value. American officials excuse the practice by claiming that the Vietnamese, as the legal authorities, have the right to destroy their own hamlets. . . . I have occasionally thought that the practice results largely from the cynicism of South Vietnamese officialdom and a superfluity of aircraft and artillery."

observed unhappily to Dayan: "We have not enough information. We act with ruthlessness, like a steamroller, bombing extensive areas and not selected targets based on detailed intelligence." Charles Mohr has described in the *Times* the human consequences of this military promiscuity: "Almost every provincial hospital in Vietnam is crowded with civilian victims of the war. Some American doctors and other officials in the field say the majority are the victims of American air power and South Vietnamese artillery."

Our strategy in Vietnam today is rather like trying to weed a garden with a bulldozer. We occasionally dig up some weeds, but we dig up most of the turf, too. If we continue the pursuit of total military victory, we will leave the tragic country gutted and devastated by bombs, burned by napalm, turned into a wasteland by chemical defoliation, a land of ruin and wreck. This is the melancholy course to which the escalation policy commits us. The effect will be to pulverize the political and institutional fabric which alone can give a South Vietnamese state that hope of independent survival which is our presumed war aim. Our method, in other words, defeats our goal. Indeed, the most likely beneficiary of the smashed social structure of South Vietnam will be communism. In our wisdom we are creating the only conditions in which China could easily take over Vietnam. "In another day," Jean Lacouture has written, "Mongol emperors sacked and massacred Asian peoples before subjugating them. In Vietnam the first part of the job would then have been done by the Americans."

"My feeling," General Wallace Greene, commandant of the Marine Corps, has wisely said, "is that you could kill every Viet Cong and North Vietnamese in South Vietnam and still lose the war. Unless we can make a success of the civic-action program, we are not going to obtain the objectives we have set." Much devotion and intelligence are at present going into the programs of reconstruction and pacification. But two factors hold up the social revolution in South Vietnam: the capacity of the enemy to slice through so much of the country with relative immunity; and, equally important, the resistance of the large landholders and leading elements in the Saigon government to any serious programs of social reform. In any case, as claimants on our resources, these programs are hopelessly outclassed by the programs of destruction. Surely the United States, with all its ingenuity could have figured out a better way to combat guerrilla warfare than the physical obliteration of the nation in which that warfare is taking place. If this is our best idea of 'protecting' a country against 'wars of national liberation,' what other country, seeing the devastation we have wrought in Vietnam, will wish American protection? What will happen to the credibility of our commitments then?[7]

And there is a deeper question, a question which already haunts the American conscience. Are we really carrying out this policy, as we constantly proclaim, to save the people we are methodically destroying, or are we doing it for less exalted purposes of our own? Are we treating the Vietnamese as ends in themselves, or as means to our own objectives? The war began as a struggle for the soul of Vietnam: will it end as a struggle for the soul of America?

---

[7] "We are here because we made a promise. We have made other promises in other parts of the world. If Moscow or Peking ever discover that the promises of the United States do not mean what they say, then this world goes up in smoke"—the Secretary of State during his visit to Vietnam in October 1966.

4.

The Price We Are Paying

Our concentration on Vietnam is exacting a frightful cost. In domestic policy, with Vietnam gulping down more than a billion and a half dollars a month, everything is grinding to a stop. Lyndon Johnson was on his way to a place in history as a great President for his vision of a Great Society; but the Great Society is now, except for token gestures, dead. The fight for equal opportunity for the Negro, the war against poverty, the struggle to save the cities, the improvement of our schools—all must be starved for the sake of Vietnam. And war brings ugly side-effects: inflation; frustration; indignation; protest; panic; angry divisions within the national community; premonitions of McCarthyism.

American public opinion, the Louis Harris poll tells us, "is rising toward increased militancy about the Vietnam war and a get-it-over-with mood." No doubt this is so: the fear of a hopeless stalemate in Southeast Asia has produced a hunger for drastic solutions. It is not so much hawks vs. doves any longer as it is people becoming simultaneously hawks *and* doves and saying, like Senator Russell, that "we should go in and win—or else get out." Among the early casualties of this get-it-over-with frenzy are likely to be our national equability, good temper, moderation and reason. And, as the frenzy gathers speed, it may well bring in its wake a new testing of the national faith in liberty.

The last such testing took place fifteen years ago. The more venerable among us may still recall the havoc—so absurd in retrospect—which a single senator then wrought in the workings of our government and the atmosphere of our society. Now, though he was unquestionably talented as a demagogue, it was not the quality of his demagoguery alone which gave Senator McCarthy his influence. It was the fact that his demagoguery incited and interpreted acute hostilities and frustrations among the American people, hostilities and frustrations generated, in the main, by our participation in the war in Korea.

All wars generate frustrations, but the Korean War was peculiarly frustrating. It was a limited war, and, though the reasons for its limitations were cogent, they were imperfectly understood by many Americans. This meant that there was spreading incomprehension and resentment over the fact that, as casualty lists lengthened, our government, renouncing nuclear weapons and respecting privileged sanctuaries, stubbornly declined to unleash the full force of our military power against the enemy. Moreover, if Communists were killing Americans in Korea, why should Americans be expected to tolerate for a moment any one at home who could be said to sound or look like a Communist? And some Americans who perhaps felt they ought to be in Korea themselves found it easy to expiate their guilt and affirm their virility by joining Senator Mc-Carthy's anti-Communist crusade. As a result, so long as the Korean War continued, McCarthy was able to influence a considerable number of his fellow citizens. He rode high in these years, leaving behind a trail of mistrust, fear and ruin. It was not till 1953, when the Korean armistice concluded the frustrations on which the Senator thrived, that the nation began to slip the bondage to hysteria and awaken from the nightmare.

The Vietnam war is just as frustrating as the Korean War and a good deal harder for most people to understand. The Korean War, after all, was a clear-cut case of invasion across frontiers; it entirely lacked the dimension of internal revolt which gives the struggle in Vietnam its peculiar difficulties. Moreover, the United States fought in Korea as the representative of the United Nations with the unqualified blessing of most of the world, while today we fight in Vietnam substantially alone. Then we had a relatively stable local government as our partner in Seoul—as against the parade of regimes in recent years in Saigon, many engaged in warfare against their own people. And then communism still seemed a united and mortal world threat, demanding the most urgent response—while today, as it degenerates into a scramble of warring tongs, it is losing its power and its momentum.

For all these reasons, the war in Vietnam may, in time, generate a higher intensity of frustration than the Korean War. And, if history repeats itself—and history sometimes does[1]—the war in Vietnam might well produce something roughly comparable to the McCarthy phenomenon of 1950–1954. As draft calls enlarge, as more soldiers disembark in Saigon, as casualties mount, as the war increasingly dominates and obsesses our national life, we can look for the appearance of associated symptoms: the oversimplification and emotionalization of issues, the exchange of invective—one side becoming 'warmongers,' the other 'appeasers'— the questioning of motives and of loyalties and the degradation of debate.

As this process continues, the emotional advantage will be increasingly on the side of the flag-wavers. Some of these will be tempted to pay off old scores as they wrap themselves in Old Glory. Conservative con-

[1] With qualifications noted below; see Chapter 7.

gressmen are already using the war in Vietnam as the excuse to oppose Great Society legislation which they would have opposed anyway; soon it may become a club with which they can assault old time liberal antagonists. Mark Twain described the process years ago:

> The loud little handful—as usual—will shout for the war. . . . A few fair men on the other side will argue and reason against the war with speech and pen, and at first will have a hearing and be applauded, but it will not last long; those others will outshout them, and presently the anti-war audiences will thin out and lose popularity. Before long you will see this curious thing: the speakers stoned from the platform, the free speech strangled by hordes of furious men who in their hearts are still at one with the stoned speakers—as earlier—but do not dare to say so. And now the whole nation—pulpit and all—will take up the war-cry and shout itself hoarse, and mob any honest man who ventures to open his mouth, and presently such mouths will cease to open.

Patriotism may become again, as Edmund Burke once wrote, "a bloody idol, which required the sacrifice of children and parents, or dearest connexions in private life, and of all the virtues that arise from those relations."

Thus the Georgia legislature has already refused a seat to a man, twice duly elected, because it disapproves of his views on Vietnam. Thus an American Communist who had won our country's second highest decoration, the Distinguished Service Cross for extraordinary heroism in the Second World War, has been forbidden burial in Arlington Cemetery. Thus a lieutenant in the

Army was sentenced to two years' imprisonment at hard labor (later reduced) and discharged from the service for taking part, while off duty and in civilian clothes, in a demonstration against the Vietnam war. Thus a ninth-grade teacher who stood silently during a flag salute at a school assembly because he did not agree with the Vietnam policy was expelled from the Las Vegas, Nevada, unit of the American Federation of Teachers, harried by anonymous phone calls and threatened with dismissal unless he promised to salute the flag in the future—which, after thirty-eight days, he did. Thus groups of protestors against the war have been beaten up in several cities; a federal judge in Philadelphia has demanded that all publicly supported colleges expel student protestors; various draft boards have terminated their deferments, presumably on the weird theory that military service is a punishment; and children, too young to be drafted, have been suspended from high schools in Cleveland and Pittsburgh for wearing black armbands in mourning for the dead in Vietnam. Thus Senator Eastland of Mississippi has introduced a bill conferring broad powers on the State Department to restrict travel by American citizens overseas—and the State Department has called for surveillance of an eminent Harvard professor on his trips abroad. A former Vice President of the United States has even detected the hand of the unsleeping Communist conspiracy in the fact that the DuBois Clubs—the Young Communist League of the 1960s, so called after W. E. DuBois, the Negro historian who joined the Communist Party before his death—should have been given a name sounding so much like that of the Boy's Club of America. This, according to the vigilant Mr. Nixon, was "an almost classic example of communist deception and duplicity."

These were still in 1966 relatively scattered incidents. The American Civil Liberties Union did not see "a clear pattern of repression" although such repression had "occurred too frequently to be classed as sporadic or isolated." But, as the sense of frustration grows, so too may these incidents. They can rapidly become the enemy of a responsible democracy. They may create a climate where people begin to refrain from saying what they believe lest they get into trouble. Before we know it, we may be developing an atmosphere which only requires a new McCarthy to become a new McCarthyism.

Vietnam thus exacts a heavy price at home. It exacts a heavy price abroad as well. On any realistic assessment, Western Europe and Latin America are far more significant to American security than Southeast Asia. Yet the Vietnam obsession has stultified our policy and weakened our position in both these vital areas. In Europe, for example, television has brought the horrors of the war into European parlors; and many—perhaps most—Europeans agreed with General de Gaulle when he said, "We find it totally detestable that a small country should be bombed by a very big one." The result has been the rise of a new form of anti-Americanism, emotional rather than ideological, leading toward a serious estrangement between Europe and America. The sense of estrangement is reinforced by the spreading impression that the United States, in its preoccupation with Vietnam, has lost interest in its western allies; and it is given a sharp edge by the fear that we are heading down the road toward war with China. When we began to bomb the oil deposits, James Reston wrote, "There is now not a single major nation in the world that supports Mr. Johnson's latest adventure in Hanoi and Haiphong." As other nations seek to disengage themselves from what they regard as an impending and unnecessary conflict, the quasi-neutralism of leaders like De Gaulle gains new plausibility.

At the same time, the war has clouded the hope, once mildly promising, of progress toward a detente with the Soviet Union. It has delayed agreements to end underground nuclear testing and to stop the spread of nuclear weapons. It almost persuaded U Thant to resign as Secretary General of the United Nations; and it probably condemns the UN itself to a time of frustration and declining influence.

Above all, it has estranged us from the future. For the future of all countries, developed or underdeveloped, depends on their youth—their young lawyers, politicians, scientists, engineers, teachers, trade unionists. These were exactly the young men and women who at the start of the sixties were beginning to look on the United States as the hope of the world; exactly those today who watch our course in Vietnam with perplexity, loathing and despair. It has become fashionable again in Washington to belittle this consequence of our Vietnam policy, to dismiss 'world opinion' in favor of the presumed realities of national power. But the American Presidents who have wielded the greatest power in the world—Wilson, Franklin Roosevelt and Kennedy—did so precisely because they never forgot that a basic element of national power is the capacity to move world opinion.

The administration has called the critics of its Vietnam policy 'neo-isolationists.' But surely the real neo-isolationists are those who have isolated the United States from its traditional allies and from the people of the world. "There is not a single independent state in Europe or in Asia," writes Mr. Lippmann, "which follows our lead. . . . No European government could survive today if it joined us on the battlefield. . . . As for the Asian peoples we are supposed to be saving, no independent Asian state—not Japan, India, Pakistan, Burma, Malaysia, Indonesia—is giving us even token support." It is the administration, and not its critics, which has raised the old nationalist standard, dropped fifteen years ago by Douglas MacArthur, of 'going it alone.' For unilateral action is the essence of isolationism, and this is increasingly the logic of our Vietnam policy.

5.
The Roots of Our Trouble

How have we managed to imprison ourselves in this series of dilemmas? One reason is a resurgence of old illusions—the illusion of American omnipotence and the illusion of American omniscience.

Our rejection of the views of our friends and allies—our conviction, as Paul H. Smith has put it, "that we alone are qualified to be judge, jury and executioner"—ignores Madison's solemn warning in the 63rd Federalist:

> An attention to the judgment of other nations is important to every government for two reasons: the one is that independently of the merits of any particular plan or measure, it is desirable, on various accounts, that it should appear to other nations as the offspring of a wise and honorable policy; the second is that in doubtful cases, particularly where the national councils may be warped by some strong passion or momentary interest, the presumed or known opinion of the impartial world may be the best guide that can be followed. What has not America lost by her want of character with foreign nations; and how many errors and follies would she not have avoided, if the justice and propriety of her measures had, in every instance, been previously tried by the light in which they would probably appear to be the unbiased part of mankind.

Or, as President Kennedy said many years later: "We must face the fact that the United States is neither omnipotent nor omniscient—that we are only six per cent of the world's population—that we cannot impose our will on the other ninety-four per cent of mankind—that we cannot right every wrong or reverse each adversity—and that therefore there cannot be an American solution to every world problem."

We have not only lost a sense of the limitations on our power but also our understanding of the uses of power. Understanding of power implies above all precision in its application. We have moved away from the subtle strategy of 'flexible response' under which the level of American force was graduated to meet the level of enemy threat. The triumph of this discriminate employment of power was, of course, the Cuban missile crisis (where the Joint Chiefs, as usual, urged an air assault on the missile bases). But President Johnson, for all his formidable abilities, has shown no knack for discrimination in his use of power. His technique is to try and overwhelm his adversary—as in the Dominican Republic and Vietnam—by piling on all forms of power without regard to the nature of the threat. His greatest weakness is his susceptibility to overkill.

Given this weakness, it is easy to see why the application of force in Vietnam has been surrendered to the workings of what an acute observer of the Johnson foreign policy, Philip Geyelin, calls "the escalation machine." This machine is, in effect, the momentum in the decision-making system which keeps on enlarging the war "for reasons only marginally related to military need."

The very size of the American military presence thus generates unceasing pressures to see all problems in military terms and to subordinate everything else to military demands. These may be demands to try out new weapons; the *London Sunday Telegraph* recently ran an informative article comparing the Vietnam war to the Spanish Civil War as a military testing ground and laboratory. Or they may be cries for 'one more step,' springing in part from suppressed rage over the fact that, with military power sufficient to blow up the world, we still cannot subdue guerrilla bands in black pajamas, without air power or artillery. Whatever the reason, Sir Robert Thompson has noted of the American theory of the war: "There was a constant tendency in Vietnam to mount large-scale operations, which had little purpose or prospect of success, merely to indicate that something aggressive was being done."

The administration has admitted that such operations, like the bombing of the north, are designed in part to prop up the morale of the Saigon government. And the impression is growing now that they are also in part undertaken in order to affect public opinion in the United States and to reverse anti-administration tendencies in the polls. Americans have become curiously insensitive to the use of military operations for domestic political purposes. A quarter-century ago President Roosevelt postponed the North African invasion so that it would not take place before the midterm elections of 1942; but today observers in Washington, without evidence of dismay, freely ascribe escalation to national politics.

The triumph of the escalation machine has been assisted by the faultiness of the information on which our decisions are based. Nothing is phonier than the spurious exactitude of our statistics about the Vietnam war. No doubt a computerized military establishment demands numbers; but the "body count" of dead Viet Cong, for example, includes heaven knows how many innocent bystanders and could hardly be more unreliable. So in the spring of 1963 the Deputy Under Secretary of State claimed that 30,000 casualties had been inflicted on the Viet Cong in 1962—a figure twice as large as the estimated size of the Viet Cong forces at the beginning of the year. So the Chairman of the Joint Chiefs of Staff could say in May 1965, "More than 50,000 South Vietnamese soldiers have been killed or wounded in battle since 1960," and the Secretary of State could say six weeks later, "From 1961 to the present . . . South Vietnamese armed forces have lost some 25,000 dead and 51,000 wounded"—a splendid increase of 50 per cent in a remarkably short time.

The figures on enemy strength are totally baffling, at least to the ordinary citizen relying on the daily newspaper. Thus President Johnson on April 4, 1966, said that 50,000 of the enemy had been killed since the beginning of the year. Four months later, the *New York Times,* on August 10, said that "according to official figures" the enemy had suffered 31,571 killed in action since January 1—a startling decline of 20,000 in the number of enemy deaths from President Johnson's April figure. The *Times* added, citing "the latest intelligence reports" in Saigon, that the number of enemy troops in South Vietnam had nevertheless increased 52,000 since January 1, to a total of 282,000. The infiltration estimate ranged from 35,000 as "definite" to 54,000 as "probably." If these figures mean anything, they suggest that the Viet Cong picked up from 30,000 to 50,000 local recruits in this period—a possibility which casts doubt on our incessant reports about the steady decline of Viet Cong morale.

Even the rather vital problem of how many North Vietnamese troops are in South Vietnam is swathed in mystery. The *Times* reported on August 7, 1966: "About 40,000 North Vietnamese troops are believed by allied intelligence to be in the South." According to an Associated Press dispatch from Saigon printed in the *Christian Science Monitor* of August 15:

> The South Vietnamese Government says 102,500 North Vietnamese combat troops and support battalions have infiltrated into South Vietnam.
>
> These figures are far in excess of United States intelligence estimates, which put the maximum number of North Vietnamese in the South at about 54,000.

But General Westmoreland told his Texas press conference on August 14 that the enemy force included "about 110,000 main-force North Vietnamese regular army troops." Then in the *U.S. News & World Report* three months later (November 28, 1966) the following exchange took place:

> Q: How many North Vietnamese regulars do you figure there are in the South?
>
> WESTMORELAND: Approximately 50,000.

The General neglected to explain what had happened to the extra 60,000 he had reported in August (and, needless to say, *U.S. News* did not ask him). Yet the American press continues solemnly to print such figures as if they meant something. Richard Goodwin has cogently summed up the condition of our statistics: "If we take the number of enemy we are supposed to be killing, add to that the defectors, along with a number of wounded much less than our own ratio of wounded to killed, we find we are wiping out the entire North Vietnamese force every year. This truly makes their continued resistance one of the marvels of the world."

Nor is our ignorance confined to battle-order statistics. An inordinate optimism has marked nearly all official statements about Vietnam since 1950—an optimism always discredited by events but somehow rarely discrediting the optimists, who continue to be heard reverently by the Congress and the press. We have been constantly told of our steady progress in pushing back the enemy; yet in bitter fact hardly more of the countryside of South Vietnam was 'secure' in 1966 than in 1965 or 1964. "In the main, and at the time that it matters most," as Philip Geyelin put it in the *Wall Street Journal* after a visit to Vietnam, "the decision-makers don't really know what they are talking about." The sad truth is that our government just doesn't know a lot of things it pretends to know. It is not discreditable that it should know them, for the facts are elusive and the judgments incredibly difficult. But it is surely inexcusable that it should pretend to know things it does not—and that it should commit the nation to a policy involving the greatest dangers on a foundation so vague and precarious. And it is even less excusable that it should pass its own ignorance on to the American people and to the world as certitude. "The air is charged with rhetoric," Richard Goodwin has written. ". . . Much of it is important and sincere and well-meaning. Some is intended to deceive. Some is deliberate lie and distortion. . . . With full allowance for necessary uncertainties I believe there has never been such intense and widespread deception and confusion as that which surrounds this war. The continual downpour of contradiction, misstatements and kaleidoscopically shifting attitudes has been so torrential that it has almost numbed the capacity to separate truth from conjecture and falsehood."

All this has produced what may, in the long run, be the most serious cost of all—a cost both domestic and foreign: the ebbing away of belief in the American government. It is an irony that a war undertaken to demonstrate the credibility of the American word should end in erosion of confidence in American integrity and purpose. When the Opinion Research Corporation conducted a poll of Western Europe in the autumn of 1966, asking under which President—Eisenhower, Kennedy or Johnson—American prestige had been greatest, the result was 74 per cent for Kennedy, 11 per cent for Eisenhower and 2 per cent for Johnson. The appearance of flim-flam, showmanship and manipulation in Washington has created a crisis of credibility from which it may take the nation a long time to recover.

6.
Is China the Enemy in Vietnam?

So now we are set on the course of widening the war—
even at the cost of multiplying American casualties in
Vietnam and deepening American troubles at home
and abroad; even at the risk of miring our nation in a
hopeless and endless conflict on the mainland of Asia
beyond the effective employment of our national
power and beyond the range of our primary interests;
even with the loss of national credibility and at the
hazard of nuclear war.

Why does the administration feel that these costs
must be paid and these risks run? Hovering behind our
policy is a larger idea—the idea that the war in Vietnam is not just a local conflict between Vietnamese but
a fateful test of wills between China and the United
States.

Our political and rhetorical escalation of the war
has been almost as perilous as our military escalation.
President Kennedy's effort was to pull Laos out of the
context of great-power conflict and reduce the civil
war there to rational proportions. As he told Khrushchev at Vienna in 1961, Laos was just not important
enough to entangle two great nations. President Johnson, on the other hand, has systematically inflated the
significance of the war in Vietnam. It is, he has said, "a
contest as far-reaching and as vital as any we have ever
waged."

The reason for this, it appears, is China. On December 23, 1964, the Secretary of State told his press
conference—as reported the next day by Chalmers

Roberts of the *Washington Post*—"that the loss of Vietnam would mean that the Red Chinese 'primitive, militant doctrine of world revolution' would not stop with the conquest of Vietnam. 'I should think,' he said, 'they would simply move the problem to the next country and the next and the next.' . . . This problem will continue, he said, until the Red Chinese decide 'to leave their neighbors alone and not to press militantly their notion of world revolution.'" "We have tried to make it clear over and over again," the Secretary of State put it to the Senate Foreign Relations Committee, "that although Hanoi is the prime actor in this situation, that it is the policy of Peking that has greatly stimulated Hanoi. . . . It is Ho Chi Minh's war. Maybe it is Mao Tse-tung's war." The object of our policy, according to the Under Secretary of State, is to "prevent Red China from establishing its hegemony over the East Asian land mass." "In the forties and fifties," according to President Johnson, "we took our stand in Europe to protect the freedom of those threatened by aggression. Now the center of attention has shifted to another part of the world where aggression is on the march. Our stand must be as firm as ever." Given this view—the view, as well summarized by U Thant, that "the conflict is a kind of holy war between two powerful political ideologies"—it is presumably necessary to pay the greatest costs and run the greatest risks—or else invite the greatest defeat.

Given this view, too, there is no reason not to Americanize the war. President Kennedy did not believe that the war in Vietnam could succeed as a war of white men against Asians. We have now junked this doctrine. Instead, we have enlarged our military presence until it is the only thing that matters in South Vietnam, and we plan now to make it still larger; we have summoned the Saigon leaders, like tribal chieftains on a retainer, to a conference in an American state; we crowd the streets of Saigon with American generals (fifty-eight at last count) and visiting stateside dignitaries. In short, we have seized every opportunity to make clear to the world that this is an *American* war—and, in doing this, we have surely gone far to make the war unwinnable.

The proposition that our real enemy in Vietnam is China is basic to the policy of widening the war. It is the vital element in the administration case. Yet the proof our leaders have adduced has been exceedingly sketchy and almost perfunctory. The American government, indeed, acts as if the proposition were so self-evident that it requires no demonstration—in spite of the fact that the countries most directly threatened by Chinese expansion, Russia, Japan and India, apparently do not accept it. If pressed, our government offers proof by ideology or proof by analogy. It does not offer proof by reasoned argument or by concrete illustration.

The proof by ideology has relied on the syllogism that the Viet Cong, North Vietnam and China are all communist states and *therefore* must be part of the same conspiracy, and that, since the Viet Cong are the weakest of the three and China is the strongest, the Viet Cong must *therefore* be the spearhead of a coordinated Chinese plan of expansion. The clichés about a centralized communist conspiracy aiming at monolithic world revolution are still cherished in the State Department, in spite of what has struck lay observers as a rather evident fragmentation of the communist world. Thus, as late as May 9, 1965, after half a dozen years of vociferous Russo-Chinese quarreling, Thomas C. Mann, then No. 3 man in the Department, could babble about "instruments of Sino-Soviet power" and "orders from the Sino-Soviet military bloc." As late as

January 28, 1966, the Secretary of State was still running on about "their world revolution," and again, on February 18, about "the Communists" and their "larger design."

While the department may have finally accepted the reality of the Russo-Chinese schism, it still does not grasp the larger implications of the shattering of communist universalism. For this schism has done a good deal more than simply to divide Russia and China: what it has done is to set all communist states free to pursue national policies. It has thereby transformed the character of the communist problem. For, in an age of centralized communist control, the extension of communism did mean the pretty automatic extension of Russian power. In the thirties or forties, if the communists took over a country, the result was to heighten the threat to the security of the democratic world. But in the age of polycentrism the extension of communism no longer means an automatic extension of Russian, or of Chinese, power. All it may mean is that a country has succumbed to a dismal and dogmatic creed, with subsequent repression for its people and losses for foreign investors; and such a development, however deplorable, does not *per se* create a deadly strategic threat to the security of the democracies.

The crucial fact is that in a world without a clear center of communist authority—and especially in countries where communism can survive only as it becomes a nationalist movement—we can no longer assume that every communist state will be a puppet or, in the lingo of Senator Dodd, a 'slave state.'[1] On the con-

[1] Those whose passion it is to eliminate Communist China as a world power must some day ask themselves whether it is really to the interest of the United States to restore Moscow as the sole and single center of communist authority and thereby assist the Soviet

trary we must expect communist states to begin to act like other independent countries. This does not mean that we can necessarily look to the multiplication of Yugoslavias—i.e., of communist nations eager to get on good terms with the west—but we can probably look to the multiplication of Rumanias—i.e., of communist nations still deeply anti-American but determined to recover control over their own polities and to assert their independence of Moscow and Peking.

The mere fact a state proclaims itself communist is thus no longer by that fact itself proof that it will serve as the obedient instrument of expanding Russian or Chinese power. The abstraction no longer settles the question. What is required is specific demonstration in each particular case. Yet the State Department (I speak of the institution; many individuals, of course, wholly understand the implications of life in the polycentrist world) continues indolently in the old course, treating Asian communism as if it were a homogeneous system of aggression. The premise of our Vietnam policy has been that the Viet Cong equal Hanoi and Hanoi equals Peking.

Obviously the Viet Cong, Hanoi and Peking have interests in common and strong ideological affinities. Obviously, Peking would rejoice in a Hanoi-Viet Cong victory. But they also have divergent interests and purposes—and the divergencies may prove in the end to be stronger than the affinities. Recent developments in

---

Union to rebuild the relatively centralized and unified international communist movement of the thirties and forties. Our natural preference for the Soviet Union in its doctrinal disputes with China should not blind us to the fact that the national interests of the Soviet Union may well be more in direct conflict than those of China with the national interests of the United States.

North Korea are instructive. If any country was bound to Peking by ties of gratitude, it was North Korea, which was preserved as an independent state by Chinese intervention fifteen years ago. If any country today is at the mercy of Peking, it is again North Korea. When North Korea now declares in vigorous language its independence of China, does anyone suppose that North Vietnam, imbued with historic mistrust of China and led by that veteran Russian agent, Ho Chi Minh, will be more reliable and slavish in subservience to Peking?

The other part of the administration case has been proof by analogy, especially the good old Munich analogy. "I'm not the village idiot," the Secretary of State recently confided to Stewart Alsop. "I know Hitler was an Austrian and Mao is Chinese. . . . But what is common between the two situations is the phenomenon of aggression." The Secretary of State had even the imagination to suggest that an exhortation to the underdeveloped world delivered in 1965 by the Chinese Defense Minister, Marshal Lin Piao, was a blueprint for world conquest comparable to Hitler's *Mein Kampf*.

The chosen technique for Chinese expansion, according to the American government, is the 'war of national liberation'—a mellifluous phrase which the Daughters of the American Revolution should not perhaps have surrendered so readily to the Communists. The Vietnam war, President Johnson told the American Legion, "is meant to be the opening salvo in a series of bombardments or, as they are called in Peking, 'wars of liberation.'" If this technique works this week in Vietnam, the administration suggests, it will be tried next week in Uganda and Peru. But, if it is defeated in Vietnam, the Chinese will know that we will not let it succeed elsewhere. "What happens in South Vietnam," the President cried at Omaha, "will determine—yes, it will determine—whether ambitious and aggressive nations can use guerrilla warfare to conquer their weaker neighbors."

One thing is sure about the Vietnam riddle: it will not be solved by bad historical analogies. It seems a trifle forced, for example, to equate a civil war in what was for centuries the entity of Vietnam (Marshal Ky, after all, is a North Vietnamese himself[2] and Pham Van Dong, the premier of North Vietnam, is from the south) with Hitler's invasion of Czechoslovakia across old and well-established lines of national division.

When President Eisenhower invoked the Munich analogy in 1954 in an effort to involve the British in Indochina, Prime Minister Churchill, a pretty keen student of Munich in his day, was unmoved. He evidently saw no useful parallel between Hitler, the man on the bicycle who could not stop, a madman commanding vast military force and requiring immediate and visible success, and the ragged bands and limited goals of Ho Chi Minh. Nor evidently could he see any useful parallel between Europe—a developed continent with well-defined national frontiers, interests and identities and a highly organized equilibrium of power—and Southeast Asia, an underdeveloped subcontinent filled with fictitious states in vague, chaotic, and unpredictable revolutionary ferment. And, if Mao rather than Ho is the Asian Hitler, even the Chinese have neither the overwhelmingly military power nor the timetable of aggression nor, apparently, the pent-up mania for instant expansion which would justify the parallel. As for the

[2] Ky's effort to pack the Saigon government with other North Vietnamese caused a cabinet crisis in the last months of 1966. Yet the American officials continue to talk as if North and South Vietnam were entirely distinct national states.

Lin Piao document, the Rand Corporation, which evidently read it with more care than the State Department bothered to do, concluded that, far from being Mao's *Mein Kampf,* it was a message to the Viet Cong that they could win "only if they rely primarily on their own resources and their own revolutionary spirit," and that it revealed "the lack, rather than the extent, of Peking's past and present control over Hanoi's actions."

In any case, guerrilla warfare is not a tactic to be mechanically applied by central headquarters to faraway countries. More than any other form of warfare, it is dependent on conditions and opportunities within the countries themselves. Defeating communist guerrillas in Greece, the Philippines, Malaya and Venezuela—defeating communist aggression in Korea—did not prevent guerrilla warfare in Vietnam. Whether there are wars of national liberation in Uganda and Peru will depend, not on what happens in Vietnam, but on what happens in Uganda and Peru.

Nor need we exaggerate the inevitability of communist takeovers of nationalist revolutions. We have been hypnotized by the notion that, when a revolution begins in an underdeveloped country, the Communists are bound to win out. But history shows this to be the exception, not the rule. "It would be a gross oversimplification," Secretary McNamara has reminded us, "to regard Communism as the central factor in every conflict throughout the underdeveloped world. Of the 149 serious insurgencies in the past eight years, Communists have been involved in only 58 of them—38 per cent of the total—and this includes seven in which a Communist regime itself was the target of the uprising." Communist strength in underdeveloped countries is ordinarily in the cities, the universities, the trade unions, not in the hills—and, where Communists wish to penetrate the normal political and institutional life of a country, there is no quicker way to destroy their prospects than by a resort to violence: cf. Indonesia and Venezuela.

One may look at Algeria, for example, or Egypt, or the countries of Black Africa, or Bolivia, or Indonesia; all these states have undergone drastic upheavals, and their nationalism has taken ardent and aggressive forms. Often these upheavals have produced regimes which do not much like the west or the United States. But the new nationalist regimes typically do not much like communism either. The striking fact of the post-war years is surely the failure of the communists to ride to power on nationalist upheavals—in short, the failure of the "war of national liberation" as a communist tactic. Where the communists have won out, as in China and North Vietnam, it is because they were able to place themselves at the head of nationalist movements during the Second World War. (The other major communist post-war success—Cuba—is a special case; Castro made his own revolution and then personally carried it into the communist empire.)

Certainly the containment of China will be a major problem for the next generation. But let us not confuse the prevention of Chinese aggression with the suppression of nationalist revolution. The containment of national communism in the polycentrist sixties will be very different from the containment of international communism in the monolithic forties. The record thus far suggests that the force most likely to contain Chinese expansionism in Asia (and Africa, too) will be not American intervention but local nationalism (plus the dogmatism and folly which have thus far made China such a hopeless washout as a revolutionary power and have alienated every Communist Party in the East except for New Zealand). Sometimes local nationalism may call on American support, but not always. Countries like Burma and Cambodia preserve their autonomy without American assistance.[3] The Africans have dealt with the Chinese on their own. The two heaviest blows recently suffered by Peking—the destruction of the Communist Party in Indonesia and the declaration of independence by North Korea—took place without benefit of American patronage or rhetoric.[4] Indeed, too overt American intervention may actually have the effect of smothering the forces of local nationalism or driving them to the other side and thereby ultimately weakening the containment of China.

In the unpredictable decades ahead, the most effective bulwark against an aggressive national communist state in some circumstances may well be national communism in surrounding states. A rational policy of containing China could have recognized that a communist Vietnam under Ho might be a better instru-

[3] U Thant has observed of his native country: "The Burmese Communist Party is still underground after seventeen years and is still illegal. . . . Burma has over a thousand miles of land frontier with mainland China. If the Burmese Government had decided at some stage to seek outside military assistance . . . I am sure that Burma would have experienced one of two alternatives: either the country would be divided in two parts or the whole country would have become communist long ago." Or, in the words of Under Secretary Ball, "The people of Southeast Asia have, over the centuries, shown an obstinate insistence on shaping their own destiny which the Chinese have not been able to overcome."

[4] It is curiously argued that the Indonesian generals would not have resisted the Communist take-over had it not been for the American presence in Vietnam a thousand miles away. This proposition omits the fact that, if the generals had not resisted the take-over, they would all have been horribly killed. They were fighting for their lives.

ment of containment than a shaky Saigon regime led by right-wing mandarins or air force generals. Had Ho taken over all Vietnam in 1954, he might today be soliciting Soviet support to strengthen his resistance to Chinese pressure, and this situation, however appalling for the people of South Vietnam, would obviously be better for the United States than the one in which we are floundering today. And now, alas, it may be almost too late: the whole thrust of United States policy since 1954, and more than ever since the bombing of the north began, has been not to pry Peking and Hanoi apart but to drive them together.

And now we are told that a higher obligation awaits us: that history has summoned America to be an Asian power—not just a Pacific power, which of course it has been since Commodore Perry opened up Japan, but a power with vital political interests and urgent military commitments on the mainland of Asia. The theory of the United States as an Asian power was the tacit point of President Johnson's Manila tour, as it has been the explicit point of Vice President Humphrey's eloquence about a Great Society for Asia. One cannot doubt the genuineness of the administration's belief that East Asia is manifest destiny's next stop.

Can Mr. Johnson and Mr. Humphrey, two astute and experienced men, really be serious about this? Evidently they are; and their Asian vision is not dishonorable. It derives from the psyche of Franklin Roosevelt rather than Theodore—from the desire, as they represent it to themselves, not to aggrandize the power of America but to help Asians become more like Americans. It is a form of imperialism unknown to Lenin: sentimental imperialism. Not perhaps unknown to Kipling: the white man's burden. This is what they mean—and they mean it decently.

But do they mean it sensibly? One can argue, I think, that the United States could embark on no more preposterous adventure in the seventh decade of the twentieth century than the salvation of Asia. This undertaking, in the first place, ignores the central historic transformation of this century—the emergence of Asia as an equal force on the world scene, which has led to the recovery by Asians of their ancient sense of ineffable superiority to the western barbarians. As long ago as 1954, when Christopher Mayhew of England suggested to Ho Chi Minh that the west had a peacekeeping role in Asia, Ho replied sardonically, "Suppose we Vietnamese—together perhaps with the Indians—proposed ourselves for a peace-keeping role in Europe. What would you Europeans think?" What indeed? How can the west continue to suppose that it can assign itself a role in Asia which Asia cannot claim in Europe or America? Nor can President Johnson really suppose that the support at the Manila Conference of four American dependencies in Asia—South Vietnam, South Korea, Thailand and the Philippines, with a total population of 103 million—offers the United States a firm moral, political or military basis for intervention.

It must be argued, moreover, that the conception of the United States as an Asian power violates the logic of our own history. For history prescribes two tables of priorities for the United States—one based on strategic significance, the other on cultural accessibility. And by both standards Western Europe and Latin America are the parts of the world which matter most to the United States. We could survive the subjection of Asia, Africa, the Middle East, Eastern Europe or Polynesia by a hostile power or ideology; but, if either Western Europe or Latin America were organized against North America, our position would be parlous indeed. And Western

Europe and Latin America are the parts of the world to which a common intellectual tradition gives us a hope of reciprocal understanding.

We express our daily concern about the underdeveloped world. But the one part of the underdeveloped world which is western in its institutions and values—and the one part of the western world which is underdeveloped—is Latin America. If we cannot relate ourselves to the democratic development of Latin America, if we cannot, as President Kennedy said in the speech launching the Alliance for Progress, demonstrate here "that man's unsatisfied aspiration for economic progress and social justice can best be achieved by free men working within a framework of democratic institutions," how can we ever suppose that we can advance the cause of democracy in the alien, mysterious and impenetrable cultures of Asia and Africa? Yet Latin America falls to the end of the queue, while all energy and concern are absorbed by Vietnam.

Expansive rhetoric is the occupational disease of national leaders. But serious leaders preserve a relationship, however tenuous, between rhetoric and reality. One cannot remember a more complete dissociation between words and responsibility than in the United States government today: official speeches are always manipulative in part, but now they are almost nothing else. The dedication of the United States to the salvation of Asia represents a translation of rhetorical extravagance into national policy. The President of the United States can hardly understand the eastern seaboard of his own country; why in the world does he think he can understand the eastern seaboard of Asia? If meant seriously, the idea of a Great Society for Asia is surely a fantastic overcommitment of American thought and resources. If meant as a rhetorical flourish, it is frivolity. However meant, the proposition demands a most rigorous and thoughtful assessment of the limits and possibilities of America's role in the world. It demands the confrontation of an issue deep in the historical consciousness of the United States: whether this country is a chosen people, uniquely righteous and wise, with a moral mission to all mankind; or whether it is one of many nations in a multifarious world, endowed with traditions and purposes, legitimate but not infallible, as other nations have legitimate and fallible traditions and purposes of their own, and committed not to an American century but to what President Kennedy used to call a world of diversity—"a robust and vital world community, founded on nations secure in their own independence, and united by allegiance to world peace." The ultimate choice is between messianism and maturity.

The argument that the United States and China must be locked in mortal combat on the mainland of Asia is not an observation but a prophecy, even if a prophecy which masquerades as historical analogy. It therefore raises larger questions about the way statesmen use history—or are used by it.

7.

The Inscrutability of History

As one who is by profession an historian and has been by occasion a government official, I have long been fascinated and perplexed by the interaction between history and public decision: fascinated because, by this process, past history becomes an active partner in the making of new history; perplexed because the role of history in this partnership remains both elusive and tricky.

It is elusive because, if one excludes charismatic politics—the politics of the prophet and the medicine man—one is bound to conclude that all thought which leads to decisions of public policy is in essence historical. Public decision in rational politics necessarily implies a guess about the future derived from the experience of the past. It implies an expectation, or at the very least a hope, that certain actions will produce tomorrow the same sort of results they produced yesterday. This guess about the future may be based on a comprehensive theory of historical change, as with the Marxists; or it may be based on specific analogies drawn from the past; or it may be based on an unstated and intuitive sense of the way things happen. But, whatever it is based on, it involves, explicitly or implicitly, an historical judgment.

And the problem is tricky because, when explicit historical judgments intervene, one immediately encounters a question which is, in the abstract, insoluble: Is the history invoked really the source of policies, or is it the source of arguments designed to vindicate policies adopted for antecedent reasons? Moreover, even when history is in some sense the source of policies, the lessons of history are generally so ambiguous that the antecedent reasons often determine the choice between alternative historical interpretations. Thus, in France between the wars Reynaud and Mandel drew one set of conclusions from the First World War, Bonnet and Laval another. Yet one cannot, on the other hand, reduce the function of history in public policy to that of mere rationalization, for historical models acquire a life of their own. Once a statesman begins to identify the present with the past, he may in time be carried further than he intends by the bewitchment of analogy.

However hard it may be to define with precision the role of history in public policy, it is evident that this role must stand or fall on the success of history as a means of prediction—on the proposition that knowledge of yesterday provides guidance for tomorrow. This is a point, it should immediately be said, on which professional historians, on the whole, have few illusions among themselves. They privately regard history as its own reward; they study it for the intellectual and aesthetic fulfillment they find in the disciplined attempt to reconstruct the past and, perhaps, for the ironic aftertaste in the contemplation of man's heroism and folly, but for no more utilitarian reason. They understand better than outsiders that historical training confers no automatic wisdom in the realm of public affairs. Guizot, Bancroft, Macaulay, Thiers, Morley, Bryce, Theodore Roosevelt, Woodrow Wilson: one cannot say that their training as historians deeply influenced their practice as politicians; and the greatest of them—Roosevelt and Wilson—were harmed as politicians by exactly the moralism from which the study of history might have saved them. But then neither was a particularly good historian.[1]

Yet historians, in spite of their candor within the fellowship, sometimes invoke arguments of a statelier sort in justifying themselves to society. Thus Raleigh: "We may gather out of History a policy no less wise than eternal; by the comparison and application of other men's fore-passed miseries with our own errours and ill-deservings." Or Burke: "In history, a great volume is unrolled for our instruction, drawing the materials of future wisdom from the past errors and infirmities of mankind." In what sense is this true? Why should history help us foresee the future? Because presumably history repeats itself enough to make possible a range of historical generalization; and because generalization, sufficiently multiplied and interlaced, can generate insight into the shape of things to come.

Many professional historians—perhaps most—reject the idea that generalization is the goal of history. We all respond, in Marc Bloch's phrase, to "the thrill of learning singular things." Indeed, it is the commitment to concrete reconstruction as against abstract generalization—to life as against laws—which distinguishes history from sociology. Yet, on the other hand, as Crane Brinton once put it, "the doctrine of the absolute uniqueness of events in history seems nonsense." Even historians who are skeptical of attempts to discern a final and systematic order in history acknowledge the existence of a variety of uniformities and recurrences. There can be no question that generalizations about the past, defective as they may be, are

---

[1] Churchill is a different matter; but he was a politician who turned to history, not an historian who turned to politics. So too was Kennedy.

possible—and that they can strengthen the capacity of statesmen to deal with the future.

So historians have long since identified a life-cycle of revolution which, if properly apprehended, might have spared us misconceptions about the Russian Revolution—first, about its goodwill and, later, when we abandoned belief in its goodwill, about the fixity and permanence of its fanatical purpose—and which, if consulted today, might save us from the notion that the Chinese Revolution will be forever cast in its present mold. Historical generalizations in a number of areas— the processes of economic development, for example, or the impact of industrialization and urbanization, or the effect of population growth, or the influence of climate or sea power or the frontier, or the circulation of political elites or entrepreneurial innovation—will enlarge the wisdom of the statesman, giving his responses to the crises of the moment perspective, depth and an instinct for the direction and flow of events. The consequences for American society of the frustrations generated by limited war—the McCarthyism effect—is probably an example of permissible generalization. Sometimes this wisdom may even lead to what Bloch called "the paradox of prevision"—to the point when men, sufficiently warned by historical extrapolation of horrid eventualities, may take action to avert them, which means that prevision may be destroyed by prevision.

The result is historical insight: that is, a sense of what is possible and probable in human affairs, derived from a feeling for the continuities and discontinuities of existence. This sense is comparable not to the mathematical equations of the physicist but to the diagnostic judgments of the doctor. It is this form of historical insight which has led in recent years to Bertrand

de Jouvenel's *L'Art de la Conjecture* and to the stimulating intellectual exercise involved in the search for *futuribles*. But *futuribles* are speculative constructions of
possible long-range futures, useful perhaps to those
who may be presidents and prime ministers in 2000,
hardly to their predecessors in 1970.

Still every day around the planet great decisions are
being made (or at least rationalized) in terms of short-
run historical estimates. The whole Marxist world, of
course, is sworn to a determinist view of the future, according to which fixed causes produce fixed effects and
mankind is moving along a predestined path through
predestined stages to a single predestined conclusion.
For the Marxists, history has become a 'positive
model': it prescribes not only for the long but for the
short run, not only strategy but tactics—the immediate
policies to be favored, courses pursued, action taken. It
is a tribute to the devotion of Marxists, if hardly to
their intelligence, that they have remained so indefati-
gably loyal to their metaphysic in spite of the demonstrated limits of Marxism as a system of prediction.

For, if any thesis was central to the Marxist vision of
history, it was that the process of modernization, of industrialization, of social and economic development,
would infallibly carry every nation from feudalism
through capitalism to communism: that the communist society was the inevitable culmination of the development process. Thus Marx contended that, the
more developed a country was, the more prepared it
was for communism, and that communism in consequence must come first to the most industrialized nations. In fact, communism has come only to nations in
a relatively early stage of development, like Russia and
China, and it has come to such nations precisely as a
means to modernization, not as a consequence of it. In-

stead of being the climax of the development process, the end of the journey, communism is now revealed as a technique of social discipline which a few countries in early stages of development have adopted in the hope of speeding the pace of modernization. Instead of the ultimate destinations toward which all societies are ineluctably moving, communism now appears an epiphenomenon of the transition from stagnation to development. Modernization, as it proceeds, evidently carries nations not toward Marx but away from Marx—and this would appear true even of the Soviet Union itself.

History thus far has refuted the central proposition in Marx's system of prediction. It has also refuted important corollary theses—notably the idea that the free economic order could not possibly last. Far from obeying dogma and perishing of its own inner contradictions, free society in the developed world has rarely displayed more creativity and vitality. It is casting as powerful a spell on the intellectuals and the youth of the communist world as the communist world cast on us during the Depression thirty years ago.

Why did Marx go wrong here? His forecast of the inevitable disintegration of free society was plausibly based on the *laissez faire* capitalism of the mid-nineteenth century. This devil-take-the-hindmost economic order did very likely contain the seeds of its own destruction—especially in those tendencies, pronounced irreversible by Marx, toward an ever widening gap between rich and poor (alleged to guarantee the ultimate impoverishment of the masses) and toward an ever increasing frequency and severity of structural economic crisis (alleged to guarantee the progressive instability of the system). This may indeed be a salient example of the "paradox of prevision"; for the Marxist forecast unquestionably stimulated progressive democrats to begin the reform of classical capitalism through the invention of the affirmative state. "The more we condemn unadulterated Marxian Socialism," Theodore Roosevelt used to say, "the stouter should be our insistence on thoroughgoing social reforms." The combination of the affirmative state with the extraordinary success of the free economic order as an engine of production—a success which, contrary to *laissez faire* dogma, government intervention increased rather than hampered—eventually thwarted the Marxist prophecy.

In the end, the Marxists were undone by Marxism. Ideology told them that those who owned the economy *must* own the state, and the state could therefore never act against their desires or interests. Yet fifteen years before the *Communist Manifesto* an American President, Andrew Jackson, had already suggested that the state in a democratic society, far from being the instrument of the possessors, could well become the means by which those whom Jackson called the "humble members of society" might begin to redress the balance of social power against those whom Hamilton had called the "rich and well-born." Thus, in the twentieth-century developed world, the economic machine drowned the revolution in consumers' goods, while the affirmative state, with its policies of piece-meal intervention in the economy, brought about both a relative redistribution of wealth (defeating Marx's prediction of the immiseration of the poor) and a relative stabilization of the economy (defeating Marx's prediction of ever deepening cyclical crisis). The last place to look for a Marxist victory is precisely the place where Marx said it would come first—i.e., in the most developed countries.

So the Marxist prophecy of a single obligatory destiny for mankind has missed in both its parts: in its prediction of the irresistible breakdown of the free economy, and in its prediction of the irresistible triumph of communism as the fulfillment of the development process. In spite of many subsidiary insights and successes, Marxism must surely stand in our time as the spectacular flop of history as prophecy. The failure, indeed, has been so complete that contemporary Marxists revile each other in seeking the true meaning of the most elementary doctrines; the more fanatical stand Marx on his head, rejecting his basic theory and arguing that communism will come "out of the countryside," not the city.

Yet the democratic world is hardly in a position to take too much satisfaction from the intellectual collapse of Marxism. It is true that our philosophical heritage—empirical, pragmatic, ironic, pluralistic, competitive—has happily inoculated us against rigid, all-encompassing, absolute systems of historical interpretation. But, though we may reject the view of history as metaphysically set and settled, we seem at times to embrace our own forms of historical fatalism, even if we invoke history less as theology than as analogy. This is only a marginal advantage. The argument by metaphor can generate a certitude almost as mischievous as the argument by determinism.

For democratic policy-makers, history generally appears as a 'negative' rather than a 'positive' model. It instructs us, not like Marxism, in the things we must do, but in the things we must *not* do—unless we wish to repeat the mistakes of our ancestors. The traumatic experience of the First World War thus dominated the diplomacy of the Second World War, at least as far as the United States was concerned. So the American insistence on the doctrine of "unconditional surrender" in 1943 sprang from the belief that the failure to get unconditional surrender in 1918 had made possible the stab-in-the-back myth and guaranteed the revival of German nationalism. The American obsession with the United Nations came from the conviction that the failure to join the League of Nations had opened the way to the Second World War. The American readiness to make concessions to the Soviet Union (as Professor E. R. May has suggested) was based, in part, on an analogy with Clemenceau's France. The American President viewed the Soviet Union as a nation which, having lived in permanent insecurity, could be expected, like France twenty-five years earlier, to value security above almost anything else. "Roosevelt," Professor May has perceptively written, "was determined to see Stalin's point of view as Wilson had not seen Clemenceau's. He was determined that, in so far as possible, the Soviet Union should have the guarantees it wanted and should not be forced into the sullen self-preoccupation of the France of Poincaré."

The Second World War, then, provided a new traumatic experience. In the years since, the consciousness of policymakers has been haunted by the Munich and Yalta analogies—the generalization, drawn from attempts to accommodate Hitler in 1938, and Stalin in 1945, that appeasement always assures new aggression. Of these analogies, Munich, as the more lucid in its pattern and the more emphatic in its consequence, has been the more powerful; Yalta figures rather as a complicated special case. I trust that a graduate student some day will write a doctoral essay on the influence of the Munich analogy on the subsequent history of the twentieth century. Perhaps in the end he will conclude that the multitude of errors committed in the name of "Munich" may exceed the original error of 1938.

Certainly Munich was a tragic mistake, and its lesson was that the appeasement of a highly wound-up and heavily armed totalitarian state in the context of a relatively firm and articulated continental equilibrium of power was likely to upset the balance and make further aggression inevitable. But to conclude from this that all attempts to avert war by negotiation must always be 'Munichs' goes beyond the evidence. No one understood this better than the greatest contemporary critic of Munich. An historian himself, Winston Churchill well understood the limits of historical analogy. So he defined the issue in his chapter on Munich in *The Gathering Storm*:

> It may be well here to set down some principles of morals and action which may be a guide in the future. No case of this kind can be judged apart from its circumstances. . . .
>
> Those who are prone by temperament and character to seek sharp and clear-cut solutions of difficult and obscure problems, who are ready to fight whenever some challenge comes from a foreign power, have not always been right. On the other hand, those whose inclination is to bow their heads, to seek patiently and faithfully for peaceful compromise, are not always wrong. On the contrary, in the majority of instances, they may be right, not only morally but from a practical standpoint. . . .
>
> How many wars have been precipitated by firebrands! How many misunderstandings which led to war could have been removed by temporising! How often have countries fought cruel wars and then after a few years of peace found themselves not only friends but allies!

Sixteen years after Munich, when President Eisenhower invoked the Munich analogy to persuade the

British to join the Americans in backing the French in Indochina, Churchill, as we have seen, was unimpressed. He rejected Eisenhower's analogy, which did not, of course, prevent Churchill's successor as prime minister two years later from seeing Nasser and the Middle East in terms of 1938 and committing his nation to the Suez adventure. This time it was Eisenhower who rejected the Munich analogy. Such incidents illustrate the depressing persistence of the mentality which makes policy through stereotype, through historical generalization wrenched illegitimately out of the past and imposed mechanically on the future. Santayana's aphorism must be reversed: too often it is those who *can* remember the past who are condemned to repeat it.

"No case of this kind," Churchill said, "can be judged apart from its circumstances." I well remember President Kennedy after the Cuban missile crisis in 1962 privately expressing his fear that people would conclude from his victory that all we would have to do thereafter in dealing with the Communists was to be tough and they would collapse. The missile crisis, he pointed out, had three distinctive features: it took place in an area where we enjoyed local conventional superiority, where Soviet national security was not directly engaged, and where the Russians lacked a case which they could convincingly sustain before the world. Things would be different, he said, if the situation were one where the Communists had the local superiority, where their national security was directly engaged, and where they could persuade themselves and others they were in the right.

Kennedy, who, like Churchill, had the mind of a first-class historian, was without illusion about the infallibility of historical analogy. The point is not terribly complicated. Burke long ago warned against the practice of viewing an object "as it stands stripped of every relation, in all the nakedness and solitude of metaphysical abstraction. Circumstances (which with some gentlemen pass for nothing) give in reality to every political principle its distinguishing color and discriminating effect." Even Toynbee, the magician of historical analogy, has remarked that historians are

> never in a position to guarantee that the entities which we are bringing into comparison are properly comparable for the purpose of our investigation. . . . However far we may succeed in going in our search for sets of identical examples on either side, we shall never be able to prove that there is not some non-identical factor that we have overlooked, and this non-identical factor is not the decisive factor that accounts for the different out-comes in different cases of what has looked to us like an identical situation but may not have been this in truth.

Or, as Mark Twain put it, somewhat more vividly, in *Following the Equator*: "We should be careful to get out of an experience only the wisdom that is in it—and stop there; lest we be like the cat that sits down on a hot stove lid. She will never sit down on a hot stove lid again—and that is well; but also she will never sit down on a cold one."

One cannot doubt that the study of history makes people wiser. But it is indispensable to understand the limits of historical analogy. Most useful historical generalizations are statements about massive social and intellectual movements over a considerable period of time. They make large-scale, long-term prediction possible. But they do not justify small-scale, short-term prediction. For short-run prediction is the prediction of detail and, given the complex structure of social events, the difficulty of anticipating the intersection or collision of different events and the irreducible mystery, if not invincible freedom, of individual decision, there are simply too many variables to warrant exact forecasts of the immediate future. History, in short, can answer questions, after a fashion, at long range. It cannot answer questions with confidence or certainty at short range. Alas, policy makers are rarely interested in the long run—"in the long run," as Keynes used to say, "we are all dead"—and the questions they put to history are thus most often the questions which history is least qualified to answer.

Far from offering a short cut to clairvoyance, history teaches us that the future is full of surprises and outwits all our certitudes. For the study of history issues not in scientific precision nor in moral finality but in irony. If twenty-five years ago, anyone had predicted that before the end of the decade of the forties Germany and Japan would be well on the way to becoming close friends and allies of Britain and the United States, he would have been considered mad. If fifteen years ago, as the Russians and Chinese were signing their thirty-year pact of amity and alliance, anyone predicted that by the end of the fifties they would be at each other's throats, he too would have been considered mad. The chastening fact is that many of the pivotal events of our age were unforeseen: from the Nazi-Soviet pact and the Tito-Stalin quarrel of years ago to such events in today's newspapers as the anti-communist upsurge in Indonesia and the overthrow of Nkrumah in Ghana (and his resurrection in Guinea).

Occasionally one reads in the American press that leading political figures in Washington are shaping their actions today by calculations with regard to the Democratic presidential nomination in 1972. I am sure that the men mentioned in such stories are themselves under no delusion about the hopelessness of such an undertaking. 1972 is as far away from 1966 as 1960 is, and no one reflecting on the unpredictability of the last six years in the United States could sensibly suppose that the next six are going to be any more predictable. I have often thought that a futurist trying to forecast the next three American Presidents in early 1940 would hardly have named as the first President after Franklin D. Roosevelt an obscure back-bench senator from Missouri, anticipating defeat by the governor of his state in the Democratic primaries; as the second, an unknown lieutenant-colonel in the United States Army; and, as the third, a kid still at college. Yet that sequence began to unfold in less time than between 1967 and 1972.

The salient fact about the historical process, so far as the short run is concerned, is its inscrutability. One must bear this in mind, I believe, when asked to accept drastic decisions now on the basis of someone's specu- lation as to what the behavior of Communist China will be a dozen years from now. In its coarsest form, this is the argument that "we must have a showdown with China before it gets the bomb." Here is the old preventive-war thesis we used to hear so often in the late forties: yet I do not think anyone can rationally contend that the world would be better off today had we dropped the bomb on Russia twenty years ago. Having been wrong so often in the past, how can we be sure we have achieved such infallibility now that we would risk the future of mankind on a guess?

Who can possibly predict with assurance that the Chinese Revolution will undertake the conquest of the world? The study of revolution has shown us that the emotional and doctrinal pitch of revolutions waxes and wanes; that, while revolutions at first may devour their children, in the end the children sometimes devour the revolutions; that even totalitarian revolutions fail at total mass indoctrination; that a successful revolution begins to develop a stake in the *status quo;* that post-revolutionary generations have their own identities and aspirations; that the possession of a major nuclear arsenal has thus far had a sobering effect on the possessor; that nations follow their historic interests rather more faithfully than they do their ideologies; and that there is no greater error than to try and deduce the policy of the future from the rhetoric of the present. Nor does the example of Hitler and *Mein Kampf* change this. Hitler was indeed the man on the bicycle; he had to keep moving. The Nazi revolution never got beyond the first messianic phase; its nature condemned it to *Götterdämmerung*. We must not forget that the Chinese revolutionary regime has already lasted five years longer than the whole life of the Third Reich. And we have seen in the case of the Soviet Union the permutation and erosion time and national interest have worked on what were once thought to be final motives and permanent objectives. With an equation so overflowing with variables, how can anyone forecast now the behavior of China twenty years from now?

History, in short, does not furnish the statesman with a detailed scenario of particular relationships or policies. Too often it equips his decisions with good rather than real reasons, holding out a mirror in which he fatuously sees his own face. This is not an argument against the knowledge of history: it is an argument against the superficial knowledge of history. The single analogy is never enough to penetrate a process so cunningly compounded not only of necessity but of contingency, fortuity, ignorance, stupidity and chance. The statesman who is surest that he can divine the future most urgently invites his own retribution. "The hardest strokes of heaven," Herbert Butterfield has written, "fall in history upon those who imagine that they can control things in a sovereign manner, playing providence not only for themselves but for the far future— reaching out into the future with the wrong kind of farsightedness, and gambling on a lot of risky calculations in which there must never be a single mistake."

The only antidote to a shallow knowledge of history is a deeper knowledge, the knowledge which produces not dogmatic certitude but diagnostic skill, not clairvoyance but insight. It offers the statesman a sense, at once, of short-run variables and long-run tendencies, and an instinct for the complexity of their intermingling, including the understanding that (as Rousseau once put it), "the ability to foresee that some things cannot be foreseen is a very necessary quality." Indeed, half the wisdom of statecraft, to borrow a phrase from Richard Goodwin, is "to leave as many options open as possible and decide as little as possible. . . . Since almost all important policy judgments are speculative, you must avoid risking too much on the conviction you are right."

Of course keeping too many options open too long may paralyze the lobe of decision and lose the game. There *does* come a time when accommodation turns into appeasement. This is the other half of the wisdom of statecraft: to accept the chronic obscurity of events without yielding, in Lincoln's words, firmness in the right as God gives us to see the right. In deciding when to decide, the criterion must be the human consequences—the results for people, not for doctrine.

Randolph Churchill's life of his father reproduces

an extraordinary letter written seventy years ago by the young Winston Churchill to a New York politician of the time, Bourke Cockran. "The duty of government," Churchill said, "is to be first of all practical. I am for makeshifts and expediency. I would like to make the people who live on this world at the same time as I do better fed and happier generally. If incidentally I benefit posterity—so much the better—but I would not sacrifice my own generation to a principle however high or a truth however great."

Such an approach may seem too modest, even, perhaps, too cynical, for those theological statesmen whose self-righteousness has almost sunk our age. Most of these confident moralists have been high priests of one or another dogmatic faith (though some, alas, have been American Secretaries of State); but all have been prepared in the best conscience and in the name of history to sacrifice their generations on the altars of their own metaphors. It can only be said that, whether they see history as ideology or as analogy, they see it wrong. Far from unveiling the secret of things to come, history bestows a different gift: it makes us—or should make us—understand the extreme difficulty, the intellectual peril, the moral arrogance of supposing that the future will yield itself so easily to us.

"I returned," Ecclesiastes reminds us, "and saw under the sun that the race is not to the swift, nor the battle to the strong, neither yet bread to the wise nor riches to men of understanding, but time and chance happeneth to them all." The Old Testament carries the case against historical generalization to the extreme. But, without going so far, we can agree that history should lead statesmen to a profound and humbling sense of human frailty—to a recognition of the fact, so insistently demonstrated by experience and so tragically destructive of our most cherished certitudes, that the possibilities of history are far richer and more various than the human intellect is likely to conceive. This, and the final perception that while the tragedy of history implicates us all in the common plight of humanity, we are never relieved, despite the limits of our knowledge and the darkness of our understanding, from the necessity of meeting our obligations.

8.
A Middle Course

The problem of balancing frailty and obligation is the essence of statecraft. Where does this problem leave us in Vietnam? For we have entered into obligations—not legal obligations under the SEATO treaty or to the succession of quasi-governments in Saigon, but moral obligations to those South Vietnamese who, under our encouragement and with the expectation of our support, have said and done things which will assure their imprisonment or death if the Viet Cong should take over South Vietnam by force. Yet the destruction of South Vietnam by the process of expanding the war is hardly a rational way to meet those obligations either. Are these the only alternatives: disorderly and humiliating withdrawal or enlarging the war?

Surely our statesmanship is not yet this bankrupt. I think a middle course is still possible if there were the will to pursue it. And this course must begin with a decision to stop widening and Americanizing the war—to limit our forces, actions, goals and rhetoric. Instead of bombing more places, sending in more troops, proclaiming ever more ardently that the fate of civilization will be settled in Vietnam, let us recover our cool and try to see the situation as it is: a horrid civil war in which communist guerrillas, enthusiastically aided and now substantially directed from Hanoi, are trying to establish a communist despotism in South Vietnam, not for the Chinese but for themselves. Let us understand that the ultimate problem here is not military but political. Let us adapt the means we employ to the end we seek.

Obviously, military action plays an indispensable role in the search for a political solution. Hanoi and the Viet Cong will not negotiate so long as they think they can win. Since stalemate is a self-evident precondition to negotiation, we must have enough American armed force in South Vietnam to leave no doubt in the minds of our adversaries that a communist government will not be imposed on South Vietnam by force. They must have no illusion about the prospect of an American withdrawal. The serious opposition to the escalation policy in the United States seeks not an American defeat but a negotiated settlement.

Therefore, holding the line in South Vietnam is essential. Surely, we already have enough American troops, firepower and installations in South Vietnam to make it clear that we cannot be beaten unless we choose to scuttle and run, which will not happen. The opponents of this strategy talk as if a holding action would put our forces under siege and relinquish all initiative to the enemy. This need not, of course, be so. It is possible to slow down a war without standing still; and, if our present generals can't figure out how to do this, then let us get generals who can. Generals Ridgway and Gavin could doubtless suggest some names. Moreover, there is a South Vietnamese army of some 600,000 men which can take all the initiative it wants. And if we are told that the South Vietnamese are unwilling or unable to fight the Viet Cong, whom they still greatly outnumber, then we must wonder all the more about the political side of the war.

The object of our military policy, as observers like Henry Kissinger and James MacGregor Burns have proposed, should be the creation and stabilization of secure areas where the South Vietnamese might themselves undertake social and institutional development. Our resources should go, in the Vietnam jargon, more to clear-and-hold than to search-and-destroy (especially when search-and-destroy more often means search-and-drive-underground). We should stop the policy of hit-and-run raids, which drive the Viet Cong out of villages one day and permit them to slip back the next and resume their work of disruption and terror. And we should certainly get rid of those "one-star generals who," in the words of Sir Robert Thompson, "regard their tour in Vietnam as an opportunity to indulge in a year's big-game shooting from their helicopter howdahs at Government expense."

At the same time we should induce the Saigon government to institute generous amnesty provisions of the kind which worked so well in the Philippines. And we should further increase the incentive to come over by persuading the South Vietnamese to abandon the torture of prisoners, a practice not only horrible in itself but well calculated to make the enemy fight to the bitter end. In the meantime we must end our own shameful collaboration with this barbarism and stop turning Viet Cong prisoners over to the South Vietnamese when we know that torture is probable.

As for bombing the north, this has become a crucial issue in the strategy of negotiation. The Johnson administration regards bombing as the key to its "quotient of pain" policy. The argument is essentially that Hanoi is counting on the protest against the war within the United States to paralyze the American government and eventually to compel American withdrawal; that it will interpret concessions—such as a suspension of bombing—as evidence of weakness; and that the effect of concessions will therefore be to lead

Hanoi to stiffen, not to moderate, its position. Thus in retrospect the thirty-seven-day bombing pause is regarded as an error. In a press conference in October 1966, when asked whether there would be a new bombing pause, the President replied, "I don't quite understand . . . why you want me to have our Marines and our airmen pause and put their hands behind their back while the other people don't pause and continue to shoot at them." Of course, no serious person has suggested that the United States should undertake a unilateral cease-fire; nor has any bombing pause been accompanied by a ban against war on the ground. But, press conference extravagance apart, a real fear remains that suspension would deter rather than hasten negotiation. The administration's conclusion is that only a hard line can force negotiation: keep up the pressure, bring in more men, step up the bombing, widen the war, until Hanoi and Peking come to their senses and stop molesting their neighbors. At some point increasing the "quotient of pain" will drive Hanoi to sue for peace.

Actually there is little reason to suppose that bombing will not continue to heighten Hanoi's resolve to fight on. The aerial war did not force the British to negotiation in 1940 nor the Germans in 1943–1945; nor, if America were being bombed today, would it produce in us anything but an absolute determination to win the war. Why do we expect the North Vietnamese to be greater cowards than we would be in like circumstance? And, as each new step in escalation fails to make much difference, the circle of targets under the "quotient of pain" policy will steadily widen—until what began as a policy of negotiation through escalation begins to turn imperceptibly into the policy which the administration has theoretically rejected: the pursuit of an illusory total military victory. Each new step, in addition, brings us closer to the point of Chinese or Russian participation in the war.

It is conceivable, moreover, to argue that there is little chance of negotiation at all so long as the bombing continues. "They will not come to the conference table on their knees," said Chester A. Ronning, who visited Hanoi in June 1966 as a special envoy from the Canadian government; so long as the bombing continues, "there is not the slightest possibility of getting talks started." The theory that concession will be construed as weakness is far more persuasive when a country confronts another country of roughly its own strength— Britain against Germany in 1938, for example, or the United States against the Soviet Union in the 1940's, or possibly the United States against China at some future point; but surely not the United States against a small country whose total population is less than that of New York or California. Moreover, if Hanoi and the Viet Cong are to be denied their dream of taking over South Vietnam, they need some concessions to save the well-known oriental face: this is a truism of diplomacy. Beyond this, it is only realistic, if irritating, to recognize that our adversaries at this point simply do not take the word of the United States any more seriously than we take their word: once again the crisis of credibility. This is doubtless why Hanoi has put such stress on the withdrawal of American troops as a condition precedent to negotiation (though eventually this will have proved to be only a bargaining point); and this is why we will have to do something drastic and different before they begin to believe that we honestly want negotiation. Stopping the bombing seems the most likely thing. Nor does the failure of the pause of 1965–1966 refute any of these points. Thirty-seven days were hardly enough even to persuade our allies that we meant business, and left them no time to move on to the next and decisive stage—that is, trying to persuade Hanoi.

The bombing policy may have increased the inconvenience of infiltration, but it has also clearly increased its energy. General Westmoreland now tells us (November, 1966) that "for the last six months it's averaged more than 7000 a month." Without bombing it might have averaged 16,000; without bombing it might have averaged 2000: who can possibly tell? The only indisputable benefits from the bombing policy have come from the (transient) pleasure it has afforded the Saigon government and the American voter. Given its limited military and political results in North Vietnam, the gains in the domestic politics of South Vietnam and the United States are hardly important enough to justify a policy which probably makes negotiation impossible and certainly contains the risk of indefinite escalation into major war. The question is by no means easy; but, of possible military strategies, the strategy directed to the physical destruction of North Vietnam would seem on balance less likely to lead to negotiation than a strategy of determined long-run defense of South Vietnam. Let us therefore taper off the bombing of the north as prudently as we can.[1]

Even as we do this, it may take a long time before our adversaries are ready to negotiate in good faith. Indeed, Hanoi has shown no real interest in negotiation thus far except as a means of legalizing a Viet Cong victory. Ho Chi Minh, moreover, has substantial reasons for resisting negotiation, even in addition to his mis-

[1] The proposal of a cease-fire on the ground in South Vietnam is very different and possibly very dangerous. Such a cease-fire should come at the end, not at the beginning, of negotiations.

trust of the American word, to his hope that the Americans will get tired and go home and to the Chinese pressure on him to keep the war going. He has twice in the past entered into negotiation with the west—in 1946–1947 and again in 1954. Each time, in his view, he was cheated at the negotiating table of the gains he thought he had made in the battlefield. He no doubt feels, like Will Rogers, that he has won every war and lost every conference.

Nor, indeed, have we offered terms which are likely to strike the other side as anything more than a means of legitimatizing not just their defeat on the battlefield but the permanent eradication of the Viet Cong as any sort of political force in post-war South Vietnam. As we question Hanoi's readiness to negotiate, we must also candidly question our own. For all our official statements about our willingness to go anywhere, talk to anyone, etc., it can hardly be said that the administration has pursued negotiation with a fraction of the zeal, imagination and perseverance with which it has pursued the war.

It cannot be said, for example, that the administration has laid fairly before the American people the occasional signals, however faint, which have come from Hanoi, as in the early winter of 1965–66, when U Thant's mediation reached the point of selecting the hotel in Rangoon where talks might take place, until we killed the idea by beginning the bombing of the north. Instead, we have repeatedly denied the existence of any peace feelers at all. When President Johnson said on October 6, 1966, "We pursue every indication that we have that might offer any possibilities, we always have an open mind, we're very anxious to find any basis for negotiation," his international audience could only gasp with incredulity. Nor, for all our declarations about "unconditional" negotiations, have we for one minute refrained from setting conditions— such as, for example, that we won't talk to the Viet Cong unless they come to the conference table disguised as North Vietnamese. Though we appear to have receded from this doctrine to the position that Viet Cong representation would not be an "insurmountable problem," our policy remains so equivocal that, given the Viet Cong's automatic mistrust of the discordant voices coming out of Washington, one can understand their impression that they have been given little solid reason to think that we mean to negotiate about anything except their unconditional surrender.

It is not hard to understand, for example, why our Manila proposal that we will remove our forces "not later than six months" after the other side pulls out of South Vietnam failed to move Hanoi deeply. If Hanoi had made the identical offer to us—that they would promise to withdraw six months after we did—we would hardly rush to embrace this as a serious proposition. Moreover, we have given several different impressions of what we mean when we ask Hanoi to withdraw "its forces" to the north. Ambassador Goldberg on September 22, 1966, spoke of the withdrawal of "all external forces—those of North Vietnam as well as those from the United States." On October 12 the Secretary of State said, "We shall leave when those invaders and arms from the North go home"; as for the "indigenous element . . . we consider it well within the capacity of the South Vietnamese to handle." But then on October 24 the Defense Department said that the conditions included "the intent that Viet Cong military units would be deactivated in any proposed withdrawal of external forces." At Manila we had spoken of withdrawing after the level of violence "subsides";

but on November 4, President Johnson, unilaterally amending the Manila offer, said that American troop withdrawal would not take place till six months after violence "ceases"—which evidently means until not only the North Vietnamese regulars withdraw but the South Vietnamese rebels give up: back again to unconditional surrender.

The future of the Viet Cong is, of course, central to negotiations, since they constitute the great bulk of the enemy in the field. But the American position here could hardly be more obscure. On the one hand, Vice President Humphrey has said that the fox should not be put into the chicken coop. On the other, Ambassador Goldberg has told the United Nations that the United States does not seek "to exclude any segment of the South Vietnamese people from peaceful participation in their country's future." "Allowing the Communists to help govern Vietnam," former Vice President Nixon has observed, "cannot be squared with the President's stated policy of no reward for aggression." But denying them a role in a government produced by free elections cannot be squared with the President's stated commitment: "We fight for the principle of self-determination that the people of South Vietnam should be able to choose their own course."

It is hard to see why we should not follow the precedent of Laos, when we admitted the Pathet Lao to the peace talks. Unless we mean to exterminate the Viet Cong, village by village, thicket by thicket, cave by cave, man by man, we must surely offer them the prospect of a say in the future political life of South Vietnam—conditioned on their laying down their arms, opening up their territories and abiding by the ground rules of free elections. Nor is there reason to see why we have been so reluctant again to follow the

Geneva Agreements and the Laos model and loudly declare neutralization under international guarantee our long-run objective for Vietnam. An imaginative diplomacy would long since have discussed the ways and means of achieving such neutralization with Russia, France, Britain and other interested countries.[2]

Does this all imply a judgment that the Viet Cong could repent and become a housebroken, democratic party in a neutralized state? Not necessarily, any more than the inclusion of the Pathet Lao in a coalition government implied such a judgment in Laos. Yet, unless we mean to exterminate the Viet Cong, we must seek terms to which their future political behavior can be held. If negotiations should lead to a provisional regime charged with the responsibility of preparing for elections, and if the Viet Cong should be given representation in that regime (and no group could be expected to take part in elections prepared exclusively by their enemies), then we should not reject that process; and, if elections should lead to a coalition government, it should be noted that coalition may well have a different significance in Vietnam from what it would have in a western party system. As Professor H. J. Spiro has pointed out, in traditional oriental society "order was maintained or restored by consensual rather than oppositional procedures. . . . Attempts to engage in [consensus-restoring] negotiations would surprise many Americans, but they would seem quite natural in the oriental context."

One cannot exclude the possibility that "consensual" procedures might work and reintegrate the Viet Cong into the national life of South Vietnam. As

[2] Lord Avon makes valuable suggestions to this end in *Toward Peace in Indochina* (Boston, 1966).

Hanoi unquestionably has its own objectives independent of Peking, so the Viet Cong may well have their own objectives independent of Hanoi. Their insistence in the *maquis* has been that they want a free South Vietnam, not a unified Vietnam under Ho Chi Minh. Even though this may be propaganda, it may also express a tension between the Viet Cong and Hanoi, a tension which in the age of polycentrist communism could help protect the independence of a postwar South Vietnam.

Denis Warner, an experienced correspondent, deeply mistrustful of Vietnamese communism, discerned in November 1966 the possibility of "an exploitable split in the Vietcong ranks." He added, "The early tendency to dismiss the Front as a wholly Communist organization is being reviewed." Conceivably, he suggests, the southerners on both sides might in the end discover they have more in common with each other than with the northerners to whom they are presently allied.

Yet other scholars—Paul Mus, for example—detect an absolutism in Vietnamese politics which rejects compromise and consensus. Still, even if the Viet Cong should prove no more capable of collaboration with democratic parties than the Pathet Lao showed themselves in Laos in 1962–1963, the experiment in coalition plus neutralization might still have its uses, as it did in Laos. There the coalition formula, by offering the Pathet Lao representation in the government, induced them for a moment to stop fighting. At the same time, it separated the honest nationalists from the disciplined Communists within the Pathet Lao, and it gave Souvanna Phouma and the neutralists the genuine neutrality of their country to defend. When the Pathet Lao, failing to take over the government from within, withdrew from the coalition and resumed the civil war, this broke their old alliance with the neutralists, and Souvanna Phouma now moved to defend Laotian neutrality not against the United States but against communism. As a result, the coalition experiment shifted the balance of forces in Laos very much against the Pathet Lao. Unsatisfactory as the situation may be there today, it is still incomparably better than the situation in South Vietnam. At least no American soldiers are dying in Laos.

One cannot, of course, expect crystalline clarity on all possible issues before a negotiation begins; we cannot lay all our cards face up on the table before the talks start. Yet we must lay down enough to persuade the other side that it is worthwhile to join the game. And we must also remember that excessive and gratuitous ambiguity will strengthen doubts about American credibility (since ideologists, of whatever faith, will always attribute contradictory or shifting positions to machiavellian intention rather than to bureaucratic stupidity)—and that it may be doing so at a time when the world has other reasons to wonder about the fixity of our negotiating purpose. For we, like they, are trapped in the classic dilemma of negotiation: we do not want to negotiate when we are behind, because the other side will hold the better cards; but we do not want to negotiate when ahead either, because, if we wait a little longer, we will be still farther ahead and can demand even better terms. Americans seem especially vulnerable to fits of military optimism. Some American officials, moreover, unquestionably fear a negotiated settlement because they doubt the capacity of any foreseeable government in Saigon to deal with a Viet Cong resurgence after the departure of American troops. Whether they admit to themselves that the alternative is an indefinite American occupation of Vietnam, I do not know, but that is what the alternative is. One feels at times that nothing would cause greater consternation in certain offices in Washington than a decision in Hanoi to go to the conference table. Indeed, American scholars who have studied the matter believe that on a number of occasions when pressure for negotiation was mounting, we have, for whatever reason, stepped up the war.[3]

On the other hand, negotiation is not an exclusive, or even primary, American responsibility. Along with a military stalemate, the other precondition of a diplomatic settlement is surely a civilian government in Saigon. The military junta headed by Marshal Ky represents almost a new class of *nouveaux* mandarins. "They are the Vietnamese," Neil Sheehan has written, "who combine the worst of two cultures—the pretentiousness of the native mandarins and the rigidity of the French colonial officers and administrators." They will "tell Americans what they think Americans want to hear"; they will promulgate land-reform and tax-reduction decrees to soothe American advisers; but "all of these measures have been sabotaged because the regimes were and are composed of men who are members of, or are allied with, mandarin families that held title to properties they have no intention of renouncing. . . . They seek to retain what privileges they have and to regain those they have lost." Their regime is pervaded by nepotism, corruption and cynicism.

Marshal Ky, moreover, has become one of those Frankenstein's monsters we delight in creating in our client countries, very much like the egregious General Phoumi Nosavan, who single-handedly blocked a set-

[3] See *The Politics of Escalation in Vietnam* by Franz Schurman, Peter Dale Scott and Reginald Zelnick of the University of California. Available in a Fawcett Premier edition.

tlement in Laos for two years. Like Phoumi, Ky evidently feels that Washington has committed itself irrevocably to him—and why should he not after the laying on of hands at Honolulu and Manila?—and that, whatever he does, we cannot afford to abandon him. Quite naturally, he takes advantage of his opportunities to get *us* to do what will serve *his* interests—which, in effect, means a determination by a Vietnamese politician to make American policy on Vietnam. Not only has he proposed the invasion of North Vietnam; but he has repeatedly proclaimed his opposition to the American pursuit of a peaceful settlement. "No negotiations with communists; never," Ky cried on his return to Saigon after Manila. ". . . We will fight to the end. . . . We don't want to meet with the Viet Cong. . . . A coalition with the communists means suicide." As for the Constituent Assembly, whose election in September 1966 excited such idealistic hopes in the United States, "the impression given by the junta," wrote R. W. Apple, Jr., in the *New York Times* (November 24, 1966) of Marshal Ky's attitude toward this valiant try at self-government, "has been one of disregard verging on contempt."

One cannot blame Ky for pursuing his own policies: one can only blame the American government for letting him try to decide American policy. And indulgence is naturally construed as complicity. Robert Shaplen reported to *The New Yorker* in August 1966 that the atmosphere there "is being compared to the miasma that surrounded Diem and his tyrannical brother Ngo Dinh Nhu" and that "many Vietnamese believe that the Americans, having embraced Ky so wholeheartedly and supported him so long, are just as responsible as his Government for the recent repressive acts." I am sure that President Johnson did not intend to turn over

American policy and honor in Vietnam to Marshal Ky's gimcrack, bullyboy, get-rich-quick regime. The time is bound to come when Ky must learn the facts of life, as General Phoumi eventually and painfully learned them.

But why wait? In our whole time in Vietnam, there has never been a government in Saigon which had the active loyalty of the peasants; indeed, in the past, when the Saigon government has recovered control of territory from the Viet Cong, its first camp-followers have often been stooges of the oligarchy collecting back rents and taxes. It might be a useful experiment to encourage a pro-peasant regime to come into existence. Only a government which enlists enthusiastic popular support in the countryside—i.e., a government not dominated by the landlords—would stand any chance of dealing with a guerrilla resurgence, even should the North Vietnam forces be withdrawn. "What South Vietnam needs," President Marcos of the Philippines has said, "is the will to fight, which cannot be exported." Instead of identifying American interests with Ky and rebuffing the broader political impulses in South Vietnam, we should long since have welcomed a movement toward a civilian government representing the significant political forces of the country and capable both of rallying the army and carrying forward programs of social reform. We should give such a government all possible assistance in rebuilding and modernizing the political and institutional structures of South Vietnam. We should encourage it to take the lead in the political and diplomatic steps necessary to stop the war. If it should favor the neutralization of its country, if it should seek negotiation with the Viet Cong, even if it should release us from our commitment to stay in Vietnam, we should not therefore think that the world is coming to an end.

Of course we cannot now see the shape of a successful negotiation: all we can do is to define its limits. For one can rarely forecast the details of a political settlement. If we widen the war, we contract the possibilities for negotiation. If we slow the war down, we may open up possibilities which we cannot presently envisage. If we have learned anything from recent experience, it is surely the difficulty of predicting the resolution of crises in advance, from the blockade of Berlin to the nuclearization of Cuba. At each point, those who could not see how the crisis could logically be resolved pressed for drastic solutions; while those who understood the unpredictability of history insisted on avoiding irreversible actions. Our need now is to create a new situation—and then to take advantage of new opportunities. This means abandoning the policy of escalation, the policy which maximizes risks without producing results. This means above all that we must oppose further widening of the war.

It is not too late to begin the de-escalation of the war; nor would the reduction of our military effort damage our international influence. "There is more respect to be won in the opinion of this world," George Kennan has written, "by a resolute and courageous liquidation of unsound positions than by the most stubborn pursuit of extravagant or unpromising objectives." If our credibility is the issue, it is rather more important that other countries believe in our intelligence and responsibility than our passion for overkill. France was stronger than even after De Gaulle left Algeria, the Soviet Union suffered no lasting damage from pulling its nuclear missiles out of Cuba. And the policy of de-escalation recommended here is, of course, something a good deal less than withdrawal.

De-escalation *could* work, *if* there were the will to pursue it . . . This is the hard question. The administration, disposed to the indiscriminate use of power, enmeshed in the grinding cogs of the escalation machine, committed to the thesis that China is the enemy in Vietnam, obviously could not turn to de-escalation without considerable inner upheaval. The issue in the United States in the months to come will be whether President Johnson's leadership is sufficiently resilient and forbearing to permit a change in the direction of policy and arrest what is coming increasingly to seem an accelerating drift toward a great and unnecessary catastrophe.

9.
Vietnam and American Democracy

We face, in short, a test of our democracy. We must not let the war in Vietnam poison our national life, as Korea did briefly in the early fifties, or as Algeria poisoned France in the early sixties. We have an opportunity to prove our national maturity and show that we can undertake a major effort abroad, as we did during the Second World War, without wallowing in hysteria at home.

What are the chances of preserving our national poise this time? There are unfavorable as well as favorable factors in our present situation as compared with that fifteen years ago. For one thing, the intensity of the national administration's commitment to the Bill of Rights can make a vital difference. The reason why the Second World War (with a few exceptions, like the internment of the Japanese-Americans) was comparatively unstained by assaults on civil freedom was the libertarianism of Franklin Roosevelt and his administration. Similarly McCarthyism was more or less contained during the Truman years. It broke out of control only when the Eisenhower administration brought an attitude of indifference in the White House and of positive collaboration with McCarthy (Secretary of State Dulles, for example) down the line. Today, while President Johnson has manfully spoken up for the right to dissent on a number of occasions, one cannot be sure to what extent his heart is always in it. There were strange notes in his Honolulu attack on critics of his Vietnam policy as "callous or timid . . . blind to expe-

rience and deaf to hope," as well as in his Chicago outburst about "nervous Nellies" who break ranks
"under the strain" and turn "on their leaders, their
country and their own fighting men." It is hardly pru-
dent for any President to insist on a conception of
unity which, on closer examination, means no more
than unquestioning acceptance of government policy.
There seems merit to the suggestion of Clayton
Fritchey, who ran public affairs at the Pentagon under
General Marshall in the early days of the Korean War:
"President Johnson and his official family are all in
favor of freedom of speech—they are only against the
exercise of it."

Moreover, the Joint Chiefs of Staff fifteen years ago
unanimously opposed the escalation of the Korean
War and thereby had a calming effect on national
opinion, especially in the angry days after the recall of
General MacArthur. But today the Joint Chiefs seem
just as unanimously in favor of the escalation of the
Vietnamese war, with all that implies. And the State
Department, which strove last time for rationality in
debate, is this time actively implying that criticism of
the war should stop because it cheers up Ho Chi Minh.
Criticism of a war always cheers up the enemy; but I
do not recall that any government official admonished
Abraham Lincoln to stop criticizing the Mexican war
on the ground that it gave aid and comfort to Santa
Anna.

Another difference between 1951 and 1967 is that
then the liberal and intellectual community was united
in the determination to maintain rational discussion.
Today some of its members seem to be vying with the
reactionaries in advancing the cause of political irrationality. This is, above all, a self-defeating tactic for
intellectuals; for, if it becomes a competition in dema-

goguery and hysteria, the anti-intellectuals will always win. One hates to see intellectuals and liberals preparing the way for a new McCarthyism by debasing the level of public discussion and substituting stereotypes for sense and rage for reason.

These explosions of political irrationality, whether on the right or on the left, have a number of things in common. For one thing, both tend to express what has been an ancient national weakness—that is, a susceptibility to the conspiratorial interpretation of history. We have always fallen too easily for the notion that complex historical developments are the result of the machinations of little groups of nasty men. This is what Richard Hofstadter has called "the paranoid style in American politics." From the clamor against the Society of the Cincinnati and the Masons to contemporary conspiratorial fantasies, whether of the John Birch Society or of the devotees of the "power elite," whether of the followers of Robert Welch or those of C. Wright Mills, conspiracy has been a familiar theme in our political discourse.

It expresses itself today in the notion on the right that the Communists are fomenting the anti-war demonstrations in the United States, not to mention the Buddhist protests in Saigon and Hue, as well as in the theory, cherished, alas, in very high places in our government, that what we face in Southeast Asia is a premeditated system of Chinese aggression, organized in Peking, for which the Viet Cong in South Vietnam are merely the pretext and the spearhead. And it expresses itself in the notion on the left that our Vietnam policy is dictated by capitalists seeking to expand profits and markets or by generals plotting a preventive war against China. Both sides refuse to see history as it really is—an untidy and unkempt process, in which decisions are taken, not according to master plans, but in darkling confusion and obscurity, and where ignorance, accident, chance and stupidity play a larger role than machiavellian calculation.

The explosions of political irrationality have another feature in common: the function in each case is more to provide internal psychic satisfaction than to advance the cause in whose name they take place—more to ventilate emotions than to influence events. Refusing a man a seat in the Georgia legislature or a grave in Arlington brings us no closer to victory in Southeast Asia than mobbing a Secretary of Defense or burning a draft card deters a President from dropping napalm bombs. The serious restraint on the movement toward a wider war has been mostly the result of the coverage and force of individuals, whether in the United States Senate or in local meetings or community teach-ins, who, acting out of a thoughtful analysis of the drift of our policy, have succeeded in bringing into existence a serious debate on our choice in the Far East. It has come, not from the outpouring of emotion, but from the application of reason.

Yet, if we have certain disadvantages today in comparison with fifteen years ago, we also have certain advantages—most notably the memory of the earlier experience. McCarthyism gave the country a kind of inoculation, and the immunity has not yet worn off, as the voters of New Jersey showed in November 1965 in rejecting the effort to make Professor Genovese's views on Vietnam the central issue of the gubernatorial campaign. A number of national figures, recalling the excesses of fifteen years ago, are showing an admirable determination to prevent a repeat performance.

These figures are not to be found in the United States where they would be found in England—that is, in the so-called Establishment. It has become recently fashionable to denounce the arrogance of the American Establishment. But one sometimes wonders whether the trouble with the American Establishment has been so much its arrogance as its cowardice—in other words, its fear of acting as an Establishment should. The point of an Establishment, I take it, is to provide support for the established values and institutions of society. This has been the triumph of the original Establishment in Great Britain. It is impossible to imagine a McCarthy terrorizing British public life: the Establishment would never permit it.

But the so-called American Establishment crumpled up before McCarthy. The great leaders of American business and the bar said hardly a word in protest. One eminent figure—whom Establishment scholars have thought to be the chairman of the American Establishment at the time—actually suggested in a public speech that the inquiries of the McCarthy committee were no worse than Senator Black's investigations into the public utility holding companies in 1935. No doubt such leaders of respectable opinion became anti-McCarthy once the crisis was over; but, whatever the retrospective courage, let us avoid the illusion that the American Establishment will be much braver the next time round. The nation will have to look to stouter and more principled figures if it is to contain another epidemic of political panic.

One place to look, I think, will be in Washington itself. Responsible men in public life recognize the damage that a new outbreak of national hysteria will do both to our own sense of purpose and to the world's confidence in our leadership. Thus Secretary McNamara in a recent speech pointedly quoted Judge Learned Hand's eloquent statement in the midst of the

McCarthy years: "I believe that community is already in process of dissolution where each man begins to eye his neighbor as a possible enemy, where nonconformity with the accepted creed, political as well as religious, is a mark of disaffection, where denunciation, without specification or backing, takes the place of evidence, where orthodoxy chokes freedom of dissent. . . . The mutual confidence on which all else depends can be maintained only by an open mind and a brave reliance upon free discussion." The Secretary of Defense then added on his own what seems a tacit rebuke of his over-zealous colleagues in the Johnson administration: "Whatever comfort some of the extremist protest may be giving our enemies—and it is clear from Hanoi's own statements that it is—let us be perfectly clear about our principles and our priorities. This is a nation in which the freedom of dissent is absolutely fundamental."

So Senator Fulbright has issued thoughtful warnings: "The longer the Vietnamese war goes on without prospect of victory or negotiated peace, the war fever will rise, hopes will give way to fears, and tolerance and freedom of discussion will give way to a false and strident patriotism." So the Executive Council of the American Federation of Teachers canceled the action of its Las Vegas local in expelling the teacher who refused to salute the flag in silent protest against the war in Vietnam. So Senator Edward M. Kennedy of Massachusetts protested to the State Department over the surveillance of the Harvard professor and brought this particular form of snooping to an end. So Senator Robert Kennedy of New York read aloud on the floor of the Senate an editorial from the *Washington Daily News* condemning the decision not to bury the Communist war hero in Arlington. "We learn from our mistakes," the editorial said "—and one of our lessons is that to hate and harry the sinner to his grave is hardly in the American tradition." Robert Kennedy was later heard to say somberly that he did not think anyone now buried in Arlington would object to the holder of the Distinguished Service Cross lying there, so he could not see why veterans' organizations were so agitated about it. So the Supreme Court has canceled the refusal of the Georgia legislature to seat a critic of the Vietnam war.

Leadership by public figures and the press offers one hope of preventing the revival of McCarthyism. And there is another favorable difference between the United States today and fifteen years ago—that is, the increased size and weight of the academic community. There are twice as many students enrolled in institutions of higher education in the country as there were a short decade ago. By the end of the sixties there will be almost three-quarters of a million teachers in our colleges and universities and seven million students. This amounts to a formidable political constituency— and one which can be counted on to be uncommonly bright, well informed, articulate and irascible. Indeed, the expansion of the academic community has already begun to affect the tone and character of our politics. It is hard to throw a stone on college campuses today without hitting a visiting politician.

The academic community will be, among other things, a constituency for the Bill of Rights. For, freedom of inquiry and dissent, if the general interest of the nation, is the class interest of the academic community. Of course, if the academic community is to strengthen the body politic against irrationality, it must clear itself of suspicion that irrationality is its own favorite form of expression. Students must have other models than Latin American universities and other ambitions than working for their L.S.D. And the faculty must stick by its professional faith in reasoned discourse and not give the impression that it regards slogan and emotion as the hot way to deal with complicated issues. Perhaps all this is too much to expect; and, in the end, the academic community, like the Establishment, will prove incapable of fighting intelligently for rational discussion.

But perhaps not. One is heartened by the way that college faculties, presidents and even boards of trustees and overseers are speaking up in defense of the Bill of Rights—and on occasions when the expression involved may have been a good deal less than rational. The New Jersey case a year ago was one notable example. In the spring of 1966 the president of the Indiana University defending the right of an undergraduate organization to invite a Communist to give a lecture, observed sensibly that "a closed campus is not a sound way to engender belief in an open society." The president of the board of trustees added, "We have strong faith in the intelligence of our students to separate fact from falsehood" and warned critics against having the university "deny the constitutional guarantee of freedom of speech in the anger and frustration of the world situation at this point in history."

I hope one is wrong in supposing that this anger and frustration, welling up as a result of the Vietnam involvement, may portend another crisis of our national freedom. But, if no such crisis comes, it will only be because individuals throughout the land take a clear and firm stand for sanity. "The men who create power," President Kennedy said a few weeks before he was murdered in Dallas in the supreme act of political irrationality in our time, "make an indispensable contribution to the nation's greatness, but the men who question power make a contribution just as indispensable." This is an exact statement of the oldest American tradition; and that tradition will live only as citizens speak out for freedom in their own communities and by their own firesides. In retrospect, we have always regretted our spasms of repression and persecution; we have gained nothing from them—McCarthy never found a Communist—and have invariably hated ourselves in the morning. Why would a nation, billing itself as the "land of the free" and aspiring to the leadership of mankind, once again parade its hypocrisies, surrender to its fears, defile its oldest ideals and disgrace itself in the eyes of the world and its own posterity?

For whatever the outcome of the Vietnam debate or of later debates that may darken our future, the essential thing is to preserve mutual trust among ourselves as Americans. Let us remember that those who take a different position—whether they want to evacuate Saigon or bomb Hanoi—may also be actuated by honorable and patriotic motives—may, whatever their degree of error, still have a genuine concern for peace and freedom. Let us always distinguish between disagreement and disloyalty, between opposition and treason. Let us never forget that complicated problems can be resolved only by reasoned analysis; and that the insistence on reason is the final hope of democratic society. If we can remember this, in whatever direction our decisions and destiny take us, we can preserve and cherish our fundamental unity of purpose as Americans.

10.
Vietnam
Lessons of the Tragedy

On March 31, 1968, President Johnson suspended the policy of military escalation in Vietnam, intensified the search for a peaceful settlement of the conflict, and announced his own withdrawal from the presidential contest. This speech may in retrospect go down as just one more incident in the long zigzag course of American action in Vietnam. It may also go down as a turning point in the postwar history of American foreign policy.

For, beyond the immediate issue of Vietnam, the March 31 speech implies a recognition, perhaps only an unconscious recognition, of a change in America's world role. It implies in particular a retreat from the universalism that has been a major strain in our foreign policy for half a century.

By "universalism" I mean the belief that the United States has an active and vital interest in the destiny of all nations. Woodrow Wilson propounded an early version of American universalism during and after the First World War. Franklin Roosevelt amplified the doctrine during the Second World War with his proclamation in 1941 of the Four Freedoms "everywhere in the world" and his warning to Churchill and Stalin in 1944: "There is in this global war literally no question, either military or political, in which the United States is not interested."

In the succeeding sections, I will attempt to disentangle the roots of American universalism and inquire why it turned into a policy of indiscriminate intervention—why the Vietnam involvement should have proceeded with such apparent logic from the American past and why decent men should have defended that involvement with such invincible self-righteousness.

1. *The Legacy of Collective Security.* The belief in the American obligation to create a general structure of world order began with Wilson. The corollary belief in the consequent American obligation to defend that structure by force at every significant point received its first powerful advocacy from Henry L. Stimson as Secretary of State during the Manchurian crisis of 1931.

The essence of the collective security position was the perception that *clearcut acts of aggression* by *major powers* constituted threats to world peace, were intolerable and required counteraction by the international community. Thus Stimson was plainly right about Manchuria, Roosevelt about Germany and Japan, Truman about Korea (for the North Korean invasion of South Korea took place at a time when communism was still a relatively unified world movement and when the extension of communism therefore meant the automatic extension of the national power of Soviet Russia).

Stimson was a man of lofty character and great moral force; and he left the imprint of his convictions on a generation of able public servants. Indeed, one can trace his influence in a personal sense even on the evolution of American policy in Vietnam. Stimson's closest associate during the Second World War was General George C. Marshall; and after the war Marshall became both the patron and the idol of Secretary of State Dean Rusk. And one of Stimson's Assistant Secretaries in the State Department was Harvey Bundy, whose brilliant sons played so vital a role in deepening the American involvement in Vietnam. But the epigones of Stimson plunged beyond his views. The expansion of Stimsonianism took two main forms, and both came to climax in Vietnam.

First, our government began to apply the collective security doctrine not just to cases demonstrably involving major powers but also to cases where major-power involvement was tenuous or speculative, or, if genuine, ineffectual and very likely doomed to failure.

Second, our government began to apply the collective security doctrine not just to cases of clearcut aggression but also to cases of internal upheaval. I do not pretend that in an age when revolution has so often been encouraged or even organized from outside, the distinction between the two has always been easy to draw. But our government in recent times—in Vietnam, in the Dominican Republic—has made no serious effort to weigh one possibility against the other. Instead, as in Vietnam, we construed almost from the start as external aggression what began and ran a good deal of its course as internal rebellion.

The result was to transform the doctrine that clearcut acts of aggression by major powers require American intervention almost into the doctrine that any form of trouble, whether external or internal in origin, whether by large or by small powers, requires American intervention.

2. *The Legacy of Liberal Evangelism.* The idea of collective security, we have noted, began with Wilson. A great and creative President, he also started another idea which ended up, after due transformation, in Vietnam. Or rather he took an old American preoccupation and gave it new significance.

The idea of America's regenerative mission to suffering mankind was not in its essence a new idea. The men who founded the American republic believed they were setting an example which in time would revolutionize the world. But they believed that America would revolutionize the world *by example,* not by Americans moving into other countries and setting things straight.

As American power grew, however, so also grew the American conviction that we must discharge our mission not only by the example we set in our own national life but by the direct tutelage—the "leadership"—we can bring to other nations. As in the case of collective security, the intellectual genealogy of liberal evangelism from Wilson to Vietnam can be traced in personal terms: from Wilson through Franklin Roosevelt, his Assistant Secretary of the Navy, to such fervent and energetic young New Dealers of the late thirties and early forties as Lyndon B. Johnson and Hubert Humphrey. It is a small step from Henry Wallace remarking to Mme. Litvinov, "The object of this war is to make sure that everybody in the world has the privilege of drinking a quart of milk a day" to President Johnson talking about TVA's on the Mekong and Vice President Humphrey saying of Vietnam: "There is a tremendous new opening here for realizing the dream of the Great Society in the great area of Asia, not just here at home." All were speaking the familiar and authentic language of American social reform.

Nothing has exalted America more than this sense of world mission—this decent and admirable feeling of responsibility for the welfare of others. It has led to acts of national generosity unparalleled in the history of man. Yet little is more dangerous than a sense of world mission pushed too far or perceived too absolutely. In this process the limited policy of helping others to help themselves has grown into the unlimited policy of imposing our own preferences on others; so that, if the Vietnamese would not do out of respect for our superior wisdom what we thought was good for them, we are determined to make them do it out of respect for our superior strength. The Army major standing in the rubble of Ben Tre summed up the ultimate logic of American messianism: "It became necessary to destroy the town to save it."

3. *The Legacy of Geopolitics.* To understand why the ideas of collective security and of liberal evangelism—ideas entirely sound and necessary in themselves—expanded beyond reason in the years after the Second World War, one must move from questions of ideology to questions of power.

For the Second World War had a devastating impact on the structure of world power. The defeat of the Axis states meant the elimination, for a while in any case, of Germany, Italy, and Japan from the global power equation. It meant, for a while, the exhaustion and demoralization of Europe, victors as well as vanquished. It meant the disintegration of the European colonial empires; it meant, in particular, the unravelling of the British Empire, which so long, for better or for worse, had provided a network of stability through what we have come to call the Third World. And as the colonial empires fell to pieces, it meant the release of confused and chaotic energies in those parts of the world no longer willing to continue under white domination.

It meant, in short, the emergence of great vacuums of power—in Europe, in Asia, in Africa. And, at the same time, the war left only two nations with the capacity to fill those vacuums of power. Only two nations—America and Russia—survived the war with strong and active military force: one with the world's monopoly of atomic weapons, the other with the world's largest ground army. Each of these nations had grown accustomed during the war to the habit of global assessment and global action. Each came out of the war with marked political and ideological self-confidence. Each was more or less in command of its own armed camp, and each in time formalized this command by setting up systems of alliance. The philosophical disagreement between a capitalist democracy and a Communist dictatorship gave edge to the structural conflict; but even without the philosophical disagreement, the existence of the vacuums of power would no doubt have sucked these dynamic states into competition and collision.

For a decade—roughly from the end of the Second War to the end of the war in Korea—these two nations bestrode the narrow world; their writs seemed to run without limits; they encountered no serious opposition anywhere, except from each other. This was the Age of the Superpowers. And this era generated in both Washington and Moscow the feeling that their appointments as Superpowers were permanent and irrevocable, that each could expect indefinitely to control events and shape destinies wherever they wished.

In Russia, Superpowership was the logical expression of an absolutist ideology that had already conferred on communism the blessing of historical inevitability. In America Superpowership, lacking a prepared ideological foundation, took the ideas of collective security and liberal evangelism and began to give them absolute form.

4. *The Legacy of Conservative Manichaeanism.* Manes, the Persian philosopher, taught long ago that good and evil were independent and co-eternal realities

locked in mortal combat. Both Superpowers tended to take a Manichaean view of world affairs in the forties and fifties. In Russia anti-capitalism had always been a central and implacable doctrine. In America anti-communism became a doctrine not nearly so central or so implacable but still sufficiently intrusive to distort judgment and to mislead decision.

Anti-communism is, of course, a moral necessity for any believer in democracy. But it is essential to distinguish between *rational* and *obsessive* anti-communism: between anti-communism as an element in a larger position, an element addressed to specific situations and graduated in mode and substance according to the character of the threat; and anti-communism as a total position, addressed to some great, all-pervading evil and requiring the subordination of every other consideration and value.

When Hubert Humphrey led the fight to throw the Communists out of the Democratic-Farmer-Labor Party of Minnesota in 1947, he was engaged in an entirely sensible exercise in rational anti-communism. When twenty years later he talked about "militant, aggressive Asian communism with its headquarters in Peking, China," and called the Vietnam war "but the most current and immediate action of militant Asian communism," he was the victim of the conditioned reflexes of an obsessive anti-communism—reflexes which had hardened with the years and which now blinded him to the way the resurgence of nationalism had destroyed the unitary Communist world.

But Dulles and Nixon and American conservatives in general were the true Manichaeans. The basic error of their obsessive anti-communism was to inculcate the view that communism was a changeless, unalterable, monolithic doctrine of total unity and total evil. This led to the conclusion that every Communist party or Communist regime must by definition forever be an obedient instrument of Soviet Russia. It was this conviction, cherished by American conservatism, of the fixed and final division of the world between the forces of light and the forces of darkness that prepared the way for Vietnam. Once again, a doctrine, rational in its essence, underwent expansion and began to be applied without discrimination.

5. *The Rise of a Warrior Class*. Thus postwar American foreign policy grew from a series of legacies—Stimsonian collective security, Rooseveltian social evangelism, Dullesian anti-communism, each bequest tempted into universalism and messianism by the power vacuums left in the wake of the Second World War. It was this combination of factors that beguiled America into a course which much of the world today regards as imperialistic and which even Americans must concede as imperial—the course which has reached its disastrous climax in Vietnam.

Yet, if there is an American imperialism, it is imperialism of a peculiar sort. Of the classical theories of imperialism, the one which throws most light on our behavior is that proposed by Joseph A. Schumpeter. Schumpeter saw imperialism as "the objectless disposition on the part of a state to unlimited forcible expansion"—a disposition created and sustained by the habits and interests of a warrior class. There would always be, he said, rational pretexts for military action—national security, treasure, and so on—but the essential urge would come from the sheer momentum of the military machine in motion. "Created by wars that required it," Schumpeter wrote of the military establishment in ancient Egypt, "the machine now created the wars it required." His account of Rome from the Punic Wars to Augustus has an uncomfortable contemporary relevance:

> Here is the classic example of that kind of insincerity in both foreign and domestic affairs which permeates not only avowed motives but also probably the conscious motives of the actors themselves—of that policy which pretends to aspire to peace but unerringly generates war, the policy of continual preparation for war, the policy of meddlesome interventionism. There was no corner of the known world where some interest was not alleged to be in danger or under actual attack. If the interests were not Roman, they were those of Rome's allies; and if Rome had no allies, then allies would be invented. When it was utterly impossible to contrive such an interest—why, then it was the national honor that had been insulted.

Are we not approaching this situation in the United States? We have been almost continuously at war since 1940; and in this generation military institutions have gained a power and cast a spell as never before in our national life. The forward role of the military has been notably evident in Vietnam. At every point along the way, they have promised that just one more step of escalation would at last bring the victory so long sought and so steadily denied. The Pentagon, in addition, has seen Vietnam as an invaluable training ground and an invaluable testing ground for new weapons and new techniques.

The military are not war criminals. They are professional men trying to do a professional job and bringing exactly the pressures that the nature of their profession prescribes. It is foolish to blame them for the advice they give. It is far more to the point to blame those who take their advice. President Kennedy accepted the recommendations of the Joint Chiefs of Staff on one major decision in his administration—the Bay of Pigs. He did not follow their advice on a major issue again— neither on Laos, nor on Berlin in 1961, nor on Cuba in 1962, nor on the Test Ban Treaty in 1963. President Johnson, on the contrary, has always flinched from overruling the Joint Chiefs.

Here lies the heart of our imperial compulsion: the momentum of the professional military in an age when international crisis has made it possible for only the most resolute Presidents to resist that pressure.

6. *The Nemesis of Universalism.* The tragedy of Vietnam is the tragedy of the catastrophic overextension and misapplication of valid principles. The original insights of collective security and liberal evangelism were generous and wise. But compulsive Stimsonianism and compulsive New Dealism, stimulated by illusions of Superpowership, rigidified by a mechanical anti-communism and pressed ever forward by the professional demands of the new warrior class, brought American universalism in time into a messianic phase. The new phase exceeded and transformed its constituent elements. Yet the existence of these traditional elements gave the Johnson administration a sense that it was executing a legacy and endowed it therefore with an overweening conviction of the rectitude of its mission, the purity of its motives, and the wickedness of its critics. It was this which must have led Secretary Rusk to say on February 9, 1968: "There gets to be a point when the question is, Whose side are you on? Now, I'm Secretary of State of the United States, and I'm on our side!"

Given the inordinate self-righteousness which would lead a Secretary of State to suggest that his critics must be on the side of Ho Chi Minh, only the abject failure of the policy could force its supporters to draw back. The failure of the Vietnam policy had long been evident to most detached observers. The evidence against the effectiveness of military escalation was just as strong, for example, on March 31, 1967, as it was on March 31, 1968; and, if President Johnson had given his speech a year earlier, many Americans and many Vietnamese, now dead, would today be alive. But in the end the failure of the policy became so plain that even the President had to admit it—everyone had to admit it except, inevitably, General Westmoreland, perhaps the most disastrous American general since Custer, and Joseph Alsop, perhaps the most spectacularly mistaken prophet since Nostradamus.

What was announced on March 31 was more than simply the collapse of the American policy in Vietnam. What was announced was the collapse of the messianic conception of the American role in the world—indeed, the end of the entire Age of the Superpowers. To understand the reasons for this collapse we must return for a moment to the Superpowers at high noon.

There were always decisive differences between the Superpowers on internal values. But their views of the world had remarkable similarities. Each Superpower saw mankind as divided between forces of light and forces of darkness. Each assumed that the opposing side was under the organized and unified control of the other. Each expected its allies to reshape themselves on its own model.

These were the dreams of glory of the Superpowers. But, alas, the world itself did not sit still; it began to change. And the most basic change of all was the rise of a new force in revolt against the reign of the Superpowers—or rather the resurgence of an older force now endowed in the years after the war with new potency and purpose. That force was nationalism: the passionate determination to assert national identity, national dignity, and national freedom of action. The rise of nationalism meant growing opposition to the United States in the western bloc, growing opposition to the Soviet Union in the Communist bloc, and growing opposition to both America and Russia in the Third World.

In the years since 1945 nationalism has redrawn lines of force around the planet. The contagion runs everywhere. Today nationalism is producing a growing will—embodied in General de Gaulle—to reaffirm European independence against the twin colossuses; it is seeking home rule in Scotland and Wales; it is dividing the country of Belgium; it is threatening Canada with the secession of French Quebec; in our own country it finds expression in the mystique of black power. And it has wrought even more spectacular changes within the empire which Stalin once ruled so calmly and implacably. The Yugoslav heresy of 1948 represented the first serious rebellion of national communism against Russian primacy. In another decade China burst forth as an independent Communist state, increasingly determined to challenge Russia for the domination of Asia and for the leadership of the international Communist movement. With the clash between China and Russia, the unified Communist empire began to break up. Albania and Rumania have long since been going their own way. The dramatic events of early 1968 in Czechoslovakia surely suggest the direction of the future.

Even Poland, even East Germany, may some day insist on national freedom.

As nationalism has transformed the democratic and Communist worlds, so too it has transformed the Third World. After the war, many people—Communists and anti-communists alike—supposed that Marxism would sweep through the developing world like a prairie fire. But since the war, communism has triumphed in only three nations in the Third World—in China and North Vietnam, because the Communists were able to place themselves at the head of nationalist movements during the war; and in Cuba, where Castro made a revolution on non-communist grounds and subsequently for his own reasons carried it into the Communist empire. For the rest, it has been a washout as a revolutionary creed.

The reason for the failure of communism in the developing world is the same as the reason for the expulsion of colonialism from that world: what the new nations want more than anything else is the assurance of their own national freedom of decision.

Nationalism has thus emerged as the most powerful political emotion of our time. And the result has been to alter the conditions which a quarter-century ago produced the Age of the Superpowers. This era came about, we have noted, as the response of two dynamic states to the vacuums of power left in the wake of the Second War. In the years since, the reinvigoration of nationalism—in Europe, within the Communist empire, in the Third World—has begun to fill these vacuums. These have been the years of the clash between nationalism and Superpowership—and the result is that the Age of the Superpowers is coming to an end.

7. *The Last Hurrah of the Superpowers.* Or at least this is evident to everyone—except to the Superpowers themselves. Both America and Russia are still operating far too much on the momentum of ideas generated in the immediate postwar years. Thus the illusion of Superpowership lies behind the American effort to determine the destiny of Vietnam—as it lay behind the Soviet attempt half a dozen years ago to enter the Caribbean, and as it lies behind current Soviet attempts to dominate the Middle East.

In 1967 Chairman Kosygin visited the United States and had a meeting with President Johnson in New Jersey. He came at a moment when Russia and America were in sharp disagreement over the two most urgent items on the meeting's agenda—Vietnam and the Arab-Israeli war. Yet in spite of this disagreement, the meeting itself was surprisingly cordial. This caused puzzlement at the time. In retrospect there is no great mystery why this should have been so. The two leaders were brought together by considerations deeper than conflicts in South Asia or the Middle East. They were brought together by a common sense of international frustration and a common fear that their mutual interests in world management were under challenge. They shared most of all a deep perplexity and anguished exasperation over the inability of their two countries to run the world any longer. The partnership of Holly Bush was above all a partnership in irritation and chagrin.

The world had for some time been approaching the point when the common American-Russian interest in global management was becoming more important than their disagreement on ideological issues or than the clash of their national interests. The irony, of course, is that these two countries were not at all concerned with collaboration during the Age of the Super-powers—at a time when such collaboration might have gone far toward ordering the planet. But as the recovery of national initiative in the rest of the world began to threaten their mutual Superpowership, the tendency grew to consider it more important to share world domination with the other than to open up the game. So, like two cartels that have stopped competing bitterly against each other for the world's supply of a vital commodity—in this case, power—they now tend to prefer to divide the market between themselves, avoiding the risk and uncertainty which would follow from the admission of new competitors.

The clearest expression of this drawing together can be seen in the attempt to limit the control and avail-ability of nuclear weapons. I do not suggest that the Test Ban Treaty of 1963 and the treaty currently under negotiation to stop nuclear proliferation are not excel-lent things in themselves. But it is important also to consider how these proposals look to the non-nuclear nations. Their obvious effect is to exclude the rest from the nuclear club and thus to preserve American-Rus-sian nuclear dominance. This is why, of course, these treaties have been so bitterly denounced by the two great rebel states—France in the Western bloc and China in the Communist bloc.

Alas, the drift of the Superpowers toward collabo-ration, generally encouraging as this new mood may be, has come too late, at least too late to save the joint hope of world domination. The pathos of the present situation is that just as America cannot unilaterally impose its will on South Asia and Russia cannot uni-laterally impose its will on the Middle East, so Amer-ica and Russia together, even if they agreed on every detail of policy and worked together to put a common policy over, can no longer settle affairs in South Asia and the Middle East. The events in the rest of the world have developed a life of their own, and they are passing beyond the reach even of joint American-Russian dictation. The influence of the Superpowers in the next phase of world affairs will become increasingly marginal.

8. *American Foreign Policy After Vietnam.* Vietnam has been a bitter experience; and I have no doubt that the nation is united behind the proposition that we must have no more Vietnams. Yet we must not let the bitterness of that experience propel us into a headlong dash from the world. A retreat to our own shores—even a retreat to our own hemisphere—is an impossible option. The consequence of Vietnam must not be resignation from responsibility. It must rather be reassessment of responsibility.

For Vietnam has demonstrated the wisdom of the statement President Kennedy made in 1961—a statement which brilliantly set forth the issues of American foreign policy in the age after the Superpowers:

> We must face the fact that the United States is neither omnipotent nor omniscient—that we are only 6 per cent of the world's population—that we cannot impose our will upon the other 94 per cent—that we cannot right every wrong or reverse each adversity—and that therefore there cannot be an American solution to every world problem.

Alas, Kennedy's profound insight was forgotten when his successor plunged ahead with the foreign policy of overkill. But today, in the melancholy aftermath of Vietnam, we must at last understand that "there cannot be an American solution to every world problem."

What are the lessons of Vietnam?

First, that everything in the world is not of equal importance to us. Asia and Africa are of vital importance for Asians and Africans, and they are of some importance for us. But they are not so important for us as are Europe, Latin America, and Soviet Russia. In the last three years we have given most of our attention and resources to a marginal problem on the mainland of Asia while our position has steadily deteriorated in parts of the world far more vital to our national security.

Second, that we cannot do everything in the world. The universalism of the older generation was spacious in design and noble in intent. Its flaw was that it overcommitted our country—it overcommitted our policy, our resources, and our rhetoric. Vietnam should teach us that in the last half of the twentieth century armed men cannot determine the destiny of a nation on the mainland of Asia. It should teach us, more generally, that the Age of the Superpowers is over, and that any American policies which involve the denial of local nationalism are doomed to failure.

Third, that we cannot be the permanent guarantor of stability in a world of turbulence. Violence is epidemic in the developing world; we cannot regard every outbreak as a summons for the American fire brigade. Not every revolution, not every change in political and economic systems, not every assertion of belligerent nationalism in a new country is necessarily a mortal threat to the security of the United States. As Robert Kennedy said, "The worst thing we could do would be to take as our mission the suppression of disorder and internal upheaval everywhere it appears."

Fourth, that military force is not necessarily the most effective form of national power. So long as we continue to define our world problems in military terms, so long will we plunge ahead into further military intervention. We must rein in our warrior class. The military hang-up of our foreign policy is an exercise in futility, even from the viewpoint of national aggrandizement. We have never had more military power in the world than we have today—and we have rarely had less influence.

Fifth, that the basis for our world influence in the coming period will lie not in our arms but in our ideas and our ideals. For the hard reality is that the Age of the Superpowers is over. As the Superpowers themselves begin to understand this, then they will recognize that in the future, world leadership will demand persuasion as well as power. Economic assistance, cultural relations: these we must strengthen as we appropriately can. But military intervention is another matter.

Of course, it is much easier in the short run to throw military weight around like an international bully than it is to appeal to the reason and conscience of mankind. But we have exerted our greatest influence in the world precisely when, as in the days of Woodrow Wilson, of Franklin Roosevelt, of John Kennedy, our leadership has commanded the confidence of ordinary people everywhere. We can restore our influence only as we begin to live up to our highest ideals in our national community and to display reason, restraint, and magnanimity in our dealings with other nations.

Index

Chase, Stuart, 145
Chayefsky, Paddy, 328, 330–32
Chevalier, Haakon, 249, 251, 260
Children of Light and the Children of Darkness, The (Niebuhr), 151
Childs, Marquis, 72
China, 323, 390, 391, 450–51n1, 517; and the Vietnam War, 420–22, 447–60. *See also* Sino-Soviet split
Christianity and Power Politics (Niebuhr), 149–50
Christians/Christianity, 125; "Christian radicalism," 135, 137; and sentimentalism, 150; socialist, 151. *See also* Social Gospel
Church and Industrial Reconstruction, The (Federal Council), 126–27
Churchill, Randolph, 96, 476–77
Churchill, Winston, 39, 96, 98–99, 392, 453, 463n1, 470, 471, 477
Civil War (U.S.), revisionist history of, 50–52; and compensated emancipation, 58; the economic exhaustion argument, 56–58; the internal reform argument, 55–56; main premises of, 52–55; as the paradigm of all wars, 213–14
Cobb, Frank, 169
collective security, 506–7
Coming Caesars, The (Riencourt), 29
Coming of the Civil War, The (Craven), 50

common man, 39
Communications Act (1934), 314
communications monopoly, 281–82
communism/Communists, x, 27, 1–6, 111, 116, 118, 156, 349; Asian communism, 376–77; and belief in God, 240–42; communist takeovers of nationalist revolutions, 454–55; and developed countries, 465–66; failure of, 237–38, 517; heterogeneity of, 323–24, 374–75, 450–52; "liberal" communism, 346; theory of the homogeneity of communist power, 399n1. *See also* Chambers, Whittaker; China; McCarthy, Joseph; McCarthyism; Poland; Soviet Union; Yugoslavia
Communist Party, 231
Compulsion, 293
Conant, James B., 236, 252, 257, 283
Conrad, Alfred, 57n2
"Conservation: Down and on the Way Out" (DeVoto), 226
conservatism, 153; American, 86–88, 92; British aristocratic, 97; and plutocracy, 97–98; revival of (*see* New Conservatism)
conservative Manichaeanism, 510–12
Conservative Mind, The (Kirk), 99
conspiracy theory, 498–99
constitutions, abrogation of, 31
consumer-goods ethos, 114–15

with democracy, 29–36; and the place of the heroic leader in classical democratic theory, 14–25; the problem of in the twentieth century, 25–29. *See also* heroes, decline of

Hickory Hills seminars, xvii

High Noon, 294–95

Hilsman, Roger, xxiii, xxiiin13, 411

Hiss, Alger, 232, 235, 237

history, 67–68, 120; and the behavioral sciences, 69–70; "boom" in, 67; and generalization as the goal of, 463; historical insight, 464–65; the inscrutability of, 461–78 *passim*; lack of creativity in modern historians, 71–72; as a means of prediction, 462; modern view of, 59–60; pseudo-history, 68; relationship of moral judgment to, 63–66; role of in public policy, 461–62; and the study of revolutions, 474–75

Hitler, Adolf, 355, 374, 475

Hofstadter, Richard, 69, 329, 498

Holmes, Oliver Wendell, 289

homosexuality, 294

Hook, Sidney, 45

Hoover, Herbert, 87

Hoover, J. Edgar, 221

Humphrey, Hubert, x, xvi, xxxiii, 457, 487, 508, 511

ideology, 32–34

imperialism, 28; American, 512–14

In the Matter of J. Robert Op-

penheimer (U.S. Atomic Energy Commission), 245

India, 27, 33, 34

individualism, 204; and ego, 134–35

Indonesia, 455, 456

Innocents Abroad (Twain), 358

intellectuals, xiii, 238–39, 286, 497–98; as "egghead(s)," 271–72, 274–75, 278, 282; and freedom of expression, 283; hatred of in American society, 277–82; reasons of for joining the Communist Party, 231; roles of, 159–60, 172–73, 190, 192–94, 289–91; and statesmen, 166–67; and *Time* magazine, 284–91

"Intelligentsia in Defeat" (Fitch), 276

Interpretation of Christian Ethics, An (Niebuhr), 136

Irony of American History, The (Niebuhr), 153–54

Jackson, Andrew, 17, 84, 416, 467

Jacksonian Persuasion, The (Meyers), 69

James, William, 44, 48, 131, 160–61, 174, 176, 192; on "toughmindedness," 243

Jefferson, Thomas, 18, 30, 84, 87, 290

Johnson, Harold Keith, 429–30

Johnson, Lyndon B., vii, xxiv, xxvii–xxviii, xxix–xxx, xxxi, 375, 377, 379, 381, 405–6, 418, 441, 443, 447, 448, 457, 485, 487, 496–97, 505, 508, 514; bombing of North

Vietnam (*cont.*)
also North Vietnam; South
Vietnam; Vietnam War
Vietnam (Binh), xviiin4
Vietnam War, vii–viii,
xxix–xxxiii, 484n1; and
American democracy,
496–504; American foreign
policy after, 520–21; and
America's role in the world,
384–85, 431n7; China's role
in, 420–22, 447–60; counter-
insurgency efforts in, 404–5,
426; false optimism concerning, 444–45; lessons of,
505–6, 520–22; and Opera-
tion Rolling Thunder (the
bombing of North Vietnam),
xxvi–xxvii, 383–84, 423–26,
481–82, 484; origins of,
387–98; the price the United
States paid, 432–39; public
frustration concerning,
434–37; the roots of the U.S.
dilemma in, 440–46; Schlesinger's proposed middle
course for, xxvii–xxxi,
479–95; spurious statistics
concerning, 442–44; U.S. involvement in, 1966– , 414–
31; U.S. involvement in
through 1966, 399–413; U.S.
troop levels in, xxvi, 379,
387, 415, 428; Viet Cong/
North Vietnamese troop levels in, 415, 443–44. *See also*
Vietnam War, legacies of
Vietnam War, legacies of: and
American foreign policy, 520;
of collective security, 506–7;
of conservative
Manichaeanism, 510–12; of

geopolitics, 509–10; of the
last hurrah of the Superpowers, 518–20; of liberal evangelism, 507–9; of the rise of a
warrior class, 512–14; of universalism, 514–17
Virgin Land (Nash), 69
Vital Center, The (Schlesinger),
x–xi, xvii
Voegelin, Eric, 284

Wadleigh, Julian, 234
Wages and Hours Act, 314, 316
Wallace, Henry, x, 508
Wallas, Graham, 161–62
Walsh, David I., 216
War and Peace (Tolstoi), 42
Ward, Barbara, 113
Warner, Denis, 489
We Accept with Pleasure (De-
Voto), 200
Weber, Max, 21–24
Wechsler, James, 72
Weeks, Edward, 332
Wells, H. G., 306
Welty, Eudora, 273
"West Against Itself, The" (De-
Voto), 223
Westmoreland, William, 423,
426, 444, 484, 515
What Is to Be Done? (Lenin),
14
"What to Tell the Young" (De-
Voto), 212–13
White, Harry, 234, 235, 236
Whitehead, Alfred North, 354
Whyte, William H., Jr., 73, 106,
299
Williams, Tennessee, 294
Wilson, Charles E., 100,
116–17, 393
Wilson, Edmund, 73, 206

Credits

The Politics of Hope

Most of the essays in this book have previously appeared, often in somewhat different form, in various magazines and books, as follows:

The Atlantic Monthly: "The Oppenheimer Case," October 1954. Copyright © 1954 by The Atlantic Monthly Company.

Culture for the Millions? edited by Norman L. Jacobs, D. Van Nostrand Company, Inc.: "Notes on a National Cultural Policy." (This essay was first published in *Daedalus,* Spring 1960.) Copyright © 1959, 1960 by the American Academy of Arts and Sciences.

Encounter: "On Heroic Leadership," December 1960, and "Varieties of Communist Experience," January 1960.

Esquire: "The Crisis of American Masculinity," November 1958, and "The New Mood in Politics," January 1960.

The New Republic: "Time and the Intellectuals," July 16, 1956. Copyright © 1956 by New Republic, Inc. "Look Back in Amazement," December 23, 1957. Copyright © 1957 by New Republic, Inc.

New Statesman: "Probing the American Experience," September 6, 1958.

The New York Times Magazine: "Invasion of Europe, Family Style," August 11, 1957.

Partisan Review: "The Causes of the Civil War," October 1949. "The Highbrow in American Politics," March–April 1953. "The Statistical Soldier," August 1949.

Perspectives USA, No. 14: "Liberalism in America: A Note for Europeans," Winter 1956. © 1956 by Intercultural

Publications, Inc. Reprinted by permission of Intercultural Publications, Inc.

Reinhold Niebuhr: His Religious, Social and Political Thought, edited by Charles Kegley and Robert Bretall: "Reinhold Niebuhr's Role in American Political Thought and Life." Copyright 1956 by The Macmillan Company. Reprinted with the permission of the publisher.

The Reporter: "The Politics of Nostalgia," June 16, 1955.

The Saturday Evening Post: "The Decline of Greatness," November 1, 1958. Copyright © 1958 by The Curtis Publishing Company.

Saturday Review: "Whittaker Chambers and His *Witness,*" May 24, 1952. Copyright © 1952 by Saturday Review, Inc.

Walter Lippmann and His Times, edited by Marquis Childs and James Reston: "Walter Lippmann: The Intellectual *vs.* Politics." © 1959 by Marquis Childs and James Reston. Reprinted by permission of Harcourt, Brace & World, Inc.

The Bitter Heritage

In writing this book I have drawn on three articles—"A Middle Way Out of Vietnam," *New York Times Magazine*, September 18, 1966; "On the Inscrutability of History," *Encounter*, November 1966; and "McCarthyism Is Threatening Us Again," *Saturday Evening Post*, August 13, 1966—as well as on certain passages in *A Thousand Days* (Boston, 1965).

A.M.S., Jr.